S. (Sabine) Baring-Gold

John Herring

A West of England Romance

S. (Sabine) Baring-Gold

John Herring
A West of England Romance

ISBN/EAN: 9783744696272

Printed in Europe, USA, Canada, Australia, Japan

Cover: Foto ©Thomas Meinert / pixelio.de

More available books at **www.hansebooks.com**

JOHN HERRING

A WEST OF ENGLAND ROMANCE

BY THE

AUTHOR OF 'MEHALAH'

A NEW EDITION

LONDON
SMITH, ELDER, & CO., 15 WATERLOO PLACE
1884

PREFACE.

(ADDRESSED TO THOSE WHO ARE NOT OF THE WEST COUNTRY.)

In a tale of the West of England in which are introduced some of the lowest types of rustic humanity to be found there, it is impossible to avoid the use of the local dialect. This dialect has, however, been modified as much as possible to render it intelligible without transforming it into the language of the schools. The vulgar dialect is regardless of gender and reckless in the use of cases. A cow is he, and a tom-cat wags her tail. At a trial in Exeter, at the Assizes, a man was charged with the murder of his wife, a woman with an aggravating tongue. The jury found a verdict of 'Not Guilty' against the clearest evidence, and, when the Judge expressed his surprise, 'Ah, your lordship,' said the foreman in explanation, 'us ain't a-going to hang he for the likes of she.' It is perhaps necessary to explain that 'the Cobbledicks' are no creation of the imagination—the clan has only been dispersed of recent years; the old man who lived in a cyder-cask is dead, but he was alive ten years ago. The clan was literally one of half-naked savages.

CONTENTS.

CHAPTER		PAGE
I.	THE COBBLEDICKS	1
II.	WHAT THE CASK DID	9
III.	WEST WYKE	17
IV.	MIRELLE	24
V.	THE OWL'S NEST	33
VI.	THAT OLD TRAMPLARA	39
VII.	THAT YOUNG TRAMPLARA	46
VIII.	CICELY	54
IX.	DOLBEARE	59
X.	A MUSICAL WALKING-STICK	66
XI.	THE GIANT'S TABLE	72
XII.	OPHIR	80
XIII.	CAPTAIN TRECARREL	86
XIV.	UNDER THE HEARTH	93
XV.	EHEU, BUBONES!	101
XVI.	TRUSTEE NOT EXECUTOR	107
XVII.	IN THE SUMMER-HOUSE	112
XVIII.	SALTING A MINE	121
XIX.	TWO STRINGS TO ONE BOW	129
XX.	GRINDING GOLD	136
XXI.	THE CUB	142
XXII.	MOONSHINE AND DIAMONDS	147
XXIII.	PASTE	156
XXIV.	THE OXENHAM ARMS	163
XXV.	A LEVÉE	169

CONTENTS.

CHAPTER		PAGE
XXVI.	THE SHEKEL	178
XXVII.	COBBLEDICK'S RHEUMATICS	188
XXVIII.	CAUGHT IN THE ACT	195
XXIX.	A RACE	202
XXX.	BETWEEN CUP AND LIP	210
XXXI.	JOYCE'S PATIENT	216
XXXII.	DESTITUTE	223
XXXIII.	TRANSFORMATION	234
XXXIV.	HERRING'S STOCKINGS	240
XXXV.	BEGGARY	247
XXXVI.	MIRELLE'S GUESTS	256
XXXVII.	A SECOND SUMMONS	263
XXXVIII.	A VIRGIN MARTYR	271
XXXIX.	WELLTOWN	281
XL.	NOEL! NOEL!	289
XLI.	WHITE FAVOURS	296
XLII.	THE SNOW BRIDE	298
XLIII.	HUNTING THE DEVIL	303
XLIV.	WILLAPARK	313
XLV.	'KINKUM-KUM'	320
XLVI.	A BAR OF ICE	326
XLVII.	WELCOME HOME	334
XLVIII.	TWO BEQUESTS	344
XLIX.	CAST UP	352
L.	TWO DISOBEDIENCES	358
LI.	TWO EXITS	366
LII.	THE RETURN OF THE WANDERER	371
LIII.	A PRIVATE INTERVIEW	379
LIV.	THE PORCH ROOM	388
LV.	NEMESIS	395
LVI.	A DEAD MAN	402
LVII.	AN ARREST	408
LVIII.	R.I.P.	419
LIX.	DIVIDING THE SPOILS	433
LX.	INTRODUCTORY	440

JOHN HERRING.

CHAPTER I.

THE COBBLEDICKS.

'Log!' said the voice of Cobbledick the Old from a cyder cask.

'I be a logging like the blue blazes,' answered Cobbledick the younger.

Then a dry and dirty hand emerged from the cask, and with a gorse bush struck at the girl—that is, at Cobbledick the younger. She evaded the blow.

'Be quiet, vaither, or I won't log no more!'

'You won't?' with a horrible curse; 'then I'll make you, if I whacks and whacks till you be all over blood and prickles. There, I will, I swear. Glory rallaluley!'

On a spur of Dartmoor that struck out into the proximity of cultivated land, stood a cromlech or dolmen—a rude monument of a lost race, reared of granite slabs. This spur of moor was a continuation or buttress of Cosdon Beacon, which, next to Yestor, is the highest point attained by Dartmoor, and is indeed the second highest mountain in the south of England.

The dolmen was composed of four great slabs of granite set on edge, two parallel to the other two, with a fifth stone closing one end. The whole five supported an enormous quoit or block, plain on the nether surface, but unshaped above. Local antiquaries, pretending to knowledge, but actually ignorant, called this erection a Druid altar, and pointed to a sort of basin on the top formed by the weather, with a channel from it to the edge, and this they asserted was a receptacle for the blood of human victims, and a means of lustration for those who stood below. Other antiquaries, knowing a great deal, and not ashamed to confess ignorance where knowledge ended and guesswork began, said simply that the monument belonged to prehistoric times, and that they neither knew who had built it, nor for what purpose it was raised. The country folk called it the 'Giant's Table.'

On the lee side of this cromlech was a cyder cask, tethered to the cromlech by a piece of cord passed through the bung-hole, and attached to a stout stick within the monument, entering between the interstices of the blocks.

In this cask lived an old man, named Grizzly Cobbledick by his neighbours. He had lived in the cask many years.

Some miles away, to the north, in another parish, that of Nymet, lived the parent stock from which he sprung, in an old tumble-down cottage, sans windows, sans doors, sans chimney, sans floors, sans everything save the 'cob'—that is, mud walls —and the ragged roof of thatch.

This hovel was what the Germans would call the 'Stammburg' of the Cobbledicks. That is to say, it was the ancestral cradle of the race; it was also the hive in which they continued to dwell. They lived there, apart from their fellows, with whom they held no communication, never entering a village nor dealing at any shop, never seen at market or merry-making, least of all at church.

Their unsociable habits went further. They allowed no one to invade their hovel and pry into their mode of living. If any of them saw a person stand still near the house to observe it, or to watch a Cobbledick at his work or his play, a yelp called the whole clan together, and with howls and curses they set on the inquisitive visitor, pelting him with stones, and flinging sticks at his head, so that he was glad to beat a retreat.

The Cobbledicks were half-naked savages. They wore, for warmth, not for decency, some wretched rags. When the scanty supply of garments failed entirely, then the whole crew dispersed over the country, hunting by moonlight for a fresh supply; they stole whatever came in their way that could be converted into covering to clothe their nakedness. Anything served—a potato-sack or a flour-bag. One or other would change into coat or gown by making in it slits for head and arms.

Once a farmer lost an oilcloth stack-covering. It was deliberately taken off his stack one rainy night before he had thatched his wheat. He recognised it torn up and utilised as curtains to the open holes that served as windows to Cobbledick Castle. The farmer prosecuted, but first a rick and then a stack was burned, and he was glad to stay proceedings and suffer the savages to keep his oilcloth, fearing for the thatch of his farmhouse, and himself, his wife and babes beneath it.

When the neighbourhood was aware that the Cobbledicks ran short of raiment, old worn garments were purposely left out at night on hedges for their use.

The migration of Grizzly Cobbledick to the parish of South Tawton took place in this wise. It marked an epoch in the history of the race. The Cobbledicks had not arrived at that stage of civilisation in which property becomes personal. Their views as to property were undeveloped. The world belonged in part to the Cobbledicks, and the rest did not. What belonged to the Cobbledicks belonged to the family, not to any individual in the family. They owned land, reclaimed from the waste long ago, clay land overgrown with rushes, partly bog; but this land was not the property of this Cobbledick or that, male or female, old or young; it belonged to all, on the principle of the Russian *mir*. Not only so, but the utensils of the house and of the farm were common; so also were the garments. The pipkin cooked for the whole family, and the hoe raised the potatoes for all to eat. The pipkin was not private property when Poll stirred it, the hoe was not private property when Dick worked with it, and the potato-sack was not owned by him or by her who wore it. If, by any chance, it were taken off, it thereby fell back into the common store.

The Cobbledicks never had been civilised. They were autochthones. The oldest inhabitant of Nymet remembered them. They did not increase much, but they did not die out. Their congeners, named the Gubbins, lived in the Lydford glens in Charles the First's reign, when a poet thus described them:—

> And near hereto's the Gubbins' cave,
> A people that no knowledge have
>   Of law of God or men;
> Whom Cæsar never yet subdued,
> Who've lawless lived, of manners rude,
>   All savage in their den.
>
> By whom, if any passed that way,
> He dares not the least time to stay,
>   For presently they howl;
> Upon which signal they do muster
> Their naked forces in a cluster,
>   Led forth by Roger Rowle.

One night a star fell from heaven and descended into the hovel of the Cobbledicks through the hole in the roof which allowed the smoke of the communal fire to ascend; and this spark sank into the heart of Old Grizzly. He was not Old Grizzly then. What his name was then in the clan never transpired.

That divine spark conveyed to this particular Cobbledick the idea of personal property. This idea, once conceived, becomes to the social body what a backbone is to the physical organism. There is all the difference in social conditions between those who have accepted personal property and those who have not arrived at it, that exists between vertebrate animals and invertebrate polypi.

Cobbledick rose from his lair by the fire where he had been snoring, caught up a female for whom he had long been sighing, stuffed a wisp of hay into her mouth to prevent her from alarming the sleepers, threw her over his shoulder, and strode out of the Cobbledick hovel.

The dispersion at Babel was caused by the discovery of the possessive pronouns.

After having carried his burden beyond earshot, Cobbledick set her down, pulled the plug out of her mouth, and said, 'If you holler, I'll smash your head. So hold thee gab and come along of I.'

The female was overawed into submission, and she paddled along at his side.

When day broke they found themselves on a shoulder of down in close proximity to Cosdon. Rambling over the moor, the woman hopping and squealing as she touched the gorse with her bare legs, they lighted on the grey cromlech, and the male, curling his tongue in his mouth, produced a loud cluck. The female, as an imitative animal, clucked responsive. 'Bags!' said Cobbledick male, and by this simple formula he had claimed the cromlech as personal property to himself, his heirs and assigns.

The idea of property had swelled to large dimensions in his heart since he had first admitted it. The tract of moor was at that time—we are speaking of seventy years ago—wholly uninclosed. Since that date many encroachments have been made, and much of the furzy waste placed under cultivation.

Xenophon opens his 'Anabasis' with the words, 'The Greeks began it.' In the record of the conquest and reclamation of the moor it stands written, 'The Cobbledicks began it.'

First they filled up the interstices between the blocks of granite of the dolmen with turf and moss, then they strewed the floor with bracken, and made bed and seat of heather. Then they marked out a portion of the moor, collected stones from off the surface with infinite labour, and fenced it round with these stones set as a dry wall. This they tilled, and their appetite for property growing, they inclosed more. The tillage was rude, but then it was the beginning of tillage to the whole Cobbledick race. It took that race six thousand years to arrive at a crooked stick with Mrs. Grizzly dragging it, and Mr. Grizzly driving with a switch, and his weight resting on the tail of the simple plough. When he took his weight off, to quicken the motions of Mrs. Grizzly with the switch, the plough levered out of the ground, she fell, and he also was thrown forward on his nose. When Grizzly left the ancestral seat, he carried with him, in addition to a woman, two ferrets in a bag, and a sharp flintstone. With the ferrets he caught rabbits, and with the stone he flayed them. Grizzly was a neolithic man.

On their first taking possession of the cromlech, Grizzly fought his wife for the sack she wore. He wanted to utilise it as a screen for the entrance. The door was to the south, but the south wind is a rainy wind and must be shut out.

Mrs. Grizzly resisted, for the same heavenly spark that had brought to him the idea of appropriating one woman as wife had carried to her also the idea of keeping as her own, her very own, the one potato-sack in which she walked and worked and slept.

This resistance on her part stimulated invention on his. He devised a screen of wattles and heather for the door, and this proved a better shelter than any sack could have made. Thus we see how the sense of property quickens invention. The heavenly spark never expired in the breasts of the Cobbledicks; they felt no desire, like the Apostles of old and reformers of the present day, to revert to the conditions from which they had escaped. The spark burned brighter: it demanded fuel. They proceeded to obtain a cow. How they procured it nobody knew, though all suspected. The Cobbledicks disappeared from Tawton parish for several days. When they reappeared they were driving a cow before them down the flanks of Cosdon. Had they fished her out of the swamps round Cranmere pool? or had they gone far, far beyond, and acquired her in the South Hams, and driven her across the moor, leaving no traces in the spongy soil and on the blooming heather whereby they might be traced, in the event of those from whom she had been acquired disputing their right to make off with her?

But if this latter were the case, what labour and perseverance it must have cost them to convey a cow across brawling torrents, over granite-strewn mountains, and through treacherous bogs!

This was the way of the Cobbledicks. When they wanted anything, they went after it over the moor. Beyond was El Dorado, between the pathless waste, a barrier forbidding pursuit. They never robbed their neighbours of anything beyond turnips and field potatoes. They had made sufficient advance along the path of social culture to recognise a sort of fellowship with their neighbours, and to respect the property of near neighbours. But this sense of fellowship did not extend beyond the moor. On the other side was a sea full of fish, into which whoever would might dip his net.

One day the female Cobbledick became a mother, and Grizzly a father.

Soon after this the wife died. Grizzly dug a hole in the floor of the cromlech, just under where the fire burned, and laid her there.

She was pleased, when alive, to sit over the red ashes, spreading out her toes, and laughing at the yellow flames. Under the hearthstone she should lie, with her face to the ashes, and her toes turned to the blaze. The Cobbledick ideas were growing. The first dawn of that sentiment which in another generation might flower into poetry had appeared in Grizzly's mind.

But the experiment was not happy. At night, as Grizzly slept, he thought he saw the old woman working her way up out of the ground, throwing the earth forth like a mole, and then peering at him from a corner. After that she dived again and disappeared. Presently he felt her heave the earth under him where he lay, and roll him over, so that he could not sleep. He was very angry, and he got a great piece of granite and beat the floor hard with it. But this was of no avail. Next night the old woman was heard scratching with her nails at the bases of the granite slabs. Once she had been given a bunch of saffron cake by a farmer's wife, and she had picked all the currants out and eaten them, before attacking the substance. She was now at work on the granite, picking out the hornblend, mistaking the black grains for currants. 'Her'll do with these great stones as her did with the cake,' said Grizzly; 'her got that all crumbled with hunting the currants, and her'll treat the stones same way, and bring the table down on our heads.'

After that he disappeared for three days, and when he returned he was rolling a cyder cask before him down Cosdon. This cask he brought alongside of the cromlech, and attached it to the old house in the manner described. He lined it with fern, and retired into it, along with the child, at night. He would no longer sleep in the stone mansion that was being undermined by the dead wife. He did not object to occupy it by day; and when he ate, he always threw some crumbs or bits of meat into the fire, to satisfy the cravings of the old woman. He supposed that she picked at the stones because she was hungry.

The child slept with him in the cyder-cask till she grew too big, and made it uncomfortable for her father. One night he had cramp in his leg, and kicked out, and kicked her forth, head over heels; then he bade her go for the future to the old house, and sleep there and be darned, glory rallaluley. Occasionally, in spring, when all is waxing and wanton, the Methodists held revival meetings on the down, and Old Grizzly was accustomed then to prowl about the outskirts of the assembly, listening to the preachers, and to the hymns and rhapsodical outcries of the converted. These camp meetings reminded him in some particulars of the ways of the primitive Cobbledicks. The new feature, unfamiliar to him, was the association of religion with these orgies.

From such meetings Grizzly had picked up a few cant expressions which he used for rounding his sentences without in the least understanding their import. If he began a sentence with a curse, he finished it with a hallelujah, much as a grocer, having put an iron weight into one scale, heaps the other with sugar till the balance is complete.

Cobbledick father and daughter were not in the unseemly condition of nudity affected by their relatives at Nymet. These latter so far resembled Adam and Eve in the period of man's innocency that they were naked and were not ashamed, but with the sense of personal property came the sense also of self-respect. The land on which Grizzly and his wife squatted belonged to the manor of West Wyke, of which the Battishills were lords, and the Squire took care that his tenants should not go unprovided with old clothes. The Battishills were very poor, and wore their garments till the last moment consonant with respectability; then they passed them on to the squatters, whom they made, if not respectable, at least decent.

'Log!' screamed the old man from the cask.

'I be a logging [1] like the blue blazes,' answered the girl, and she spoke the truth.

She was seated with her back to one of the great stones of the 'Giant's Table,' with a bare foot resting on the cask on each side of the restraining rope. She worked her feet alternately, so as to produce a vibratory motion in the barrel from left to right. The old man liked being rocked to sleep; he exacted the task of his daughter; and only when he began to snore and ceased to swear dare Joyce Cobbledick desist from logging and retire to her own lair.

The evening had fallen. The sun was set, but a haze of light hung like a warm hoar frost over the head of Cosdon, though darkness had settled down in the valleys, and the village of Zeal began to twinkle out of all its windows.

The air was still. The rush of the stream over the granite masses that choked its course was the only sound audible, save the fretting of the cask on the turf in its oscillations.

The girl was tired, and one of her feet was bleeding. She had cut it with a sharp stone that day.

Joyce Cobbledick was aged eighteen. She was a tall, well-built girl, with bright colour, a low forehead, and dark eyes. Her hair was as uncombed and uncared for as the mane of a moorland pony. It was dark brown. Her jaws were heavy and her cheek-bones high, like those of her ancestry. There was some beauty about her—the beauty of a fine animal; she was perfectly supple in every limb, admirably proportioned, easy and even graceful in her movements, unrestrained by shoes and cumbrous clothing. Her face was even fine, but there was nothing like intelligence illumining her dark eyes.

She wore a thin print gown, and that was in tatters from her knees by scrambling through hedges to steal turnips, and brushing through gorse brakes after rabbits.

Presently the girl intermitted her trampling movement, believing the old man to be asleep.

The stars were coming out. The one street of Zeal, lying between rich meadows and wood, was like a necklace of diamonds embedded in black velvet.

Joyce leaned forwards to listen if her father were snoring. All was still in the cask, preternaturally still.

She bent her head lower. Then, suddenly, with a roar,

---

[1] To '*log*' is to rock. Thus a logan stone is a rocking stone, and a woman logs her baby in its cradle.

'Darn your eyes, glory rallaluley!' an old grey, frowzy head and face shot out of the barrel, and with it a long arm. A heavy blow of the furze bush fell across the girl's head and cheek, making her cry out with pain.

She recovered her position in a moment, and dashed her feet together savagely at the cask. The violence of the action was more than the cord could endure, already fretted against the rugged edges of the granite blocks. It snapped, and in a moment the cask was driven forward by the impetus of Joyce's angry kick. It rolled over and over; ran down a bank, then along an incline of smooth turf, dashed against a stone which somewhat diverted its course, bounded into the high road, where it shot forth its tenant, and continued its course in rapid revolutions down the road that here ascended from the valley. Joyce uttered a cry, sprang to her feet, and ran after the rolling barrel towards the highway, and there saw her father lying stretched across the road, stunned and speechless.

CHAPTER II.

WHAT THE CASK DID.

As Joyce stood on the bank about to leap down into the road to her father's assistance, she was arrested by a sight calculated to fill her with dismay. A chaise drawn by a pair of horses was approaching from the direction of Okehampton at a brisk pace. The cask was in full career down the road, gaining velocity as it rolled. A curve hid it from the postillion, and Joyce stood breathless, powerless to warn the post-boy or arrest the cask, watching for the result.

The boy was in spirits; he cracked his whip, and stimulated the horses—fresh from the stable at Okehampton—to take the hill in style. The cask was whirling on. Then it reached the sweep in the road, and it went direct against the bank, danced light-heartedly up it, reeled back, swung itself round and shot straight down the road at the horses. In another moment it was on them, leaping at them like a tiger at the throat of his prey.

What followed was so sudden, and the light was so imperfect, that Joyce could not quite make out what she saw. She heard a loud cry from the post-boy, who was thrown. Whether one of the horses went down and floundered to his feet again she was not sure; she believed it was so. Next moment the chaise was off the road, the two frightened animals tearing away with it over the common. Forgetful of her father in the excitement of the spectacle and in dread of the final catastrophe, Joyce ran after the carriage, which she saw bounding over heaps of peat that had been cut and laid to dry, lurching into hollows, jolting over tufts of gorse, and jarring against stones.

Then she saw against the light of the horizon the figure of a man emerging from the window of the chaise, trying to open the door. Almost simultaneously the wheel of the carriage struck a huge block of granite, and in an instant the chaise was thrown on one side, the horses were kicking furiously, and the whole converted into a wreck of living beasts and struggling men and splintered fragments of carriage.

'Ho, heigh! stay them osses,' yelled the post-boy, who had picked himself up and was running over the down. 'Sit on their necks; kip 'em down.'

Joyce ran also, and reached the spot soon after him.

The postillion went straight at the horses, regardless of everything else, and cut their traces; whereupon they ran off, and he careered in full pursuit after them.

'Leave the beasts alone, boy,' shouted a young man who had disengaged himself from the shattered carriage, and was helping out a young lady. 'Leave the beasts and come here.'

'No, no, sir! The osses fust. Them's my concern.' And away went the boy.

'Here, girl,' said the same young man to Joyce, as she came up; 'help me.' He signed to her what to do, to raise a man who was lying motionless among the fragments of the carriage, to carry him a little distance, and lay him on the turf at full length.

'Stay by him whilst I go for the young lady.'

Joyce nodded.

The young lady was seated on the rock that had upset the carriage.

'What frightened the horses?' she asked.

'I do not know. Are you hurt?'

'My foot is sprained. I cannot walk; but no bones are broken, of that I have satisfied myself. How goes my father?'

'He is seriously injured.'

'He did wrong to try and open the door. The carriage must have fallen over on him.'

'Will you remain here whilst I go back to him?'

'Certainly. The moss is soft as a cushion on this stone.'

'Your father, I fear, is seriously hurt. As you say, he was leaning out of the window when the coach turned over, and it went down on the side where he was.'

'Bring me my cloak from the chaise. It is chilly, and the spot is desolate. Il me donne les frissons.' She spoke with wonderful composure. She might have been on a picnic, and the dish with the chicken pie broken; yet she had narrowly escaped death herself, and her father was lying dead a few feet from her. The young man looked at her face, a little surprised at her perfect coolness. The face was wax-like, of transparent whiteness; there was no colour in it. But then she was cold and possibly frightened, though betraying no fear in her manner. Her features were regular and of extraordinary beauty. Her eyes were large and the lashes long; her hair abundant and black. Of emotion in her face there was none.

'I remember my father said he had suffered from the rheumatism. Pray take him from off the grass.' The young man thought to himself, 'He will never suffer from that more,' but he made no answer. He went back to the man lying on the turf, knelt over him, and examined him. Joyce stood by with arms folded.

'Is there any house near to which this gentleman could be removed?' he asked.

'West Wyke,' answered Joyce.

'Where is that?'

She made a motion with her chin, indicating the direction.

'And is there a gate to be had on which I can lay him?'

She jerked her chin again.

'Now, sir,' said the post-boy, coming up, 'I've got the osses quiet, what can I do for you?'

'This gentleman must be removed at once on a hurdle or gate. Run and bring me one.'

'Be he hurted cruel bad?' asked the boy.

'He is dead.'

'Deary me!' exclaimed the post-boy. 'What a mussy it weren't one of the osses. Make us truly thankful. I'll get you a gate.'

'I'll help you,' said Joyce. 'You don't look a sort to carry a gate. Do you call yourself a man or a rat?'

Presently the two returned with a hurdle; that is to say, Joyce was carrying one on her head, casting occasionally a contemptuous glance at the dapper little fellow at her side.

'Is my father able to speak yet?' asked the lady.

'No,' answered the young man. 'Do not be alarmed. We must carry him to a house, where he can be put to bed, and then we will return for you. Do you mind being left alone, or can you walk as far as to the house?'

'I have already told you that I cannot walk. You are forgetful, monsieur.'

'Then this girl will remain with you till we return.'

Very well. If she likes to remain she may remain. It is her affair.'

The young lady spoke with a foreign—a French accent, which was pretty. Indeed, there was a foreign grace in her attitudes, and taste in her dress, which showed that, if an Englishwoman, she must have lived a great deal in France.

The gentleman returned to Joyce; he was a tall and fine young man, with dark hair and moustache and frank blue eyes.

'Will you remain here with the lady while we go on to the house?'

Joyce nodded and went over to the rock on which the young lady was seated. She planted herself before her.

'The 'ouse to which we must carry the gent be yonder,' said the post-boy. 'I seed him as I went for the gate.'

'Do not be alarmed if we carry your father.'

'I shall not be alarmed.'

Then, the post-boy going before and the young gentleman following, they proceeded very gently to carry the motionless form in the direction of West Wyke.

Joyce remained with the young lady; she studied her with great attention from head to foot. The sky was clear, and there was still much light entangled in the upper atmosphere. The whole of the north was full of silvery twilight.

'I niver seed a born leddy afore so close,' said Joyce.

'I am a born lady,' replied the other, haughtily.

'Did I say you wasn't? Have you any other rags on but what I sees?'

'Rags!' indignantly. 'What do you mean, girl?'

'Look here,' said Joyce, 'I hasn't. Fust comes the gown, and then comes I. Down in the good land to Zeal and Tawton, where the lanes be cut deep, I seed there be nethermost hard rock, then over that comes shellat, then a sort of gravelly trade (stuff), then a top o' that meat airth; and over all, like the gown, the waving green grass. Up here on the moor t'ain't so. There's the granite and then the moss, and if you scrats through the moss you comes right on and on to the stone. That be like us as lives up here, vaither and I, but wi' the quality it be different, as lives in lew (sheltered) places; they has more coverings nor us, night and day, I reckon.'

'You have no more clothes on you than that thin gown?'

'No, us be like moor rock, fust the moss, then the stone.'

'Are you begging?'

'I never axes for naught; what I wants I takes.'

The lady shivered and drew back on her seat. She was disgusted with the appearance, and offended at the rudeness of the girl.

'Why don't clothes grow on our backs, thick and warm as the wool on sheep, the fur on rabbits, and the moss on moorstones? 'Twould come handier,' observed Joyce Cobbledick.

The lady made no reply.

'Wot's that man, that young man as spoke to you and I?' asked Joyce.

'I do not know his name.'

'He don't belong to you?'

'Most certainly not,' with a contemptuous shrug.

'Where did you get mun?'

'He is travelling with us—that is all. He joined my father in taking a chaise from Launceston.'

'Why didn't y' travel by the mail-coach? Her goes by ivery day.'

'The coach had left Launceston when we arrived there from Falmouth, so we engaged a chaise. My father was in haste to reach Exeter, and that person joined us. I do not know his name, neither do I care. My father satisfied himself, I presume, of his respectability. That is all.'

'Where do'y come from, mistress? Over t'other side of the moor, I reckon.'

'I come from France.'

Joyce was puzzled. Her geographical knowledge was too limited for her to know of France.

'I reckon that be a long way off, t'other side o' Prince's Town and the prisons, surely. Be there savages in them parts?'

'Savages! certainly not.'

'There be here. I be one. I be a Cobbledick, and the Cobbledicks be all savages. But vaither and I be better nor the rest out Nymet. They be savages and no mistake.'

'I have no doubt of it.'

'I say, young lady, is that man as they carried on the gate to West Wyke your vaither?'

'He is my father.'

'Did he bang you about much? Did he whack you often wi' a bunch of vuzz? Not but you'd mind over much wi' all them pack o' clothes to your back.'

'Certainly not.'

'Did you have to rock him to sleep o' nights in a barril?'

'No.'

'Mebbe you niver had much dodging out of the way of the stones he throwed at your head?'

'Of course not.'

'My old vaither doth all these to me. He whacks me wi' brimmles and vuzz, and he throws turves and stones at me, and I has to rock mun every night or he wouldn't sleep a wink. Of all the proper blaggards in the world there ain't an ekal to vaither. But I reckon vaithers is vaithers all the world over. They be all like oaksticks, some crookeder nor others, but none straight. You don't mind over much what has happened to yours?'

The young lady only imperfectly understood the girl, owing to the rudeness of her speech and her strong provincial brogue.

'There be my old vaither rolled out of his barril right across the high road, and I don't know if he've a broke his neck or no; and I don't kear hover much, no more nor you does because your vaither ha' gone and done the same.'

'What do you mean, girl?'

'I mean what I sez. I know what broke necks mean. I ha' broke the necks o' rabbits scores and scores of times. Him's just the same, ivery bit and croome.'

The young lady shuddered. She did not cry, but her breath caught in her throat.

'Mon Dieu! Ce n'est pas vrai! Comme cette fille me fait peur!'

'What be that jabber about? You oughtn't to mind.'

'For the love of God, girl, do not frighten me. It is wicked —it is cruel. It is not true.'

'Not true!' echoed Joyce; 'I knows it be. I knows a broke neck in a man as in a rabbit.'

'Be quiet. If you want money, *en voilà*, take and leave me tranquil.'

Joyce struck her hand aside.

'What'll you do wi' he now? Mother be poked under the

hearthstone, where the fire can warm her. But when Old Grizzly goes, I shan't put he along o' mother. He can't sleep under the table now, and her'll lead'n a life of it, if he be put under the hearthstone along of she. Her niver worrits me, but her don't leave old vaither alone not one minnit of nights. Her does it because he knacked her, and beat her scores and scores o' times when her were alive. Now her thinks her turn be come. But her's got no vice in her. It be all play, only vaither be that crabbed he don't put up wi' it. When Old Grizzly goes, I'll up wi' his heels and send him into a bog once for all. He'll be wet and cold there, I reckon, and the moss grows so thick over them quaking bogs, that once in there be no getting out, no more than when you're gone under the ice on Rayborough Pool. Then he'll leave me in peace, I reckon.'

'You will do that, you long cripple (viper), you!' screamed the old man, who had overheard the arrangements planned for his interment and disapproved of them. 'You will do that!' He rushed on Joyce from behind, raining furious blows on her with his fists. 'You will stog me in a bog, will'y? I'll put you in fust, curs'd everlasting rallaluley if I don't.' The old man yelled with fury. He stepped backwards and leaped at Joyce, and beat and swore.

The young lady was frightened, and cried out for help. The horrible old man seemed to her to be some superhuman apparition rising out of the moor soil—a vampyre, a ghoul from a cairn, come to destroy the wretched girl before her.

'You chuck down thicky (that) stone, vaither?' cried Joyce, as he stooped and took up a piece of granite in both hands.

'I won't, I won't. I'll mash you first, you unnat'ral varmint! You nigh upon killed me by rolling me over and over in the cask, and shan't I nigh upon do the same by you? Glory rallaluley, blast me blue!'

Joyce was unquestionably stronger than old Cobbledick, and might have disarmed him, but the divine spark had been communicated to her; it flickered faintly in her dim soul, and a dumb instinct forbade her raising her hand against her father. She had borne his brutality for many a year, and had not resented it. She was his child, for him to deal with as he thought best. The sense of property had become strongly rooted in the minds of this branch of the Cobbledicks, and as forces are correlated, and heat, and light, and electricity, and sound are but the same force acting in different ways, so was it with the sense of possession. In the breast of Joyce it had transformed itself into a consciousness of filial duty.

Joyce put up her hand to ward off the blow.

Then the young man who had carried the injured gentleman away arrived, running up, summoned by the cries, and with one stroke of the stick he held in his hand, he made the old man drop the stone.

'In another moment he would have beaten out your brains,' said he, panting.

'I reckon he would,' observed Joyce.

The old man howled with pain, dancing about holding his arm where struck.

'Who are you? What are you doing here?' asked the gentleman.

'Never you heed he,' said Joyce. 'Hers old vaither.'

'Help me away from this horrible place,' entreated the lady; 'I have fallen among savages in a dreadful wilderness. Am I in England, in Europe—or is this the wilds of Northern Canada?'

'She is lame,' said the young man to Joyce. 'Assist me in conveying her to the house yonder.'

Joyce put herself submissively on one side.

'How is my father?' asked the young lady.

'No better,' he replied.

'This strange girl tells me he has broken his neck.'

He was silent. He could not tell her the truth. It must be broken gently to her.

'I should wish to know if it be so.'

'Let us hope for the best. I have sent the post-boy to Okehampton for a doctor. He will know better than I what is the matter, and what must be done.'

'But you can surely tell me whether he be alive or dead.'

'He is still unconscious.'

'I know he be dead,' said Joyce roughly. 'What's a broke is a broke, and his neck be broke as sure as a bit o' cloam. I told her so.'

'Is he dead?' again asked the young lady.

She was now being carried to the house. There was no tremor in the arms that rested on the shoulders of her bearers.

'I asked you a simple question. It is unmannerly to refuse an answer.'

'I believe he is dead,' said he with an effort.

'I am very sorry,' was her calm reply.

The young man stopped; the girl Joyce stopped also. The twilight from the north-west was full on the white lovely face; there was no expression of distress on it, none of grief—not a trace of a tear in her large dark eyes.

'Why do you not go on? I said I am very sorry, naturally. He was my father. What else should I say?'

CHAPTER III.

WEST WYKE.

THE young man and Joyce conveyed the lady between them under a low embattled gateway into a small yard or garden—it was too dark to distinguish which—and halted in the porch of a house.

Joyce said: 'Stay, I go no vurder. I niver ha' been inside a house and under hellens (slates) afore, and I bain't a going now.'

The door opened and a blaze of ruddy light fell on them. A young lady had opened to admit them.

'There be Miss Cicely Battishill,' said Joyce. 'Sure her will take my place once for all.'

'Another step more, girl,' said the young man to Joyce, 'and our burden is in a chair.'

'Why do'y call me a gurl?' asked Joyce. 'I bain't a gurl. I be a maiden. There be maidens in these parts, and no gurls. I dunnow, but the leddy I been a helping may be a girl; hers different from I; I be a maiden.'

'Never mind distinctions,' said the young man impatiently. 'Go on another step.'

'No, I'll put my head under no hellens. I be a savage,' said Joyce obstinately. 'You go on yourself, and get Miss Cicely to help.'

'I will take your place, Joyce,' said the young lady at the door, and she assisted the strange pale girl to come in.

The young man looked back over his shoulder, and said, 'Thanks for your help as far as it went, maiden.'

Joyce stood without, the red light on her, with the dark garden, the moor, and the night sky behind, her strange face appearing even handsome in the glow, and the flicker reflected in her dull eyes.

C

The figure struck the young man with an evanescent sense of pity. She seemed an outcast—desolate, friendless.

Then the door closed, and the light was cut off. But Joyce did not leave. She stood in the porch with her arms folded looking over the black garden wall at the wild blacker moor beyond, over which the wind was soughing. She was lost in a day-dream unintelligible to herself.

The light from the window streaked the garden and fell on an orange lily that stood out luminous and fiery against the inky background of foliage and wall. The stars were coming out in the sky. Joyce remained motionless, with her eyes on the fiery flower.

In the meantime the pale young lady was conveyed to a seat by the fire. The porch door opened immediately into the hall or parlour. This was a small low room, irregularly built, with a bay in which was the window. It was so small that with twenty people within it would be crowded inconveniently; it was so low that a tall man could touch the ceiling.

The hall was panelled throughout, very unpretentiously, with plain black oak; there was no carving except over the great fireplace, where was a coat of arms, once heraldically emblazoned, but now obscured by smoke. The coat was curious. Azure, a cross crosslet in saltire, between four owls argent, beaked and legged or.

On the walls were hung a few old portraits in tarnished oval frames. The paint was cracked and peeling off.

The ceiling was crossed by moulded oak beams of great size, black with age and smoke.

A tall, very thin gentleman, Mr. Battishill, the owner of the house, and squire of West Wyke and lord of the manor, had been seated in a high-backed leather-covered chair beside the fire. He started up and offered it to the young lady, with many rather uncouth bows. This gentleman was old; he still wore his hair tied back by a black riband, though the fashion had gone out. His suit was rusty, his boots were split in the upperleather, and the elbows of his long coat were patched. His face was peculiar. The nose was pointed and aquiline, and, as forehead and chin receded, it gave his head the appearance of that of a bird. The eyes were very wide open, prominent, and of the palest grey. His hair was frosted with age.

The expression of his eyes was one of eager inquiry. His mouth was weak, and the lips were incessantly quivering. There was a kindly look about the feeble mouth which assured those who studied the face that a kind heart was lodged within, and showed them that the qualities of this organ were superior to those of the head.

Mr. Battishill's daughter Cicely was a fine girl, about the same age as Joyce—eighteen. She was somewhat stoutly built with hair of a glowing auburn, almost red, but not harshly red, rather of the richest, sunniest chestnut. Her complexion was of that quality seen nowhere but in Devon; transparent, delicate, white, with the brightest, healthiest, purest colour conceivable; a face in which the mounting of a blush had all the beauty and splendour of a sunrise. Her eyes were hazel, dancing with life and intelligence. There was buoyant good nature in every line of her face. At the present moment her expression was that of distressed sympathy with the lovely girl just introduced into her father's house.

The contrast between the two was striking. The new comer was absolutely colourless. Her hair was dark, almost if not wholly black. She was very slenderly built, her hands were long, and the fingers fine and tapering. The hands indicate culture and purity of race; those at which Cicely now looked were hands belonging to a lady of high nervous sensibility and perfect breeding. Her features were regular, and singularly delicately and beautifully cut. The eyes, when raised, sent a tremor to the heart of him on whom they rested; they were deep, full, and mysterious. A soul lay in those unfathomed pools, but of what sort none might guess. There was nothing in the expression of the face to assist in the inquiry. And yet the face was not a blank page and therefore uninviting. The expression that sat on it was one of reserve, and therefore as provoking as those wonderful eyes.

Cicely was frank and impulsive; her heart was visible to all the world, she had no reserve whatever; what she thought she said; and her heart spoke through her eyes,—a genial, affectionate heart, fresh and simple.

The pale young lady was evidently relieved by being placed in a chair by the fire. Her foot had pained her; it was now rested on a footstool.

'I beg your pardon,' said Mr. Battishill, 'I did not catch the name. It is such a pleasure to me to know to whom I am able to offer hospitality. It places persons on a footing of friendship at once when they are able to address each other by name.'

'My name is Mirelle,' said the young lady, without raising

her eyes from the fire or moving a muscle of her face. 'My mother was the Countess Garcia. She married my father, a Mr. Strange. It is not necessary in Spain to take the paternal name; I prefer to be called Mirelle Garcia de Cantalejo. Cantalejo is territorial.'

Mr. Battishill listened with open mouth and staring eyes, and drew himself up. A distinguished guest this!

'And Canta——'

'Cantalejo,' interrupted Mirelle, 'is in Segovia—in Old Castile of course. We belong to the purest of the ancient Castilian nobility. Cantalejo belonged to the family from the earliest period; it is even said that when Saint Jacques came to Spain he was the guest of my ancestor, and that is why we bear an escallop on our coat. Cantalejo belonged to us till the sixteenth century.'

'And now?'

'It has ceased to belong to us for three hundred years. But before that we exercised sovereign powers in the country; we coined our own money, and hung malefactors on our own gallows.'

'Your poor father,' began Mr. Battishill, his nervous mouth working and his eager eyes staring, 'that is, Mr. Strange—I think you said Strange——'

Mirelle bowed an affirmative.

'Your poor father, Mr. Strange, lies, I fear, in a very sad and precarious state. He has been placed in the spare bed-room upstairs, and the doctor has been sent for, but cannot well be here for an hour.'

'I am told that my father is dead,' said the young lady composedly. 'I am very sorry. And what increases my desolation is that he was a heretic.'

'You love him?' whispered Cicely, looking pained and puzzled.

'I have always prayed for him, and I will pray for him still,' said Mirelle. 'He did not know the truth, so his invincible ignorance may save him.'

'You would hardly like to see him now,' suggested Cicely.

'No, perhaps to-morrow.'

'You love him?' persisted Cicely.

'Of course,' answered Mirelle. 'It is my duty. But you must understand that I have not known him except by name till last fortnight. I had not seen him at all till a fortnight ago, when he came to Paris to take me away from the Sacré Cœur.'

The young man had been watching her face intently. He had seemed more pained than Cicely at her want of feeling. Now he drew a long breath, a sigh of relief; these words of Mirelle explained her coldness.

'I am sorry that he is dead,' she went on, 'but he ought not to have married my mother.'

'We cannot regret that,' said Mr. Battishill with awkward gallantry, 'since to that we are indebted for the pleasure of making your acquaintance.'

Mirelle considered for a moment, then she said simply, 'You mean that I should not have existed. True; I did not think of this.'

Mr. Battishill and the young man were unable to repress a smile. She was a curious mixture of simplicity, reserve, and frankness. The reserve was exercised over her feelings, but she was perfectly frank about her thoughts.

'Have you ever been to Cantal——? I have not quite caught the name.'

'I have never been in Spain at all,' answered Mirelle.

'Where, then, have you lived?'

'In Paris. Where else should I live? One lives in Paris, one exists elsewhere.'

'But your father?'

'Mr. Strange was a Brazilian diamond merchant. I mean a merchant of diamonds living in Brazil. My mother married him there. It was very good of my mother, but she was an angel. He was rich—*comme ça, mais bourgeois.* When I was born, my mother came to Paris to have me properly educated, and I lived there till the good God took her. I have been at school with the English sisters of the Sacré Cœur. When my father came to Paris he took me away, to bring me to his home in England.'

'Where is his home?'

'He has none; he would make one. He has retired from his business.'

'What relations has he? They should be communicated with.'

'I do not know that he has any. My mother never spoke of my father's relations. She knew nothing of them; she did not want to know them. In this world everything is on shelves, and the things on each shelf are kept to themselves. Where they get mixed there is inextricable confusion. Above, angels; then kings, nobles, bourgeois, peasants, monkeys, and so down to the lowest form of life—those laid on the floor. My father's relatives were not noble.' Then suddenly, 'Are you noble, sir?'

Mr. Battishill threw up his head proudly. 'My family is gentle, and of ancient degree,' he said. 'We appeared in the Heralds' Visitation of 1620 in four descents, but I have title-deeds that show we were lords of the manor of West Wyke from the time of Edward the Third.'

'Those are your arms?' asked Mirelle, looking at the chimney-piece. 'What birds are those?'

'Owls,' answered Mr. Battishill proudly; 'owls argent, beaked and clawed or.'

Mirelle contemplated the owls, then looked at the gentleman, with his blank eyes, beak-like nose, and grey hair. Her lips twitched slightly, but she was too well bred to smile.

'The bird is dedicated to Minerva. It is the symbol of wisdom,' she said.

'The Battishills were ever owls,' said he proudly. Then he asked, glancing at the young man, 'Is this gentleman your brother?'

Mirelle looked up full for the first time into the young stranger's face.

'He is no relative of mine. I do not even know his name.'

'My name,' said he, stepping forward, 'is John Herring.' He was interrupted by a laugh from Mirelle.

'Herring!' she exclaimed, 'Quel drôle de nom! That is a fish they split and pickle, and pack in barrels, is it not?'

The young man coloured.

'The name is bourgeois—Herring!'

The young gentleman drew back, wounded. He said nothing more about himself, but asked Mr. Battishill in a low voice for a lantern.

'The trunks and portmanteaus are lying with the broken chaise, and I must see to their being placed under shelter and in security. Are there men about the premises who can assist me?'

'There will be some difficulty about finding a man,' answered Mr. Battishill. 'We do not keep one in the house, and the cottages are at a distance. You will not find your way to them by night. Do not trouble about the trunks; leave them till morning. No one will touch them.'

'I prefer removing them. When the post-boy returns from Okehampton with the doctor, I will secure his assistance.'

Cicely had lighted a lantern whilst her father was speaking. She offered it to John Herring. 'I will go for you to the cottages,' she said; 'I will send some men to help you.' She accompanied him to the door. 'It is quite right that the things should not be left out all night on the moor. There are tramps on the Exeter road, and the Cobbledicks are close by.' She opened the door, and the light fell on Joyce.

'Why, Joyce, you here still? I thought you had gone back to the Giant's Table.'

'If I were to go back to vaither, he'd kill me. I ha' lost he his old barril, and him won't sleep under the table a'cos mother be there wi' her playful ways, tormenting of he.'

'What do you mean, Joyce?'

'I means this, miss. His barril be rolled away down hill, and I dunnow where her be rolled to. Where be vaither to sleep?'

'Under the Giant's Table.'

'That won't do, 'cos o' mother. Her be lively o' nights when vaither be there. 'Tain't wickedness, it be her playful ways. Her leaves me alone right enough. But vaither won't go there. Now if he might sleep i' one o' your linnies[1], he'd be right vast enough as a nail in a door.'

'By all means, let him sleep there, Joyce,—at least for a while, till you can recover the cask.'

'Then I can go back to he. If I hadn't that to say, he'd ha' killed me. Now he'll go snuggle into the straw like a heckamall[2] in a rick. That's beautiful!'

'Joyce,' said Cicely, 'this gentleman is going to the broken carriage. Perhaps you can assist him to remove some of the trunks. They must not be left out where they are.'

'There be some scatt right abroad,'[3] answered Joyce; 'I seed mun, and the things be coming out like.'

'More the reason why they should be collected and brought under cover.'

'I'll go right on end,' said Joyce. 'And vaither may sleep in the linney?'

'Yes, he may.'

'Oh, rallaluley, he'll be glad!'

So Joyce led the way, followed by Herring, and Miss Cicely Battishill went in quest of assistance.

[1] Lean-to sheds.
[2] A heckamall or heckanoddy is a tomtit.
[3] Broken to pieces.

When Herring and Joyce reached the scene of the accident, they discovered Old Grizzly hopping about amidst the wreck, pulling the pieces of the broken carriage apart. He had made some clearance in the confusion, but not from disinterested motives. Everything in the shape of cushion and cloak had disappeared, and the old wrecker was engaged in collecting chips of the broken wood for firing.

John Herring did not notice particularly what he was about; it was too dark to distinguish much. He went directly to the boxes.

Of his own goods there was little to take care of save one valise, and that was safe. The rest of the trunks and portmanteaus belonged to Mr. Strange and his daughter. The trunks lay, some still corded, on the top of the chaise, others thrown off, one with its lock sprung. This box had either been very much shaken by the fall, or Grizzly's arm had been turning it over, for the lid would no longer close over the confused and overflowing contents.

Grizzly Cobbledick decamped when he saw the lantern brought to bear on the wreck. Joyce called after him, but he made no reply. Then she went in pursuit to announce to him the glad news that he was to sleep in the straw of the calves' linney at West Wyke.

'I wonder,' mused John Herring, 'whether that old rascal can have stolen anything of value. If he has, there is no one to bring him to book. The owner is dead, and the daughter probably knows nothing of the contents of the boxes.'

If he had known!

CHAPTER IV.

MIRELLE.

It is aggravating to the reader to be asked to move backwards when he has been well started in a story. He resents it as he resents the backing of a train when he has left the station where he took his ticket, and is impatient to reach his destination.

The author is aware that he is trying the patience of the reader when he asks him to turn into a side alley which bends in the same direction as his starting point. He would avoid asking him to turn if it were possible to do so. But it is not always possible. To a drama, to the farce of half an hour, is prefixed the list of characters. In taking up one of Lacy's acting copies, the reader learns at a glance that Box is a journeyman printer, and Cox a journeyman hatter, and that Mrs. Bouncer is a lodging-house keeper. He learns a great deal about them before he comes to a word of dialogue. He is informed that Box wears 'small swallow-tailed black coat, short buff waistcoat, light drab trousers (short turned up at the bottom), black stockings, white canvas boots with black tips, cotton neckcloth, and shabby black hat;' further, that Cox is apparelled in 'brown Newmarket coat, long white waistcoat, black plaid trousers, boots, white hat, black stock;' that Mrs. Bouncer is costumed in 'coloured cotton gown, apron, cap, &c.' He feels at once that he knows all about these characters. He reads their past in their costume, they wear their souls on their limbs. Note that 'turned up at the bottom'—the words illumine the abysses of the character of Box, and make them clear to us.

But the novelist is debarred what is allowed the dramatist. He must haul up his curtain on a situation without an introductory word, and then, when the reader is puzzled as to the characters, antecedents, and purposes of the *dramatis personæ*, he is obliged to step forward, stick in hand, as in a waxwork, point out the several personages and describe them. This is the way of novelists. It is a bad way, it is inartistic, but it is exacted by the reader.

Now, in describing the characters of a novel it is not sufficient to give minute accounts of the costume—in the case of the Cobbledicks this is done in a word; the author is required to give his readers a key to the inner mechanism of his puppets, to show why they walk or pirouette, and what may be expected to be the limits of their powers. He can rarely do this without retrogression.

That Mirelle may be understood and not be judged with undue severity, we must step back to a period before her birth; but we shall be as rapid in our survey as we can, and shall resume the thread of our story after a very short divagation.

The Countess Garcia de Cantalejo was a poor Spanish lady sent out to Brazil by her relatives, who were by no means near, to be got rid of by marriage, malaria, or mosquitoes, as might be, but anyhow to be got rid of.

She was handsome, but, like the milkmaid in the ballad, 'her face was her fortune.' Now in Spain pretty women abound, and ugly women are exceptional. Marriageable men look out more for money, which is scarce, than for beauty, which is a drug. Money, moreover, they know, in prudent hands will wax; beauty they know, however well conserved, will wane.

In Brazil she was seen and admired by Mr. Strange, a diamond merchant, and she consented to give him her cold hand, intending at the earliest opportunity to supplement it with the cold shoulder. She married him, because no one else would have her, and because he was well off. She was proud of her family, and it was a condescension on her part—like that of the sun which stoops to kiss the puddle—for her to link the proud name of Garcia with that of Strange, and Cantalejo—which was territorial, with a blank, for the Stranges had never owned any more ground than the six foot allotted them as graves, and that only till they had mouldered. They had made, but not coined, their money, certainly never had hung men on their own gallows.

'Mr. Strange and the Countess Garcia de Cantalejo lived together for a few years like oil and water. At length the Countess became the mother of a daughter, who was baptized Mirelle at the font in the Cathedral of Bahia, by the Cardinal Archbishop himself. After this Donna Garcia informed her husband that their separation was inevitable. The child could not be decently suckled, weaned, and educated in a colony, certainly not in a city so mean as Bahia. The child, the heiress of the coronet and of the name with its territorial tail, must go to Europe.

The Countess did not purpose returning to Spain; there were circumstances attending her departure from her native country which had embittered her against her relatives there. No; she would go to Paris, the centre of the civilised world.

Mr. Strange raised no objections. He was weary of association with a woman full of caprice, of fading charms, and of intolerable pride. He was a reserved and a disappointed man. To every bird comes its time of song; to the swan only at death, to the nightingale in balmy spring while mating; it is only the chatterers that chatter ever. The song time, the flowering time, the moment when the dullest life breaks into poetry, is the moment of love. Mr. Strange had gone through this and had been disenchanted, and thenceforth hi slife became dull, prosaic, without melody and colour, unimpassioned. His heart had flamed, and his wife had extinguished its fires with ice.

Mr. Strange had no love for babies. Babies are to men

objects as offensive as naked infant rabbits. A doe eats her young rather than expose them to the strange eye before their fur is grown. If women were as wise as does they would never exhibit the contents of their nursery till the children could talk and run about.

Mr. Strange heard a squalling in the house ; the object his wife had produced was thrust under his eyes and nose with indecent haste. It dribbled when teething, erupted with the thrush, and had a difficulty in keeping down its milk. Consequently, when the Countess proposed to remove the babe to Paris, Mr. Strange gave a cheerful consent, and this consent was made doubly cheerful by the certainty that the mother would accompany her child.

If Mr. Strange acted in a somewhat callous manner in granting this separation between himself and his wife and child, he was in other particulars generous. He made the Countess an allowance which, for his circumstances was handsome, and as the child grew, and greater demands were made on his purse, he met these demands without remonstrance.

Arrived in Paris, the Countess Garcia had not long to swim before her feet touched ground. She had a perfectly legitimate right to her title, her pedigree was unassailable, her manners were polished. She appeared at the balls of the Spanish ambassador, and associated with the best French and Spanish families belonging to the old noblesse. It was well known that she had married a moneyed Englishman, of no birth, nor station, nor religion. It was known that she had married for money. No one spoke of Mr. Strange. The great people among whom she moved would as soon have inquired about a boil that troubled her as about the husband whom 'for her sins' she had saddled on her. No persons of breeding invite their friends to introduce them to the family skeleton.

Mirelle was brought up by the Countess to think of her father as a man who had taken a mean advantage of her mother's poverty. He was her father by sufferance; *de facto*, alas, not *de jure*. She had inherited her mother's complexion, eyes, and hair; the blood in her veins was her mother's, Spanish and aristocratic; her sentiments were her mother's, as also her prejudices and her faith. It was hard to say what she derived from her father except her living and schooling, for which he paid. For that she owed him nothing. He was fulfilling his duty, and a privilege he ought to value. What was he, to be the husband of a Garcia and the father of a Garcia? He was English, he was a heretic; worst of all, he was bourgeois.

The Countess bought herself silks with Mr. Strange's money, wore the diamonds he sent her, hired good rooms in an aristocratic quarter, and paid for them from his remittances. She had nothing whatever of her own. She owed him everything to her handkerchiefs and her shoestrings. She knew this perfectly, and writhed under the knowledge. The greater the debt she owed him, the deeper the detestation with which she regarded him. Each present he sent her was repaid by instilling a drop of bitterness into the heart of his child towards him.

One stipulation with regard to his daughter's education Mr. Strange had made. He insisted that she should have an English nurse, and that when she grew older she should have English playmates and English governesses. When old enough to go to school her mother sent her to English nuns, because Mr. Strange refused to allow her to go to any other convent than one of English sisters. Thus it was that Mirelle grew up to speak English fluently and well, and to thoroughly understand the tongue. But of English ways of thinking and of feeling she had not the faintest conception. Proud, cold, selfish, and bigoted her mother had been, and the ambition of Mirelle was to model herself on her mother. Thus she, too, became proud, cold, selfish, and bigoted. It was not her fault—the fault lay in her training.

The Countess was a woman of the world, who combined religious zeal with worldly self-seeking. She was a vain woman, and though she did her utmost to conserve her beauty, it withered, and the child blooming into lovely maidenhood at her side made the contrast distressing, because noticeable. This was the reason why she placed Mirelle in a convent in her fourteenth year. She saw the girl often, but never, if she could help it, was seen in her company.

This separation from her mother was of advantage to Mirelle. It preserved her simplicity. There was no craft in her; she was absolutely guileless, distressingly frank, and innocent of the trickery as well as of the wickedness of the social world. She was cold, because the spring had not yet come to her frozen heart. She loved her mother, but without passion, for her mother was too selfish to awaken passionate love. Her nurses and governesses had changed so often that she could not count them. Among the cold sisters, lilies of virtue, the exhibition of emotion was, if not sinful, yet smacking of imperfection. Natural affections were weaknesses of the moral spine, to be conquered by wearing a perpetual back-board.

Suddenly the Countess died—died in her chair before the looking-glass, reciting the Litany of Loreto, whilst her face was being enamelled. The beautifier entreated Madame la Comtesse not to draw her mouth down on one side, it was cracking the enamel before it was dry—just when she had arrived at the 'tower of ivory.' Then Madame la Comtesse gave a gasp and the enamel came off, washed away from her brow by the sweat of death, and running in a milky river down her nose and cheeks, and dripping on the peignoir under her chin. The beautifier rang the bell, and said, 'Sacré mille diables! To whom shall I send in the bill? Madame is no more in condition to pay.'

When Mr. Strange heard of his wife's death, he settled his affairs in Brazil. He was a strictly conscientious man, and he felt that now it was his duty to look after the child. He had no idea that the child had sprung up into maidenhood, and was a tall, lovely girl, lovelier than her mother had ever been. His wife had not taken the trouble to send him a miniature of his daughter. Miniatures are expensive, and the Countess wanted all the money she received for herself. She did, indeed, once send him a bit of her hair, tied with blue silk; but then, that cost nothing. Mr. Strange thought of his child as a limp piece of mortality in a long white garment, with a frill round the red head like that put round a ham-bone—a thing of squeals, that in its squealing showed a pair of toothless gums, a quivering red tongue, and a crinkled white palate. He could hardly believe his eyes when introduced to his daughter. She received him with perfect self-possession, without raising her eyes from the ground to look at him, for the sisters had taught her the custody of the eyes. According to S. Paul, there is but one Man of Sin, and he is in the future; to the religious all men are men of sin, and in the present.

Mirelle curtsied gracefully. She spoke the best copybook sentiments of filial respect, and assured him (out of the Catechism) of the obligation to filial duty under which she lay.

Then he took her away from the nuns of the Sacred Heart, and carried her about Paris, sight-seeing, in the hope of making her unbend.

The decorator sent in a bill for two thousand francs, his charge for beautifying madame, hoping to get fifty, and ready to accept five. Mr. Strange tore the bill, and lit his cigar with it.

An old woman who had laid madame out asked five francs for her pains, then timidly produced a lock of hair she had cut off madame's head as she laid her in the coffin. The hair was beautiful still! and, oh! madame had looked so sweet, so peaceful, like a holy angel, actually young again. Then Mr. Strange took the lock reverently, turned his face away, and did not speak. Something in his throat troubled him. He thought of twenty years ago—of the time when his heart bounded, of the singing of the nightingale, of the flowering of the wheat, of the short dream of poetry. Then he recovered himself, and put something in the old woman's hand. The old woman went chuckling away. When she reached the street she said, 'That was a brave invention. Madame's complexion was that of a toad's belly. She was hideous as a monkey. I could not pick the paint off her skin. Some adhered, the rest flaked away. That lock of hair was part of her false front. Mon Dieu! how soft men's hearts are!' Mr. Strange speedily discovered that he and his daughter had about as many subjects in common as an Esquimaux has with a native of equatorial Africa. She was above all things a Catholic, he a Protestant. She was religious, and because religious, somewhat conscientious. He conscientious, and, because conscientious, somewhat religious. His religion was to his life what stockings are to a traveller's portmanteau, something to fill corners with where nothing else will go. With Mirelle religion was the chief packing of her life, and this was a condition incomprehensible to her father. She had artistic instincts; she loved pictures and music. Now, pictures and music happen to be two things not to be got in Brazil, except in such an execrable state of degradation as to be unendurable. But he liked the theatre, and to attend the theatre Mirelle considered wicked. Mirelle had learned history from the sisters of the Sacré Cœur that is, she had learned that every modern political idea is positively evil, that absolutism is ideal perfection, that the mediæval times were the only times in which it was worth living, for then the popes gave and withdrew crowns, kings kissed their feet, and emperors held their stirrups. She had been taught geography out of French manuals, and had learned that France is to the rest of the European powers as the sun to the planets; from it they derive their light, and about it they rotate.

Mirelle had her acquaintances, the Princess L'Amoureuse, Prince Punchkin, countesses, baronesses by the score, the mothers and aunts of her schoolfellows, and friends of her mother. Not one of these was known to Mr. Strange even by name, and when she spoke of them she might have been, for aught he cared, reciting the list of European lepidoptera.

Even in their eating their tastes were opposed. Mr. Strange was fond of pickles, Mirelle loved sweets. Chillies tickled his palate, chocolate soothed hers; crystallised angelica carried her into heaven, and plunged him into purgatory, for he had a hollow tooth. Mr. Strange endeavoured to talk to Mirelle of her mother. Now that the Countess was dead, some of the old romance that had surrounded his wooing reappeared, and his heart softened to the memory of the woman. Mirelle was ready enough to speak of her, but she had nothing to say that vibrated a chord in his heart. She spoke of her mother as a fashionable lady, living in society, dressing for balls, driving in the Bois de Boulogne, or holding a plate at the door of the Madeleine—not of her as a woman feeling, loving, suffering.

This condition of affairs was becoming intolerable. How was Mr. Strange to live with a young lady with whom he was utterly out of sympathy, whose head was where his feet stood, and her feet at his head? They saw different worlds, they breathed different air.

The first thing to be done was to get her away from France. That was a plain necessity. On English soil common interests might spring up.

Mr. Strange had a friend of former times living at Avranches, a friend of whom he had lost sight for many years. He knew his address, and he knew also that he was married to a French lady.

Mr. Strange's nearest relative, a cousin, had lived formerly at Falmouth, and, he supposed, lived there still. Mr. Strange resolved to visit his old friend at Avranches, and go on in the packet from St. Malo to Falmouth. He would consult both on what was to be done with Mirelle. He had other reasons, which will appear in the sequel.

So he hurried away from Paris, and went to Avranches. His old friend was delighted to see him, shook hands—both hands—with the utmost cordiality, asked half a dozen times after his wife and children, and forgot as frequently, when told, that his wife was dead and that there was but one child, a daughter. He insisted on carrying his dear friend Strange with him to the café, and on his drinking with him a glass of *eau sucrée* flavoured with syrup of orange, and eating with him sponge biscuits. Would he further, in recollection of old times, favour him with a game of dominoes? The Frenchified Englishman did not introduce Mr. Strange to his wife, or ask him to bring Mirelle from the hotel to his house, and finally, looking at his watch, remembered he was due to take his wife a drive, shook hands with his dear old friend with effusion, and begged, if he were again passing through Avranches on his way to or from Brazil, not to omit to call and drink again with him sugar and water and eat a sponge cake.

Mr. Strange departed, his grave face looking graver. After a rough passage, in which Mirelle suffered extremely, and her father smoked and looked at the waves unconcernedly, they arrived at Falmouth. Cato, when at sea, jumped overboard, saying he would rather die than endure another half-hour of sickness. Cato was a stoic philosopher, Mirelle was neither a philosopher nor a stoic. She was profoundly wretched, and looked ghastly when she landed in a drizzle at Falmouth. Thus her first arrival in England was not encouraging. Mr. Strange inquired for his cousin, and learned that he was no longer at Falmouth; he had removed to Launceston. Mr. Strange heard such an unsatisfactory account of his cousin that he was greatly disconcerted. His cousin's name was Trampleasure. He found a universal consensus of opinion at Falmouth that Mr. Trampleasure was a man unprincipled and unscrupulous, and that he had moved to Launceston only because he had made Falmouth too hot for him.

Mr. Strange remained a couple of nights at Falmouth, and then took coach to Launceston. There he neither called on his cousin nor stayed. He found at the inn a young gentleman equally anxious with himself to push on to Exeter, and he offered him a seat in the chaise he had hired. Thus it was that Mr. John Herring was with him and his daughter when the accident occurred. Before leaving Brazil Mr. Strange had made his will, bequeathing everything he possessed to his cousin Mr. Sampson Trampleasure, and to his Avranches friend, in trust for his daughter, and had constituted them her guardians. This will was in his desk. He did not unpack his desk at Falmouth and cancel his will; there was time enough to do that on his arrival at Exeter. Man proposes: God disposes.

CHAPTER V.

THE OWLS' NEST.

WEST WYKE is a perfect specimen of a small country gentleman's house of the sixteenth century. Two or three hundred years ago every parish in the West of England contained several gentle families, not acred up to their lips, but with moderate possessions. These small squires farmed a large part of their own estates themselves, gave moderate portions to their daughters, who were not ashamed to marry yeomen and even tradesmen, and their younger sons went to sea, or were apprenticed to merchants in the towns.[1]

When the heralds came round to hold their courts and examine into the claims of gentility and right to bear arms, these squires rode to court with their title-deeds in their saddle-bags and their signet rings on their hands, and showed convincingly that they had held their acres for many generations and had borne coat armour. Hard drinking, gambling, an extravagant style of living, have destroyed these little gentry, and the same causes have effected the extermination of the yeomanry.

In the parish of South Tawton two hundred years ago there were seven families of gentle blood—the Weekes of North Wyke, the Burgoynes of Zeal, the Northmores of Will, the Oxenhams of Oxenham, the Battishills of West Wyke, the Mylfords, and the Fursdons. All have gone; their place is only known by the old houses they have left behind, and a few tombstones with their heraldic bearings on them in the church. The grand old mansion of the Weekes is now parted in twain, one half a farmhouse, the other a labourer's cottage. The park is cut down, the ceilings are falling, the panelling is decaying. The house of the Burgoynes is now a village tavern; Will, a cottage, its grand old gateway levelled with the dust; West Wyke is a farmhouse.

If we would know how our gentle ancestors lived, let us

[1] Thus, in the Visitation of Devon of 1620, a Cholmondeley enters his brothers as 'silkman on London Bridge,' and 'prentice in London,' and a Wolston registers his sisters as married respectively to a 'labourer' and a 'clothier'; a daughter of Glanville married a blacksmith of Tavistock.

look closely at West Wyke—it deserves a visit and a description.

The house stands on the moor, in the midst of a little patch of reclaimed land. The situation is too lofty and exposed to allow of trees to flourish. A few ash stems attempt to live there, and they are twisted from the south-west. A few feet below the surface the roots reach the rock, and when the tap-root touches stone the doom of the tree is sealed.

West Wyke House was built in 1583—the date is on it—by William Battishill. It is a house which a substantial farmer nowadays would scorn to inhabit. It consists, on the basement, of one hall, a ladies' bower, a kitchen, and a large dairy—that is all. And that is the basement plan of many hundreds of similar mansions in the West, once tenanted by proud squires and their ladies, well born, well bred, and well attired. Look at their portraits—they were gentlemen of breed and honour, they carry it in their faces; they were ladies of pure and noble souls, refined in mind, simple in life. It is written on their brows.

In 1656 Roger Battishill, the reigning lord of the manor, walled in a garden in front of the house, and at the side built an embattled gateway, only twelve feet high to the crown of the battlements; a gateway of shaped granite blocks and carved granite mouldings; and over the centre, proudly also sculptured in granite, the arms of Battishill, the cross crosslet in saltire between four great owls. He planted the garden with lilies, white and orange, with honesty, golden-rod, and white rocket. These flourished here, sheltered from the winds by the inclosing walls; and a monthly rose ran up the side of the house, about the hall window, and bloomed up to New Year's day.

No road led to the embattled gateway. No carriages were used in those days, and for the horses' hoofs there was the spongy turf. When a rough track had been trampled through the moor grass, and made black with oozing peat water, the riders rode afield and made another way till the first had grassed itself over again.

Observe the date on the embattled gateway. Charles I. was executed in 1649, Cromwell had issued his edict in 1655 for exacting the tenth penny from the Cavaliers, in order, as he pretended, to make them pay the expenses to which their mutinous disposition exposed the nation. To raise this impost, which passed by the name of the decimation, the Protector appointed major-generals, and divided the kingdom into military jurisdictions under them. These men had power to subject whom they would to decimation, and to imprison any person who should be exposed to their jealousy or suspicion. Now Roger Battishill had been a Royalist, but his twin brother Richard had been a Roundhead. There were two other brothers, Robert and Ralph. Now, when the commissioner came to Okehampton to levy decimation, he summoned Squire Battishill before him; whereupon the four brothers, all habited in grey, with very erect hair, protruding ears, and staring eyes, and a general puzzle-headed expression in their faces, appeared before him, and so bewildered the commissioner with their Roger and Richard, and Robert and Ralph, and their extraordinary likeness to each other, and their profound puzzle-headedness, which made it impossible for Roger to speak without involving Richard and Robert and Ralph, and so through the rest—that he dismissed them undecimated, fully impressed that the Royalist was Ralph, who, being only just of age, could not have been in the past a dangerous recusant. Thereupon the four brothers rode home to West Wyke, hooting with joy, and in commemoration of this achievement set up the embattled gateway, to shut themselves in and the world and politics out for ever. Over the gateway they carved the four owls, their arms, said Roger and Richard, and Robert and Ralph—their own portraits said the malicious world of South Tawton.

Some account of the hall has been already given. In our day the oak panelling has disappeared as fuel for the great hearth, but in the granite mullioned window is still preserved in stained glass the cognizance of the Battishills, the four owls impaled with, azure, three towers argent, on which are squatted three white birds.

A gentleman of the present day, if not exacting, might possibly accommodate himself in the lower part of the house, but would hardly acquiesce in the upstairs arrangements, for there all the bedrooms were *en suite*. In the centre slept the squire and his lady, when he had one; on the right were rooms for the men; in the furthest slept the apprentices, in the nearest the sons and brothers of the family. On the left were three rooms all in communication. The first was the state guest room, the next that allotted to the young ladies; beyond that, over the cow-shed, the room for the servant maids.

We have a great deal to learn from our ancestors, and we

are learning much. We copy their architecture, we reproduce their dyes, we affect their costume, but we do not go back to their sleeping arrangements.

Some days passed. Mirelle remained at West Wyke; John Herring was lodged in the inn at Zeal, not far distant in the valley. He devoted himself to the affairs of Mirelle. Mr. Battishill was most kind, but quite unable to be of real use. He was prepared to discuss with Herring what must be done, and he would undertake to do what he thought desirable, but he never did anything. The dead man might have lain a month, three months, a year upstairs, before Mr. Battishill took steps for his interment. He had a theory of his own relative to the disposal of the dead. He believed that elm was an unsuitable wood for the making of coffins. Alder was the proper timber, because alder grew in swamps, and was presumably damp-resisting. It was in vain that Herring explained to him that alders did not attain a sufficient size to be sawn into planks. That was because alders were not suffered to grow; they were treated as weeds and cut down. 'Grow them,' said Mr. Battishill; 'give them time and see for yourself.' He would have allowed the dead man to occupy the spare room till the alders were grown.

Then, again, he had a theory that coffins ought to be filled with that powerful antiseptic, brown Norwegian pitch, pitch from the pine, none of your villainous coal tar, but brown pitch like old treacle. And so on, from coffins to alders, and to Norway tar, and the dead man waiting for the alders to grow and the pitch to be extracted. John Herring was obliged to see to everything, to arrange with the undertaker, and to fix the funeral. Then, again, Mirelle might have remained on till she married or died for all that Mr. Battishill would have done to discover her relations; perhaps it would have been better had it been so. We take infinite pains to do what is just and kind, and find afterwards that everything would have been better had we put our hands in our pockets. We give in charity and pauperise; we effect reforms which bring in a state of affairs worse than existed before. There is more mischief wrought by doing good than by doing nothing.

Before the funeral, Herring discovered that the deceased had an account with an Exeter bank. He found this through a letter in the pocket-book of the deceased addressed to him in Paris from Exeter, acknowledging the receipt of several thousand pounds, transferred by a Brazilian bank, and notifying the opening of an account in Mr. Strange's name.

Herring communicated with this bank, stated what had taken place, and the banker allowed him to draw a limited sum for funeral expenses. The young man requested, even insisted, on Mr. Battishill being present when he examined the dead man's pocket-book and purse, and he required him to sign a statement of the amount of money found on him.

Mirelle remained perfectly passive; she took her residence with the Battishills as a matter of course. The accident had happened near their house, on their land; it was only proper that they should shelter her. If she gave the matter a thought, this is the result of her cogitation, but actually it did not trouble her. She had always been provided for, and had never had to consider how she was to be provided for. She did not excuse herself for taking advantage of the hospitality of strangers, for it did not occur to her that such an excuse was necessary. Herring was obliged to take on himself what Mirelle omitted. He apologised for her. A strange chance had constituted him her guardian, at least for a while. She allowed him to arrange everything. If he asked her to advise him as to her wishes, she replied that she was without any; he must act as he thought proper. She knew nothing of the ways of England; he must do whatever was conventional.

It did not enter her head that his journey was interrupted on her account, and that he was put to very serious inconvenience by his difficulty in leaving her without a protector. To trust Mr. Battishill to do what was requisite was to trust a piece of bread and butter not to fall butter downwards.

Mirelle took it for granted that Herring was doing his duty or following his pleasure. She accepted his services as she accepted those of the girl who blacked her boots. Each fulfilled a function for which they were called into existence. She neither thanked him nor rewarded him with a look. What he was like she did not know, neither did she care. He wore very big and shapeless boots, but that was proper; boots like these became a bumpkin.

At the funeral he wore black, and gave her his arm. He and she were the sole mourners. She did not wish to attend. She supposed that only men attended the funerals of males; but when it was explained to her that this was not the custom in England, she submitted.

Mr. Battishill did not follow the coffin. There was a difficulty with him about black clothes. He had one best suit, but that was dark blue with brass buttons. He was not provided with ready money, and a new suit of clothes would cripple him for some years, as it would have to be paid for in instalments, a leg and an arm at intervals of a quarter; the coat-tails at equal and similar intervals. Mr. Battishill did not like to admit this, so he was prostrated with a convenient attack of the gout the day before the funeral, and sat in his chair with the lame foot swaddled on a stool before him. We laugh at the shifts of the gentle poor, and label them meannesses, whereas they are necessities. Cicely remained at home. There was but one servant kept at West Wyke, a cook, housemaid, parlour maid, kitchen maid, laundress, condensed into one, and Cicely had sufficient to do to keep the house in order. A funeral, moreover, entails extra work—eating, drinking, and doleful making merry.

Herring gave her some money from Mr. Strange's purse, telling her that it was to be spent on things necessary, and would be accounted for to the executors. It was not right nor reasonable, it was not in the least necessary, that the Battishills should be put to expense by reason of the funeral of a man who was an entire stranger. The deceased was well off, and the small expenses of his funeral would be nothing deducted from the six thousand pounds which they knew was at the bank, and would go to his daughter.

Cicely frankly accepted the money, and made greater preparations than she could otherwise have made. She put more saffron and currants in the cakes, and with these necessary condiments the luxury of candied peel. Instead of providing cyder she put sherry on the table, and gave the bearers and undertaker cold round of beef instead of squab pie.

As Herring and Mirelle left the churchyard after the funeral, she took her hand off his arm, and in their walk back to West Wyke she was interested in the ferns and mosses of the banks. Herring spoke to her occasionally, trying to begin a conversation; but she answered shortly, and either dropped behind to examine a fern or was arrested by the view through a gate, plainly showing him that she declined to converse.

When they were on the moor, John Herring suddenly stopped and picked a tuft of white heath. He offered it to Mirelle, and she accepted it indifferently.

'Although this be a day of sadness, Countess, yet here is an omen that some brightness is in store for you. It is said in the West that the white heath brings good luck to the person that secures it.'

'You found it, monsieur, not I.'

'But I pass on my luck to you. Keep it; I hope it may always spring up in your path as it has this day.'

She made no reply, but gathered a sprig of pink heath.

On reaching the gate of West Wyke Cicely met them; she had been looking out for their return.

'Voyez!' said Mirelle, 'I have picked a lovely bouquet of ferns and moss and wild flowers on my way. We have no ferns in France, at least I have never seen such. In this one particular you surpass us.'

She showed her bunch. The white heath was not there.

'Oh! exclaimed Herring, incautiously, 'the best flower of all has fallen—the white heath.'

'So it is,' said Mirelle. 'I am sorry; my hand was full.'

'Shall I go back for it?'

'No, it has fallen in the mire, and is trodden under foot. I shall doubtless find my own good luck some day myself.'

CHAPTER VI.

THAT OLD TRAMPLARA.

As they entered the garden, Mirelle was about to take Cicely's arm, and walk round it with her, looking at the flowers, when John Herring stayed her—

'Excuse me, Countess, I must trouble you one moment. I think it time that we should make an attempt to find out your father's relatives or connections in England.'

'I do not suppose that he had any.'

'Why not?'

'He did not speak to me of any. Besides, these people do not hang together like persons who have pedigrees.'

'But something must be done. Whither are you to go? What is to become of you?'

'Comme le bon Dieu veut!'

'You cannot remain here till some one turns up to claim you.'

'Why not?'

Mr. Herring was staggered. He could not reply, and say

that she was trespassing on the hospitality of entire strangers. She turned to continue her walk.

'That is a fine orange lily,' she said to Cicely.

'You must really allow me to detain you,' pursued Herring. 'All I ask now is, may Mr. Battishill and I look through your father's desk that is in his trunk? His bunch of keys has been given to you. Will you open the desk, or shall we do it with your sanction?'

'Do what you like, Mr. Fish.'

Cicely looked reprovingly at Mirelle, and ventured on a correction. 'Mr. Herring, you mean.'

Mirelle's cheek tinged faintly.

'I beg you pardon, sir. Your name had escaped me. I am not yet familiar with English names, which seem to me harsh or grotesque. I remembered that you belonged to the fishes, but to which particular family of fish I did not recall.'

Herring bit his lip, then said quietly, 'Would you prefer opening your father's desk yourself, Countess?'

'Mon Dieu, non!'

'Then will you give me the key, and allow us to examine the contents of the desk?'

'Certainly. But I do not know which is the key. Here, take the bunch, and do as you will.' Then she turned impatiently round, and walked away.

When Herring had entered the house, Cicely said gently, 'I think, Mirelle, you are bound to try and remember poor Mr. Herring's name.'

'Why should I? It in no way concerns me.'

'But you hurt his feelings. I saw he was pained.'

'Oh, but no! that is not possible. He cannot care about such a droll name. Herring!—red herring—pickled herring! —the thing is ridiculous. When the name is historical, then —c'est bien autre chose. But when it is ignoble, and, in addition, is ridiculous, what is there to be proud of? If there be no pride, there can be no wound. These people, moreover, have not the feelings that we have—I mean about their names. I should resent it were I called anything but what I am. But then the Garcias fought the Moors. Don Luis de Garcia with one blow cleft a Saracen through his turban, 'twixt his eyes, to the very saddle, and the saddle itself was cloven. We had the saddle and the sword in our armoury three hundred years ago. We held the county of Cantalejo, we coined our own money, and hung on our own gallows. But the Herrings! they swim in the vast sea along with the sprats and the congers, the common plaice and the little dabs. They have no history. They spawn ten thousand at a time; they are the bread of the nobler fish. No—a Herring has no cause to be offended if his name be forgotten. There,' Mirelle laughed, 'I have said my say.'

'He is a gentleman,' said Cicely, with some warmth; 'I know nothing of his family, but I judge by his manners and appearance.'

'I have noticed neither. I do not consider those who in no way concern me. I cannot describe to you the colour of the eyes and hair of the postillion who upset us, and I know and care as little about the nobody who had the bad fortune to be upset with us. Il m'ennuie, c'est tout dire.'

'He has been very considerate towards you. He has done a great deal for you deserving of gratitude.'

'For what else did the good God create men but to be useful—to assist the ladies? He made the dog the servant of man, and man the dog of the woman. The man does not thank or consider the dog that fetches him a stick out of the water, and the woman has no occasion to pat and praise the man who executes foolish trifles for her. If the dog shakes himself near his master, when emerging from the water, then the stick he brought is applied to his sides, and when the man makes himself over officious, woman turns her back on him.'

'You have an odd idea of the reason why men are placed in the world.'

'I have a perfectly just idea. At the convent of the Sacré Cœur the good sisters kept several tame men. There was old Jean who sawed the firewood for them, and ancient Jacques who gardened. There was even a devout sweep who cleaned their chimneys, and though his face was black, his soul was white. There was a venerable chaplain who heard confessions, and there was a domesticated notary who did their legal business. The sisters worried these men a great deal, especially the notary and the confessor; the latter made a good end in a lunatic asylum. They all took it in good part. Their backs were made to bear their burden.'

'You will not forget his name again?'

'Whose name? What! ce bon Poisson! I will remember for your sake.'

John Herring brought down the dead man's desk into the hall, that Mr. Battishill and he might examine its contents together. Mr. Battishill hastily put his leg up as Herring entered.

'Sorry that I could not attend the funeral,' said the old gentleman, 'but the sins of the fathers are visited on their children. I endure the gout because my father and grandfather tippled port. Sit down, Herring, and I will tell you a good story. In the grand old days when there were many squires about here, and the Knapmans were at Wansdon, and the Whiddons at Whiddon, the old Squire Knapman was getting into a bad way financially, like me. He was invited to dinner at Whiddon, and drove there in his great coach. After dinner, Squire Whiddon saw him into his overcoat in the hall, and was about to accompany him to the door when old Knapman said, " No, no! you will catch cold! keep in, man." But the squire was too hospitable for that, and he attended Knapman to the coach. "Don't come out, for heaven's sake, you will get your death of cold," said Knapman. "Why!" exclaimed Whiddon, "what is the meaning of this, Knapman? Going to ride on the box instead of inside, a night like this?" "I prefer it," answered Squire Knapman, proceeding to ascend to the box. But Whiddon would not allow it; he went to the coach-door and opened it—when, lo! he found it full of hay.'

'How came that?' asked Herring.

'Why, do you not see? Old Knapman was badly off for hay for his horse, and when he went out anywhere to dinner he told his coachman to fill the carriage with hay from his host's rick, and himself went home on the box.'

'A good story, sir; but I think we had better examine the contents of this desk before we tell any more.'

'Sit down, sit down, man. Do not drive the willing horse, and let an old man give you a piece of advice. Let well alone, and do not precipitate yourself, as Orlando says, "from the smoke into the smother."'

'But you forget, sir, this that you advise me to leave alone is not well at all. The young lady is an orphan, and we know nothing of her relatives.'

'Go on, then! How full of briars is this working-day world! What do you propose to do with the lady?'

'I cannot tell till I have ascertained whether she has relatives in England.'

'If she has not, she must be made a ward in Chancery, or you must marry her, and so take her affairs into your own hands.'

'Mr. Battishill!' John Herring flushed to his temples and looked down.

'I am putting an alternative case. Now, to make her a ward in Chancery is to put a fly into a cobweb. Her few thousand pounds will be bled away. By-the-by, talking of thousands, do you know anyone inclined to speculate in silver lead? I have a rare lode on my property, but I have not the means to work it. I have set three men on the shode, and they have been engaged there for several days. There is no mistaking that grey-blue stuff that comes up. But I cannot go on myself. If I could, the property would be cleared in no time. As it is, I am crushed by that damned old Tramplara. Do you remember how Sindbad had to carry the Old Man of the Sea on his shoulders who picked all the apples and ate them himself, whilst Sindbad perished of hunger? Do what he would, Sindbad was powerless to dislodge the horrible creature astride on his back.'

'Yes, I remember.'

'Well, I am in the same predicament; I have got that old Tramplara on my back.'

'Who is Tramplara, sir?'

'Tramplara! Not know Tramplara? I thought every one knew and had felt him. He is a Cornish lawyer, who lived at Falmouth, till Falmouth passed him on to Launceston, having had enough of him. He has lent me money. He knew that I wanted to improve my property; I was hot on draining at one time, and thought if I drained my marshes I should till my purse. But, Herring, draining does not pay in all lands It don't pay in clay at all. The only thing I drained effectually was my pocket. Then I was drawn on to speculate in Cornish mines that old Tramplara whispered great things of to me. As a particular favour he put me up to splendid investments before they were opened to the public. By all the saints in Cornwall—and they are more numerous than those in Paradise—that mining did for me completely.' The old man stamped his gouty foot on the ground. 'It was a swindle. And now I am entangled in the toils of old Tramplara, and cannot get out. Ah! Herring, if I could but work the lead mine myself, I should clear myself of Tramplara. But I cannot do it; the cursed rascal robs me of all my rents, and I am unable to nurse the mine until it can run on its own legs. I must call in strangers to form a company, and that means they are to swallow the cup and give me the dregs. Moreover,

I am afraid of Tramplara finding it out. If he does; if he suspects what a lode there is at Upaver, he will foreclose, take the property, and work the mine himself.'

'I have no capital at my disposal,' said Herring.

'I do not suppose you have. But only think! Supposing that Mr. Strange had come here alone, to recover of his fall, and that I could have induced him to sink some of his thousands here! Come along with me; I will take you to Upaver and you shall judge for yourself.' The old man jumped up, and walked across the hall to his hat.

'Your gout, sir!'

'Oh, that is all right now. A walk will do it good.'

'Another time, Mr. Battishill. Just at present we must examine the desk, and see if we can find any clue to the family of Mr. Strange.'

'To be sure, to be sure,' said Mr. Battishill, returning to his chair. 'You drew me off our business. Open the box and get the matter over.'

Herring was trying the keys. Before he had found the right key, Mr. Battishill put his hand on the bunch and said, 'By the way, before we go on with our inquiry, tell me, do you belong to the Herrings of Codrington?'

'I did not know there were Herrings there.'

'No; I do not mean now. In 1620 Hugh Manning, of Newton Bushell, married Elizabeth, daughter of John Herring, of Codrington, in Devon; so it stands in the Visitation, under the Manning pedigree. I do not think much of your family not appearing in that Visitation, as some good Devon families just emerging from the yeoman class, or not caring to appear at the court of the heralds, are left unregistered. It was so in this parish. Neither the Oxenhams nor the Northmores appeared, and yet they held lands here from time immemorial.'

'Had we not better seek out the Strange family, instead of exploring the past of the Herrings? The latter will keep.'

'You are right, quite right, my young friend. Good Lord, what pertinacity you have. It is like that of a ferret hanging on to a rat. Open the desk.'

The desk contained a considerable number of papers, almost all connected with business, and in a foreign language—Portuguese—which Herring could not read.

Mr. Battishill leaned back in his chair and looked before

him out of the hall window, lost in his meditations. He muttered something impatiently.

'I beg your pardon,' said Herring looking up. 'Did you address me?'

'I?—no,' answered Mr. Battishill. 'I merely said, " Damn old Tramplara!"'

Herring resumed his examination.

'The scoundrel has his claws in my neck, and the mischief is he is dragging more than myself down. There is poor Cicely as well.'

'Can you decipher these letters?' asked Herring, holding out a couple of papers to the old gentleman; 'they are written either in Spanish, Italian, or Portuguese.'

'I cannot say. My knowledge is limited. "Ignorance is the curse of God, knowledge the wing whereby we fly to heaven." I once read Latin, but that was long ago. I may remember a few words of French. "Dieu et mon droit," that means "God and my right." "Honi soit qui mal y pense," that means something about the Duchess of Gloucester's garter. No, this is Chinese to me. "There is no darkness but ignorance."'

'Hold!' exclaimed Herring; 'here is his will. Shall we look at it?'

'By all means. No other document is so likely to help you to what you want to discover. Give it to me.'

The will was very short. Mr. Strange had drawn it up himself before sailing for Europe. The substance has been already given. Mr. Strange left everything he possessed to Mr. Eustace Smith, of Avranches, gentleman, and Mr. Sampson Trampleasure, of Falmouth, solicitor, in trust for his daughter, Mirelle, till she attained the age of twenty-three, and empowering them to expend from it such moneys as were needed for her entertainment and education. They were constituted sole guardians, trustees, and executors.

Mr. Battishill uttered a groan.

'That scoundrel again!'

'But, sir, this is Trampleasure, not Tramplara.'

'It is the same. He writes himself Trampleasure, but nobody dreams of calling him anything but Tramplara.'

'He is constituted her guardian.'

'Yes; but associated, fortunately, with another, Mr. Eustace Smith.'

'But should he renounce?'

'Then good-bye to Mirelle's six thousand pounds. It will go down Wheal Polpluggan.'

'Wheal what?'

'Wheal Polpluggan, that engulfed my money, and me.'

CHAPTER VII.

THAT YOUNG TRAMPLARA.

'WHAT is to be done?' asked Herring. There was a small black square ruler on the table, belonging to Mr. Strange's desk. He took it up and played with it, now balancing it across his finger, then standing it up on the table, with the end in his palm.

'Let things take their course,' answered Mr. Battishill. 'I advise with Gloucester, "Thy greatest help is quiet."'

'I will write to Mr. Eustace Smith at once.'

'Do so. If he renounces, mark my words, Polpluggan swallows the young lady's fortune. Friend Herring, I have the eyes of my heraldic cognizance, and can see in the dark. A wonderful mine, Polpluggan. The amount of capital sunk in it must have constituted a silver lode somewhere.'

'When I have heard from Mr. Eustace Smith I will communicate with Mr. Trampleasure—not before. I suppose I am justified in doing this?'

'Justified! Certainly. I have never seen Polpluggan myself. It is situated in the Scilly Isles. Of these there be forty; but I have been unable myself to make out in which Polpluggan lies, whether in Presher, or Bryher, or Annette, or Tean, or Great Gannilly, or Little Gannilly, or Gweal, or Withial, or Ganniornich, or ——'

'I beg your pardon. May I borrow some notepaper?'

'By all means. There is some. The beauty, or the mischief of the matter is, that the lode of tin is in the granite and under the sea. Mining in granite is costly, and the proximity to the sea dangerous, entailing extraordinary precautions. The water gets in. Now when this takes place there follows a call on the shareholders for pumping it out. Every great storm drowns the mine and fills the shareholders with despair; the pump goes down into their pockets. Then the tin vein does not yield as at first. Once there were bunches like those of Eshcol, the dividends were seven, seven-and-a-half, eight, eight-and-a-quarter, going, going, going up, and then, slow but sure, as the miners sank their shaft so did the shares sink, and the dividends with them, till they reached zero. After that, a rapidly swelling minus quantity.'

'I have written the letter. Have you sealing-wax?'

'There it is. Now the beauty, or the mischief is—beauty from the Tramplara, mischief from the Battishill point of view —that old rascal so fired my imagination, and was so accommodating, that I borrowed the money of him to sink in Polpluggan. If I had speculated with my own little savings—but no! I had no savings—that would have been bad enough, but to speculate on borrowed capital is ruinous. That rascally old Tramplara led me on till he led me into his trap, and then snap, the door shut behind me, and I am fast. Poor West Wyke! Poor Cicely! Poor—' he looked at the stained coat in the window, 'poor ancestral owls!'

A shadow fell across the table from some one passing the window.

'Good God!' exclaimed Mr. Battishill; 'here comes that young Tramplara.'

A rap with the handle of a riding-whip on the hall door, and, without waiting for a response, Tramplara entered. He was a young man, good looking, with dark hair and eyes, and a dark moustache. His cheeks were florid. He had been drinking, and that gave a gloss to his face and an uncertainty to his eye. He came in with his hat on. He wore a short coat, knee breeches, and tall boots.

'I say,' he began roughly, 'what is the meaning of this? There have been those—with an oath—Cobbledicks inclosing a fresh piece of the down. I won't have it. They will establish rights, and it will be hard to displace them. Their fences must be tore down.' His pronunciation was West country, his grammar occasionally so.

'Have you observed that Mr. Battishill is in the room?' asked Herring, quietly. He had just sealed the Avranches letter.

'I see him right enough. I was addressing him, not you.'

Herring looked at the old gentleman; he had become limp. His jaw had fallen, and his hands trembled as he laid them on the arms of his chair.

'Then perhaps you will remove your hat, Mr. Tramplara.'

'I object to be so called,' answered the young man sharply.

'My name, sir, is Trampleasure, and only those who can't spell call me otherwise.'

'Very well, Mr. Trampleasure; will you remove your hat?'

'Who are you? I don't know you. Never had the pleasure of seeing your face that I am aware of. What may your d—d name be, hey?'

'Sir,' said Herring, rising, 'I will stand no insolence. When you ask my name properly, you shall have it.'

'O Lord! who cares a brass button what you be called? Keep your name to yourself if you like.'

Herring walked straight up to him, composedly and firmly, looked him full in the eyes, and said, 'You have been drinking. Remove your hat, or I will knock it off.'

Tramplara took off his beaver and put it testily on the table.

'I am not a bad fellow,' he said, 'when asked a civil question, but I object to be bullied.'

Then he seated himself near the table, looking sulky.

'I am Mr. Sampson Trampleasure, junior, gentleman,' he said. 'Now perhaps you will tell me your name.'

Herring gave him in return his sur and Christian names.

'Never heard of you,' said Tramplara. 'What are you doing here?'

Herring made no reply to his impertinence.

'I say,' began the young man again, in a loud tone, 'I won't have those Cobbledicks encroaching. I saw that old Bufflehead, Grizzly, but could not make him understand, or leastways he wouldn't understand.'

Mr. Battishill bridled up feebly. 'You are premature, Mr. Sampson; West Wyke is my property, and I have the right to settle on it whom I choose.'

'Oh, ah! that's good,' said young Tramplara. 'Yours on sufferance. You know well enough that my governor has his foot under your chair, and can kick you over any day he has a mind to.'

'When he does that he can deal with the Cobbledicks as well. Naked came we into the world, and naked we shall go out, Battishills and Cobbledicks together.'

'That'll soon take place unless you shell out. You know what I have come about.'

Mr. Battishill's brief indignation and assumption of dignity expired. He put his hand into his pocket, and drew forth his handkerchief, and wiped his lips.

'You have come on an unfortunate day, Mr. Sampson. We have had a death in the house.'

'I don't care whether there be a death or a birth,' answered the young man rudely. 'I know one thing, if I do not go back with the interest due last Lady in my pocket, there'll be pretty summary dealings in a place and with persons not the other side of London, nor in China, nor New Zealand, nor Bra——! Why! how in the name of Ginger came this into your hands?'

His eye was resting on the will that lay open as John Herring had left it when extracting from it the address of Mr. Eustace Smith. He put out the crook of his whip and drew it over to him. 'Ten thousand crocodiles! There is my name in it. Sampson Trampleasure, of Falmouth, Solicitor. No! that is my father. Last will and testament of James Strange, of Bahia, Brazil! Why, that's a kinsman of ours. My grandmother was a Strange. How the devil came this into your hands?'

Mr. Battishill looked at Herring. Herring was disconcerted. The surprise and indignation caused by the intrusion and insolence of the young man had prevented him from recollecting to fold up and put away the document.

'Writing to one trustee,' said young Tramplara, taking up the letter, 'and in duty bound about to write to the other when interrupted by me. I will save you the trouble. But how came this into your hands? Will you answer me that?'

'I have already told you, Mr. Sampson, that there has been a death in the house. An unfortunate and melancholy accident took place last Friday, a carriage was upset near this house, and a strange gentleman killed. He was brought here, and has been buried to-day.'

'That was Mr. James Strange?'

'It was. He was a gentleman who, according to his daughter's account, had lived many years in Brazil as a diamond merchant.'

'I know that. He was my father's first cousin; consequently he was—blowed if I know—but cousin of some sort, and about the only relative on that side I had. What did he die worth?'

'That will be for your father to ascertain,' said Herring.

'It seems to me a most extraordinary thing to find a will of one not even remotely belonging to you lying on your table where it might be torn to light pipes with.'

'The reason is very simple,' said Herring. 'Mr. Battishill

and I knew nothing about Mr. Strange, and his daughter seemed to be equally in the dark about his relatives.'

'What, is that pretty girl in the garden along of Miss Cicely his daughter?'

'That young lady is his daughter. Mr. Battishill and I examined the papers of the deceased. Most were in Portuguese, which we were unable to read. From the will we gathered who were the trustees and guardians of the lady. That was what we sought, and that was what we have ascertained.'

'Well, this is a rise,' said young Tramplara. 'This is like going out after a partridge and starting a pheasant. But never mind. I keep my game in my eye. You will have to unburthen your pockets, Battishill, old boy!'

'Has the sea broken in on Polplugggan?' asked Mr. Battishill dolefully. He knew well enough that the visit did not relate to Polpluggan, but he tried to put off the worst.

'Polpluggan,' said the young man, with a touch of melancholy in his voice; 'Polpluggan is swamped outright. The mighty Atlantic has got on top of him, and is pouring himself down his throat. There ain't no more pumping to be done there, more's the pity.'

'No more calls, then, on the shareholders?'

'No.'

'Nor dividends either?'

'Oh dear no. What's lost is lost. Polpluggan was a very pretty thing; but there—his day is over, more's the pity.' He sighed. 'He was as fine a fellow in the way of tin as you might wish to look on. But with the best intentions you can't go after a lode into the bowels of the stormy deep. The public don't like it; and when you call on them every month to pump out the ocean, they turn unpleasant, and apply live coals to your tail and make you squeak. No—Polpluggan is no more.' Then with a boisterous laugh and a slap on the table, 'Never mind the death of Polpluggan, old chap. We aren't seen the end of Cornish mining yet. There are many more, bigger nor Polpluggan, looming in the future. But that's neither here nor there. What I've come about is the interest that ought to have been paid last Lady.'

'It has been a bad time, Mr. Sampson. The sheep have been cawed, and I have done all I could to save them. It was the rain last fall and all the winter that did it. I kept them off the clay land, and I tried every remedy I could think of. The last, and that which promised best, was bruised box leaves.

We cut off all our box borders in the garden, used every green sprout and leaf, but it was not sufficient. The poor beasts picked up a little on it, but no lasting cure was effected, and they just rotted away.'

'Oh, blow the sheep!' said young Tramplara, coarsely. 'It ain't them I want, but the money.'

'But I have not got the money,' sighed Mr. Battishill. 'If I could have sold my sheep I could have paid. But not only so. The farmer at Upaver has lost his sheep as well, and several bullocks to boot, so that he has fallen behind with his rent. It is a very extraordinary thing that my sheep should get cawed, for I have never known such a thing happen before in this high land. Down in the valley on the clay is another matter. But you never saw any of that blue grass on my upland, which is the signal Nature throws out that no sheep are to draw nigh. It has always been said that peat——'

'Faith! it is only a matter of time. A year or two don't matter particularly,' said Sampson Tramplara, 'sooner or later scatt you go. If you chose to speculate you must look out for the consequences. You ought to know what mining means at your age. You don't think to walk over a bog, and not get stogged.'

'Your own father urged me on. But for him I would have had nothing to do with Polpluggan.'

'Nor with draining either?'

'That was my blunder. Polpluggan was the pit down which I fell hopelessly, and your father led me to the brink and pushed me over.'

'There are plenty to keep you company, if that be a consolation,' said young Sampson. 'Now it has just come to this. You don't suppose my father hasn't lost also in Polpluggan, do y'. I can tell you he has—a brave bit of money too. He wants his money as much as you do; and he will have it too.'

'You must have patience; all seasons are not bad.'

'But if you nip your fingers you squeak. My father is nipped pretty tight, all along of Polpluggan. You see he has another mine in view, and it wants capital to get that floated.'

'Look here,' said Mr. Battishill, desperately. 'If it comes to that, and he wants another mine to start upon, let him come to me. I will put him upon a lode, a real lode, and I stake my life there is silver lead, and plenty of it, at Upaver.'

'That won't do,' said Tramplara. 'It isn't what comes out of a mine that makes it pay, but what is put into it. You don't understand these things, or you would never have gone head over heels down Polpluggan. There is nothing to be had from you, so I don't mind saying it. And you are an old friend, and are sucked dry, and about to be turned inside out.'

'There is no water that can drown my mine.'

'More is the pity. It is just the water that makes it pay. But come! It is too late for you to learn the alphabet of mining.'

The bottle of sherry that had been purchased for the funeral was on the table, along with some glasses. Without invitation the young man poured out and drank.

'There's sixty pounds goes home in my pocket, or it don't. And if it don't, worse luck for you.' He put his hand to the bottle. Herring drew the decanter from his reach.

'What do you mean?' asked Tramplara. 'Give me the sherry this moment.'

'You have been drinking before coming here,' said Herring, 'and you shall not further insult Mr. Battishill by becoming drunk in his presence.'

'What is that?' shouted young Sampson. 'Hey! what a moral man we have here. All for total abstinence, I presume.'

He jumped up, whip in hand, and switched the whip two or three times before him; then, looking Herring full in the face, with an insolent smirk on his lips, clapped his hat on one side of his head, and planted himself before him with legs astride, his left hand on his hip, and the right hand brandishing the whip.

Instantly Herring twisted the whip out of his hand, and knocked his hat off his head with it across the hall. Then he handed him the whip again, coolly, in a manner that meant, 'Touch me with it, if you dare.'

Tramplara's face became mottled.

'Thank you, Mr. Herring, thank you,' said Cicely, who entered at that moment with Mirelle. Her cheeks were prettily dimpled, the brightest colour glowed in her face, and her eyes danced with delight.

Tramplara drew back, grasping the whip by the middle, clenching his teeth, and looking quickly from one to another in the group.

'Come into the little drawing-room,' said Mirelle, composedly, 'I dislike being present at vulgar brawls. These two young men have forgotten themselves; perhaps next they will proceed to box, which is a disgusting sight.'

'Stay one moment,' said young Sampson. 'Ladies, you must hear the truth at once. Miss Strange is my cousin. My father is her guardian. She shall not remain in this house any longer. I will take her away with me to Launceston, where my mother and sister will receive her. I have just read her father's will. It is all right, ain't it, Mr. Battishill? Besides, this house is not likely to be able to afford her hospitality and shelter any more. Is it not so, Mr. Battisbill? So pack up your duds, missie, and be ready to start to-morrow. I will bring a chaise out of Okehampton.'

'I am not going with you,' answered Mirelle, coldly, and without looking at him.

'Oh, ain't you though? I am your cousin, Miss Strange, and am come to fetch you away.'

'I know nothing about you,' said Mirelle with perfect composure. 'You are not my cousin. I am not Miss Strange. I am the Countess Mirelle Garcia de Cantalejo.'

'You have had your answer,' said Herring to the young man. Then, turning to the ladies, 'Now, Countess, and you, Miss Battishill, I must ask to withdraw. I want a word myself with this—person.'

Cicely smiled at him, and drew Mirelle away.

Herring watched them depart, but his eyes were upon Mirelle, not Cicely.

Then, going to the table, he drew a cheque book from his pocket, and wrote on it an order for sixty pounds, payable to Mr. Battishill.

'Will you kindly endorse this, sir?' he asked of the old gentleman.

Mr. Battishill, hardly comprehending his purpose, complied.

'Now,' said Herring to young Sampson Tramplara, 'take this, and write out at once a receipt to Mr. Battishill.'

'I refuse it,' said Sampson, sullenly. 'How am I to know that you have so much money in the bank, and how do I know that your cheque will not be dishonoured?'

Herring pointed to the little black ruler.

'You will sign the receipt at once, or I will break this ruler across your head.'

Tramplara made no further remonstrance. With a hand that shook partly with anger and partly with fear, he complied.

'Very well,' said Herring, 'now go. Pick up your hat, it is in the corner, and take yourself off.'

Tramplara sulkily obeyed. When he reached the door he turned, his face white, his hands quivering with passion.

'The time will come, Mr. Herring, when it will be in my power to repay you this, and then, by God, I swear——'

'What do you swear?' Herring held up the black ruler.

Tramplara shut the door, and was gone.

CHAPTER VIII.

CICELY.

WHEN John Herring turned to look at Mr. Battishill, he found the old gentleman fallen back in his chair, his face distorted, and scarcely conscious. He saw at once what had happened. The excitement had brought on a stroke.

Herring went into the kitchen and called the maid.

'Make no noise; help me.'

She assisted him to remove the master upstairs. He sent her for the doctor, and then tapped at the door of the parlour, that he might break the news to Cicely.

Two days later Mr. Battishill was sitting up in his own room, decidedly on the mend. The attack had been slight, nevertheless it was a seizure, a first—and such are warnings of others in store. Cicely came down into the hall to meet Herring, who had walked up to West Wyke from Zeal. where he was staying. She went up to him, and he noticed that there were tears in her eyes.

'Mr. Herring,' she said, 'my father is better. I am glad to have a moment in which I can leave him and speak with you alone.'

'I am entirely at your service,' he said.

She looked into his eyes with her frank, bright smile—a luminous smile that flickered through a veil of tears.

'I know that perfectly, Mr. Herring, and have no scruple in making use of you. Here you have remained in our neighbourhood, instead of going on your way about your own concerns; you have spent the greater part of every day with us, instead of seeking to amuse yourself—all because you knew that your assistance was needed. That is not the way with many young men. Another in your place would have taken his valise and gone by the next coach after the accident, and left Mirelle to shift for herself. You have been everything that is kind and considerate to Mirelle—I beg her pardon—the Countess Garcia.' A smile twinkled in her pleasant face. 'And this emboldens me to appeal to you in my trouble.'

Herring was about to protest his own readiness, but she put up her hand to stop him, and went on:—

'You have been foolishly generous, Mr. Herring. You have advanced sixty pounds to my father, to stave off the ruin that is impending. It is of no use. Do not venture to do this again. You ought not to have done it even once. However, let me clear off the debt in part immediately. I have butter-money—not the entire sum, not even a half.'

'Dear Miss Battishill, I will not take it.'

'Let us understand each other,' she said; 'do not interrupt me. I have had a little battle with myself upstairs before I could nerve myself to meet you. I do not know why it is that gentlefolks shrink from speaking of money matters one with another. Now I am wound up, and can go on ticking, but if you say a word, it is like putting a feather among the wheels, it arrests the movements, and the clock ceases. What I have to say must be said. Mr. Herring, it will not do to lend us money, we are hopelessly involved to the Trampleasures. Nothing that you can do will save us, without involving you in our disasters. My dear father has relied on the hereditary wisdom of the Battishills,' she looked up at the stained glass in the window, and the pretty dimple came in her rosy cheek. 'Those heraldic owls have done us harm. They have bred in our hearts the belief that Wisdom went with the cognizances, and had set up her temple at West Wyke. My dear father always supposed that he was about to make his fortune by the application of the hereditary wisdom to the development of the resources of the property, or else in speculations in mines. Alas! an owl can see in the dark, but not even one of our owls in the darkness that envelops Cornish mining. My father was led on by Mr. Trampleasure, who flattered him by appealing to his judgment in various matters, and now we are dipped past recovery. The Tramplaras will take from us everything—the dear old house, our moors, our little farms. I have foreseen this for some time, and I have known that it is inevitable. Sooner or later the crash must come, and it is better that it should come now, rather than later when my father will be less able to bear it.'

Herring made another effort to interrupt.

'No,' she said again, with a faint smile, 'let me go on

ticking. You have advanced my father sixty pounds. Next Michaelmas he will have to meet another demand for a larger amount. There are thousands of pounds owing to Mr. Trampleasure, of which this is the interest. He may call in that debt at any time, and then—how are we to meet it? All the money my father borrowed is gone without having been of the smallest advantage to us—gone in unfortunate ventures which have engulfed everything. The dear old man would do the same thing to-morrow if he were able. He is now full of the notion that he has discovered a silver lead mine at Upaver, and he may try to persuade you to embark in it. Do not be persuaded. Do not listen to him. Nothing that my father touches ever succeeds. As long as I can remember he has been on the point of making a fortune, but has invariably missed the point, and fallen after each venture into deeper disaster.'

'I have been to Upaver. I walked there yesterday, and saw what had been brought up. There is silver lead there, of that I am certain.'

'Have nothing to do with it,' said Cicely. 'Fortune's wheel has been on the turn for the Battishills for some time, and always downwards. Promise me to banish Upaver from your mind. Promise me not to put your money into it.'

'I have no money to put in.'

'And never, never again lend my father money—or me, however earnestly I may beg for it. It is of no good; we must go down, down, down. Most of us small Devon gentry are like buoys moored to a sandbank. Every wave goes over our heads. We are never wholly above water. After a while the canker gets into our hearts; we break away from our sandbank, and drift away—away into the vast unknown. We Battishills are about to drift; decay has set in. Nothing but a miracle can save us, and the age of miracles is over. There, take my butter-money, it consists of eighteen pounds, no more; I shall, however, be able to pay you two pounds in a fortnight, and you shall have the rest, if I can possibly manage it, next year. I cannot promise an earlier payment. Take it.'

Herring drew back his hand.

'Take it,' said Cicely. 'It is stocking money. An old stocking is the surest of banks; it never breaks.'

'No,' said Herring, 'you want the money. I am not a rich man, by any means, but I am not so hard pinched that I cannot lend a trifle. You will hurt me if you refuse the loan.'

'I said to myself when I came down that we should fight,'

said Cicely; 'but I will not suffer you to conquer me. Do you not understand that I have pride, and that it is the part of a gallant gentleman to humour it?'

'Give me the money,' said Herring. 'One thing, however, I will not promise. You asked me never to listen to you again if you begged a loan. This money and more will always be at your service on an emergency.'

'That is settled,' said Cicely with a sigh of relief.

'Now we come to a second matter; again I appeal to your good nature. Look at this letter. My father has received it from Mr. Trampleasure, requesting him immediately to bring his ward—Miss Strange as he calls her—to Launceston, along with her boxes and her father's papers. The will must be proved and an inventory of goods taken for probate. Mr. Trampleasure does not offer to come for Mirelle himself, he expects my father to conduct her to Launceston; he knows that the demands he makes on my father must be complied with. Now it is out of the question that the dear old man should take this journey in his present condition of health, and I dare not leave him. There is no one we can trust except yourself. It is true I might write and say that my father is ill and unable to travel; then Mr. Trampleasure would be forced to come himself, but I dread an interview between my father and the man who has ruined him. In his present weak state and partial convalescence, it would not be wise. The doctor says he must be kept from everything liable to excite him. So I fall back on you. I told you that I knew you were ready to do whatever is kind, and because I know this, I make no scruple in using you. Was I not right?'

'I will do what you wish—gladly.'

'And,' said Cicely, hesitating and colouring, 'as you return on your way to Exeter, you will call on us again? You cheer my father, who quite counts on your visits, and, I am not ashamed to confess it, I want advice. There is no one in this neighbourhood I can speak with on these matters. Accident or Providence—I believe the latter—has brought you here, and made you a welcome guest, and has constituted you almost the confessor and adviser of the house.'

'I will certainly see you again.'

'By the time you return an answer will have arrived from Avranches, and we shall then know whether Mirelle will have another protector, or must be left to the uncontrolled disposal of the Tramplaras.'

'Yes,' said Herring impetuously, 'if only for that I must return. It is too dreadful to think that she who has been accustomed to the purest and most refined surroundings should be thrust into association with persons like Mr. Tramplara and his son, and that her property should be intrusted to a man who plays ducks and drakes with all the money that he gets a chance of fingering.'

'I am glad you feel warmly in this matter,' said Cicely, laying a slight touch of sarcasm on the words 'feel warmly.' 'Mirelle will apparently need protector, confessor, and adviser as much as we, if not more so.'

'She is so helpless, so solitary,' explained Herring.

'By the way, chivalrous defender of unprotected maidens,' said Cicely, brightening up, 'you come to us like the mysterious knight in a romance, we know not whence, nor whither you go. It shows how utterly selfish we have been, how centred in our own troubles, that no one has cared to inquire whether you too have troubles, and whether you are alone in the world.'

Herring smiled. 'There is no mystery about me; I am plain John Herring, nothing more. I eat, I grow, I sleep, I talk. Troubles!—no, I have none. Alone!—well, yes, that I am. You and the Countess I find acting in tragedies, but my part hitherto has been in a farce.'

'And you so little regard your good luck that you offer it to the first girl you meet.'

'What do you mean?'

'Only the sprig of white heath,' said Cicely, laughing.

Next day Mirelle left West Wyke in company with John Herring in an open caleche. Cicely parted with her in a friendly manner, but without great cordiality. The coldness and pride of Mirelle repelled her, and she did not like her contemptuous treatment of Herring. Yet—strange mystery that the female heart is—she would have liked it quite as little had Mirelle gratefully accepted his services.

She resented also her want of tenderness towards her father. Cicely could not understand it. But then she had been brought up with her father, knew him, respected even his weaknesses, and loved his many virtues. She was unable to understand that a like great love could not grow out of the acquaintance-ship of ten days, passed in coaches, steam-packet, and hotels. She judged Mirelle more harshly than justly. That is, she judged her as one woman judges another. As Mirelle was driven away Cicely turned back towards the house, saying, 'She is an icicle; she freezes my blood.'

Herring turned to Mirelle and said, 'How kind, and good, and simple Miss Battishill is.'

'I have never before seen such red cheeks,' answered Mirelle. 'Do you think she paints?'

CHAPTER IX.

DOLBEARE.

A BRIGHT day, with a few fleecy clouds drifting before a west wind. A sky bright as that which overarches a young heart. The prospect as smiling as that which opens before youth. Barriers bathed in sunlight and indistinct in haze. Clouds without threat of rain casting cobalt-blue shadows.

The wild range of Dartmoor rose into peaks, with gullies seaming their sides, down which the Taw and the Ockments rushed foaming from their cradles. A glorious scene inviting exploration, an enchanted land calling the traveller to enter its seclusion and dispel its mysteries. Bathed in sunlight, enveloped in that finest haze that pervades the air on the brightest day in the West Country, who would suppose that all he saw was barrenness and naked desolation?

'Do you see that castle rising out of the woods?' asked Herring, pointing to some ruins of a keep on a hill to the left of the road, after they had passed Okehampton. 'That castle belonged to the Courtneys. There is a story of a certain Lady Howard who lived there in the reign of James I.'

'I have not heard of him. Was he an English king?'

'He was king of England. He was the father of the ill fated Charles I.'

'I have heard of him. He married a French princess, so he comes into history.'

'Lady Howard was married four times; she had one daughter by her first husband, whom she hated.'

'Perhaps she only despised him because he was not noble, and had taken advantage of her poverty to marry her.'

'On the contrary, she was rich, an heiress, and her first husband was a son of the Earl of Northumberland.'

'Then I understand nothing about it,' said Mirelle, leaning back in the carriage as if the story had ceased to interest her.

'When she was married to her second husband she refused to see her daughter. The poor girl came here to Okehampton; some relations sought to effect a reconciliation. She was introduced to her mother under a feigned name—here, in this castle, and Lady Howard did not know her. But when the daughter fell on her knees to her mother and entreated recognition, Lady Howard started to her feet with an exclamation of aversion, and attempted to leave the room. The girl clung to her, entreating her love, as the unnatural mother was escaping through the door. But Lady Howard flung together the oak valves as she escaped, and they caught the daughter's arm between them and broke it.'

'She was a bad woman; but she is expiating her crime in purgatory.'

'Her purgatory is a strange one,' said Herring. 'Every night she drives along this road from Okehampton Castle to Launceston Castle in her great coach drawn by four headless horses, with a skeleton driver on the box, and her favourite bloodhound runs beside the coach. When they arrive at Launceston the dog plucks a blade of grass from the mound on which the keep stands, and then they return in the same way to Okehampton, which they reach before break of day. And she is condemned to do this nightly, till every blade of grass has been plucked off Launceston Castle hill; and that will not be till the end of the world, for the grass grows faster than the hound can pluck it.'

'Have you ever seen the carriage with the lady in it?'

'No. During the war French prisoners have been confined in the dismantled castle, parts of which have been converted into prisons for them, and several who have died in confinement are buried in Okehampton churchyard.'

Mirelle shivered.

'I would not, I could not lie here. I should be wet under this dripping sky. Poor men! Why did you not tell me this before, and I would have visited their graves and prayed over them in their native tongue? It contracts my heart to think of them, lying here, away from la belle France, and the golden sun, and the vineyards, and the waving corn, and the scent of incense, and the shadow of the cross.'

'The sun shines here. It is shining now.'

'*It*,' said Mirelle. 'You are right when you say *it*, not *he*. In France he shines, he laughs, he illumines, he warms and even burns. He is always in the sky. Here you have a phantasm of the sun, without power and blaze and fire. I do not call that the sun; it is a make-believe, a constitutional monarch allowed to peep out between the clouds now and then, not reigning by right divine, dispelling the clouds.'

Herring looked round at the girl in astonishment. She was echoing sentiments she had heard in the convent and among her mother's aristocratic acquaintance. 'And,' she went on, 'your church is the same—a phantasm, a mock sun. When the servants of Saul came to seek David, Michal, his wife, took a log of wood and put on it a bit of goat's skin, and threw over it the bedclothes. Then the servants said, It is David asleep. And that was what your Reformation consisted of. You substituted a log for the living body. But why should I speak to you of all this? You and I use the same names for expressing different ideas. You have never eaten grapes off a vine, nor figs warm with the kiss of the sun on their cheeks; and by grapes you mean raisins brown and dried, and by figs withered fruit packed in wooden boxes. When I speak of the sun, I mean something indescribably glorious; you, a round tuft of cotton wool up in the clouds, that you can see sometimes when supremely lucky. So in other things; what you mean by a king and a church are altogether different; pale ghosts of what I mean by the same words.'

Herring was amused, and not a little perplexed. She put him down with an air of superiority, as a schoolmistress would put down a boy in her class who had made a stupid blunder, which merited a whipping, but was let off with degradation.

After some pause in the conversation he ventured to remark, 'You will not deny that this scenery is lovely.'

'It is beautiful in feature, but wanting in colour. I could cry out for my paint-box, and spill the colours over the scene to make it perfect. My master taught me, when I learned to paint, that shadows were to be made of carmine and ultramarine. There are no such colours here. Shadows must be put in with Indian ink. I could copy all the tints with a child's fifty-sous box of paints, warranted free from poisonous matter, as also from all real colour. Besides,' she added, 'Venus when she rose from the sea must have been intolerable till dried. Your land is fair, but everlastingly dripping.'

She spoke without a smile. Herring turned his head aside to laugh,

So they went on; he telling her traditions to while away the journey, she setting him down.

At length they arrived at Launceston.

The town is curious, perched on a height, rising precipitously out of the valley of the Kensey, and culminating in a rock that has been shaped by the hands of men, and crowned by a circular keep of concentric rings of masonry.

The main street of Launceston is entered under an ancient gateway. Scarcely another English town has such a picturesque and continental appearance.

On the steep slope of the hill, clinging to its side, was the quaintest conceivable house—a long narrow range of gables, roof and walls encased in small slate-like mail armour. In front of the house is a narrow terrace, with, at one end, a sort of summer-house, furnished with fireplace and chimney. Below this terrace the rock falls abruptly to the valley. The foundations of the houses in the street above are higher than the tops of the chimneys of 'Dolbeare,' as this picturesque old house was called.

In Dolbeare lived the Trampleasures, as they called themselves; Tramplaras, as the world called them. Herring knew little of Launceston, and he had some difficulty in finding the house.

The door opened to them, and they were introduced into a hall, with stairs branching off on either side. Then a stout red-faced man, with perfectly white hair, burst out of the adjoining room, with a noisy shout of 'Oh, here you are at last! Come to my arms, Cousin Strange.'

Mirelle drew back before the coarse man.

'I say,' pursued he with effusion, 'what's your pet name, darling? Let's be cosy and familiar at starting. What are you? Mirrie? Rellie?'

Mirelle turned to ice. 'You have mistaken the person,' she said. 'I am no cousin. I have no other name than that of Countess Mirelle Garcia de Cantalejo. I have come here till my affairs are settled, and then I shall go elsewhere. I pray let this be understood from the outset. I am not a Strange, and we are not relations.'

The old man stood open-eyed and open-mouthed without speaking, and then burst into a roar of laughter, which made his face blaze a fierce red, horrible against the snow of his hair and whiskers. His eyes were black, with a cunning twinkle in them. His hands were large, the fingers short and fat, the palms very wide. Altogether a repulsive old man, to whom the hoar head was no crown of glory, but he a dishonour to hoar hairs.

Mirelle contemplated him with undisguised aversion. Then she turned to Herring and said, 'I cannot lodge with this person. Take me back to the Battishills.'

Herring did not know what answer to make.

'Pray, who are you?' asked the old man. 'Brother or lover of the lady? Perhaps a cousin whom she does condescend to recognise; a Parley-vous Mossou, hey?'

'My name is Herring,' said the young man, gravely. 'Mr. Battishill is ill, and Miss Battishill cannot leave her father. Consequently they asked me to escort the Countess to Launceston.'

'The Countess!' exclaimed Mr. Tramplara. 'Oh, Ginger! a live Countess in the house. Lord! the little rooms won't contain her. We must throw out bow windows. Come here, Orange, come here, Polly, and see a live Countess.'

As he called, a feeble old woman, in a big cap with lilac ribands and a pink bow under her chin, appeared at a side door, and with her the daughter whom he called Orange. The latter entered the hall.

'Father,' said Miss Orange Trampleasure, reproachfully, 'you are too boisterous with the young lady. Do you not see? She is tired with her journey, and your noise frightens her.'

'Frightens me!' repeated Mirelle, with perfect composure. 'Non, il ne me fait pas peur—il me révolte.'

'Come with me, cousin,' said Orange. 'Let me take off your things, and show you your room.'

Mirelle hesitated.

'My dear,' Orange went on, 'there is no help for it. Whether you like it or not, here you must stay; you cannot go back to the Battishills. It is unreasonable to expect them to take charge of you. Besides, your father committed you to us.'

'My father has left a gentleman in France my guardian equally with this person here.'

'Then you must stay with us till he has been communicated with,' said Orange. 'Come with me.'

Mirelle allowed herself to be conducted upstairs.

Old Tramplara went into a muffled convulsion of laughter. He winked at Herring and said, 'She's a queer piece of flesh, ain't she—full of French hoity-toity? We must take all that out of her, and make good English homespun take the place of mouslin-de-laine, parley-vous, bong-soir, mossou!' Then the old man curtsied and grimaced, and went into attitudes.

'So,' said he, 'you be the gent that has escorted my Lady High and Mighty here! My son said something about you. You gave him a rap over the knuckles, hey? Serve the beggar right. He had been drinking, I'll swear. He said he had come across a temperance fellow who had insulted him. And you also, I suppose, are the party that have been paying sixty pounds for old Battishill; lending him the money—making him a present of it, I should rather say—for he who lends to him don't hear the chink of his coin again. I suppose you have plenty of brass to throw away. Well, there be better investments than West Wyke, I can tell'y. I wish I had been by to have tipped you a hint. Herring is your name! I wonder whether you are any relation to old Jago Herring, of Welltown?'

The young man did not enlighten him.

'Look here,' said Mr. Trampleasure. 'Stay and pick a bone of mutton with us at supper. Don't be shy about meeting Sampson. He ain't here, now at least—and what's more, he's not the fellow to bear malice. Lord bless you! if he were a bit rampageous, it was because he had been drinking; and as Moses who was the meekest of men said, when the liquor is in the manners is out. But the contrary is also true—and I Sampson Trampleasure say it—when the liquor is out the manners return. And, though I ain't a Moses, and a prophet, and all that sort of thing, yet I've a pretty shrewd head of my own, and what I say is worth attending to. Come along, Herring, and have a bite with us all, and see the young lady nestle into the bosom of the family. By Grogs! I've lost my manners though. Here's Mrs. Trampleasure, and I've never introduced you to her. Mr. Herring, Mrs. Tram, the flame of my youth, the solace of my age—eh, old woman?'

'Have done wi' your funning, Tram,' said the old lady, giggling feebly. 'Will you step in, sir? It gets chilly of an evening, and a fire is agreeable, sir, especially when one is troubled with a cold in the head.'

'Look here, Herring,' said Trampleasure, familiarly. 'You are not returning to West Wyke to-night. That is impossible. You are going to sleep at the White Hart or the King's Arms, that is certain. Well, it ain't always lively of an evening at an inn. You can plead no engagement, and therefore I will take no excuse. You stay with us and save your pocket the cost of supper. If you are fond of music, we'll give you some. "Music hath charms to soothe the savage breast," you remember the text—in Malachi, I believe, and he was the last of the prophets. If that was the last thing he ever said it was the truest. Is her Serene Highness at all in the tum-tum way?'

'I really cannot say.'

'Because, if she is, she's where her talent will be drawn out. I play the bass violin, Sampson is a Boanerges on the flute, and Orange can do pretty well on the harpsichord. But there she comes herself, all along of her Ladyship. Come in, Herring, this is Liberty Hall, with no more forms and ceremonies in it than in the Tabernacle in the Wilderness.'

He drew the young man into the sitting-room. 'There's another musician in the house,' he said, 'but of him, mum. He don't let himself be heard often, thanks be.'

Herring reluctantly submitted. He was repelled by the old man, but he was concerned for Mirelle. Could she endure this association? Was the daughter, Orange, better than her father, or was she equally vulgar? The mother was feeble and commonplace, not obtrusively offensive. He would like to be satisfied that in Orange poor Mirelle would find a refuge and a support against the coarse father and from the brutal son.

He could learn this only by staying, and he therefore accepted the invitation, though not with the best grace.

The table in the little dining-room was laid with a white cloth, and there was a dish with a cold leg of boiled mutton on it at the head. Cheese, butter, and bread were dispersed, not arranged, on the surface of the table. In the centre stood a plated cruet-stand with old mustard turned brown in a pot, and a bottle of sauce down whose sides the sauce had trickled and caked.

Mirelle entered with Orange, pale, her long dark lashes drooping on her cheek. She was ashamed, perhaps afraid, to look up. Herring thought he saw something on the lash. A tear?—hardly a whole tear. A brilliant, not a diamond.

The room was comfortable. It was panelled with painted wood of Queen Anne's period, the mouldings heavy and the panels large. The room was low. A fire burned in the grate.

Orange Tramplara came up to Herring.

'You have had a long journey—tedious also,' she said.

'Not tedious by any means. That was impossible in such company.'

'Well, long. I wish we had known for certain that my cousin would be here to-night, then we would have had a warm supper ready.'

F

'Don't bother with excuses,' burst in old Tramplara. 'Men do not heed what they eat, but what they drink. Cold mutton is a very good thing, especially with a glass of hot grog on the top.'

Herring looked steadily at Orange. She was a tall, stoutly built, handsome girl, with black hair, florid complexion, and very beautiful dark eyes. Her lips were crimson, ripe and sensuous. She had a fine throat and a swelling bust. Herring could make out nothing more. Men cannot read women's characters from their faces. It is well that they are denied this faculty, or the race would become extinct. 'Marriages,' says a proverb, 'are made in heaven.' No—marriages are made in Paradise—the paradise of fools.

Whilst Herring studied Orange ineffectually, she was making her own comments on him. She read more of his character than he had been able to decipher of hers. But he had deciphered nothing. She saw that he was good-looking, honest, and amiable, and that he did not lack ability. She read good-nature in every curve, and turned contemptuously away. Good-nature is weakness.

'Come along,' said Mr. Tramplara, 'the travellers want to peck. Sit you all down. "For what we are going to receive." Under-done, missie? or tasting of the butcher's fingers, eh?'

CHAPTER X.

A MUSICAL WALKING-STICK.

As Herring sat at table, he noticed opposite him, hung against the wall, a large pastille portrait of a gentleman in a red coat, with powdered hair. The face was refined.

By way of conversation, Herring asked Orange, who sat next him, whether this were a family picture.

'What—this, this?' said Tramplara, taking the answer out of his daughter's mouth. 'Nobody knows who the red man is.'

'An ancestor, however, I presume,' said Herring.

'Lord bless you! no; he don't look like an ancestor of our family. No flesh and blood and muscle and go-ahead there; all thinness and fine bone and whimsy, very well for show, but no use for work. Though I do not know who the party was, yet I do know something queer about the picture. This house don't belong to me, I rent it; and in the lease that picture goes with the house, and so does a bundle of old walking-sticks that we keep in the attic. Now ain't that curious? I reckon the sticks belonged to that old fellow in the red coat, but I can't say. He and the house and the sticks go together. You can't rent the house without the sticks and the picture. The sticks are not worth much; they would not fetch half a crown, the whole lot of them, at a sale. There is one with a head I thought was silver gilt, but it is no such thing, it is gilded copper; there is a second, mottled with things like trees on it; and there is one, and that the queerest of all, has an ivory handle with holes in it, like a flute, but with tongues to them like those in an accordion, so that anyone up to that sort of thing might play a tune on it. Sampson could do it if he tried, but there is a reason why he don't try. It is all cursed superstition, but still it won't do to tempt Providence; that is my doctrine, and I challenge Scripture to make better. What—no appetite?' he asked, when Mirelle declined a slab of cold mutton placed before her. 'Come, come, we must get hearty to our meat in Old England, and have no pecking of crumbs and nibbling of salads here, like birds and rabbits.' He ate himself and said, 'Missie! you don't get mutton like this in France. I've been in Paris, and I ought to know. I dined in the Palley-royal, and I said to the garçon—garçon! By the way, missie! what is the name you call yourself by? Garçon, garçon?'

'Garcia,' answered Mirelle, haughtily.

'Garcia, is it? Well, garçon means waiter, so I take it Garcia means bar maid, eh? Why, there are the boys. I hear them in the hall. Excuse me a moment, I want a word with Sampson.' Down went his knife and fork, and the great fellow dashed noisily out of the room.

The situation for Herring was not pleasant, but young Tramplara relieved him of his embarrassment the moment he entered by going directly to him with extended hand: 'Very sorry I wasn't polite t'other day; but there, forgive and forget, as the footpad said to the traveller when he relieved him of his purse.'

'No, no, Sampy,' put in his father; 'you are out there, my boy. Verify your quotations, say I. That same sentiment proceeds from Shakespeare—one of the writers of the Apocrypha,' he added, in explanation to Mirelle; 'not quite a prophet, but tinged with the prophetic fire.'

Herring frankly accepted the apology. Young Tramplara was followed into the room by a gentleman, tall, with light hair and very light moustache, a military air, and a handsome face and figure.

'Miss Strange,' said old Tramplara, 'let me introduce my friend, Captain Trecarrel. Captain Trecarrel, Miss Strange, *alias* the Countess Garcia de Something-or-other-unpronounceable. Same, Mr. Herring. Take a chair, Trecarrel, and try your teeth on the mutton. Miss Strange is the daughter of my first cousin, Jimmy Strange. "Though lost to sight, to memory dear," as the sacred penman has it. The young lady don't fancy her name somehow, it isn't high-flavoured enough for her foreign ideas; however, she is a Strange, so sure as lamb is young mutton.'

Captain Trecarrel declined.

'What—no meat! Oh, a Friday. You Catholics——'

'Vous êtes Catholique, monsieur?' asked Mirelle, suddenly waking into interest.

'Si, mademoiselle.'

'Et vous parlez Français?'

'Assez bien.'

'Tenez. Quand on sait penser en Français, on n'est plus bête, et quand on est Catholique, voilà l'âme qui vit.'

Herring noticed the look of surprised admiration with which Captain Trecarrel contemplated the wax-like face before him. He saw also the smile that leaped into her eyes when the Captain confessed his religion and spoke in French. She had accorded *him* no smile. Orange also noticed the admiration awakened in the Captain, and the encouragement given him by Mirelle. Her cheek darkened and she bit her lip.

'No parley-vous here, please!' said old Trampleasure. 'No one any more mutton? Well, a merciful man is merciful to his beast, says Holy Writ, and so say I. Bella, take out the meat for your own supper.' When the red-haired servant, who walked from her shoulders, had cleared the table, and had put another log on the fire, and impregnated the atmosphere of the room with a scent of yellow soap, Tramplara said: 'Now for some music. Do you tum-tum, missie?'

Mirelle did not notice the question.

'Beg pardon, Countess Garcia de Candelstickio. If you don't play yourself, perhaps you will enjoy good music when you hear it? Now then, Orange, sit you down. Sampson, get out your flute, and here is my bass viol, big and burly, and sound in the wind as jolly old Trampleasure himself.'

'Do you play at all, Countess?' asked Herring.

'Occasionally; according to where I am. I am not Orphée. I do not pretend to tame the beasts.'

'Come along, Captain, you must not absent yourself from the concerto. Can you manage any other music than blowing your own trumpet?'

'If Miss Orange will supply me with a comb and some silver paper, I can give you a rude imitation of the pan-pipes.'

Orange became grave at once. 'Do not jest on that subject, Captain Trecarrel.'

'No, no,' threw in Trampleasure, 'it is all cursed superstition, but still, "Let sleeping dogs lay," as Chalker observes in the "Canterbury Tales."'

'What do you mean?'

'You have heard of the old gentleman in red who is said to walk here,' answered Orange, in a subdued tone. 'The tenants who had Dolbeare before us let the walkingsticks lie at the agent's, and they were fairly routed out of the house by the noises.'

'It was rats,' said Trampleasure; 'women are cowards about noises.'

'What has this to do with my impromptu musical instrument?' asked Captain Trecarrel.

'This,' answered Orange; 'whenever there is any great misfortune about to befall those in the house, a sound is heard going through it such as that you proposed to make. What is singular is that one of the walking-sticks that goes with the house has some such a musical instrument in the handle.'

'Who is supposed to walk and pipe woe to the house?' asked the Captain.

'That red man hanging on the wall behind you.'

Every one turned to look at the picture.

'He appears harmless enough,' said Trecarrel.

'Has anyone heard his music?'

'None of us have,' answered Orange; 'but it has been heard by others before we came here.'

'It is a strange story,' said Trecarrel. 'It reminds me of the tenure of Tresmarro, not far from here. There the house is let with a human skull. The farmer there, not liking the object, buried it; but noises of all sorts, voices, knockings, tramplings, heard at night, made the place unbearable, so he dug up the skull and restored it to its niche in the apple chamber, where it stands now, and then the disturbance ceased.'

'Come, never mind about the ghosts,' shouted old Tramplam, 'we want music;' and he drew his bow across the bass viol, making the room resound.

Captain Trecarrel drew his chair beside Mirelle. Orange saw this, and said, 'Captain, to your post of duty. I want you to turn over the leaves whilst I play.'

A look of annoyance came over his face; he rose, and took his place by the piano.

The concert began. The flute was out of tune, the bass viol roared and drowned the piano. Mirelle shuddered, and drew back against the wall.

'Are you fond of music?' asked Herring, during a pause.

'Of music, yes. Of noise, no.'

'Countess,' said he in an undertone, 'before I leave allow me to ask of you a favour. I go to-morrow, and perhaps shall not see you again.'

'Most probably not.'

'It pains me to see you thus left with uncongenial surroundings. Your position here may become unendurable. Should you, at any time, need help, and you think I can give you assistance, do not fail to summon me.'

'You are very good to make me the offer, but I am hardly likely to make use of it. I shall not remain in this house a moment longer than I am obliged. I have another guardian living at Avranches. As we passed through the place, on our way to England, my father called on him. When he is ready to receive me I will go to him, and leave England for ever.'

'But suppose he declines to act?'

'He cannot decline. My father saw him at Avranches.'

'We will hope for the best. But on the chance of your desiring independent advice, will you take and keep my card? My address is on it—that is, the address from which letters will be forwarded to me.'

'I thank you. I will preserve it,' said Mirelle stiffly. 'For myself it will be needless, but I will recommend your firm to my acquaintances, and I hope obtain some orders.'

Herring looked puzzled. Mirelle took the card and twirled it in her fingers without glancing at it. She was annoyed with what she regarded as an impertinence.

With a crash on the piano, a shriek from the flute, and a bellow from the bass viol, the symphony concluded.

John Herring rose to depart. The musicians were engaged on their instruments. Captain Trecarrel was leaning over the piano, talking to Orange. As Herring rose, Mirelle rose also. She knew he was going to depart, and that, perhaps, for ever.

She was relieved to think so.

He ventured to hold out his hand. Purposely she avoided seeing it, but, raising her eyes, she looked him in the face. Wondrous, mysterious eyes they were. They dazzled Herring. This was the second time only that he had met her look.

'I am very anxious about your future, Countess.'

'I pray you give it no thought. My future is in my own hands alone; it cannot concern you.' She slightly curtseyed.

Then there came a faint musical strain as on some reedy instrument stealing through the house. It was heard outside the door, in the hall, then it passed round the room and went on into Mr. Trampleasure's office beyond; a strange music, distant yet near, so distant that the ear was sensible of an effort to hear it, yet so near that the vibration could be felt. The air played was familiar; a solemn, quaint old melody, associated with these words:—

> Since first I saw your face, I resolved
> To honour and renown you;
> If now I be disdain'd, I wish
> My heart had never known you.

Orange turned pale. Old Tramplara was startled. Mirelle and Herring did not at first realise that this was the music that had been alluded to at table. Some moments elapsed before those in the room had recovered from their surprise sufficiently to speak, and then only Orange had the courage to refer to it. She turned sharply, almost fiercely, on Mirelle, and said, 'It is you—you! who have brought this on us.'

'Brought what?'

Orange was too agitated to explain. 'I have told you what this means,' she said.

'What have we here on the floor?' asked Tramplara, in a shaking voice.

'A card,' answered Mirelle. 'Mr. Herring's address.' She raised it and read:—

> 'Lieut. Herring, 25th Reg.
> 'Welltown,
> 'N. Cornwall.'

'Why!' she exclaimed, supremely shocked, 'he is an officer in the army, and I thought he was a *commis voyageur* for some grocery or drapery business. Where is he?'

John Herring was gone. She had not even thanked him

for what he had done for her, and he had done for her, and would do for her, far more than she knew. However proudly she may have resolved to hold her future in her own hands, that future was in his.

'Herring!—Welltown!' echoed Mr. Trampleasure: 'why he is the son of old Jago Herring after all.'

'Twenty-fifth!' echoed Captain Trecarrel: 'why, he must have been at Waterloo.'

'Waterloo, by all the rules of military science, ought to have been a victory to the Emperor,' said Mirelle. 'Indeed, it was a victory, but the arrival of the Prussians, and thereby the preponderating numerical power brought to bear against our troops when exhausted, compelled them to retreat.'

'Sampy,' said Trampleasure, in an undertone to his son, 'I had a peck or two at old Jago, and there must be flesh on the bones of the son. The old fool has sent his son into the army to make a gentleman of him. Quick! run after him, my lad, and beg him, whenever he passes through Launceston, to give us a call, and see how the Countess Candelstickio is picking up her crumbs.'

CHAPTER XI.

THE GIANT'S TABLE.

HERRING drove back next day to West Wyke. He was not in good spirits; he had not slept much the night before. The thoughts of Mirelle, of her isolation in the midst of coarse, sordid natures, of her exposure to the impertinence of Sampson, junior, and the vulgarity of the elder Tramplara, had kept him awake. His sole hope lay in Orange, that she might prove a refuge and protection for Mirelle. The Countess had repelled him. She had not even thanked him for what he had done for her. She had treated him as a travelling bagman, had absolutely declined his proffers of friendship. Was it likely that they would meet again—that he should again look into those dark, inscrutable eyes? She filled all his thoughts. He could give attention to nothing else. Poor Mirelle! Unsuited utterly by her bringing up for battling with the realities of life. Reared in purest cloudland, she was translated to grossest proseland. Nursed in a convent, she found herself suddenly at its spiritual and moral antipodes. She had spent her life hitherto secluded from the rush and roar of life. Now she was plunged in the swirl of the current, and knew not how to swim. Poor Mirelle! Herring sighed. He was thinking of her when he reached West Wyke, and Cicely's cheerful voice roused him from abstraction.

She met him in her frank and genial manner, and showed how pleased she was to see him. What a contrast between his reception to-day and his dismissal over night! Then a frost had fallen on his heart, now a sunbeam thawed it. And yet he could not avoid contrasting Cicely unfavourably with Mirelle. Cicely was eminently sober, sensible, and practical; perfectly natural, entirely without disguise. Mirelle was dreamy, unreasonable, unpractical; her nature altered by her education, her character a riddle. Cicely had her congeners everywhere. Herring had met a thousand equally fresh and charming girls; hers was the type found in every manor house and parsonage of Old England. These girls are sweet, wholesome, but not piquant. Every one knows what they are; the sounding-line goes to the bottom of their souls at once, and all the way through fresh and crystal waters. But Mirelle was mysterious. Herring had never met with one like her. He could not fathom her; he dare not even cast the plumb. That she had a shrewd spirit he saw; that she had depth of character he suspected; that she was good as an angel of God he was so convinced that he would have died for his faith. He liked Cicely, he loved Mirelle. He could imagine nothing about Cicely; he knew all. He knew nothing about Mirelle; his imagination could soar in contemplation of her, and see her still above him.

Mr. Battishill was delighted to see Herring. He took the young man's hand in his. He would not let it go, but kept shaking it, and repeating how pleased he was to see him. Herring was touched. There was something in this reception like a coming home. Then they got to talking about Mirelle. A letter had come from Mr. Eustace Smith, a peppery, indignant letter, refusing to have anything to do with executorship to the deceased's will, trusteeship of his property, and guardianship of his child. Consequently Mirelle was left wholly at the mercy of Tramplara. Nothing further could be done by Mr. Battishill or by John Herring.

'Do you understand Mirelle?' asked Cicely of the young man.

'What do you mean by understand? I cannot answer you without a definition of terms.'

'I mean—— What is your opinion of her?'

'I should like to know yours first, Miss Battishill.'

'That is not fair. However, you shall have it. I think Mirelle has no heart. She has been brought up by a selfish mother, and by sisters who, in their religious way, are selfish also. She is one of those persons whom it is impossible to love, for there is nothing lovable in her. But it is quite possible to pity her, and pity her I do from the bottom of my heart. Her character is as cold and colourless as her exterior.'

'You misread her,' said Herring, 'or I am vastly mistaken. She has a heart, a very warm and tender heart, but it sleeps like a flower-bed under the snow. It is a heart full of promise——'

'How can you say that? Have you dug through the snow to explore it?'

'I should say, full of possibilities. She is not really selfish —I mean, she is not naturally selfish, but she has not been placed in a position where she can attach herself to any person. She has been reared to love ideas, not individuals—the Church and la belle France, and to these ideas she has attached herself warmly. With us the object of education is to enlarge the sympathies; with those who have trained her it has been the object to narrow them. Each system has its advantages, and each its defects. If we enlarge the sympathies they run shallow, if they be narrowed they become intense; and the men and women who make their mark, who influence the destinies of their fellow-men, are those of one idea and fiery prejudice. Mirelle is self-restrained without being reserved. She is frank as to her thoughts and impenetrable as to her feelings. What she believes to be true she speaks with crudeness, because she is unaware that the world will only accept the truth cooked and sauced. She is wholly ignorant of life, more so than a child with us of fourteen, because an English child lives in its home, with brothers and sisters, and its associates are of every sort and degree. Mirelle has had no home, all her associates have been of one type, of one class, and of her own sex. She has never been brought into contact with the poor, and has never associated with men. The defects you notice are superficial, and will fade as she grows older and gains experience.'

'You judge her more kindly than I,' said Cicely. 'But that is like you. You are always generous. Men see the good side of women, and women only the worst side of their sisters.

Woman is to man like the moon, always showing one face, and that serene and luminous. That there is another, systematically turned from him, passes his philosophy.'

'I grant the likeness,' said Herring, vehemently. 'But why should that other side be dark and unsightly? No; Paradise is on the unseen face.'

'Omne ignotum pro magnifico,' said Mr. Battishill; 'I remember so much Latin.'

'You would like, Miss Battishill, to drag the moon down out of the sky and turn her round and show me a desert of lava.'

'I should like to see exactly what the moon is made of. I see volcanoes and chasms on this face, I cannot suppose green hills and flowery plains on the other. She naturally shows us the only decent face she has.'

'There we differ as the poles,' said Herring, warmly. 'I prefer to see her far, far above me, and I do not wish to bring her down to my level. I idealise her hidden side, and believe I do not see it because of my own unworthiness.'

'Let us change the topic,' said Cicely,' or we shall quarrel, and I cannot afford that.'

'By all means,' answered Herring, 'and so, tell me, has anything been seen of that strange girl who helped me to carry the Countess to your door?'

'What! Joyce?'

'Yes, I think that was the name you gave her.'

'No, I have been too occupied with my father to think of her. She is more than half a savage, and lives with her old father in a Druidical monument called the Giant's Table, not far from here.'

'If I had not come to the rescue in time, the wretched old man would have killed her. I am not altogether easy in my mind. The father was beside himself with rage, though what had angered him did not transpire.'

After he had eaten—for Cicely insisted he should not go out till he had been given a meal—Herring went in search of Joyce. His purpose was to give her a crown for her assistance; he judged from her appearance that she was wretchedly poor. Moreover he was desirous to see that the girl had not been ill-treated by her father after his protection was withdrawn.

The moor was ablaze with the gorse in full flower. The air that is wafted from the Spice Islands cannot be more fragrant than that which played over these masses of growing gold.

Herring had no difficulty in finding the Giant's Table. The little clearing effected by the Cobbledicks lay as an island in the moor. Their rude stone fences walled out the gorse gold and the rosy heather. Adjoining this inclosure was the grey mass of granite stones set on edge, capped by an enormous block; the interstices were filled in with moss. Herring looked round. Not a human being was visible; no one worked in the clearing. A faint sweet smoke hung about the mysterious old monument, showing that a peat fire burned within.

The young man walked round the cromlech and discovered the entrance. Within it was dark. His eyes were dazzled with the gorse bloom. He saw the smouldering embers of a turf fire, and the smoke crept out at the doorway, which served equally the purposes of chimney, window, and door. Then he stooped and entered.

'Is any one here?'

'Here be I,' answered a voice from the further end.

'Who? Joyce?'

'Yes, sure.'

'Why, Joyce, what are you doing here? What! lying down? Are you ill?'

'I be broked all to pieces,' she answered; 'I be going to die.' Her voice was hoarse.

'Good heavens, Joyce! how has this occurred?'

He went to the upper end of the cromlech, and knelt by her. Now he was able to see. The girl lay on the cushions of the chaise, and some of the rugs were thrown over her.

'How has this come about, Joyce?'

'I won't tell'y, unless you swears not to let the constable know. I don't want no hurt to come to vaither of this. Vaither were here a minute agone, but I reckon he seed you acoming, and so he sloked away. Hers afeared the constable'll be after'n all along o' doing this.'

'But what has he done to you, child?'

'He's a'most scatted me to bits,' she said. 'Look'y here!' She held out her arms. Both were broken below the elbows, and the hands hung limp and powerless. 'I'd angered 'n; and yet, t'warnt my fault neither. The coord snappt acause the coord were wore out. But never heed that. You won't tell o' he? See now; say after me, "Blast me blue if I does."'

'My poor girl, I will not tell.'

'Say what I sez: "Blast me blue, and glory rallaluley!"'

'There's no necessity for that. You may trust my word.'

'He'd a right to do it,' argued Joyce. 'I be his daughter, and a vaither may do what he minds to wi' his child. That's reason.'

'I dispute that. He had no right whatever to maltreat you. But, tell me, have you had no doctor to you? Your bones must be set.'

'A doctor won't do me no good, maister. I never seed a animal as had been mashed that hev come right again. 'Tain't in nature. I be going to die right on end, I be. But I don't wish vaither no hurt for it. I be his daughter, and he has a right to do as he pleases.'

'Joyce, when was this done?'

'When were this done? Why, that night the carriage were overset and the man killed.'

'What! all that time ago, and nothing done to your arms! Did not your father put splints on them?'

'What be they? Vaither can't mend nothing. He've abroked and tore down scores and scores of things, but he've amended nothing.'

'And no one has been here to help you?'

'Nobody niver comes here. My vaither be a sight better now than he were. I tell'y how that comed about. I'll tell'y the whole tale right on end. When I returned home after I'd a' been to West Wyke wi' you, carrying the lady wi' the white face, him were a' lying in wait for I, and when I comed up, then he set on me wi' a great stone, and he hurted me all over, and broke what he could break. You see I'd a angered 'n, and he forgot himself. I've a forgot myself a times too. After that I crept in here, and laid me down by the turve fire. But vaither, he wouldn't come in, he stood and peeped in at the door. I seed 'n, and I sed, "Vaither! Miss Cicely sez you may go and sleep in the calves' linny among the straw, and it will be warm and comfortable for'y, vaither, better nor the old barril was. So you go along, and let me bide quiet and die in peace." Then he went. In the night I were that burning hot I could not sleep, and I opened my eyes, and there I seed old mother wot be buried under the hearthstone; her were a heaving up in the midst of the fire. I seed her head sticking straight out of the burning turves, and her looked hard at me; her face were red as live coals. Then her went on heaving and pushing till her'd a worked herself right out of the earth, in the midst of the fire, and the burning turves tumbled this way and that as her comed out. Then I seed that her old gown were flickering wi' blue light, just as you've seed old touchwood. Her comed to me and her kissed me, but sure her lips were like fire, and they burned me. Then her sed, "Joyce, tell your vaither that I be acoming after 'n if he does you any more harm. I knows where he be, in the linny, lying warm in the straw. But I'll make 'n warmer. I'll throw fiery turves in among the straw, and he'll burn, he'll burn, he'll burn!" As her were a saying of that her went backerds into the fire, and down through the turves, and they closed over she just as afore. But I heard her still a mumbling to herself under the hearthstone, "He'll burn, he'll burn, he'll burn!"'

'Oh, Joyce, you were fevered and wandering in your mind,' said Herring, who belonged to the nineteenth century after Christ. The condition of Joyce's mind was that of a savage three centuries before Christ.

'After that,' she went on, 'I told vaither all, and he hev come here and been very good to I. You see he be mortal afeered o' being caught asleep in the linny in the straw by mother wi' a flaming turve in her hand. He thinks her won't make much worrit o' nights, becos of disturbing me. And then he laughs and sez, "Mother be that pleased I hev a given her summat to play with, and her be a playing wi' that an won't trouble no more."'

'Joyce, your father must be very sorry for what he has done.'

'He is that for sartain. All becos you see he've a got to do everything himself now. Afore, I did a deal of things. I got up the taties, and I baked 'em in the ashes, and I milked the cow, and I did scores and scores of things. But now that I hev my arms a broke it puts a deal o' work on vaither. Her hev to do everything from morning to night. And vaither be getting an old man, and not up to work as he were years by. He feels it, sure, very much, and wishes he hadn't a done it now. But wot's the good o' wishing. Wishing won't mend broken bones.'

Herring was kneeling by her. He could not understand the girl. Was she delirious, or was this the outpour of her reasonable soul? He put his hand on her low forehead, brushing up the shock of coarse hair. He wished to feel her pulse, but could not touch the artery in the broken hand. She lay very still with her eyes fixed on him.

'You are feverish,' he said. 'I am going to fetch a doctor.'

'I say,' exclaimed Joyce, vehemently, 'you've swore not to tell the constable of vaither. If you were to do that, I'd never be friends wi' you more.'

Friends with him! The poor savage and the lieutenant in His Majesty's service! Herring was unable to suppress a smile.

'Joyce,' he said gravely, 'you must have those poor arms patched up. The surgeon must attend you. I shall have you carried hence. No doubt Miss Cicely will know of a cottage where you can be received.'

'No,' she said hoarsely, even fiercely, 'I'll go over no drexil (threshold). Let me lie here and die where I've a lived.'

'But I insist on a doctor attending you.'

'What can a doctor do for me? It ain't in nature. What be broke be broke; be it a leg, or a neck, or a arm, or a heart, it be all one. What be a broke be a broke for ever and ever, Amen.'

After some difficulty he persuaded her to consent. Then he ran off to South Tawton for a surgeon. He returned with one rather over an hour later. Then he stood outside whilst the medical man entered the den and examined the patient. Presently he was called.

'She is severely bruised, but no other bones are broken except those in her arms. She is obstinate, and I cannot induce her to allow me to put splints on and bandage the arms.'

'Oh, Joyce! if you wish to be well you will submit.'

'I don't care one way or other,' said the girl sullenly. 'I wouldn't give the turn of a turf whether I lived or whether I died. Wot's life to me? It ain't anything I cares for.'

'But I do care very much about it, Joyce. You must have your bones mended and get well to make me happy.'

'You care, do'y? Then I'll live. There!' She held out her broken arms, but as suddenly drew them back. 'I won't hev the doctor touch me. Blast me blue if I will. If I be to get well and live, then you must make me well and live, and none else. Take my hands and do what you will. You may cut 'em off and I won't cry. You may tie 'em up and I'll say nort.'

The surgeon said to Herring, 'You had better humour her. She is not a rational being.'

So Herring put the splints in place, and bound the bandages tightly round them.

Joyce watched him with her large animal-like eyes fixed on his face. A feverish fire was burning in them, giving them a factitious light. She did not withdraw them from him for a moment.

'You're right for sartain,' she said. 'If I'd ha' died, what 'ud vaither ha' done? And her be growing a brave age.'

Then, still kneeling by her, Herring spoke with the surgeon about the girl, as to what was to be done with her arms and what she was to eat. Suddenly he exclaimed with a start and recoil, 'Good heavens, Joyce! what are you doing?'

He looked at her. A human soul was struggling to emancipate itself from brute instinct. He saw it in her feverish eyes. She had them fixed on him as those of a dog look at its master—and *she was licking his hand*.

CHAPTER XII.

OPHIR.

'SAMPY, my boy,' said Tramplara the elder, 'improve each shining hour, says Paul, afterwards called Saul, and he couldn't have given a better piece of advice if he'd been paid to do it. Since Polpluggan has been blown I have had nothing to do, and I want not only to follow Paul's advice and improve the shining hour, but do better, and improve the overcast and rainy ones. You and I, Sampy, are the men to whom the future belongs, the representatives of the age, and it will not do for the likes of us to keep our light under a bushel. That ain't Scriptural, and it ain't advantageous neither.'

'All right, gov'nor. What is this the preface to?'

'Sampy,' said Tramplara, confidingly, 'we must start another mine.'

'What—tin? lead? manganese? copper?'

'Better still, my gosling.'

'I don't know what you can have better except coal, and coal don't luxuriate alongside of granite.'

'Gold—the noblest of metals—gold.'

'Oh, ah! gov'nor, that won't do. There's no gold to be found here.'

'Why not?'

'Why not? Because no folks are fools enough to sink it in such a venture as gold mining.'

'You are wrong. There is one quality I can always rely on—as the Apostle says, "Folly never faileth, everything else may vanish away." If you appeal to men's reasons, it is like looking for ghosts in haunted tenements; they are supposed to be there, but never found when wanted. Human folly is like Dozmare pool, it is unfathomable, though you let down into it all the bell-ropes of Cornwall. You can set up windmills in Essex, for there the wind always blows; and you can establish water wheels in Cornwall, for the rain supply is inexhaustible; and you can float speculations where you will, and the fools will keep them going. In the story of the Fisherman in the "Arabian Nights" the fish that have been scraped and disembowelled and put in a frying-pan over the coals stand up on their tails and say, "We are doing our duty. If you reckon we reckon; if you fly we mount and are content." Now those fish we are told were men. And men are just the same now. They do their duty in coming to be scraped and gutted and roasted, and what you pipe they repeat; they have no pleasure apart from yours, and they rush into your hands to be cleaned out, just as the martyrs asked to be tortured.'

Sampson junior nodded.

'What is it that Solomon said, "A fool and his money are soon parted"?'

'I say, gov'nor, it is dry work listening. Let us have in some grog.'

'Bring the spirits out of the cupboard and ring for Bella to give us sugar and hot water. Are you listening to me? What I say is important. I am leading you after gold.'

'All right; but you were speaking of human folly.'

'Human folly is the cable[1] that incloses the ore. It is not for nothing, Sampy, that I have been regular at chapel and paid for my pew at Salem. Mr. Israel Flamank, the minister, is a very good man; a sort of cedar in Lebanon, always green, and he is as soft as butter and as easy to make a pat out of with, at pleasure, a crown or a goose at top. There are in the world good men of whom with Scripture it may be said, "It were better that a millstone had been hanged round their necks than they should have learned to read and write." For, you see, Sampy, they read a great deal without knowing the relative value of what they read, and they write the first craze that comes into their heads to set other fools crazy after them. When there is a choice of herbs set before an ass, he prefers a thistle, because as Shakespeare sings, "It is his nature to." You may take my word for it, gosling, there is a parcel of people in this world with an exuberant fund of piety in their constitutions, just as some children are born with water on the brain. And as these have no definite belief, the pious element within washes

[1] The rock altered by the vein of ore it surrounds is termed by miners the cable.

about, unable to settle. When you was a boy, Sampy, it was your delight to make silver trees. You had a fluid clear as crystal in a bottle, and into it you introduced a scrap of carpet thread, and all at once the metal held in solution crystallised about the rubbish you had inserted, and built round it a mass of sparkling metal, hard as steel and shining as silver. It is the same with folk of the calibre of Israel Flamank. Their dilute piety is ready to settle round any trashy notion that gets into them, and rear about it a tree of fantastic conviction. Flamank has done a deal of crystallising since I have known him, about all sorts of odds and ends. First he was a total abstainer, then a vegetarian, then he found the gospel in the pyramids, and now he is all for the Phœnicians.'

'But, father, what does this concern us?'

'Everything, my son,' said old Tramplara, with sunny self-complacency. 'Fill your glass and listen. Do you know what the Phœnicians were?'

'I don't know, and don't care.

'Then I'll tell you. The Phœnicians were next-door neighbours to the Jews, and, what is a wonder, were on speaking terms, and did each other little neighbourly acts, which shows they lived in the Dark Ages. You don't happen to know anything about the Cassiterides, do'y, Sampy?'

'Not a farthing. Had they anything to do with the Phœnicians?'

'Oh, what an ignorant boy you are! You are living in the midst of the Cassiterides, and don't know it. Cassiterides is the Phœnician for Devon and Cornwall. It means the place whence the Phœnicians drew their tin; and where the Phœnicians went the Jews went also. Marazion, as every fool knows, is called also Market Jew, because the Jews came there to buy metal for Solomon's temple. You haven't a Bible, have'y, Sampson junior, ready to hand?'

'I doubt if there be such a thing in the house.'

'There is, though, only I don't know where it be stowed away this present moment. I bought one for taking the level of the Phœnicians under the guidance of the Reverend Flamank. Now Solomon; you've heard of Solomon?'

'Which, the pawnbroker?'

'No; Solomon the wisest of men, and because the wisest the richest. He sent a navy of ships with his own men and Phœnicians to get gold for the temple at Jerusalem and his own house. There is one thing strikes an earnest inquirer like

me about King Solomon, and makes me admire the beauty of
his character greatly. When he were building the temple he
built his own palace at the same time, and didn't make of 'em
separate accounts. So the Jews gave profusely for the building
of their temple, and how much of that subscription went to the
King's house, I reckon Solomon himself would have been
pushed to answer. He was seven years building the temple,
and thirteen years over his own palace, and when you know
that, you can guess how the material went. But that is neither
here nor there. I was just giving you a sample of the wisdom
of Solomon. Well, the ships of Solomon came for gold to
Ophir, and fetched thence four hundred and twenty talents of
gold-dust; that, Israel Flamank tells me, is nigh on fifty-three
thousand pounds weight. Think of that! Now where gold
came from, there gold is to be had.'

'But where did it come from?'

'From Ophir, to be sure. We must find Ophir.'

'Governor, that won't do. You and I are not going to
leave Old England gold prospecting. You are too old, and I
am disinclined.'

'Didn't I tell you we were in the Cassiterides?'

'Yes; but Cassiterides is not Ophir.'

'But Ophir may be in the Cassiterides.'

'Gold never was found in the West,' said Sampson junior,
shaking his head.

'There never was any tin in Wheal Polpluggan,' said the
old man, who turned blazing red with suppressed laughter.
His sides shook, his white hair gleamed ghastly against his red
skin. Then he broke into a roar, and slapping Sampson on the
knee, he shouted, as he waved his glass of grog over his head,
and spilled the contents on his silver hair and gleaming cheeks,
'To the prosperity of Ophir! Drink, Sampy, drink! to
Ophir, the Ophir of Solomon in the West Country.'

'Polpluggan was tightly salted,' said young Sampson, 'and
salted only with tin. Besides, Polpluggan was in the Scilly
Isles, some forty or fifty miles from Penzance. There were many
who would rather jeopardise their money than risk their breakfast in a rough passage. But gold——' He shook his head.

'We'll salt Ophir when we have found the spot.'

'What! with gold dust? You'll sink a fortune in that,
and the success is doubtful.'

'It is bound to succeed,' answered the father. 'My boy,
I've come to see that there is a pan of cream has not been

skimmed yet, and I hope, if I live long enough, to skim it. There is not much more to be done at those pans we have gone over hitherto. We must try a fresh one. I'll tell you what that big rich pan is; it is the big rich pan of religious fanaticism. I'll take a lesson from the rats. The rat when he has an eye on the cream sits down with his back to it, and looking up at the wall lets drop the end of his tail into the cream; then he pulls it up with a shocked and bashful air, sucks it, and lets it down again, and in half an hour he has cleared the pan of all but sky blue.'

'I don't see how it is to be done,' said young Tramplara, meditatively.

'You are young and inexperienced,' answered his father. 'You haven't sounded the depths of human folly yet. Lord bless you! I've been surprised myself at its profundity. And when we come to religious folly, my private conviction is that it goes down through the world and out at the other side. It is like the well of Zem-zem, that has no bottom. I have not been an earnest inquirer at the feet of the Reverend Israel Flamank for nothing. Whilst kneeling to him I have been like a shoemaker taking the measure of his foot. I know the sort of gate he will clear, and where the bellweather goes all the flock will leap. You listen to me and I will give you a parable—a mighty comforting one. There was an old manganese mine long disused, and the adit ran level out into a meadow where some bullocks were feeding. One hot day, when the flies were troublesome, one bullock took refuge in the adit, and when the others saw that in they walked after him, each thrusting forward the fellow before him. Presently they got frightened with being so far from the light, so the foremost bellowed, and the second bellowed, and this was repeated to the last, who, in mighty alarm, dug his horns into the hinder quarters of the bullock in front, and he repeated the performance on the one before him, and so on, driving one another further and further into the heart of the mine. Well, they got so far that there was no getting them out, and the owner had to kill them where they were. They were too frightened to back, and to turn was impossible. Sampy, that good foolish Israel Flamank is just like the leading bullock. He'll go into Ophir eagerly, and all his congregation after him, thrusting one another on, and we shall have the slaughtering of them. They will be too compromised to back when they find themselves in the wrong place.'

'But how about the salting?'

'There are various sorts of salting. You only know one sort. You have seen Polpluggan salted with tin ore brought from elsewhere, and basketfuls drawn out of the shaft that had been previously put in. That is one sort of salting, and I allow that with gold this would come expensive. I shall have to manage more economically. My dear boy, when fools are hungering to be deceived, they are not particular about the meat that feeds their folly. They don't inquire if the mutton comes of rotten sheep.'

'How shall you float it?'

'Nothing easier. Let us find Ophir, and the Reverend Israel will do the rest. He conducts a religious paper, entitled "The Western Cornucopia," much read by those of his persuasion, and throughout the West of England. I like that word persuasion, Sampy. When I hear a man talk of his persuasion, I feel that he is persuadable to any sort of suicide. Now, let me get my truck on Israel's rails, and it will run down by the law of gravity.'

'But where will you light on Ophir?'

'I do not know yet. I am an earnest inquirer, and I have been sitting with the Reverend Flamank many an hour, as solemn as a Quaker, over our Bibles, making it out. I'm hard to believe, he eager to convince. He has no idea that I am leading him on; he believes he is driving me. Now and then, as the light of nature prompts, I throw out a suggestion, and he snaps at it enthusiastically, appropriates it, and reproduces it as an original inspiration. Country folks will tell you that every cloud brings with it wind. That is the reverse of the fact. It is the wind that brings the cloud. So in this case there occurs a little mistake as to which is the impelling power. The Reverend Israel has shown me that the situation of Ophir is pretty accurately indicated. It is said in Scripture that Ophir lies between Mesha and a mountain in the East called Sephar. Now, with my incenting, the Reverend Flamank has arrived at this—that Mesha is the village of Meshaw, near South Molton, and that Sephar is Sheepstor, which is a mountain due east of Launceston.'

'It is due south of Meshaw.'

'Yes, but it is due east of Salem Chapel. People always reckon from where they are themselves. You see the line uniting them passes through Crediton, South Towton, Cosdon

'By the way, father, Squire Battishill told me he had found a silver lead mine at Upaver.'

'Upaver!—Upaver!—Ophir! Ophir! Sampy! By the wisdom of Solomon, we have spotted Ophir!'

CHAPTER XIII.

CAPTAIN TRECARREL.

CAPTAIN TRECARREL was Captain only in the militia, yet he flourished his captaincy with as much pride as if he were in the regulars. He was Trecarrel of Trecarrel, the head of one of the oldest families in Cornwall. When we say that, we mean that he was head in the sense of a tadpole's head, which is head and nothing else. Trecarrel was head, and nothing else. There was no tail of younger brothers and sisters dependent on the property. But then the property barely supported the head, and by no possibility could have sustained the burden of a tail.

It was not always so. At one time the Trecarrels were the chief family in the neighbourhood, and Sir Henry Trecarrel, Knight, at his proper cost, to the glory of God, and in honour of St. Mary Magdalen, rebuilt the parish church of Launceston in the most sumptuous manner he was able. Not one stone was set in the fabric that was not the finest granite, and not one block was unsquared and unsculptured; the sculpture was as delicate as the grain of the granite would allow, with trees distilling balsam, plumes and palm-branches, with the arms of Trecarrel, and with minstrels harping and playing the rebeck, the tabor, and the bagpipe. Under the east window in a niche was sculptured the recumbent effigy of that most yielding of saints, the Magdalen, wrought in the most obdurate of stones. The pinnacles and gurgoils were all cut out of the same material with infinite labour, and at extraordinary cost.

The church was not quite finished when the Reformation came. Then the King's Commissioners paid a visit to Launceston and swept from the church its valuables in silver and gold, for the filling of the royal exchequer and for the abolition of idolatry. After the Commissioners had departed, a rabble followed, headed by one Bunface, a butcher, who burst into the church and destroyed what the King's Commissioners had spared. They smashed the stained glass in the windows, and broke the legs of the Christ on the rood, but left the thieves on either side unmolested. They extinguished the perpetual lamp and spilled the oil over the chancel floor. They threw down the altar, and, having broken open the shrine, cast the sacrament under their feet. They knocked the heads off the apostles, and lastly, with a lever, overthrew the font, and in so doing exceeded the intentions of the Reformers, who having destroyed five sacraments, and reduced a sixth to a stump, elected to maintain the seventh intact. After that the party rang a peal in the tower and finished the evening by getting uproariously drunk at the Pig and Whistle.

Bunface never again appeared in church, for though the Government passed a law to force the people to attend divine service and receive the sacrament, under pains of fine and imprisonment, just as children have to be whipped to make them swallow medicine that is necessary but nasty, yet Bunface could not be induced to put in an appearance. 'Let me burn the Bible, or break the Commandments, or test my cleaver on the minister's head, but if this be denied me, if there be no more destroying to be done, then I'd rather pay my fine than go.'

When Sir Henry Trecarrel refused to sit in the church under the preacher, and take the sacrament at the mean table under the pulpit, the magistrates cautioned him, and when he disregarded their monition they fined him, and when he paid the fine and continued recusant they threw him into the common gaol, and there, after languishing two years, he died of the gaol-fever.

Sir Harry Trecarrel was succeeded by his son, who suffered also in purse and liberty for his attachment to the old religion. He was convicted of harbouring a Popish priest, and of hearing mass in his private chapel. The priest was hung, drawn, and quartered—that is to say, he was cut down the instant after he had been slung up, sliced open, and his heart torn out of his breast whilst still palpitating. That was the way in which recusant priests were dealt with by that bright Occidental Star, good Queen Bess. Mr. Henry Trecarrel saved his neck only by the surrender of one of his best manors.

In the civil wars Trecarrel made large sacrifices for the King, and was accordingly dealt with as a Malignant by the Protector. Confiscation and fine diminished his estates still further. On the Restoration he went to London, and laid the record of his services and sufferings at the feet of Charles II. The King commended his loyalty, and promised him, if he would take holy orders, that he would recompense him with at least a canonry; but as Trecarrel was unable to do this, being a Papist, he was dismissed with, as his sole reward, a portrait of the royal martyr, full length, in which the lower limbs were so adjusted that, had they been true to life, the royal martyr could neither have walked nor sat on his throne. The Trecarrel of the reign of George I. gambled away everything that had been left except the house and home barton of Trecarrel, which were inalienable. This Captain Trecarrel had inherited from his ancestors, together with the picture of Charles I. with distorted limbs, the Catholic faith, and the Trecarrel blue eyes and beauty—but chief of all these things, in his estimation, were the hereditary blue eyes and beauty.

Captain Trecarrel's income was small, so small that he could not marry on it. He was obliged, therefore, to look out for a wife with money.

Now, as has been said, nature and his ancestors had bestowed on him aristocratic good looks, and he was admitted by the ladies of the neighbourhood to be the handsomest man they knew.

He was aware of his beauty, he knew precisely the effect he could produce on the female heart by a look out of his blue eyes, blue as the borage blossom. There was not a marriageable girl who would not have abjured her faith, have adored Mumbo-Jumbo, if required, to become Mrs. Trecarrel of Trecarrel. The Captain knew his value, and was not impatient. The young ladies of good birth in the neighbourhood were neither heiresses nor well dowered. He looked further afield, and was caught by the handsome face of Orange Trampleasure, and by the handsome fortune with which popular opinion endowed her.

Old Tramplara was thought to be enormously rich, and to be eager to marry his daughter well, and to be ready to pay for the blood and position that would come to the family through a good alliance.

Captain Trecarrel was not a man to feel deeply. He liked Orange, and that Orange liked and admired him was obvious to his blue eyes. But then, he was accustomed to be liked and admired, and he had only to smile and look languishingly to draw to him any amount of affection from any number of marriageable girls. He looked for something more substantial than liking and admiration.

After much hesitation, Trecarrel proposed to Orange Trampleasure and was accepted on the spot. But the proposal was only the first scene in a long drama, and the second scene did not pass with the same rapidity and success. Captain Trecarrel had no intention of being married till he was quite satisfied as to the sum of money Orange would bring with her. Old Tramplara spoke grandiloquently, and made large promises of what he would leave her when he was not himself in a position to enjoy his money. But this was not what the Captain wanted—which was something present, not prospective. At last he did get the old man to name a very liberal dowry, and when he next asked in what shape this dower would come, he discovered an eagerness on the part of his prospective father-in-law to pay it in Patagonian securities. Now Patagonian bonds were not at par. They had been declining very steadily in the money market, and when the South American State deferred meeting its coupons with punctuality, the drop had been nearly to zero, for it was anticipated that Patagonia was meditating repudiation.

Mr. Trampleasure supposed that the Captain was unaware of this, but Trecarrel was not as innocent as his blue eyes led people to suppose. He was one of those few men who know exactly on which side their bread is buttered; and Captain Trecarrel knew further, what very few people do know, how to eat bread and butter with most satisfaction to himself. An adult eats his slice with the butter uppermost, but a child turns the buttered side down. By so doing he extracts from it the utmost enjoyment it is capable of giving, for by this expedient the tongue is brought into immediate contact with the butter. Captain Trecarrel was not going to eat his bread with thin Patagonian scrape over it, instead of yellow English gold. Those innocent blue eyes of his could see as far into a millstone as the keen sloes of Mr. Trampleasure. Consequently, till that Patagonian business was satisfactorily settled, Captain Trecarrel held aloof from hymeneal felicity.

The arrival of Mirelle and her admission into the family at Dolbeare were opportune. Captain Trecarrel was struck with her beauty, but then, he was struck with the beauty of every girl whose looks were pleasing. But what struck the Captain far more than her beauty was the opportunity this arrival afforded him of rousing the apprehensions of Orange and her father that he might slip through the meshes of their net.

He resolved to pay his court to Mirelle, to exhibit a lively interest in her, to wake up a little convenient jealousy in the bosom of Orange, and to give the father clearly to understand that he himself repudiated Patagonia.

The curious mixture of simplicity and shrewdness in Mirelle

amused him. It was a real pleasure to him to converse with her, and a particular pleasure to look into those deep eyes and speculate what lay beneath.

Once a month a priest came to Trecarrel on a circuit through the north of Cornwall, and said mass in the chapel near the house. On these occasions Mirelle walked over to Trecarrel. Trecarrel lies, like most old manor houses, in a hollow. A small stream dribbling through the hollow constituted the only attraction which could lead a gentleman to build his stately mansion in such a spot. A stately mansion Trecarrel must have been in its prime. The great banqueting hall was of hewn granite, with granite windows and doorway and chimney-piece. A little chapel stood south of the hall, also of cut granite. The mansion-house itself is, at the present date, reduced to a fragment of the great house that once occupied three sides of a quadrangle. At the time of which we are writing it was more than dilapidated, it was falling into utter ruin. There was no glass in many of the windows, and the roofs were breaking down. Next to the hall the glory of Trecarrel was the gate-house of granite, with a richly sculptured doorway of the same intractable material, moulded deeply, with strawberry leaves carved in the hollows of the mouldings. The Trecarrel who gambled pulled down the gatehouse because coaches could not pass beneath the arch; but when he had pulled it down he had not the power or the means to remove the huge blocks, and so he left them encumbering the ground where they had fallen, and there at the present day they lie, rankly overgrown with nettles.

Captain Trecarrel could not suffer Mirelle to walk home unattended when she made her monthly pilgrimages to his chapel. She was always pleased to see and converse with him. He was her equal, a gentleman and a Catholic—the two qualities which made them akin and separated them from the ignoble and unbelieving around. In these walks the Captain told Mirelle the story of Sir Henry Trecarrel and the building of Launceston Church, and the way in which the work was arrested. He told her what his ancestor had done and suffered in the civil wars, and he showed her one day in the hall the sole reward he had received for his sacrifices. Mirelle was able to sympathise with the misfortunes of the house; she also represented a generous race, that had fought the Moors, had ruled a county, coined its own money, and set up its own gallows. In that last particular the Garcias and the Trecarrels had differed.

The Garcias had hung men, the Trecarrels had had much ado to keep themselves from being hung.

The story of the self-sacrifice of the Trecarrels for Church and King stirred the soul of Mirelle, ready to warm to all that savoured of heroism; and she looked on the Captain as the noble representative of a glorious line of confessors and martyrs. She fondly deemed him made of the same stuff, ready to lay himself down on the altar if need be. But no! Trecarrel was wholly free from the spirit of self-sacrifice. He would not surrender his independence for five thousand pounds in Patagonian bonds. During one of these walks the Captain ascertained from Mirelle that her father had left her six thousand pounds, not in Patagonian bonds, but in hard cash. Six thousand pounds! That was one thousand above the sum that Orange was promised. Six thousand pounds in coined gold, with his Majesty's head on each piece, God bless him! Trecarrel's tone assumed more tenderness, a softer light shone out of his celestial eyes, and he slightly squeezed the arm that was on his own under the big umbrella, as he paddled with Mirelle to Launceston under a Cornish drizzle and through West Country mud.

That night the Captain did not sleep. He tossed on his bed. He sat up and hammered the pillow into shape and put it under his neck. Then he got up and drank cold water. Then he tried to count sheep going through a gap in a hedge. All was in vain. He could not sleep and he could not count the sheep, because his mind was active. He was stung into wakefulness by the consideration whether it would be possible for him to be off his engagement to Orange, and on with one to Mirelle. It would not be consistent with his honour as a gentleman and an officer (though only in the militia) to become engaged to Mirelle before breaking with Orange. It would also not be proper for him to break with Orange; but it would be perfectly honourable for him so to conduct himself as to force her to break with him. He made no doubt that Mirelle would have him. No woman could refuse him, with his eyes and name, his profile and his position. Besides, Mirelle manifestly liked him. She made no secret of the pleasure she took in his society. Now the only means of effecting a rupture with Orange was for him to pay marked attentions to Mirelle, and to wane in his attentions to herself. Orange would then speak to her mother, and the mother would communicate her daughter's trouble to the father, and then a crisis would be attained. The father would either break off the match, in which case he would be free to address Mirelle, or, in his dread of losing such a son-in-law, he would drop the Patagonians and offer ready money. Orange and five thousand pounds; Mirelle with six! There was no comparing the lots.

Captain Trecarrel turned the situation into an equation. As Mirelle is to Orange, so is 6,000 to x.

$$\text{Mirelle} \times x = \text{Orange} \times 6,000l.$$
$$\text{or } \frac{M}{O} = \frac{6,000l.}{x}$$

Now Orange was of an inferior social grade, and this difference could not be estimated under 1,000*l.* Then Orange had incumbrances, in the shape of very vulgar parents and a cur of a brother. This could not figure at less than 1,000*l.* Orange was plump, and plump girls become obese women; a serious detriment that could only be covered with another 1,000*l.* Mirelle was a Catholic, and her faith was worth 1,000*l.*

The equation therefore stood thus:—

$$\text{Mirelle} + 6,000l. = \text{Orange} + 10,000l.$$

'Hah!' said Captain Trecarrel, as he hammered his pillow with both fists. 'I'll not take Orange under ten thousand pounds, I'm confounded if I will.'

It must not be supposed that Orange Trampleasure was ignorant of the walks taken by the Captain with Mirelle. Captain Trecarrel did not desire that she should remain in ignorance of them, and when he escorted Mirelle home he came on with her to the house to pay his respects to Mrs. Trampleasure, and inquire after her cold in the head and her bronchial tubes. He usually remained on such occasions for the early dinner, and spent the afternoon with the girls in the garden-house when it rained, or strolling with them in sunshine through the Castle grounds.

At these times he was civil to Orange, and even attentive, but he let her plainly see that when engaged in conversation with her his eyes and thoughts were roving, and roving in the direction of Mirelle. Orange would not have been a woman, and a loving woman, if she had not observed and been hurt by this.

Orange had set her heart on marrying him, not only because she oved him, but also because she was ambitious. She had mor e culture than her father and mother and brother, and she felt their coarseness. She disliked their friends. She was a

proud girl, and when the prospect opened before her of becoming
Mrs. Trecarrel, she resolved to make this the means of shaking
herself free from the sordid society in which she had been
forced to move, and to take her place, as of right, in a class
above it in culture, in traditions, and in aspirations.

Orange volunteered to walk to Trecarrel with Mirelle on
her monthly expeditions, and the offer was frankly accepted.

Mirelle did not know that her cousin was engaged to Trecarrel, she had not been let into the secret; Orange was not
of a confiding nature, and the intercourse between her and the
Captain had of late been strained. Mirelle regarded him as a
friend of the family; she rather wondered what he could find in
the Trampleasures to make him seek their society, but she entertained no suspicions of a nearer tie than friendship.

The jealousy of Orange was roused. She became less demonstrative in her affection towards Mirelle, but she was not
unkind. She harboured bitterness in her heart, but it was not
suffered to brim over her lips. The only token she gave of
wrath and jealousy was a heightened colour and a dangerous
flicker in her eye, whenever subjected to one of those slights
which are only perceptible to the eye of love. Trecarrel
noticed this, and was content. He would achieve his end by
means strictly honourable. Mirelle was unconscious and unsuspicious of what was going on around her. She liked the
Captain, she told Orange as much, without colour rising in her
transparent cheek or lowering her eye. She liked Orange, who,
if not cordial, was kind, and who proved a very serviceable
screen against the brutality of her father and brother. That
the Captain was playing her off upon Orange for his own selfish
purposes, and that deadly jealousy and hate against her were
being kindled in the bosom of her cousin—of this Mirelle was
unsuspicious.

CHAPTER XIV.

UNDER THE HEARTH.

JOHN HERRING visited Joyce daily. He had no choice. She
would allow no one else to touch her bandages. He was impatient to prosecute his journey, but was detained by this poor
savage, who refused doggedly to allow the doctor or Cicely to
touch her arms. Herring remonstrated, and insisted that he

must go. Cicely Battishill volunteered to take his place. Then Joyce became wild, she tore at the rags with her teeth, and would have ripped them off and relaxed the splints, and undone all that had been done for her broken bones, had not Herring hastily promised to remain and attend to her daily, and so with difficulty allayed her apprehension and anger. He was particularly anxious to be in Exeter, but he could not risk the health of Joyce by deserting her in this juncture. He was held captive at West Wyke, held in captivity by Joyce's broken hands. The reason why he was impatient to go forward was that he had been summoned to Exeter to rejoin his regiment, then quartered there. The morning following the accident he had applied for an extension of leave, but no answer had come to his application. He knew that he ought to be with his regiment. He would get into trouble for his absence, and yet—he allowed himself to be detained. The call of humanity was one he was unable to resist. He was good-natured, that is—weak. The strong men are the selfish men. Herring's simple and kindly heart was interested in Joyce, but perplexed and pained. He had no experience of life, and no knowledge of its problems. He had never before been brought in contact with a character utterly rude and destitute of that elementary knowledge which we take for granted is as universally diffused as the atmosphere. He sat under the Giant's Table and talked to Joyce, asked her questions, and endeavoured to draw out the thoughts of her clouded brain. But the profound ignorance, the gross barbarism of her mind and manner of thought amazed him.

He saw nothing of Old Grizzly, who, as Joyce expressed it, 'sloked away' whenever he came in sight.

'Joyce,' said Herring one day, as he knelt by her, having just bandaged her arms, 'do you know the difference between right and wrong?'

The question was called forth by some words of the girl showing a startling ignorance of the elements of morality.

'In coorse I do,' she answered; then sitting up on her bed of heather, 'I'll tell'y how I comed to know. I were once in a turnip-field fetching a turnip for our dinner. There were a wooddoo (dove) running up an oak hard by, and he sings out, " Tak' two, Joyce, tak' two;" and in an old holm tree sat a raven, and her shooked her head and said, "Very wrong, Joyce, very wrong." But I minded more what the wooddoo sed, and I took two. Then as I were climbing over the hedge, I dropped one turnip back in the field whence I'd took 'n; and the wooddoo called again "Tak' two, Joyce, tak' two." "So I will," sez I, and I pitches on my feet again in the field where the turnip had fallen to, and as I picked 'n up, in at the gate comed Farmer Freeze, and he seed me and set his dog Towzer on me, and my legs be scored now where Towzer set his teeth in me. After this I knowed never to believe wooddoos no more when they sez "Tak' two." The raven were right. I shud ha' tooked one or three or five. I knows now that it be wrong to take even numbers of aught, and right to take odd.[1] For you sees,' she continued earnestly, 'if I had taken only one turnip, I'd ha' been over the hedge and away avore Farmer Freeze comed in; but as I minded the wooddoo, and waited to take two, I were tore cruel bad by Towzer.'

Herring looked in her face with wonder.

'Joyce,' he said, 'is this possible? Pray, have you ever heard of God?'

'Who be he?'

'He is above the sky.'

'What, over the clouds, do'y mean?'

'Yes.'

'I've seed 'n scores and scores o' times.' (Here we must note that by this expression Joyce meant 'any number of times.' She could not count above ten, the number of her fingers, and a score was her highest reckonable number, for that was the number of her fingers and toes.) 'You mean the sun as goes running everlasting after the moon; she be his wife, I reckon.'

'Why so?' asked Herring, with a smile.

'Becos her be always a trying to get out of his way.'

'Did your father ill-treat your mother?' he asked.

'In coorse he did, though I can't remember much about it. Her was his wife, and he had a right to.'

'Do you mean that he beat and kicked her, as he has beaten and kicked you?'

'Kicked!' echoed Joyce. 'Who ever sed as he kicked mother or I. It be gentlefolks and wrastlers as kick; us has nothing on our toes, and so us don't kick for fear of hurting 'em.'

'Does your father often beat you?'

'As he likes, but that don't matter now.'

'Why not?'

'Becos I don't belong to 'n any more.'

[1] This story was told the author by a poor Devonshire labourer. He believed he had understood the language of the birds.

'What! emancipated at last, Joyce?'

'I belongs to you.'

'To me!' Herring drew back, staggered by the thought.

'A coorse I do. Vaither a'most broked me to pieces, and I'd a died, but you mended me up and made me to live again. So it stands to reason that I don't belong to vaither no more, but belong to you. 'Tes clear as a moor stream. I can see the reason on it as sartain as I can a trout in a brook. I've been a thinking it over and over, and I never could reckon it right out. Then, one night mother began to grub her way up by thicky stone. I seed her grey hairs coming out o' the ground, and I thought 'twere moss; but after some'ut white and round like a turnip comes, and I sed to myself, "How ever comes a turnip to be growing here, under the Giant's Table?" Presently I seed her eyes acoming up, and then I knowed it were mother. Then I went over and I helped her wi' a rabbit's leg-bone. I scratched the earth away, so as her could get her nose and mouth out of the ground, and her were snuffling like a horned owl.'

'My dear Joyce, you were dreaming.'

'It were true—true as I see you here.'

'But, Joyce, how could you have helped her out of the ground, as you say, with your arms broken?'

Joyce was puzzled. Like other savages, she had not arrived at that point of enlightenment in which dream and reality are distinguished.

'I don't know nothing about that,' said Joyce, 'but it be true what I ses. I know that very well. Let me go on. At last when her could speak plain, her sed, "Joyce, you belong no more to Grizzly, you belong to the young maister." So I sez to her, "How can that be?" Then her answers, "You mind the old iron crock as were chucked away by the Battishills. They'd a broke 'n, and wanted 'n no more. Then your vaither found 'n and mended 'n up somehow. There her hangs now wi' turnips and cabbidge a stewing in her over the fire. Do thicky crock belong to the Battishills now any more? No, her don't, they broke 'n and chucked 'n away. Her belongs to Old Grizzly for becos he took 'n and patched 'n up. That be reason," sed my mother, "for sartain." And what her said be true and right. So I belong to you.'

'But I decline the honour, Joyce,' said Herring, laughing.

'Will you beat and break me and cast me away, like as did vaither?'

'I beat and hurt you! God forbid, my poor child.'

'Then till you does, I belongs to'y—that's sartain!'

She laid herself down on the cushions with the action and tone of voice that implied the matter was concluded past contradiction.

Here was a state of affairs! A state of affairs sufficiently startling. A few weeks ago John Herring had been his own master, with no one depending on him, and without responsibility. Now he was in a measure responsible for three girls. Mirelle, it is true, had asserted her independence, but she had nevertheless imposed on him obligations. Cicely made no scruple of declaring that she relied on him for direction, not to be got from a father never very dependable, and now enfeebled in mind and body. Joyce now informed him that she had transferred her allegiance to him from her father, and he had seen so far into her dark mind as to perceive that what she said she meant, and what she meant she acted on.

'Here,' said Joyce, 'you put your hand on my elbow.'

'Why on your elbow?'

'I can feel there what I want to feel. My hands be as hard as my feet, and they don't feel much. When I wants to know if the porridge be scalding, or whether I can eat 'n, I don't put a finger in, I put my elbow. Now do as I ax'y. Put your hand there.'

She made Herring place his hand above the splints on the elbow. Then she fixed her eyes on him and asked, 'Wot's her name?'

'Whose name?'

'Her wi' the white face?'

'What—Mirelle!' The name dropped involuntarily from his lips.

'You may take your hand away,' she said, 'I know what I wanted to know.'

'What did you want to know, Joyce?—the name?'

'Ah! I wanted to know more nor that; and I've a learned all in a minute.' She paused, still intently watching him. Presently she asked, 'Where did you take her to? Where do you live? Did'y take her to your own home?'

'No, Joyce, of course I did not.'

'Why of course? You likes her more than any other.'

'I—I—Joyce! are you daft?'

'I bain't daft,' answered the girl. 'What I've a found out I know. My elbow told me the truth. When you had your hand on my arm one day I said to'y something about Miss Cicely, and your hand were quiet as if I spoke about a tatie to one wi' a full belly. But when I axed about the Whiteface—I cannot mind her name—then you gave a start, and your hand shooked. We'm friends, you and I, and you won't hide nothing from me. Where be Whiteface to now?'

'I took her to some relations—cousins of hers.'

'Ah! we've folks (kindred) too out to Nymet, but ours be reg'lar savages. We have clothes to our backs, and taty ground, and a new take. I reckon Whiteface's folk be of other sort.'

'Of course they are. She is comfortable and well cared for by them.'

'Why didn't they come and fetch her away when her father broke his neck, instead of leaving you to take care of her and take her away?'

That was not a question Herring could easily answer.

Joyce did not wait for a reply. 'No,' she went on ''twere you as cared for her and did iverything for her, as you've a cared for and done iverything for me. But me you think on just now and then, and her you'll be thinking on night and day, I know that very well. It be natural, and I say nort against it. And how be't wi' her I wonder. Did her tell you afore her left how good you'd been, and how her'd niver niver forget what you'd a done for her?'

'No, Joyce.'

'Didn't her then look you in the face as I do now, and if her didn't say it in words, let you see in her eyes that her thought and felt it?'

'No, she did not look at me at all.'

'See there now!' exclaimed Joyce. 'I be nort but a poor savage, but I be better nor her. I know what be right and vitty (fitting)—and her don't.'

'Of course you know what is right, with the guidance of wooddoves.'

'It were the raven, not the wooddoo,' said Joyce, eagerly. 'The wooddoo told me wrong. The wooddoo sed "Tak two, Joyce, tak two." But that's no count. It'll come right wi' Whiteface and you in the end. Her'll find them folk of hers not like you, always a thinking and caring for her, and then her'll remember you and think on you, just as I do lying here. Be you a going?'

Herring had risen from his knee as if to leave.

'Stay a bit longer,' pleaded Joyce. 'Do'y know what it be after it hev been raining all day, and cold and wisht, out comes the sun afore he goes down, and the clouds roll away, and Dartmoor seems to be all alight, and then for the glory and the beauty and the warmth you forget all the time o' cold and darkness and rain? It be so wi' me. Here I lies and I sees none but vaither, and her grumbles becos I can't work, and when vaither bain't here I sees nobody, and it be wisht, I reckon, till you comes; and then I be that full o' gladness and joy I remember no more the time o' loneness and pain and trouble. You'll bide a bit longer, won't'y?'

'I really cannot stay, Joyce, with the best will to pleasure you, I cannot.' The demonstrative admiration and affection of the poor creature confounded and distressed him.

'I've more to tell'y,' Joyce continued. 'I've that to tell'y which be most partikler. Do'y know what vaither did to make mother lie quiet? He gived her some'ut. But her bain't no more a child to be amused wi' toys like them. May be for a night or two her sat and turned 'em over and was kept quiet wi' looking at 'em. But it bain't the likes o' them as will make mother still and sleep o' nights, instead of rooting about in the earth under the table like a mole.

'What does she want, Joyce?'

'Her wants you to do it. You mun lift the hearthstone and say glory rallaluley, and Our Vaither—kinkum kum over her. Her told me so herself. I cannot do it. I don't know the words. I've just picked up a word here and there when the Methodies ha' been out on the down, singing and preaching, and hugging and praying. You can say kinkum kum over mother and make her lie quiet and sleep.'

Poor dark soul! Joyce had no knowledge of God, and very dim, perverted conceptions of right and wrong. Her only faith was in troubled spirits, and that was no faith, but a confusion of mind between death and life, and dreaming visions and sight when waking. Her sole idea of prayer was a spell to lay the restless dead. Herring's heart was softened by compassion for the girl. She watched the expression of his face very intently, somewhat mistrustfully, fearful of a refusal, and, worse than all, of ridicule. But though Herring did meditate refusal, no thought of the ludicrous in her request stirred a muscle of his mouth. He was grieved for her, and he was touched by her ignorant simplicity.

'Poor Joyce!' he said, and knelt down by her again. 'Poor Joyce!'

Then he tried to soothe her and turn her thoughts into another channel. She, however, persisted in forcing the task on him of saying sacred words over a dead and buried woman. When Joyce had made up her mind to anything she was inflexible. Herring was being forced into one position, then into another, for which he was unsuited. Joyce had made him her doctor, her nurse, her guardian, and now she made him her priest. He was good natured, and good nature is weakness.

After holding back he at length, out of pity, and to humour the headstrong girl, did as she required. She made him raise the hearthstone, and trig it up with a piece of granite. He could not lift the stone out of its place, though Old Grizzly had been able-armed enough to do this unaided. Then Herring knelt and gravely said a prayer—*the* prayer.

Joyce was satisfied.

'That be right,' she said. 'Now mother don't want her toys no more. There be a stick wi' a crook to the end i' thicky corner.'

'I see there is.'

'Fetch 'n, and scrabble with 'n under the hearthstone.'

'What for?'

'Do as I tell'y. You'll see what for fast enough. Hav'y got the stick? Now thrust it well in, and poke about till you comes to some'ut hard.'

Herring groped as bidden, rather uneasy in his mind at what he was doing, lest he should rake out the bones of the dead woman.

'Do'y feel nort?'

'Yes; there is something there hard and heavy.'

'Vang 'n in to'y.'

Herring obeyed. There certainly was something there. As the crook struck it, it sounded like a metal box. After some working with the stick he managed to get it out. It was a small box of japanned iron, which had been locked, but had been battered till the lock had given way. The lid accordingly was loose.

'Open it,' said Joyce. 'Vaither found 'n the night o' the axidenk. He found 'n in one of the boxes that had gone scatt wi' falling from the carriage. He thought there might be some'ut in him, and so he tooked 'n away and brought 'n here, and wi' a bit of stone knacked the lock all abroad. I see 'n do it.

That were after he'd a broke me to pieces. When I came by
my wits I seed old vaither sitting by the fire and working
till he'd a got the lid started, and then he looked in and seed
what were there, and he sed he'd give me some if I'd take 'em.
But they wos no good to me, and I couldn't a done nort wi' 'em
with both my arms broke. I couldn't move my fingers, and I
were that deadly ill I didn't care for nort but to lie quiet and
die right on end. So then, after a bit, vaither sed he knowed
what he'd do wi' 'em as they were no good to he. He'd give 'n
to mother, her'd play wi' 'em o' nights and be quiet. So he
heaved up the hearthstone—vaither be a deal stronger than
you—and he shoved the box under, just over where mother's
heart be. There, look'y what brave fine things they be.'

Herring had opened the box. He looked in in speechless
amazement. Then he raised a tray and looked further, and beneath the tray was more still.

Presently he found his tongue, drew a heavy breath, and
said, 'Good heavens, Joyce, these are diamonds. There are
thousands of pounds worth of diamonds here.'

'They be brave shiney stones.'

'They are diamonds.'

'Well, you may take 'em. They belongs o' rights to the
Whiteface. You can take 'em and give 'em to her or keep 'em
yourself, just as you likes.'

CHAPTER XV.

EHEU, BUBONES!

WHEN Balboa, from a peak in Darien, discovered an ocean un-
troubled by waves, unstained by the shadow of a cloud, he
named it the Pacific. John Herring's exploration of life was
the reverse of Balboa's course; he had left behind him the
Pacific Ocean, in which he had hitherto sailed, and he had
sighted the sea of storms. Balboa had little idea of the extent
of the watery tract he discovered, and Herring had but a faint
suspicion of the nature and fretfulness of the sea on which he
was about to embark. A few weeks ago the problem of life
had seemed to him a simple addition sum; he was about to
discover that it consisted in the extraction of surds, which
when extracted prove dead and dry symbols. 'Vanity of
vanities,' said the Preacher, after he had worked at the sum all

his days; the conclusion of the whole matter is, 'all is vanity.'

With a sense of alarm Herring became aware that Joyce had put into his hands more destinies than her own. Mirelle's future was contained in a little casket of which the lock was broken, and which was placed at his unchallenged disposal. The fortune that had been confided to the trustee under the will was certain to be engulfed as the ship that strikes the Goodwins. Here, however, was the bulk of her property, providentially saved from the grip of Tramplara, and lodged in honest hands. What was he to do with this? Was he justified in retaining it till Mirelle should need it, and then delivering it to her untouched, or was he bound to deliver it to him who was constituted legal trustee by the will of her father?

The conflict stood between moral and legal obligation. It was a question whether, if he acted in accordance with legal obligation, he would not be morally guilty were Mirelle's entire fortune made away with.

A week or two ago, had the question been proposed, If you find a guinea, should you return it immediately to the owner or keep it till you think the owner needs it? Herring would have been ready with an answer that cost him little consideration. Now he was not sure that the ready answer was the right answer. Life is not a simple matter; it is a veritable problem. The problem of life is the Pons Asinorum.

He met Cicely at the gate of West Wyke. She was looking distressed, and she touched his arm. 'I want a word with you. Look here.' She held out a letter.

'I have ventured to open it. The letter is addressed to my father, but as it has the Launceston postmark, and I knew the handwriting to be that of Mr. Tramplara, I did not show it to my father. I opened it. Was I right? I feared it might contain something to distress him, and I found the contents more distasteful than I had anticipated. I was right, was I not, to open the letter?'

A week ago, if asked, Is anyone justified in opening another person's letter? Herring would have answered in the negative. But now, all the cut and dried precepts of morality he had learned began to fail him. They did for copybook slips, not for rules of life.

'You have something in your hand, Mr. Herring,' said Miss Battishill, observing the iron box. 'Is that yours?'

He hesitated. Is it justifiable ever to tell a lie? Is it justifiable to evade the truth, and so deceive? He had no doubts on this head a week ago. He doubted now, and did evade giving a direct answer.

'The box is broken, and I am going to have the lock mended.'

'But, Mr. Herring, you have just come from the Cobbledicks.'

'Yes,' he answered, and then hesitated. He was unaccustomed to fence with the truth. 'When the accident took place, the box was lost somehow, and Joyce has found and restored it me.'

'I hope you have lost nothing of value from it.'

'I have lost nothing from it,' he replied. 'But never mind the box now, Miss Battishill. Tell me what it is that now occasions you trouble.'

'Old Mr. Tramplara has written a peremptory letter to my father, calling up all the money that he has advanced him on the security of the property.'

'And your father is not in a position to pay?'

'I am sure he is not. The letter must be answered, and that speedily. I need your advice. I dare not let my dear father see the letter; the result might be fatal in his present state.'

'No,' answered Herring, 'he must know nothing of the demand.'

'But if we do not meet this call, and meet it we cannot, Mr. Tramplara will turn us out and sell the estate.'

'Is there no way of avoiding this? Cannot a portion be sold to clear the rest of incumbrance? What amount does your father owe?'

'I do not know. Will you ascertain that from him, and then consider with me what must be done? If we are forced to leave West Wyke, it will kill papa.' Then her tears came.

'Miss Battishill,' said Herring, in great distress—he was unaccustomed to woman's tears, and therefore moved by them—'dear Miss Battishill, do not give way. We will find some mode of escape. I will do my utmost for you; be very sure of that.' He took her hand and pressed it. She returned the pressure, and, looking up into his eyes through her tears, said, 'You give me confidence, you are so strong and sure.'

'I strong! I sure!' exclaimed Herring. At that moment

he was feeling the weakness of his principles and the uncertainty of his course.

'Go in, and talk to my father,' she said, 'whilst I try to forget my troubles among my flowers.' Then with a relapse, 'Oh, Mr. Herring, I do so love this sunny south garden, and the old house, and the heathy moors, and Cosdon reigning like a king over all. It will go nigh to break my heart as well as my father's, if I am forced to leave West Wyke.'

'We must put faith in the future,' he said.

'I did believe in the future till of late, but now my path lies under eclipse.' She paused and sighed. 'But after all, is it worth while deferring to tell my father? He must shortly know the truth. It is only a matter of weeks.' She made a little effort to control her emotion. 'You decide whether he is to be told or not. I am not competent to form an opinion. I shrink from agitating papa, lest it lead to another stroke; if however this must be done——' She turned sharply away, and signed to him with her hand to leave her and go indoors.

Herring entered the hall.

Mr. Battishill was in his arm-chair. He was much enfeebled by his seizure, but though his utterance was not as clear as formerly, his loquacity was undiminished.

'Mr. Herring,' he said somewhat peevishly, 'I have been left a long while alone, and yet not altogether alone, I have had Shakespeare and my own thoughts to company. But alas! as Lear says, "My wits begin to turn—I will be a pattern of all patience, I will say nothing." Herring, sit down in that chair and have a talk. I wish you had known us in better days, and when my wife was living. We had more of an establishment then. Now there is only a maid-of-all-work, then we had a cook and housemaid, and a nurse for Cicely. I do not think we were the happier for having so large an establishment. I believe it killed my wife.'

'What, sir?'

'The servants killed her. I have puzzled my brain to know which were created first, the beasts, or the parasites on their backs; but of course it was the beasts, for they could do without the parasites, but not the parasites without the beasts. So I believe that the common ruck of humanity was made to feed on the noble specimens of the kind. We, the aristocracy, exist not for ourselves, to enjoy our lives and follow our wills, but for our servants, to support them and be subject to their whims. That which the palmer worm hath left hath the locust eaten, and that which the locust hath left hath the canker worm eaten, and that which the canker worm hath left hath the caterpillar eaten. My dear wife always insisted that this was an Oriental and prophetical manner of describing the servant nuisance. That which the housemaid has left the cook carries off, and what the cook spares the kitchen-maid embezzles, and what the kitchen-maid leaves the charwoman whips off in her basket under her shawl. My poor dear wife fought a long battle to keep the house up, but in vain. The aristocracy I explained to her are the pigs and poultry of mankind, kept and fattened to be eaten. She succumbed at last, and when, dear soul, she was dying, almost the last words she said were, "Where I am going there will be no servants." In this hope she made a happy end.' The old man paused and wiped his eyes. 'When the first woe was ended, then came the second.'

'What was that?' asked Herring.

'That was Tramplara, of course. I was pretty well in Tramplara's web before the first woe was overpassed.'

'May I ask the amount of your indebtedness to Mr. Trampleasure?'

'Lord bless you!—you ask me more than I can answer. I have borrowed so often, and when I have not paid as I expected, I contracted an additional loan,—like an owl that I was. Pace, Bubones!' the old man touched his forehead as he looked at the heraldic glass. 'However, if it be an amusement to you I give you full liberty to overhaul my desk.'

'It would be as well if I were to get your indebtedness into shape,' said Herring. 'If I can be of any help to you in this way, command me.'

'I don't see that you can help me; I am past that.'

'It struck me, sir, that by the sale of a portion of your property you might be able to wipe off some of the debt.'

'Wipe off the debt! as soon wipe a child's nose dry. I said to a little urchin one day, "Blow your nose, and cease snuffling." "Please, Squire," he answered, "it ain't no good, it won't bide blowed." It is the same with my accounts. I have tried to wipe off my debts several times, but the debtor side keeps running. Look at my books, you will find the figures show as remarkable a tendency to turn one way as do the heads of the trees at this elevation.'

'You will then allow me to overhaul them.'

'Certainly, if it will give you pleasure. There is no accounting for tastes. There is an old woman in one of my cottages who has a bad leg, and insists on showing it me. I say to her, "Betty, keep that for the doctor, it revolts me." It is the same with a gentleman's accounts. They are his running sore. But he is wiser than Betty, he covers it up. If you are a doctor of sick ledgers, by all means examine, and I wish you joy.'

Herring was now staying at West Wyke. He went carefully over the accounts of Mr. Battishill, and found them to be in utter confusion. The old man kept receipts sometimes, but not invariably. He received his rent when he could get it, and by instalments; his tenants were always behindhand because punctuality of payment was not insisted on. It took Herring some time to arrive at a just idea of what the old gentleman owed, and he was startled at the amount. He also obtained an approximate value of the estate. It was clearly impossible for him to meet his liabilities.

Herring saw no course open except the disposal of the property, or part of it.

The estate was small, it had been reduced, and the land was of inferior quality. It was possible that the sale of Upaver alone might suffice to clear off the mortgages, but then it was doubtful whether Mr. Battishill and his daughter could live on at West Wyke, farming the barton, when Upaver was sold. To farm without capital, and without being able to superintend the workmen, meant to sink deeper into the bog after having been extricated from it. The wisest course for Mr. Battishill would be to sell the entire estate, and retire to a cottage on what remained of the purchase-money, after all the liabilities he had contracted had been discharged. He was reluctant to propose this, and yet it was the proposal which would be most advantageous to the old man.

'Well,' asked Mr. Battishill, a few days later, 'my good friend, what has come of this pondering over my papers? You have grown portentously dull, and left all the talking to me.'

'The case is hopeless,' said Herring, sadly.

'I knew it was,' said the old man, with a look and air of discouragement. In spite of his words, he had nursed a hope that Herring would by some feat of ingenuity find a mode of relief, and would assure him that the situation was not desperate.

'"I by neglecting worldly ends, all dedicated to closeness and the bettering of my mind . . . by being so retired, in old

Tramplara waked an evil nature." My situation is not unlike that of Prospero—here I dwell with my Miranda. Well, well! what will be must be—

> He that has and a little tiny wit,—
> With heigh, ho, the wind and the rain,—
> Must make content with his fortunes fit,
> Though the rain it raineth every day.'

The old man, though discouraged, did not believe that the case was desperate.

'Never mind,' he said, 'the world of West Wyke will hold out my time. There is but one thing that I ask of Providence, and that I am sure Providence will not deny me. I desire nothing but to die here and be laid with my ancestors. Do you know what our motto is? You would never guess, "Eheu! Eheu! Eheu!" I suppose that was given as resembling the hoot of an owl, but it was ominous. Poor Cicely! she will not be able to carry the ancestral house with her when some Ferdinand comes to carry her off. She will take with her nothing but the owls, and he who marries her will bear those owls on an escutcheon of pretence on his own coat. So at last, at last, it will come to this, that the white owls who have nested here in honour for so many centuries will spread their wings and seek a perch elsewhere. Eheu! Eheu! Eheu, Bubones!'

CHAPTER XVI.

TRUSTEE NOT EXECUTOR.

ALTHOUGH John Herring had been devoting his attention as closely as possible to the affairs of Mr. Battishill, and had found them an engrossing study from the confusion which pervaded them, he had not been able to shake off the sense of responsibility incurred by the possession of Mirelle's diamonds. Joyce had constituted him trustee of the fortune of this maiden. Mirelle had two trustees now, as her father had intended, but John was trustee without the knowledge of the other, and over a fortune of the existence of which that other was happily ignorant. Tramplara was trustee by virtue of the testament of Mr. Strange, John Herring by virtue of the caprice of Joyce.

Herring satisfied his conscience that he was acting rightly in retaining the jewels. He knew that they could not be safely intrusted to Mr. Tramplara. When he turned the matter over in his mind, he thought he could make out the course of events which had influenced Mr. Strange. This gentleman had called at Avranches on Mr. Eustace Smith, the co-trustee, but he had not called on Mr. Trampleasure when he passed through Launceston. There must have been a reason for this. He had probably heard in Falmouth sufficient as to the character of Tramplara to determine him to cancel his name from the will, as a person not to be trusted with the fortune and destiny of his only child. It was clear from Mr. Eustace Smith's letter that he had not been consulted when Mr. Strange saw him at Avranches. The deceased must, therefore, have determined, when renewing his acquaintance with him, not to trouble him with the executorship or guardianship of his child. Mr. Strange had, no doubt, intended to draw up a fresh will when he reached Exeter. As we know, Herring's conclusions were correct. Cruel fate had cut the father off before he could rectify the error into which he had fallen. Now a happy accident had constituted Herring guardian of the major portion of Mirelle's property.

John Herring had confidence in himself. It was impossible for him to commit a dishonourable action. The diamonds were as safe in his hands as in the strongest bank cellar. He believed the trust was given to him by Providence. He was a simple-hearted young man, and believed in Providence. He recognised in this rescue of the jewels, and their committal to his custody, an interposition of Heaven in behalf of the orphan. Whom could Providence have chosen more trustworthy than himself, and more interested in the welfare of Mirelle? The more he considered the situation the more convinced he became that a finger out of heaven was pointing to him a plain duty, and that he could not shirk that duty justifiably. But he had no desire to shirk it. He was anxious and interested about Mirelle. He was certain that Tramplara would risk her fortune in some rash venture. He had heard of the man. He now remembered that his father had lost money by him. Tramplara would take the coin intrusted him, put it in a handkerchief over the table before the eyes of his victim, and, presto! it was gone, and the kerchief empty. A clink under the table told that the coin had fallen into the conjuror's pocket. It was not possible for John Herring, knowing the character of Tramplara, and suspecting that the deceased had desired to cancel his will, it was impossible morally, for John Herring to surrender to him the trust now committed to him.

Of all men, he, John Herring, was the most calculated to look after Mirelle's interests, for he loved her better than any one else in the world could love her. John Herring being, as has been said, very simple, thought that duties rose to the surface like earthworms to be taken by the crows. Here was an obvious duty which had worked up under his eye, and he swooped down on it, and made it his own immediately.

But if Mirelle was his first care, the Battishills formed his second. Without any seeking on his part, they had thrown themselves on him, and he could not without cruelty withdraw his support. He saw a good and kind, if somewhat fantastical old man and his sweet helpless daughter, menaced with the greatest of evils—banishment from their home, to become outcasts in the world, with no income, or very little, to sustain them; he struck down by sickness, and she too ignorant of life to know how to meet it, weighted with the burden of a paralysed father.

What was he to do?

Then a bright idea struck him. He would try to help Mirelle and Cicely at once. To do this he must go to Launceston, and to go to Launceston he must obtain leave of absence from Joyce.

John Herring was now, for the first time, opening his eyes to the fact that to be good-natured and ready to oblige all those appealing to him was to involve himself in many difficulties. Among swimmers they who are drowning lay hold of him who maintains himself above water; it is necessary, though painful, to give each a kick in the face and send him to the bottom, if the swimmer will reach the shore himself alive. It is only the selfish man who can sing as he walks in the face of the robber. He has nothing to give, what he has is too ingeniously stowed away to be discoverable. Life is a Hounslow Heath where footpads beset every road, and, where they leave a gap, beggars step in. And these demand and take from the traveller everything he has, and kick him, when stripped, off the heath, with a jeer, into the black beyond.

A kind-hearted man such as John Herring does good to others as he *would* be done by. Would is in the optative and ever unfulfilled mood. It is not the criminal who is stung by remorse; the only crime that brings self-reproach is generosity to a brother in need. The glow that succeeds a good deed is the sting of repentance for having done it.

Of all this Herring was ignorant. Puppies are born blind,

but when thrown into the water that is to drown them they open their eyes. Herring was beginning life. He must pay his footing.

If Herring had not been ridiculously simple, he would not have gone to the Giant's Table and explained to Joyce that he could not attend to her arms for a couple of days. Would young Sampson have done this, or Captain Trecarrel? They had their eyes open, and allowed none to catch their ankles as they swam. Herring took pains to make Joyce understand that she must be patient, and not by impatience undo the good already done her.

She was stubborn and despotic.

'Joyce,' said he, 'I am going to see Mr. Trampleasure. Do you know him?'

'I know 'n,' she replied. 'He were here yesterday along with vaither. Vaither went off with 'n up the Coomb by Rayborough.'

'Mr. Tramplara was here!'

'Yes, he were. He came down on vaither hard, and sed he were going to turn us out of our land, and tear down the Table, and send us out without home or ground of our own.'

'This is strange. He did not come near West Wyke.'

'I reckon not. He said as how he were going to turn the Squire and the young lady out as well. He said we might give 'em shelter under the Table for a bit till he knocked that all abroad too.'

'Why did he go to Rayborough?'

'I reckon he were searching after some mine. But I don't know. He scared vaither pretty smart; but he got vaither at last as meek he would do anything he were axed. Then Tramplara made 'n come along of he on to the moors, and I seed mun no more.'

'Joyce, I hope to save West Wyke for Mr. Battishill, and that is why I am going to Launceston. If I succeed, then you also will be safe from disturbance. Your Table will not then be thrown down.'

'Squire won't hurt of us—t' I know by; he never did nobody harm, he.'

'Then, Joyce, you understand, I shall not return till the day after to-morrow, and you must let the doctor or Miss Battishill attend to your arms.'

'I won't.'

'But you must. I tell you I cannot be here.'

'You may go.'

'Thank you for giving me my furlough,' he said with a smile. 'But, as you see, when I am absent you will have to be attended by some one else.'

'Neither vaither, nor doctor, nor Miss Cicely shan't touch me, not by the blue blazes. I tell'y you may go, and my arms shall bide as they be. They won't take no hurt. I shan't do nort to 'em till you comes back. There, that's settled.'

Herring informed Mr. Battishill and Cicely of his meditated expedition to Launceston to see Mr. Trampleasure. He told them that he was in hopes of bringing him to another mind about the mortgages, but he did not enter into the particulars of his scheme, nor did he tell them what he had learned from Joyce relative to Mr. Trampleasure's visit the day before and exploration of Upaver. Herring conjectured that the old man had seen the ore brought up from the mine recently opened, and was eager by foreclosing to secure it for himself, having formed a high opinion of its value. Herring went again that evening to Upaver and explored the workings, taking with him one of the labourers Mr. Battishill had employed on it. The man was familiar with mines, and was confident that the lode was good. The 'shode' had led to as beautiful a 'bunch' as a man might hope to see in a lifetime. A fortune was to be made at Upaver.

To his surprise, Herring learned from the man that though Mr. Trampleasure had passed the workings, he had not paid them any attention, but had gone farther up the glen. But then, as the miner said, with a jerk of the chin, there was nothing lying about which might lead anyone to suspect what was below. All the samples were buried or hidden in the gorse brakes.

Herring carried off with him some of the best specimens of pure ore, and, on his return to West Wyke, showed them to Mr. Battishill, and told him his opinion of the mine. He said that he was confident, if a respite could be obtained from Tramplara, and a company be formed to work the mine, that the royalties on the lead extracted would speedily clear the property of its burdens.

The old man was elated. He talked over the prospect, offering many suggestions, some utterly unpractical, and his hollow cheek flushed with excitement.

'Ah!' said he, 'if Tramplara knows about that lead he'll

not grant a respite, but be down on me at once if he sees profit to be got by it.

> 'I'll have my bond: I will not hear thee speak:
> I'll have my bond; and therefore speak no more.
> I'll not be made a soft and dull-eyed fool,
> To shake the head, relent, and sigh, and yield
> To Christian intercession.'

The old man shook his head. 'No, Herring, you will not prevail on him with prayers. "It is the most impenetrable cur that ever kept with men." No, you must attack his self-interest if you will bend him, and how you will manage that passes my conception.'

'But suppose I say to Tramplara, Here is the money.'

Cicely looked sharply up from her work.

'Mr. Herring, you made me a promise.'

'My dear,' said Mr. Battishill, 'you have often let me see that you disapproved of my speculations, as if I must be blind. But see! here at last, in Upaver, I have hit on one that will succeed.'

'You have hit on it, father, for others to make fortunes out of it. You have hit on it as West Wyke is slipping from us.'

CHAPTER XVII.

IN THE SUMMER-HOUSE.

As John Herring entered the gates of Dolbeare, he saw Mirelle go into the summer-house. This summer-house stood at the edge of the terrace between the garden-gate and the house.

He desired to see her alone, and therefore, before going to the front door, he turned to the garden lodge and stood in the doorway.

Mirelle saw him and bowed slightly. Herring went in, and up to her. Then, after a moment's hesitation, she held out her hand.

He took it, but he might as well have touched an icicle. No token of pleasurable recognition appeared in her face.

'You are surprised to see me,' said Herring, 'I dare say.'

'Not at all,' she answered. 'Why should I be? I know nothing of your movements. If you had told me you were going to Moscow, and I had seen you start in that direction, I should be surprised to see you here now; but as I know neither where you live nor the places you frequent, there is nothing in your reappearance to justify surprise.'

'I have come to-day from West Wyke.'

'Indeed! I hope you left all well there.'

'Only fairly so. You have not heard what happened to poor Joyce.'

'I do not know who poor Joyce is.'

'Joyce is that wild girl who helped you to West Wyke on the evening of the accident.'

'I remember an uncouth and unmannerly *paysanne*. Is her name Joyce? I did not know it. If I had heard it, the name escaped my memory. Joyce! what is the derivation of the name Joyce?[1] Joieuse, I presume—a singularly inappropriate name in this case.'

'Very much so, poor child. That brutal father of hers broke her arms, and otherwise seriously injured her.'

'Indeed! These savages have their ways.'

Herring was shocked at her want of feeling.

'You do not seem to feel for her, and yet she helped you, as you may remember.'

'Of course I am very sorry. I am sorry when I hear a mason has fallen off a scaffold, or a child has tumbled into a well, or a horse has broken his knees; I am sorry when a donkey is roughly treated. But unless I am acquainted with the mason, and the child, and the horse, and the ass, I do not feel more than a transient pity. You possibly have seen sufficient of this wild girl to possess some interest in her; I know absolutely nothing of her. How, then, can I feel for her more than I do when I say I am sorry?'

'May I take a chair?'

'Certainly. Sit down, and we will talk. I have something I wish particularly to say to you. I am sorry that I let you go the other time without thanking you formally for having rescued me from the broken carriage, for having seen to the funeral of my poor father, and for having conveyed me hither to the care of these people here.'

She spoke without any expression in her tone, simply as though repeating a lesson learned by rote. When she had spoken, she drew a long breath like a sigh of relief. She had discharged a duty. It was off her mind, and she was free.

[1] In the South Tawton Register stands this entry under Baptisms: 'Jocosa, anglicè Joyce, daughter of ——,' &c. It was formerly a common name in Devon.

I

'You see for yourself, Mr. Herring, that the feelings of the heart are too sacred to be dispersed over the earth, to be scattered like coins amidst a crowd of beggars. One meets with some thousands of persons in the course of existence, and cannot cut one's heart into little bits and present each with a portion. We must reserve it for true friends, and give it them entire. Those who pass us by, and whom we see but for a while, are like the figures of a magic-lantern slide; they make us laugh, or they interest us for the moment, and then are forgotten. When we hear that a slide is broken, we ask, which? The man driving a wheelbarrow, or the old woman who desired she were pope, or the cabbage that becomes a tailor? When we are informed, we do not weep, we merely say, It can be replaced.'

'I hope you do not class the Battishills among your magic-lantern slides.'

'No, I know them, and they have been kind to me. I even liked Mr. Battishill. He has his ideas.'

'And Miss Cicely?'

'She is rustic and good-hearted. But she does not think. She has no knowledge of books. She could be made passable if sent to school, but must be recreated to be given ideas. Besides, I am not fond of the plump and the *ingénue*.'

'You have not asked after Mr. Battishill. If it be not too great an effort for your memory, you will recall that he had a stroke before you left West Wyke.'

'Do not be sarcastic I remember that perfectly well. If you will trouble your memory, you will recall that I did, on first learning you came from West Wyke, ask after Mr. and Miss Battishill. I remember that he had a paralytic stroke, but I recall as well that he showed good signs of recovery.'

'I am afraid, Countess, that he stands the chance of another stroke; for he is menaced with a great evil, and any profound agitation is likely to bring on a second seizure.'

'I am very sorry to hear it.'

'His affairs are involved to such an extent that it will be necessary for his property to be sold, and he will have to leave West Wyke.'

'Then he can go and live in France; anywhere must be better than that dismal old house on a barren moor. It is best that it should be so. He will escape from a dungeon.'

'You do not understand that his heart is bound up with West Wyke, and that to transplant him from the home of his ancestors will be to kill him.'

'He thinks West Wyke a Paradise only because he has never crossed the Channel. When he reaches a nook where the sun shines and the flowers ever bloom, he will thank Heaven for having released him from his prison and exile in that wretched house and on that howling waste.'

'Countess, you are young, and have no conception of the power that association has on the old. You can begin life anywhere, and everywhere hopes and interests start up. To the old it is not so, they are without hopes, and their only pleasure is in recollection. To the aged the looking back is almost as sweet as the looking forward is to the young.'

'Then let him sit down in an arbour of roses, and dream of the past there; not in a dingy old parlour with smoked ceiling, and the rain pattering against the window.'

'I fear that he will be turned destitute into the world, or, if not destitute, nearly so; and to a broken and sick man that means death.'

'He can hardly be worse off elsewhere than he is now.'

'He will have to go into a new home and accommodate himself to that, at a time of life and in a condition of health unfitting him for a change. You are unfeeling, Countess.'

'Pardon me, I am not. I know Mr. Battishill, and I respect his many good qualities, but I cannot put myself in his frame of mind. It seems to me that, were I he, all thought of being allowed to leave such a spot, with the world before me, would fill me, if sick and dying, with new life. I would start up in my bed and cry out, Take me to France; there I know I shall be well.'

'As he does not know France, he has no such desire. And he is too old to acquire new tastes. There comes a time when the mind as well as the body is tired, and all it asks is to be given rest. New scenes, new associates, new habits exact too much of the exhausted spirit. Have you not seen a feeble flame extinguished by fresh fuel being put round it with the hope of coaxing it into a blaze? This is not all; the rupture of old associations is the rupture of the thousand filaments the tree root has woven in the soil about it. Break these, and though the tree be transplanted from cold clay to richest loam, it will die. Think of your own forefather when he lost Cantalejo. Think how his heart ached, how he turned to take a last look at the ancient walls, and could see nothing, for, strong man as he was, his eyes were full of tears. He knew that with him his entire posterity was banished for ever.'

'I can understand that,' said Mirelle, sadly; 'never more able to coin his own money, nor hang anyone on his own gallows.'

'And your ancestor went forth hale and able to meet the world, and conquer himself a new place in it.'

'Yes,' said Mirelle, raising her head proudly, 'he was a brave soldier. He fought, and was killed in the wars.'

'But this poor old man is broken with years and infirmities.'

'It is the will of God.'

'He dies, and his daughter is cast adrift, without means, and ignorant of the world.'

'Do not speak to me of her. She is the embodiment of prose—pleasing and entertaining, but still prose. The world is prosaic, and she will always find a hole in it into which she can fit. It is those with ideas, the originals and the poets, who are adrift and homeless. Every gate is closed to them.'

'Countess, think of that evening when the accident took place, and your poor father was killed. You were left on the moor, knowing nothing of the place where you were, or of the people among whom your lot was to be cast. What if, by an unlucky chance, I had not been present to assist you, and the Battishills had not been ready to receive you? What would you have done on that moor, alone, without adviser, without home and without money? The savages would have fallen upon you—that ruthless man who has smashed the bones of his own daughter would not have spared you.'

Mirelle shivered.

'You may well shudder; I do not know what would have become of you. But a merciful Providence interposed in your behalf, and raised up to you friends who have cared for you.'

'Yes,' she said, 'I see that. I see that now.'

'Cicely Battishill is like to be placed in a very similar position; to be left homeless and friendless in the world, standing by a father, who, if not dead, is as bad as dead for all the help he can afford her. She cannot become a governess and earn her bread, she has her father to nurse. Now, Countess, when you think of your own condition on that eventful night, and of what might have become of you unless the Battishills had thrown open their door to you and cherished you, then, perhaps, you will be able to realise the condition of Miss Battishill, who, though she may be prosaic, as you say, is a delicate maiden, and has the nurture of a gentlewoman.'

'Mon Dieu! que puis-je faire, moi! You speak to me as

though I could save them. I can do nothing, with the best desire to help them. I cannot invite them to make this their refuge. This is not my home. It is simply a menagerie in which I am allowed a cage among the bears.'

'I think it is your *duty* to do what you can to assist the Battishills.'

'Show me the way, and I will not shrink from performing any duty. But you must see I am unable to help these good people.'

'Not altogether unable, Countess. Your father has left you several thousand pounds, which are in the hands of Mr. Trampleasure, in trust. He must invest them for you. He is also the man who has a hold on the estate of the Battishills. Get him to take your money, or as much of it as is needed, in payment of the sum owed him by Mr. Battishill, and to transfer to you his claims on the property. That is, let him transfer the mortgage on West Wyke from himself personally to himself as trustee for you. Then you will be mistress over the estate of the Battishills, and if you will not foreclose, I can promise you that the interest shall be regularly and punctually paid. I am certain that the investment is sound. By this means you will be benefiting the Battishills and yourself simultaneously.'

'I understand nothing about mortgages, investments, or interest. I leave that to others. If this proposal of yours enable me to wipe off an obligation I owe to those who have been kind to me, I accept it gladly, and if it be a duty I shall make it a matter of conscience to fulfil it.'

'It is a duty. At least I think it is. Judge for yourself. You see your benefactors the Battishills in distress, and you have it in your power to rescue them from ruin at no cost to yourself. It seems to me that no duty could be put in a plainer form before you.'

'Mr. Trampleasure is in the house. He will have to be consulted. We cannot act without him. Will you summon him hither, and we will arrange the matter on the spot. You will not find me one to shrink from the discharge of a duty.'

John Herring left Mirelle, and did as she desired. He found Mr. Trampleasure at home, as she had said. He was engaged with his son in the dining-room on some plans, and they had a bottle of spirits and a jug of hot water on the table at their elbows, though the time was early in the afternoon.

Old Tramplara greeted Herring with effusion, the young one sulkily. Herring told the father that the Countess wanted to speak to him in the summer-house for a few moments, if he would oblige her with his presence.

'See what comes of having a live Countess in the house,' said the old man, laughing; 'I have to dance after her. Now, if she had been plain missie, she would have come here to see me.'

Then he accompanied Herring to the summer-house. This house was, in fact, a room of fair size, furnished with a fireplace and carved mantelpiece, that contained a quaint old painting on panel. The windows were large, and that to the south-east overhung the precipice, and commanded a magnificent view down the valley of the Tamar and up that of the Lyd to the range of Dartmoor, which rose as a wall against the horizon, broken into many rocky peaks, a veritable mountain chain.

Mirelle had a chair and table in this window, and was engaged on the manufacture of tinsel flowers for the chapel at Trecarrel.

The table was covered with scraps of foil and bits of coloured silks; and the snippings strewed the floor.

'Well, Serene Highness de Candlestickio!' exclaimed the old man, noisily, as he came in, with a burst of laughter; 'what does your consequentialness desire? Some wires to stick them gewgaws on?'

Mirelle shrank before the uproarious old man, and spoke in her coldest and most reserved manner.

'I have sent for you, Mr. Trampleasure, about my money which has been intrusted to you. Mr. Herring has been advising me how to dispose of it.'

'Oh, indeed; very good of Mr. Lieutenant Herring.'

'I do not myself understand these matters, and so I have requested Mr. Herring to explain my wishes to you. It seems that Mr. Battishill is in trouble, and owes you money.'

'That is true as gospel,' said Tramplara; 'he owes me an imperial bushel of it. There are some persons who have a liking for borrowing, and much prefer that to paying. Mr. Battishill is one of these, and I have been his victim. And although David does say, "Blessed is he that borroweth and payeth not again," yet that is one point on which David and Sampson Trampleasure are at issue.'

'Mr. Battishill is prepared to pay regularly the interest on the loans he has contracted,' said Herring.

'But, my dear lieutenant,' said Tramplara, 'I happen at

this moment to be in immediate want of a very large sum of ready money. I call on Battishill to refund what he has borrowed. He can't do it, and I sell up.'

'You are very hard. Are you aware that he has had a seizure, and is ill?'

'Can't help that, lieutenant, I want money. You saw sweet Sampy and me engaged on some plans when you came into the room. Well, we are in for a venture, and shall want money to carry it out.'

'What the Countess proposes——'

'Oh, blow your Countesses,' said young Tramplara, putting his head in, and then following with his body. 'There are no Countesses in this shop. The lady yonder is Miss Strange, only daughter and heiress to James Strange, Esquire, of Bahia, Brazil.'

'Shut your trap, Sampy,' said his father. 'No impertinence here. Manners before ladies of the tip-top aristocracy, please. What do you say, sir, about the proposal of the Countess?'

'I decline to discuss this matter before your son,' said Herring, indignantly. 'It in no way concerns him, and he was not invited to be present.'

'The business is Trampleasure and Son,' said young Sampson. 'The firm bears that name throughout the county.'

'But the firm has nothing to do with the affairs of the Countess Mirelle Garcia.'

'Oh! I beg pardon,' said the young man. 'The trustees and guardians of her ladyship are Trampleasure and Herring —more correctly, Herring and Trampleasure.'

'I have no further right to interfere,' said Herring, with difficulty retaining his composure, 'than as spokesman for the Countess, who has empowered me to act in her name. Have I your authority for what I say and do, Countess?' He turned to Mirelle.

'My full authority,' she answered. 'I have requested you to speak my wishes in this matter to Mr. Trampleasure. As for his son, I must request him to efface himself, and not to trouble his head with my affairs.'

'Go, Sampy,' said his father. 'Good angels attend you.' The young man withdrew sullenly. 'Now then, Lieutenant Herring, I am at your service.'

'The Countess wishes that her money, left in your hands as trustee, may be invested in the mortgages on the West Wyke estate. These mortgages you hold. Five thousand pounds are owing to you, and you are in immediate need of the money. Take five thousand of her money, and transfer to her the claims on West Wyke.'

'Oh, ah! When is she likely to get her interest? You had to help the Squire out of one hobble, and he will be dropping into another shortly.'

'I can answer for it that the interest will be paid punctually and in full.'

'I don't approve of the investment. I don't regard it as sound.'

'I wish it,' said Mirelle.

'My dear pet and pearl of the aristocracy,' said the old man, 'I am solely responsible for what is done with the money. I must look after your interest in the matter. Why, if I yielded to your request, you would get only four and a half for your money, and I can assure you of seven.'

'She would prefer the smaller sum on this security than the larger on one more risky.'

'Risky, risky! what?—Ophir a risk! My dear Herring, I know better than you where security lies. The young lady's money will be invested in a gold mine—in the gold of Ophir! I said seven per cent., but I am sanguine of a rise to ten, fifteen, twenty, twenty-five. What do you think of that, eh?'

'Mr. Trampleasure,' said Mirelle, 'if I have any voice in this matter——'

'You have none—none whatever.'

'And if I particularly entreat you not to run risks with my money in gold or other mines, but to dispose of it for the relief of the Battishills——'

'Then I shall turn a deaf ear to you. I am responsible to no one. Your father has left me supreme judge in the matter, and I shall act as my own conscience and your interest direct.'

'Surely, Mr. Trampleasure——'

'Surely you cry to a stone wall. I shall discharge the obligation your father laid on me with strict fidelity. I am a man of wide experience, and I venture to think that Mr. Herring's knowledge of money investments is recent and partial. I object to his interference, and, but for the respect I owe to the memory of his father, Jago Herring, I should resent it.'

'I have no right, I admit,' said Herring, 'other than that I derive from an interest in the welfare of both the Countess and the Battishills, and from the request she has made me to speak in her name and make a proposal which will benefit both parties.'

'I refuse what is offered,' said Tramplara, his natural insolence breaking through the varnish of politeness he had assumed. 'I refuse to be dictated to; and I shall act as I choose with both missie's money and with that owl of a Squire.'

'One moment,' said Herring, whose cheek was flushed with anger. 'I ask one question of the Countess. Is it still your wish that the Battishills be saved from ruin?'

'Certainly I wish it.'

'Allow me to ask further, supposing the means of relieving them were at your disposal, would you act in the way I have suggested? That is, supposing you had money independent of Mr. Trampleasure, would you invest it in the West Wyke mortgages?'

'I would do so.'

'You are quite sure of your own mind?'

'I do not speak without meaning what I say.'

'Then, Mr. Trampleasure, you shall not lay a finger on the estate. It is safe. The money shall be forthcoming on the day you name to receive it.'

'Are you going to find it?'

'That in no way concerns you.'

'If you are, you are softer than I supposed.'

'The money will be ready for you.'

Mirelle rose, and, stepping up to Herring, held out her hand. There was more feeling in her voice and warmth in her hand than before.

'I thank you, Mr. Herring. I am not ungrateful.'

'What for?' asked Tramplara, rudely.

'For crossing your plans,' she said, and turned to look out of the window at the view.

CHAPTER XVIII.

SALTING A MINE.

TRAMPLARA paid several visits to Upaver without calling at West Wyke, sometimes alone and sometimes along with his son. He did more than visit Upaver; he got some men to break ground there and begin a mine, without asking permission of the landlord, Mr. Battishill, or letting him know what he was about. The farmer who rented Upaver held his tongue.

One day, however, old Tramplara came to West Wyke House, along with a person whose looks betrayed what he was—a dissenting minister; in fact, the Reverend Israel Flamank.

Mr. Battishill was by no means pleased to receive Tramplara. A mouse is not elated at the sight of the cat.

Nothing, however, could be more friendly than the manner of Tramplara. He was gushing and jovial. He presented his friend Mr. Flamank, under whom, he said, to his soul's welfare he had sat, one whom he should always regard as, under Providence, the man who had brought him to realise the great value of eternity and the infinite nothingness of to-day. Then followed a great deal of this sort of unctuous flattery, 'laid on with a trowel' and sticking wherever applied. Mr. Battishill looked on with amused surprise to see how readily Mr. Flamank accepted the splashes, coarse and thick as they were.

Then Tramplara addressed himself directly to the Squire.

'You must allow me, Battishill, to shake your hand once more; you must indeed. My friend and shepherd, Flamank, has made a discovery—a discovery of such moment that I doubt not it will astonish you. That it will please you, I do not doubt either. Flamank is a divine who has made prophecy his special study, and his knowledge of Bible history and geography is simply surprising. By the way, before I tell you what his find is, will you let me know whether you really propose to pay me back in full what I advanced some years ago?'

'I shall not be able to do so,' answered Mr. Battishill, 'but a friend has offered to find the money, and to relieve you of the mortgages.'

'You mean young Herring.'

Mr. Battishill nodded.

'But where the devil'—Mr. Flamank started and looked remonstratingly at Tramplara—'where in Deuteronomy—I said Deuteronomy,—he can have come upon the money, I can't think. I did know something about old Jago Herring, his father, and I thought he had been a plate licked pretty clean. I did not suppose there was much fat left sticking. But I dare say the old woman had money.'

'What old woman?'

'Mrs. Jago Herring, the lieutenant's mother. And as there was no daughter, her money naturally came to him. It is possible that is how he must have come by it. Where is he now?'

'In London, I believe. He left a week or two ago.'

'I may take it for granted, I suppose, that the money will be forthcoming?' asked Mr. Trampleasure.

'I do not doubt it. Mr. Herring is a man of his word,' answered the old Squire.

'I congratulate you, Battishill.' Mr. Battishill winced each time he was addressed with familiarity. 'I congratulate you. It would have gone hard with me to sell you up. I would not have done it unless forced to do so. What drove me to threaten was need of money, and the occasion of needing it I leave to my reverend friend here to unfold. Whether I am wise in trusting him, I cannot say. But what is a pastor for but to lead? But I must open the case, he is too modest to tell the tale, as it redounds to his honour and is a brilliant example of sagacity. I must tell you, Battishill, that I have been privileged to attend his Bible lectures, and he has deeply impressed me with the greatness and commercial enterprise of the Philistines.'

'Phœnicians, of course,' said Flamank.

'Phœnicians, of course—you see, Squire, I'm not well up in the story. I follow my guide, but all this lore is puzzling to me. Well, you know the Phœnicians came to Cornwall to fetch tin and gold, and that Solomon's servants came along with the servants of Hiram for the purpose, and they brought the tin and the gold to Jerusalem for the temple.'

'Mr. Battishill must have heard of the Phœnicians,' said Mr. Flamank, now on his particular ground, and able to trot. 'From them we derive clotted cream. It is a singular and significant fact that clotted cream is made nowhere in the world except in Devon, Cornwall, and Phœnicia. That is a well-established fact, and it speaks volumes in favour of an early intercourse between the Cassiterides and the natives of Tyre and Sidon. The Cassiterides have been for some time identified in the minds of antiquaries with Devon and Cornwall. The only difficulty in the way is this. The Cassiterides are described by the ancient geographers as islands. But the difficulty vanishes when closely considered. The Phœnicians ascended Brown Willy and Cosdon, and from these heights saw the sea on both sides, and, not supposing they were in an isthmus, they hastily and incorrectly concluded they were in an island. But the fact of clotted cream being found only in Phœnicia and the West of England is, to my mind, absolutely conclusive. A point not considered by antiquaries has arrested my attention. The point is, that the Jews came with the Phœnicians, and that they actually formed permanent settlements in our West Country.'

'Jews, Jews!' put in Tramplara: 'they would go after tin anywhere.'

'Look at Marazion,' continued Mr. Flamank; 'the Bitter Waters of Zion. The place bears the stamp of its origin in its name. There is Port Isaac, also, no doubt named after the patriarch, and Jacobstow, and, touching memorial, Davidstow, so called after the sweet psalmist by the servants of his son Solomon. There is a hamlet of Herodsfoot, and a village of Issey, that is, Isaiah, and St. Sampson, after the strongest of men. Still more remarkable is the fact of the Israelitish colonists founding a parish which they called Temple, because they were at the time engaged on building that wondrous structure in Jerusalem. Redruth derives its name from the ancestress of David, and we still speak of sending persons to Jericho, which is a farm not far distant from Launceston. A careful study of the Scriptures led me some time ago to this conclusion, that what the profane writers call the Cassiterides are, in the sacred page, called Ophir.'

'Ophir—"over the sea and far away!" You recall the text, Squire,' interjected Tramplara.

'Our friend's familiarity with the Scriptures is late, and not as accurate as might be desired,' apologised Mr. Flamank, with a look of pity cast at Tramplara. 'Suffice it that, led by a delicate chain of evidence as clear and unmistakable as that of clotted cream, I was led to seek Ophir in these western counties. You will recall that the inspired penman lays down the situation of Ophir with great nicety. It lies between Mesha and Sephar. Now Mesha is undeniably Meshaw in North Devon, and Sephar is Sheepstor in South Devon. Draw a line between Meshaw and Sheepstor, and it passes over Cosdon.'

'Why, bless my heart,' exclaimed Mr. Battishill, 'you are not going to find Ophir here!'

'We have found it,' said the dissenting minister, gleefully. 'The identification is complete. Do you happen to see my "Western Cornucophir"?'

'Cornucophir, what is that?'

'My paper—a monthly originally entitled the Cornucopia,

because of the abundance of good things it contained. When this surprising discovery dawned on me, I changed the name to Cornucophir—Cornu, for Cornubia, Cornwall, and Ophir, for the Land of Gold. The combination is happy.'

'But you are looking for Ophir in Devon, not in Cornwall.'

'Devon was included in Cornwall till the time of Athelstan, who drove the Britons back over the Tamar, and restricted them to Cornwall. Tamar'—Mr. Flamank paused and rubbed his hands—'there again, the river called after the daughter of David and twin sister of Absalom. Having arrived at this remarkable discovery by an exhaustive process and irrefragable evidence, in which every step is capable of being demonstrated with mathematical certainty to Christian believers, I begged Mr. Trampleasure, who has wide experience in mines——'

'Polpluggan,' groaned Mr. Battishill.

'As in Polpluggan, as you rightly observe, to examine the line between Meshaw and that mountain in the east, Sheepstor. Mr. Trampleasure is not as sanguine in this matter as I am. He is hard to be convinced even now; I am not sure that his faith is firm. Whilst we were discussing the nature of the land between Meshaw and Sheepstor—he resolutely refused to explore the red sandstone and clay land, maintaining that gold is never found except in the proximity of granite—he told me of a farm of yours called Ophir.'

'Ophir!' exclaimed the old gentleman; 'I have no such farm.'

'Excuse me,' said Mr. Flamank; 'you have, and I have been over it myself, exploring the ground for gold.'

'I believe you call the place Upaver,' said Tramplara, with a twinkle in his eye, which watched the Squire intently.

'Upaver! You have not been hunting up my silver lead mine, have you?'

'Silver lead, no!' answered the pastor; 'we have been hunting for gold.'

'But this is stark nonsense,' exclaimed Mr. Battishill; 'the place never was called Ophir. It is, and always has been, Upaver.'

'Upaver and Ophir are all the same, just as Sheepstor is the same as Sephar. I asked the farmer the name of the place, and without hesitation he said that he minded in old times it was called Ophir, but that the maps spell it with an *U*.'

'He has not been fifteen years on the farm, and I have been here seventy.'

'He has heard from the oldest inhabitant.'

'I am the oldest inhabitant,' protested Mr. Battishill. 'I can show you, moreover, leases of a hundred and two hundred years ago, in which it is called Upaver.'

'The leases were drawn up by lawyers ignorant of the pronunciation of the name. What the farmer told me was confirmed by another man, an old wild-looking creature, almost a savage. He also said the place was called Ophir, and he clenched his statement with a dreadful imprecation on all those who called it otherwise. What is more, he showed me a silver coin he had found, and I bought it of him for five shillings. If you will examine it, you will see Hebrew characters on it. I have seen this coin figured in Commentaries on the Bible; on the obverse a vase, the pot of manna, I presume, on the reverse a flower, Aaron's blooming rod. It is a shekel. Now I ask you, how came a shekel to be found at Ophir unless the Israelites had been there to drop it?'

Mr. Battishill took the coin, and turned it over in his hand. He was puzzled.

'That man you describe is old Grizzly Cobbledick, who lives under the Giant's Table.'

'I have seen the Giant's Table. It is an Israelitish monument, a Gilgal. There are many such in Cornwall, as well as upright stones—the same that Jacob set up and anointed with oil.'

'There are plenty of these upright stones on Dartmoor,' said Mr. Battishill. 'On the side of Belstone Tor is a circle called the Nine Maidens. The story goes that they were damsels so fond of dancing that they would not desist on the Sunday, and in consequence were turned to stone. And it is said that even now on Sunday at noon the stones come to life and dance thrice round in a circle.'

'I must make a note of this for my article in the "Western Cornucophir." I pray you to observe the continuance of Sabbatical ideas, an evidence of Jewish teaching; and of the resistance to it on Belston Tor, a mountain dedicated to Bel or Baal, the Sun God of the Phœnicians.'

'But you are holding back from Mr. Battishill the most important discovery of all,' said Tramplara, who saw that the old gentleman was not much impressed by the biblical and antiquarian theories of his visitor.

'At my request, and against his own convictions,' continued Mr. Flamank, 'my good friend Trampleasure searched Ophir for gold. A more qualified person could not have been found, for he is thoroughly conversant with the metals and their ores. He brought me one day some sand, granite washings, with grains in it that certainly looked like gold. We tested them with nitric acid, and, sure enough, they proved to be gold. I had no rest in my mind till I had persuaded Mr. Trampleasure to accompany me to Ophir, and to assist me in the examination of the place. He conducted me to the spot where he had found the gravel, and there we searched and I found this.'

He held out some shining yellow cubes.

'That is mundic,' said Mr. Battishill; 'it looks like gold, but is worthless.'

'So Mr. Trampleasure said. He laughed at me for my mundic find, but I could hardly be convinced that it was not gold. However, later, I found these grains. Here they are in my kerchief, with the quartz and mica as I took them up. I did not find much, but still, enough to show that the metal is present.'

He spread out his handkerchief on the table. In the midst of the coarse white gravel were certain yellow granules that looked like gold.

'You found this in Upaver valley?' asked Mr. Battishill, in great surprise.

'Yes, I was more successful than Trampleasure. But then I worked in faith, and he was dubious, so I dare say looked with less eagerness.'

'This is very extraordinary,' said the old gentleman. 'I never suspected the existence of gold on my property.'

'Why not?' asked Trampleasure. 'Gold is always found in connection with granite.'

'That is true; but none has been found hitherto in Devon.'

'And yet the whole valley has been streamed by miners in olden times. Their mounds of refuse are traceable all the way to the source of the stream. No gold has been sought because none was expected to be found. The Bible has led me, by a course of inductive evidence, to the identical spot whence came the gold that overlaid the temple, and that made the shields with which Solomon adorned the walls of his palace.'

'Whence that gold was got, more gold must be obtainable,' put in Tramplara; 'especially with our modern appliances.'

'It is most amazing,' said Mr. Battishill. 'Bless me! I

wish I were well enough to get out; but I am stricken, and can only creep about with the aid of a stick. I should like myself to examine the place where you say you found the gold.'

'Surely you cannot doubt my word,' said Mr. Flamank. 'I can give you the best possible proof of my sincerity. I am ready to embark my little savings to the last penny in the mines of Ophir, if you will consent to their being worked.'

'I have no objection whatever, so long as I am not asked to risk any money in them myself.'

'Look you here, Squire,' said Tramplara; 'let us strike whilst the iron is hot. I am as anxious as the Reverend Flamank about Ophir. You can lose nothing, and may make a pot of money. I have brought with me a lease; read it. I will pay you a yearly rental of a hundred pounds, and you shall have the usual royalties on the gold raised. Then I will undertake to form a company to work the mines of Ophir. Not one penny can you lose by it. If you choose to take shares you may run some risk, not otherwise. If the mine proves a success, your fortune will be made, and so will mine, and those other lucky devils——'

'Lucky what?' inquired the startled pastor.

'Lucky devotees, I said. I said devotees distinctly. Those lucky devotees who took shares in Ophir. "Out of the hills ye shall dig brass," said the great lawgiver, and his prophecy will be fulfilled, for brass in colloquial English means money.'

Tramplara took a lease out of his pocket and opened it before Mr. Battishill.

'Read it—nothing can be fairer.'

'Father,' said Cicely, who had come in, 'please do nothing till Mr. Herring returns. Take his advice before signing any document.'

'Nonsense, my dear; I can lose nothing. I shall not take a share, and I may gain thousands of pounds.'

'If you will work the mine yourself, do so,' said Tramplara; 'if not, let us work it. The religious public is already screwed up to a pitch of screaming excitement. The "Western Cornucopia"——'

'Cornucophir,"' corrected the pastor. 'Besides, I object to the term screaming excitement.'

'It is allegorical and Oriental—Phœnician, in fact,' explained Tramplara. 'The "Cornucophir" has been leading them on week by week, expecting the discovery of Ophir. Now all is ready for the announcement that it has been found, and with that announcement we must publish the prospectus of the Ophir Gold Mining Company. If you do not accept my terms, all I can say is, the place will be invaded by religious gold-diggers, who will turn everything topsy-turvy and carry off every particle of gold they find without giving you any share in their spoil.'

'I will sign the lease; it is only for a year,' said Mr. Battishill, eagerly; 'but I can take no shares, I have not the money.'

'I will take as many as I can,' said the minister. 'Ophir must succeed.'

'Now then!' shouted Tramplara, waving the lease over his head. 'Now for the run of gold. Blow the trumpet in Zion; call the solemn assembly of sharetakers together. I shall be ready for them with my crushing machines. Hoorah for the gold of Ophir, and the fortunes that will be made out of it!'

CHAPTER XIX.

TWO STRINGS TO ONE BOW.

CAPTAIN TRECARREL had the good luck to find Mirelle alone in the garden house, engaged on her flowers. She had not been taught to do useful work. She cut out lace patterns in paper, and made imitation flowers. She could play and sing, but there was no piano in the garden house, and she spent most of her time there, so as to be away from the rooms frequented by Trampleasure senior and junior.

Captain Trecarrel was playing his cards very carefully. He did not intend to be off altogether with the old love till he was quite sure that it was to his pecuniary advantage to be on with the new. He was curious to know in what Mirelle's money had been invested. This was not easy for him to find out. He could not inquire of old Tramplara.

After turning the matter over in his head, the Captain resolved on trying to ascertain what he desired to know through Mirelle herself, who was too simple to suspect his purpose.

He took a seat by her in the window. She smiled at him, and made room beside her.

'I have been thinking a great deal about you, Mirelle,' said he. He had slipped into calling her by her Christian name, and she did not resent it. 'And the more I think of you, the more I pity you. Your poor dear father made a sore mistake in confiding you to the care of these Trampleasures.'

'They were his relations,' she said.

'True; but then you are so utterly out of place among them. You are unable to sympathise with them——'

'Fortunately.'

'Fortunately, indeed, or you would not be charming. A grievous error has been committed, I may even say that a great wrong has been done you, unintentionally, and the consequence is that you suffer. I see it in your face.'

'Captain Trecarrel,' said Mirelle, 'I once thought to myself, suppose Heaven were to rob me of all means, and I were obliged to be a servant maid in the kitchen, then I thought how utterly unable I should be to live in such a place, not because it was a kitchen, but because of those I should have to associate with. I and they would have no interests, no pursuits, no ambitions, hardly a thought in common. To all intents I might as well live in a stable with horses, or in a fowlhouse surrounded by cackling pullets. I should not mind in the least shelling peas, for I could think my own thoughts whilst so engaged; but to be encompassed with others who think no thoughts, who have no ideas worth uttering, who live as to their outsides, and have no inner life, that would be unendurable. I find myself now in such a situation. The Trampleasures and I do not see the same sights nor hear the same sounds. We have not even the sense of smell in common, for Mr. Tramplara and young Sampson like to sniff brandy and puff bad tobacco, and I am convinced that Orange and her mother do not dislike these, to me, intolerable odours. In the garden is a sweet rose and a bed of mignonette. I have not once seen a Trampleasure apply his nose to a flower. We have the same organic structure, and are classed together in natural history as belonging to the same genus, but there the similarity ends. The likeness is superficial, the dissimilarity is radical. The likeness is physical, the dissimilarity psychical. The Trampleasures are animals made in the likeness of man. I am human, made in the likeness of God. I can see what is beautiful in nature and art. I can feel music in my soul, I have aspirations beyond making money and getting married. I have interests beyond the claque of Launceston gossip. But these Trampleasures have no sense of beauty, no poetical instinct, no spiritual aspirations. Orange is the best of them, but in her I only think I perceive a soul, I am not sure that it exists. God took some of the beasts he had made and bade them stand up on their hind legs, that they might look at heaven instead of contemplating earth. But their souls did not stand up also. The result was the ape. There are men, likewise, not superior. They walk on two feet, but their souls run on all fours.'

'Poor Mirelle!' said Trecarrel, looking tenderly at her out of the Trecarrel blue eyes. 'Yours is a cruel fate.'

'Yes, it is cruel, and, but for this summer-house where I can be alone, would be insupportable. Life to these Trampleasures, and people cast in their mould, is a harpsichord on which they drone a strain void of invention, freshness, and thought. When you have heard their performance—it is the song of life—you are aware that you have listened to a succession of notes unworthy of being termed a melody, in chords undeserving of being designated harmony. When one with higher thoughts sits down to the same instrument and plays a piece like a sonata of Beethoven, they yawn and say, " Let us have something out of the Beggars' Opera!"'

Little did Mirelle guess how mean and commonplace was the barrel-organ tune that Captain Trecarrel cared to play on his harpsichord of life. Because he was a gentleman by birth, and a Catholic in faith, she supposed that he stood, like Saul, a head and shoulders higher than the vulgar beings that surrounded him and her. We shall see, in the sequel, how egregiously Mirelle was mistaken.

'Is there no escape for you?' asked the Captain.

'I see none. I should like to return to Paris, to the convent where I was reared, but Mr. Trampleasure will not hear of it. I should be quite content to be a nun.'

'A nun!' exclaimed Trecarrel. 'Oh no, no! dear Mirelle, that must not be. With your gifts of mind and soul and person, you are suited to live and shine in the world.'

'In what world? This mean, dull English world?'

'Your place is here. Your heart has not yet spoken. You are still young. Some day you will make a good man happy, and you will find your proper sphere of usefulness, with a congenial spirit at your side, not in shelling peas, but in spreading enlightenment among the dark and erring souls around you.' His voice shook. He took her hand, and he felt it tremble in his.

K 2

'No, Mirelle, you were not born to wither in a convent unloved and unloving, Excuse me if I give you my opinion with great plainness. You are here without a guide. These Tramplaras cannot advise you, because they cannot understand your position. Trust me as a brother. Let us regard each other in the affectionate and familiar light of brother and sister—that is our relationship in the faith. Allow me to counsel you. My heart aches when I think of your loneliness. I place myself at your disposal: trust me, and suffer me to be your adviser.' He raised her hand to his lips, and kissed it fervently. The little hand shrank back, and when he looked up he saw alarm in her dark eyes.

'A brotherly kiss,' he said, reassuringly, 'the seal of our bond, nothing more. Shall it be so?'

'The seal will not need renewal,' she answered.

He saw that her eyes were filling. He knew that she liked him; he was doing his best to make her love him. It would be easy for him to advance from brotherly to loverlike affection, and it was quite possible to remain stationary on fraternal regard. This he thought to himself, and he said in his own soul, 'Bravo, Trecarrel! you have not compromised yourself by a word.'

'And now, dear sister Mirelle,' he said, with his sweetest smile, 'the thing I desire to know is, What has become of your father's money?'

She was surprised. He saw it; but he went on quietly, 'You see in what a brotherly and practical spirit I approach your affairs. I want to know exactly how you stand, for—between four eyes be it spoken—I am not satisfied that a certain whitehaired person who shall be nameless is the most prudent man to be entrusted with money. He sank a large sum in Patagonians which might just as well have been sunk in Cranmere pool. If he made a fool of himself with his own money, he may play the fool also with yours. For how long is he your trustee?'

'For five years. I am eighteen, and I do not come of age till I am twenty-three.'

'Unless you marry.' Trecarrel sighed, and looked hard at the distant peaks of Dartmoor.

'I do not think there is anything about my marriage in the will, which I have read, and I know the contents.'

'Oh!' said the Captain, and his mouth went down at the corners. 'You do not come into possession at marriage.'

'I believe not—not till I am three-and-twenty.'

The Captain released the tips of Mirelle's fingers which he had seized when he put the question.

'Then Tramplara has the entire and uncontrolled disposal of the money for five years, and if you were to marry now you would still have to wait five years till you got it—if you got it, in the end, at all.'

'I suppose so.'

'Do you happen to know what the old fellow has invested your money in? I ask as a friend, because I wish to protect your interests, and to advise you what you should do.'

'I have already had an adviser here—Mr. Herring: he was anxious about the money.'

'He was, was he?' Captain Trecarrel drew nearer, with revived interest, and again attempted to possess himself of the hand, but failed.

'Yes, he appeared very anxious.'

'On what grounds? What possible right had he to inquire about it?'

'He expressed friendly regard for me.'

'A sort of brotherly interest?' inquired the Captain.

'No,' answered Mirelle, curtly, and drew herself up. The Captain looked hard at her.

'Have you given him any encouragement? Have you allowed him any right to interfere?'

Mirelle's cheek coloured, and a haughty flash came into her eye.

'Captain Trecarrel, I do not comprehend you.'

'My dear Mirelle,' he said in a gentle, soothing tone, 'do not misunderstand me. What I mean is harmless enough not to offend you. Did you ask his advice, and in your first loneliness give him such occasion as to suppose that he was necessary, that as a pert and pushing cock-sparrow he has hopped in where not wanted, since you have come under the protection of others?'

'No,' answered Mirelle, 'I have always kept him at a distance. When he has volunteered help it has been declined. He came here about the money not for my sake only, but for the sake of some friends whom he wanted to assist out of a difficulty.'

'Oh! he wanted to help friends to your money! How disinterested and how benevolent!'

'He wished to have my money invested in mortgages on the estate of West Wyke.'

'What did Mr. Trampleasure say to that?'

'He absolutely refused. He said he had a better investment in view, one that would render double.'

'What was that?—not Patagonia?'

'No; Ophir.'

'What! The gold mines of Ophir?'

'Yes, my money is to be put into that.'

Captain Trecarrel vented a low whistle, and stood up quickly. 'Dear Countess, always command my services—as a friend,' he said. 'Excuse my flight, I must have a word with Tramplara at once.'

He hurried from the summer-house, and entered the front door of Dolbeare. He was so often there that he no longer went through the formality of ringing. It was Liberty Hall, as Tramplara assured all his friends.

He tapped at the dining-room door and went in.

There he found Mr. Tramplara smoking and working at accounts. Orange sat near the window; she had been speaking with her father, and had been crying. Both father and daughter rose hastily as the Captain came in, and Trecarrel had sufficient penetration to see that he had been their topic.

'Halloo, Captain!' exclaimed the old man, turning almost purple. 'Talk of the—hum, and he is sure to appear, as the psalmist says. The very man I wanted to see. How are you?'

Orange slipped out of the room.

'Sit down, Captain, and let us have a talk. Fact is, I want particularly to have a bone picked with you. There is Orange, poor girl, wasting to a shadow. You are not dealing fairly by her; you are engaged, and yet you won't come to the scratch. She says you are tateytating with the other party on the trotters, as Mirelle calls the pavement, and give Orange the gutter to walk in. That won't do.'

'You entirely mistake me,' said Trecarrel, his blue eye becoming cold; he drew himself up, and began to point his moustache, whilst he looked Trampleasure over contemptuously. 'Do you dare to insinuate that I—a gentleman, a Trecarrel—am behaving otherwise than honourably? I love your daughter as much as I loved her at first; but you and I are men of the world, and we both know that love and onions are poor commodities on which to keep house. You are well aware what my circumstances are, for I have concealed nothing from you; and you must therefore know that I cannot, as a gentleman and a man of honour, invite a lady to share my future with me unless she be prepared to provide pepper and salt with which to season the onions.'

'I know that. Orange is not penniless.'

'No, but Patagonian bonds are not nourishing, Mr. Trampleasure.'

'Who said that Orange would bring nothing else with her?'

'You offered me five thousand pounds with her in securities which are worthless.'

'I offered you those bonds before I knew they would depreciate so greatly. They may recover any day.'

'I incline to wait for that day before setting up house with Miss Orange.'

'Nonsense, Trecarrel. If you won't take these bonds, you shall have some sounder stuff. I am a man of my word. I said I would give Orange five thousand pounds, and five thousand she shall have, the day she is married.'

'In bonds?'

'In shares, if you like, in one of the most promising of all ventures.'

'In Ophir—no, thank you.'

'You are a fool to refuse them. Why, man! have you read the "Cornucopia"? Have you seen the prospectus of the company?'

'Mr. Trampleasure, I will have no paper at all. Give me with Orange the sum of five thousand down, and insure me five thousand more when you are dead, and I will ask her to name the day.'

'You are mercenary.'

'I am practical. You know that Trecarrel will support a bachelor—that is, keep him in mutton chops and fried potatoes, and a new coat twice a year. I will give you a sample of my penury. Whenever I have apple-tart for dinner, I think twice before I indulge myself with clotted cream over it. My circumstances will not allow me to support a wife and family. I am bound to look ahead, and to consider my wife's interest as well as my own. I cannot offer her the humiliations of poverty.'

'Well, well,' said Tramplara, 'you shall have the money down.'

'Your word?'

Tramplara held out his hand, 'I give it you.'

'I should prefer it in black and white,' said the Captain.

'You shall have it in yellow and white,' said the old man. 'And now in return you shall grant me a favour—your name as a director of the Ophir Gold Mining Company.'

'My name is Trecarrel,' answered the Captain, freezingly.

'I know that well enough—that is why I want it.'

'And that is precisely why you shall not have it.'

'You refuse me this favour?'

'Emphatically. I do not believe in Ophir.'

The old man drummed with his fingers on the table, and raised his eyes furtively to the Captain, met his cold, supercilious stare, and dropped them again.

'Well! go into the drawing-room, and patch up the rent with Orange.'

Then, when the Captain was gone, Tramplara laughed heartily. 'By Grogs!' he said, 'who would have thought the fellow so keen? He don't look it.'

The Captain found Orange standing in the drawing-room leaning against the mantelpiece, tearing a white lily that she had plucked out of a vase into many pieces. Her fingers were stained with the pollen. Her cheeks were flushed, and an angry glitter was in her eyes, twinkling through tears of mortified pride.

Trecarrel had not much difficulty in changing the expression of that handsome face, and before he left the reconciliation was complete, sealed with a kiss, and the day was named.

CHAPTER XX.

GRINDING GOLD.

IN a remarkably short space of time two 'leats,' that is, channels of water, had been brought from Rayborough Pool along the side of the moor to the site of the gold mine. Buildings had been erected, wooden sheds run up and tarred, and a crushing machine was in operation. One stream of water was conducted over a wheel, and the wheel set in motion half a dozen hammers that pounded the granite; then the granite thus pounded was passed under an iron roller which effectually reduced it to powder. This powder was made to slide through a trough into water brought by the second leat, and the water, as soon as it received the pounded quartz, became milky. The milky water overflowed into a second tank, depositing in both much that was held in solution, and then ran away into the river, which it discoloured for some distance down.

Old Tramplara looked regretfully at the white water. If Ophir had been nearer Plymouth or Exeter, he might have sold it as milk.

The deposit in the tanks was subjected to a second and, indeed, a third washing. It was washed and rewashed till all the quartz had been carried away and nothing remained but glittering gold.

The excitement created by the discovery of Ophir was prodigious. The neighbourhood came to see the works. The miners extracted granite, and placed the pieces under the stampers, and then transferred the gravel into which they had been pounded to the roller. Anyone might watch the process. Everything was above board; there was no attempt at concealment. Only, no one was allowed to approach the precious deposit unattended by the overseer. Any respectable person was allowed to follow the washing and drying to the final process, where nothing remained but the costly yellow grains. All he had to do was to write for permission to Mr. Tramplara, or to send in his card at the works, and leave to go over the entire mine—without any reserve—was freely accorded. The number of crowns and guineas pocketed by the very respectable overlooker ripened the fruits of civilisation in him. He became courteous, eager to instruct, pious, and sober. Christian graces grew on golden roots. There was a fixed time in the day when visitors were given admission to the mine.

The limitation of time was rendered necessary by reason of the crowd of visitors eager to examine the works, and the consequent interference with the working. The regulation was reasonable and unassailable. Another rule was made that no one was to be allowed to go within arm's length of, nor to handle the gold after final washing. The overseer, however, made exceptions in favour of every respectable visitor, letting him understand that the exception in his case was unique, and only granted because of his—the visitor's—really extraordinary respectability. He was allowed to gather up in his palm and turn over with his finger the golden dust, and the polite and pious overlooker always reaped a rich harvest from this exceptional favour.

Readers of the 'Western Cornucophir' came from all parts

of Cornwall; serious men, with heavy brows, big jaws, and firm lipless mouths. Women also—married women, likewise serious, (unmarried women, speaking broadly, are flighty,) in rich but sober dresses, arrived in chaises, wearing spectacles and false fronts, and having bibles in their pockets, and vinegary attendants carrying shawls, and guardians of their virtue. There were many Methodical Christian and Unmethodical Christian, and Primitive Christian, and Latter Day Christian, and Universal Christian, and Particular Christian, and Ne-plus-ultra Christian ministers, all intensely interested in Ophir, taking up the matter as one of *stantis vel cadentis ecclesiæ*. These were treated with exceptional courtesy at the mine, by express command of Mr. Tramplara. They were shown everything. They were set to work themselves in the adit. They galled their soft palms in picking at the gold vein, or granite supposed to contain the vein of gold. They carried the lumps of their own extraction to the crusher. They watched them being pounded and rolled, not turning an eye away the whole time. They assisted at the washing. They picked out the gold themselves from the pan, and were liberally allowed to carry home with them each at least a guinea's worth of the precious grains. Thereupon each became in his special circle an agent of the company. And Methodical Christian, and Unmethodical Christian, and Primitive Christian, and Latter Day Christian, and Universal Christian, and Particular Christian, and Ne-plus-ultra Christian applications for shares poured in by every post.

But the greatest hit of all was the solemn opening and dedication of Ophir.

A huge tent had been hired from Exeter, capable of seating many hundred persons. Bunting in profusion, of every colour, fluttered from it. Over the entrance rose a flagstaff from which waved a gold-coloured banner adorned with the Seal of Solomon.

A cannon had been brought from Exeter, and it was discharged at intervals. The Okehampton band was engaged, and it played out of tune alternately with a military band from Exeter, which played in tune, and rivalled it in the worthlessness of the music performed.

The day was magnificent. An autumn day, with a glorious sun illumining the moorland rosy with blooming heather; as though raspberry cream had been spilt over the hill-sides. The scarlet uniforms of the band, the gay colours of the flags, the white tent, the glitter of the falling water over the wheel, combined to form a charming scene. All Okehampton, all North and South Tawton and Chagford was there, and many also from Tavistock, Launceston, Moreton Hampstead, and Exeter. The people were scattered over the moor slopes, listening to the music which was not worth listening to, in the way in which English people do listen—that is, talking the whole time; they raced and rolled over on the short grass, and strewed the hillsides with sandwich papers and empty ginger-beer bottles. Ginger-beer bottles! ay, and bottles of cold tea. For Ophir was a great Temperance mine, and the dedication of Ophir a Temperance demonstration, Ri-lid-de-riddle-roll! Who cannot rollick on ginger-beer? Who that is by nature inane can fail to make an ass of himself when out on a holiday on cold tea?

Ophir was a great Temperance mine. All the washers were sworn in as total abstainers. As was stated on the prospectus, the workings were to be carried on only with water. 'We may as well fish in two ponds, Sampy,' said old Tramplara; 'let us angle for the Temperites as well as for the Israelites.'

Thus the dedication of Ophir was not only a grand religious demonstration for all those who looked for Israel in England, but also of those who have supplanted the Ten Commandments by one, 'Thou shalt not drink fermented liquor.' Old Tramplara was desirous to have the mines blessed by ministers of all denominations—twelve, if possible, to represent the twelve tribes. He had therefore applied to the bishop of the diocese, and requested his presence for the opening of the proceedings. But the bishops of the Anglican Church are not the tugs that lead, but the boats that follow, popular opinion. They bless nothing till authorised to do so by the daily papers, and as the daily papers had not yet spoken on the subject of Ophir, the bishop was in the bewildered condition of the priest of Delphi when the oracle is silent. If Ophir were to prove a magnificent success, he would never forgive himself for not having been at the opening. If it proved a disastrous failure, he would never forgive himself for not staying away. So he temporised, after the manner of weak men and weak classes of men; he discovered that he was due at the opening of a (barrel) organ at the Land's End on that particular day, and he wrote a letter full of apologies, expressive of his warmest interest in the proceedings, promising his heartfelt prayers, invoking the most solemn blessings on the gathering, and then ate his breakfast, devoured the 'Times,' and forgot everything about Ophir and the barrel organ at the Land's End.

But though the bishop of the diocese was unavoidably absent, representative pastors of all the Christian denominations in the West were present, and prayed and harangued to their hearts' content, and ate and drank to their stomachs' content as well.

The tent was filled to overflowing. Grace was said simultaneously by twenty-nine ministers to avoid giving offence by exalting one above another. A noble collation had been provided. Waiters dressed like clergymen attended on the guests. 'Lemonade, sir?' 'Gooseberriade, ma'am?' as they uncorked long-necked bottles with gold foil about the throats, and poured the effervescing drink into champagne glasses. 'Temperance cake, miss?' with an offer of an inviting dish of sponge-cake sopped in—well, non-alcoholic brandy—and with flummery over it to hide its blushes.

Reporters were present from every West of England paper and several London journals as well. These gentlemen were supplied freely with 'gooseberriade,' and grew cheery in spirit, and red in face, and watery in eye, and uncritical in disposition under its influence. They began to believe in Ophir as much as a reporter can believe in anything. And when, on raising the napkins under their finger-glasses, each found a ten-pound note, the enthusiasm of the press for Ophir bordered on fanaticism. After lunch, the entire party sought the mine, and those who could get in hammered at the stone, and there was much ado in wheeling to the stampers the 'gozzen' that had been extracted.

Tramplara particularly urged on the reporters to dig and wash for themselves, and they complied with his request. The prayers and blessings of the pastors of discordant Christianity had been of avail. Never before had the rock yielded so much gold. There it was—in glittering granules—strewing the washing floor. The rock had been quarried by ten reporters, seven pastors, and one old lady, with a grim face and severely plain, untrimmed costume. The stone had been wheeled by them to the crushers, at that time clear of every particle of stone. The grim old lady had not wheeled, but carried her specimens in her gown, exposing thereby some elaborate lace frills beneath it. The entire party saw the granite thus extracted washed in several waters. They washed it themselves, no workman touched any part of the machinery, or dipped a finger into the water, and there—there was the gold—gold-dust in abundance. There could be no deception. There was no room for deception.

John Herring was there also, looking on, much puzzled.

He had not been at the lunch, but had strolled to Ophir after it. His lead mine was not advanced. No company was formed to work it. Who would look at lead when gold was available? He watched the whole process critically, and was convinced that there was no deception in what passed under his eye. There the gold was. Every one present was given a grain as a memorial of that day. The whole affair was marvellous. The expense to which Tramplara had gone was prodigious. Would he have thrown his gold away in shovelfuls unless he were sure of getting gold out of the mine? Herring was young and simple. He was right. Tramplara would not have gone to this lavish expense unless he had made sure of getting gold out of the mine. But then, it did not follow that he was going to extract it from the granite. Some things are softer than granite, and the gold may be got easily enough by those who can touch the vein.

'What! Lieutenant! you here?' exclaimed Mr. Trampleasure, coming up to Herring, looking flushed and glossy. 'Glorious day, this. Wonderful discovery, this Ophir. "Thither the tribes go up!" said the prophet, speaking of this day and the way in which they went into the tent to their dinner. Come in and have a glass of wi—, of something comforting but not exhilarating. Come in, my dear lieutenant; there is only the band there, making clean the cup and the platter, when their betters have done.'

'No, thank you,' answered Herring, 'I have had an early dinner. Besides, I must trouble you no longer to style me lieutenant.'

'Why so?'

'Because I have sold out.'

'Sold out! Become a civilian again!'

'Yes. I have things to attend to which demand my presence here. I am going to work the silver lead.'

'My dear fellow, don't throw money away on that. Take shares in gold.'

'I prefer lead.'

'Herring, is that why you are taking up the mortgages on West Wyke?'

'Partly.'

'You'll never work the lead yourself? You have no experience. However, we will talk of that another time. Are you likely to be in Launceston next week?'

'Yes. I shall go there to pay you the mortgage money.'

'Very well. We are going to have a kick about on Thursday—the first dance in the season. There is a reason: Orange is engaged to Captain Trecarrel. Will you come?'

Herring thought a while before answering.

'Look here! I will tell that little bleached puss of a missie to expect you, and put your name down as her partner for the first caper.'

'I will come.'

All at once the Reverend Israel Flamank was seen flying down the valley, with coat tails expanded like wings, and his white tie loose and flapping. He was shouting and waving his arms.

What was it? Had he been bitten by a serpent? Had he found a nugget?

When he came up, he was breathless and of inflamed countenance. At length he gasped—'I have been privileged to discover it!' Then he paused again. A circle formed round him.

'A do-deka-penta-hedron,' he said. Then seeing the reporters with their notebooks in hand and pencils pausing in mid-air, and fearing that their knowledge of Greek surpassed his (he need have entertained no apprehension), he added simply, 'Solomon's Seal carved on a rock.'

The whole crowd went after him. Here was a wonderful coincidence! Coincidence! Avast! Conclusive evidence that the servants of Solomon had worked at this identical place. The symbol of Solomon, the interlacing triangles, cut in imperishable granite, was there as an eternal witness to Ophir.

Herring did not follow the troop: he turned to go back to West Wyke. He was not eager to inspect the 'Dodekapentahedron.'

CHAPTER XXI.

THE CUB.

MIRELLE was conscious of a change in Trecarrel towards her. She ceased to engross his attentions, which were now directed towards Orange. She could not recall anything she had said or done that would account for this change. When the Captain was alone with her, he was full of sympathy and tenderness as before, but this was only when they were alone. Trecarrel argued with himself that it would be unfair and ungentlemanly to throw her over abruptly; he would lower her into the water little by little, but the souse must come eventually. Some of the martyrs were let down inch by inch into the boiling pitch, others were cast in headlong, and the fate of the latter was the preferable, and the judge who sentenced to it was the most humane. Mirelle suffered. For the first time in her life her heart had been roused, and it threw out its fibres towards Trecarrel for support. She was young, an exile, among those who were no associates, and he was the only person to whom she could disclose her thoughts and with whom she could converse as an equal. He had met her with warmth and with assurances of sympathy. Of late he had drawn back, and she had been left entirely to herself, whilst his attention was engrossed by Orange Tramplara.

But Orange, with no small spice of vindictiveness in her nature, urged the Captain to show civility to Mirelle. She knew the impression Trecarrel had made on her cousin's heart, and, now that she was sure of the Captain, she was ready to encourage him to play with and torture her rival. Women are only cruel to their own sex, and towards them they are remorseless.

'Do speak to Mirelle; she is so lonely. She does not get on with us; she does not understand our ways—she is Frenchified,' said Orange, with an amiable smile. The Captain thought this very kind of his betrothed, and was not slow to avail himself of the permission. Nevertheless, Mirelle perceived the insincerity of his professions. She was unaware of the engagement; this had not been talked about, and was by her unsuspected. Orange was well aware of the fascination exerted over Trecarrel by Mirelle; she knew that her own position with him had been threatened—almost lost. She was unable to forgive her cousin for her unconscious rivalry; she did not attempt to forgive her—she sought the surest means of punishing her. Mirelle was uneasy and unhappy. She considered all that had passed between her and Trecarrel. He had not professed more than fraternal affection, but his manner had implied more than his words had expressed. She became silent and abstracted, not more than usual towards the Trampleasures, for she had never spoken more than was necessary to them, nor had opened to them in the least, but silent before Trecarrel, and abstracted from her work at all times. The frank confidence she had accorded him was withdrawn, their interchange of ideas interrupted. She found herself now with no one to whom she could unfold, and she suffered the more acutely for having allowed herself to open at all. She began now to wish that John Herring were nearer, and to suspect that she had not treated him with sufficient consideration.

Mirelle was not jealous of Orange; she was surprised that Captain Trecarrel should find attractions in her. Mirelle had formed her own conception of her cousin's character; she thought her to be generous, warm, and impulsive; coarse in mind and feeling, but yet kindly. How could a gentleman such as the Captain find charms in such a person? Mirelle did not see the money, nor did she measure correctly the character of Orange.

About this time young Sampson Tramplara began to annoy her with his attentions, offered uncouthly. The youth was perfectly satisfied with himself; he believed himself to be irresistible and his manner to be accomplished. He was wont to chuck chambermaids under the chin, and to lounge over the bar flirting with the 'young lady' at the tap, but was unaccustomed to the society of ladies, and felt awkward in their presence.

Mirelle at once allured and repelled him. He could not fail to admire her beauty, but he was unable to attain ease of manner in her presence. She seemed to surround herself with an atmosphere of frost that chilled him when he ventured near. After a while, when the first unfamiliarity had worn off, through meeting frequently at meals and in the evenings, he attempted to force himself on her notice by bragging of his doings with dogs and horses, addressing himself to his father and mother, but keeping an eye on Mirelle and observing the effect produced on her mind by his exploits.

After that he ventured to address her; to admire her embroidery, her tinsel flowers, her cut-paper lace, and to pass coarse flatteries on them and her; and when this only froze her into frostier stiffness, to attempt to take her by storm, by rollicking fun and insolent familiarities.

He was hurt by the way in which she ignored him. He never once caught her eye when telling his best hunting exploits; his raciest jokes did not provoke a smile on her lips; he could extract from her no words save cold answers to pointed questions.

Her position in the house became daily less endurable, and she could see no means of escape from it. She had appealed to her guardian to allow her to return to the convent of the Sacred

Heart, but had met with a peremptory refusal. A fluttering hope had sprung up that Trecarrel might be her saviour, a hope scarce formulated, indistinctly existing, but now that had died away.

Once she appealed to Mr. Trampleasure against his son. She begged that he would insist on young Sampson refraining from causing her annoyance by his impertinence. But she obtained no redress. 'My dear missie, the boy is a good boy, full of spirit. He comes of the right stuff—true Trampleasure, girl! We don't set up to Carrara marble here. You must treat him in the right way. Flip him over the nose with your knitting pins, or run your needle into his thumb, and he will keep his distance. You can be sharp enough when you like, and say words that cut like razors. Try some of your smartness on Sampy, and he will sneak away with his ears down. I know the boy; he is not smart at repartee. You should have heard how Polly Skittles set him down t'other day.'

'Pray, who is Polly Skittles?'

'The barmaid at the Pig and Whistle.'

'I decline absolutely to take lessons from a Pig-and-Whistle barmaid how to deal with a booby.'

'Missie!' exclaimed the old man, flaming red, 'you forget —he is my son.'

'No one could possibly doubt it,' said Mirelle, and walked away.

After that, so far from old Tramplara making his son desist from annoying Mirelle, he egged him on to it. The old man's pride was hurt at the scorn with which the girl treated him and his son—a scorn she took no pains to conceal.

'Look you here, Sampy,' said Tramplara, 'if the girl is to be had, you had better say Snap. There is her six thousand pounds, which must be kept in the family. True by you, it is now sunk in Ophir; but I expect some day to bring it out of Ophir turned into twelve thousand. If she marries, her husband will be demanding the money, and that might lead to unpleasantness. As Scripture says, "Live peaceably with all men," and I say the same, when money is involved. I will tell you something more. I do not believe, I cannot believe, that six thousand pounds represent the total of old Strange's estate. There must be more money somewhere—perhaps in a Brazilian bank; and all that is wanted is for one of us to go over and find out. You won't convince me that a diamond merchant doing a roaring trade for a quarter of a century made no more

L

than six thousand pounds. I have always heard that the diamond trade is a very beautiful and delicate business, giving rich returns. With caution you manage to get as many diamonds out of the niggers as from their masters, and you pay five shillings to the former where fifty pounds won't satisfy the latter. I leave you to guess what profits are made. If we had not our hands full of Ophir, I would go myself to Brazil, or send you, to see about James Strange's leavings. Six thousand pounds! Why, that is what he sent over to meet present contingencies. He intended drawing the rest when settled. Mark this, Sampy. Should a breath of cold air come down off the moors on Ophir, and somewhat chill that warm concern, so as to make it advisable for either or both of us to take a turn out of England—Brazil is the word.'

'Have you written to Brazil?'

'Of course I have. To the English Consul at Bahia, and have offered to tip him handsomely if he sends me word that old Strange left money there. But I have had no answer as yet.'

As the attentions of young Tramplara became more offensive and more difficult to avoid, Mirelle appealed in despair to Captain Trecarrel.

'My dear Mirelle, what can I do? He is the son of the house, and I visit there. If I were to quarrel with him, I should be forbidden the house, and then,' with a tender look out of the Trecarrel blue eyes, 'I should see no more of you.'

'I thought gentlemen could always take action in such matters. Voyez! In France I step up to a gentleman, and say, That person yonder has looked at me insultingly. Then the gentleman who is a perfect stranger goes across the street and knocks down the insolent one.'

'That would involve an action for assault, and the estate would not bear it,' said Trecarrel, sadly. 'If it were worth a couple of hundred more, I might do it. I know an excellent fellow who knocked a young farmer head over heels in the graveyard on leaving church, because he had looked from his pew admiringly at the young lady this gentleman was about to marry. He compromised the matter by getting a commission for the young farmer, but it cost him a lot of money. These are not the days, my dear Mirelle, when *any* man may be heroic; heroism is only compatible with a balance at the bank. I'll tell you, however, what I can do, and that I will do, as it falls within my means to do it. I will invite young Sampson to a supper at the King's Arms, and I will then talk the thing over reasonably with him. Put your mind at ease. I have great influence with the cub, who looks up to me as a sort of model, and I do not doubt that I shall induce him to desist from his attentions.'

But Captain Trecarrel had overrated his influence. The cub continued his offensive conduct.

One day when he had intruded on her in the summer-house, where she was writing at her desk—her father's desk—she suddenly recalled Herring's interference at West Wyke.

'What—writing a love-letter,' asked young Sampson, lounging on the table opposite her, and trying to look into her eyes. 'Oh dear, how I wish it was to me!'

Mirelle lifted the flap of the writing-case, and took out the small square ruler, and with her finger pushed it across the table in the direction of Mr. Sampson, without raising her eyes from the writing.

Young Tramplara looked at the ruler, then at Mirelle. She took no more notice of him, except that she wrote on a piece of folded paper the name and address of John Herring, and when Sampson attempted again to speak she tossed the paper before him and pointed to the ruler.

He rose scowling. He perfectly understood what she meant: another impertinence, and she would write to John Herring to break that ruler across his skull. Her coolness, her utter contempt for him, the galling of his pride, filled him with rage; but he was a coward, and so he rose from his seat, thrust his hands into his pockets, and sauntered out of the summer-house whistling 'The girl I left behind me.'

CHAPTER XXII.

MOONSHINE AND DIAMONDS.

MIRELLE and Orange were dressing for the ball in the same room; that is, Orange had come into the room of Mirelle for her to do her hair. Mirelle was perfect in this art; her delicate fingers turned the curls in the most graceful and becoming arrangement. This was an art above the sweep of the powers of the maid-of-all-work. Orange, in return, offered to do Mirelle's hair.

'But Mirelle, my dear Mirelle! You look like a ghost, all

in white. Not a particle of colour! It does not suit you; you are so pale. Good heavens! let me look at your hands.' Orange took the long narrow fingers in hers, and held the delicate hand before the candle. It was transparent, and thus only did it show a rosy red.

'Unless I had seen it, I would not have believed that there was blood in you,' said Orange; and then she glanced at herself proudly in the cheval glass. 'Do look at me, Mirelle. I am glowing with life. See my lips, my cheeks—how warm they are! My eyes flicker, whereas you are as though spun out of moonshine. There is not the faintest rose in your cheek, and your lips alone show the least tinge of life. Your eyes have no sparkle in them; they are dark pools in which nothing lives. I wish you would stand between me and the lamp; I believe I should see the light through you. Whoever saw flesh like yours? It is not flesh, it is wax. You must paint. You are unendurable like this—like a corpse of a bride risen from her coffin come to haunt the living.'

'I shall put on my diamonds,' said Mirelle.

'What diamonds?'

'My mother's.'

'I did not know you had them.'

'Yes, I kept them with my own things, in my own box. When my mother died they were committed to me.'

'You cannot wear diamonds; a girl in England does not put on jewellery.'

'I am going to wear them.'

Then Mirelle opened a little case, and drew from it a coronet and a necklace of diamonds.

'Fasten the crown about my head,' she said; 'I can put the necklace on myself.'

Orange stepped back in astonishment. She had never seen anything so beautiful.

'Why, Mirelle, they must be very valuable. How they twinkle, how they will sparkle downstairs among the many lights.' Then with a touch of malice, 'What will Captain Trecarrel think? Now you look like a queen of the fairies. He will fairly lose his heart to you to-night.'

She saw a spot of colour come into each cheek. It angered her, and she went on with bitterness in her soul, 'You know that you belong to his class; and he will think so as well to-night. I suppose he and you will despise us humble folk who have to do with trade and business, and you will have eyes only for each other. What a couple you will make, side by side, he with his aristocratic air, and you bejewelled like a princess!'

She looked at herself in the glass and then at Mirelle, and was reassured. No comparison could be drawn between them. She, Orange, was splendid. She wore pink with carnation ribands, and a red rose in her hair, another in her bosom. Her dark and abundant hair and her large dark eyes looked well, set in red. The colour in her cheeks was heightened. Her bosom heaved, she had a fine bust and throat, and her features were handsome. There was life, love, heat in her. Who could care for a snowdrift—nay, for a frozen fog, though it sparkled?

'Come down, Mirelle: it is time. I have already heard one carriage drive up. How we shall get every one who is invited into this house I do not know.'

'I will go down presently. You go on without me. I am not wanted as yet.'

Mirelle did not descend for half an hour.

When she entered the room where the guests were assembled, it was full. She did not look round her except for a seat, and when she had discovered one she walked to it. She knew nothing of the persons there: they were excellent on their appropriate shelf, but their shelf was not her shelf.

Trecarrel and Herring were both present, and saw her. They had been watching for her to come in. Her appearance surprised them. In the well-lighted room, in her white muslin, with white satin bows, and with her head and delicate throat glittering with diamonds, she seemed a spirit; a spectral White Lady. Her face was as colourless as her dress, save for the fine blue veins that marked her temples. She seemed too fragile, too ethereal to belong to the earth. Her beauty was of an order rare in England, unknown in the West.

Captain Trecarrel started forward. 'Countess Mirelle,' said he, ' you are unprovided with a flower. Am I too impertinent if I offer you one? I thought you might possibly be without, and I have brought you a spray of white heath. Will you accept it?'

She raised her eyes, smiled somewhat sadly at him, and took the sprig with a slight bow. Then she put it to her bosom. As she was doing so, her eye encountered that of Herring, who stood by. She recalled his offer of white heath made on the day of her father's funeral.

'It brings good luck,' said Trecarrel. The same words that Herring had employed. Mirelle's hand trembled, and she looked timidly, flutteringly, at Herring.

'Ah!' said he, 'all the bells have fallen off.'

Then she said, in a half-pleading tone, 'Mr. Herring, I was once very rude and very wrong when I refused the same from you. Now I am rightly punished.'

She removed the sprig. 'You see, Captain,' she said, as she handed it back to Trecarrel, 'the heath has rained off all its white bells. I am not destined to receive good luck from either you or Mr. Herring. I thank you for the kind attention. I cannot wear the heath now.'

'Are you engaged for the first dance?' asked Herring.

Mirelle looked at Trecarrel, who turned his head away. He must, of course, open the ball with Orange. After a pause, in a tone tinged with disappointment, she said she was not engaged, and Herring secured her.

The appearance of Mirelle in the ball-room caused general surprise. It was an apparition rather than an appearance. The prevailing opinion admitted her beauty, but decided that it was of too refined and pure a type to be pleasing; it was a type suitable for a statue but not for a partner. Men love after their kind; blood calls for blood, not for ice.

The ladies discussed her diamonds, and concluded unanimously that they were paste. No one allows to another what he does not possess himself.

'You know, my dear, she comes from Paris, and in Paris they make 'em of paste for tenpence to look as natural as real stones worth a thousand pounds.'

'But her father was a diamond merchant.'

'True by you, but these stones were her mother's I make no doubt, and that mother was a gambling old Spanish Countess, who would sell her soul for money. I've heard Mr. Trampleasure say as much.'

'She don't look as if she had any constitution to speak of,' observed one old lady.

'That transparent skin,' answered another, 'always means that the heart is bad. I ought to know, for my uncle was a chemist. The highest person in the land—and when I say it, I mean the highest—came into my uncle's place one morning and asked for a seidlitz-powder, and he took it on the premises, and he told my uncle that he never took a better seidlitz in his life.'

'She is proud as Lucifer,' said one. 'Look! she's gone and refused Mr. Sampson Tramplara. That is too bad, and she owes her meat and bread, and the roof that covers her, to the charity of his father.'

'He is getting angry,' said the lady whose uncle was in the chemical line. 'Sampson is not one who can bear to be treated impolitely.'

'She will dance with no one but that strange gentleman whom they call Herring, and Captain Trecarrel. Stuck up because of her rank, I suppose.'

'Ah! as if her rank was anything. The highest in the land spoke quite affable to my uncle, and said his seidlitz was the best seidlitz he had ever drunk.'

'Do you call Mr. Sampson handsome?'

'Handsome! I should rather say so; and better than that, he will be rich.'

'Better than all, he will be good,' said a serious lady, Mrs. Flamank, impressively.

'The highest in the land put down twopence for his seidlitz like any other man. But that seidlitz cost my uncle five-and-twenty pounds, for he paid that sum for a Royal arms, lion and unicorn and little dog all complete, to put up over his shop door; and an inscription, "Chemist (by appointment) to His Royal Highness." But I never heard that it brought him more custom. Still, there was the honour, and if that were a satisfaction to him, I don't blame him.'

'What do you think of Orange Tramplara hooking the Captain?'

'The hooking was quite as much on his side as on hers. He is poor as a rat, and she wants position, so the transaction is one of simple sale and barter.'

'The highest in the land,' began again the lady whose uncle had been a chemist; but at these words the ladies broke up their party round her, and escaped to other parts of the room.

Sampson Trampleasure would not take his refusal. He stood by the side of Mirelle, his cheek flushed, and his eye twinkling with anger.

'I don't see why you should dance with some gentlemen and refuse others,' he said sulkily.

'I have refused no gentleman,' answered Mirelle, looking across the room.

He was too stupid to understand the rebuff. He persisted

in worrying her. 'Well,' he said, 'if you won't stand up with me, you must let me take you to supper.'

She was silent a moment, raised her eyes timidly and entreatingly to John Herring, and said, 'I am already engaged.' Herring coloured with pleasure and stepped forward to her assistance.

'You must not tease the Countess,' he said. 'She confesses that she is not strong and able to dance often. She has fixed on the number of dances she will engage in, and more fortunate applicants have forestalled you, and put their names on her card. You have only yourself to blame that you did not press your claim in proper time.'

'I say,' observed Sampson, with an ugly smile on his lips, 'Mirelle, don't you go dancing too often with Trecarrel. Orange won't like it. When a girl is about to be married to a man, she don't like to have another girl coquetting with her deary.'

'Mr. Sampson Trampleasure,' said Herring, stepping forward, 'this is your father's house, and I——' but Mirelle's hand grasped his arm, and arrested what he was about to say. He looked round. At the same moment a pair of waltzers caught Sampson, and with the shock he was driven into the midst of the whirling circle, when he was struck by another couple, and sent flying at a tangent to the door.

Herring looked at Mirelle. She was trembling slightly, and her face was, if possible, whiter than before. Dark shadows formed under her eyes, making them look unusually large and bright.

She did not speak, but continued grasping Herring's arm, unconscious what she was doing; he could feel by the spasmodic contraction of her fingers that she was more agitated than she allowed to appear. He stood patiently at her side, seeing that she was distressed, and supposing that the insolence of young Tramplara was the occasion of her distress.

Presently she recovered herself enough to speak. She put her handkerchief to her brow, and then, with feminine address, gave her emotion an excuse that would disguise its real cause.

'He offends me,' she said; 'I am unaccustomed to this sort of treatment. Some persons when they go among wolves learn to howl. With me it will be a matter of years before I can school myself to endure their bark. I have lived hitherto in a walled garden among lilies and violets and faint sweet roses, and suddenly I am transplanted into a field of cabbages, where some of the plants are mere stumps, and all harbour slugs.' She paused again. Just then Trecarrel came up. She let go her grasp of Herring's arm. She had forgotten that she was still holding it. Trecarrel came smiling his sunniest, with his blue eyes full of languor. As he approached she shrank back, and then drew herself up.

'I think, Mirelle,' said he, 'you are engaged to me for the next quadrille.' He was looking at her diamonds and appraising them; and he wondered whether, after all, he had not made a mistake in taking Orange instead of Mirelle.

'If I were her husband,' he considered, 'I could keep a tight hand on Tramplara, so that he could not very well make away with the six thousand pounds. I wish I had known of these diamonds a few weeks ago.'

Mirelle looked at him steadily. She had by this time completely recovered her composure. 'Am I to congratulate you, Captain Trecarrel?'

'What on?' he asked.

'I have just learned your engagement to Orange.'

'That is an old story,' he said, getting red; 'I thought you were admitted into the plot six months ago.'

'I did not know it till this minute.'

'There is the music striking up. Will you take my arm?'

'I must decline. I shall not dance this quadrille. See, Orange is without a partner.'

She rose, and to avoid saying more walked into the hall, and thence, through the front door, upon the terrace. The moon was shining, and the air without was cool. In the ballroom the atmosphere had become oppressive.

'Would you kindly open the window?' asked Orange, turning to Herring, and casting him a smile. She was standing up for the quadrille with her Captain. The young man at once went to the window and threw it open.

The night was still without. A few curd-like clouds hung in the sky; the leaves of the trees, wet with dew, were glistening in the moonlight like silver. Far away in the extensive landscape a few stars twinkled out of dark wooded background, the lights from distant villages.

There was a vacant settee in the window, and Herring sat on it, leaning on his arm, and looking out.

Poor Mirelle! What could be done for her? Her position was intolerable. The only escape that he could devise was for her to return to West Wyke. But was it likely that Mr.

Trampleasure would consent to this? And in the next place, would Cicely Battishill care to receive her?

'Mr. Herring,' said Orange, 'a gentleman is needed to make up a set. May I introduce you to Miss Bowdler?'

Of course he must dance, and dance with the fascinating Bowdler—a thin young lady, with harshly red hair, red eyelashes, a freckled skin, and eyes that had been boiled in soda. Miss Bowdler was the daughter of a banker, an heiress, and Trecarrel had thought of her, but could not make up his mind to the colourless eyes and red lashes.

Herring danced badly. His thoughts were not in the figures, nor with his partner. He mistook the figures. He spoke of the weather, and had nothing else to say. Miss Bowdler considered him a stupid young man, and that this quadrille was the very dullest in which she had danced. When it was over, he returned to the window, and as there was an end of the settee unoccupied, and the rest of it was occupied by the chemist's niece and a raw acquaintance to whom she was telling the story of the highest in the land—' And when I say the highest, I mean the highest,'—and his seidlitz, Herring was able to take his place at the window without being obliged to speak to any one. He looked again into the moonlight, and towards the dark woods of Werrington, still revolving in his mind the question, What was to become of Mirelle? He saw that she would take the matter into her own hands and insist on being allowed to go elsewhere. She could not remain in a house where the son was allowed to treat her with insolence. She would like to return to France, to her dear convent of the Sacré Cœur. The thought was dreadful to Herring, for it implied that he should never see her again.

He fancied, whilst thus musing, that he heard voices on the terrace, and next that he caught Sampson Tramplara's tones. He did not give much attention to the sounds, till he heard distinctly the bell-like voice of Mirelle, ' Let go this instant, sir !'

He sprang to his feet and was outside the window in a moment. He had been sitting looking in the opposite direction from that in which he heard the voices; now he turned in the direction of the garden house.

At the door of this summer-house he saw young Tramplara, and the white form of Mirelle. The moon was on her, and her head sparkled with the diamonds of her coronet, but there was no corresponding sparkle about her neck.

Herring flew to the spot, and saw that young Sampson had snatched the necklet from her throat. The diamond chain hung twinkling from his hand.

'Restore that instantly,' said Herring, catching the young man's hand at the wrist. 'You scoundrel, what are you about?'

'Keep off, will you!' said the cub. 'I should like to know your right to interfere between me and my cousin, Mirie Strange. I only want to test the stones of her chain. The chaps in the dancing-room say they be paste and a cussed sham. I reckon their mothers have put them up to it. I've got a bet on with young Croker, and I want to try if they'll scratch glass, that is all. So now will you remove your hand and take yourself off?'

Herring doubled up Tramplara's hand, and wrenched the necklace from it.

'Take your chain, Countess. And now for you, you ill-conditioned cur, I warn you. Touch her again, and I will fling you over the wall. Offer her another insult, and you shall suffer for it. If I spare you this time it is because this is your father's house, and I have been his guest. But I will not eat at his table again, that I may reserve my liberty of action, and have my hands free to chastise you should you again in any way offend the Countess Mirelle Garcia.' He turned to Mirelle. 'I once before offered you what help and protection it was possible to me to render, and now I renew the offer.'

'Oh, Mr. Herring,' said she, 'before, I refused your offer very ungraciously. I said then that I was able to help myself. I did not then know the rude elements with which I should have to contend, and I was unaware of my own weakness. Now, with my better knowledge, I accept your offer.'

'Thank you,' he replied: 'you make me this night a very proud man.'

'Mr. Herring,' she pursued, 'I will give you at once the only token I have that I rely upon you. This person who snatched the jewels from my neck, if capable of such an act as that, is capable of another.' Her voice came quick, her bosom heaved, the angry blood was hammering at her temples. 'I do not believe that these diamonds are secure in this house. If he could wrench them from my throat, he would take them from my trunk. Voyez! je vous donne toutes les preuves possibles que j'ai de la confiance en vous.' She disengaged the tiara from her hair. 'There, there!' she said hastily, 'take both the crown and the necklace. I intrust them to you to keep for me. I know that I can rely upon you! I do not know in whom else I can place trust. All are false except you : you are true.'

'Countess! I cannot do this.'

'Why not? Do you shrink already from exercising the trust you offered?'

'Not so, but——'

'But I entreat you,' she interrupted with a trembling voice. 'Ces diamants-ci appartenaient à ma mère—à ma chère, chère mère; c'est pour ça qu'ils ont tant de valeur pour moi.' She forced a smile and made a slight curtsey, and turned to go.

Young Sampson Tramplara was standing near, scowling. Mirelle's eyes rested on him.

'Mr. Herring,' she said, 'should I need your help at any time, may I write?'

'Certainly, and I place myself entirely at your service.'

Young Tramplara burst into a rude laugh.

'The guardianship of the orphan was committed to Tramplara, then it passed to Tramplara and Herring, and now, finally, it is vested in Herring alone.'

To what extent the guardianship of that frail white girl had passed to Herring, to what an extent also he had become trustee for her fortune, neither she nor Sampson Tramplara guessed. He had uttered his sneer, but the words were full of truth.

Then there floated faintly on the air, whether coming from the house or from without could not be told—mingling with the dance music, yet distinct from it—the vibrations of metallic tongues in a musical instrument like an Æolian harp, and the tune seemed to be that of the old English madrigal—

> Since first I saw your face, I resolv'd
> To honour and renown you!
> If now I be disdain'd, I wish
> My heart had never known you.

CHAPTER XXIII.

PASTE.

MIRELLE was subjected to no annoyance after the ball, for both old Tramplara and his son were at Ophir nearly the whole of their time. They returned occasionally to Launceston, but never together. One was always left in charge of the mine, and this was usually young Sampson. When he did come home, he kept out of the way of Mirelle, and old Sampson was too much engrossed in his gold mine to think of her.

She lived in the house, but hardly belonged to it. Her life was apart from all its interests, pursuits, and pleasures. She spoke little and showed herself seldom. Orange was full of her approaching marriage, and could give attention only to her dresses. Her friend and confidante, Miss Bowdler, was constantly there, discussing the bridal garments and the costume of the bridesmaids. In her own little pasty mind Miss Bowdler harboured much rancour and verjuice. She was envious of Orange's happiness; she had herself aspired to Trecarrel, and she felt no tender delight in the better success of Orange. But she disguised her spite for the sake of Sampson, whom she hoped to catch, now that Trecarrel had escaped her net. Orange knew perfectly the state of the Bowdlerian mind, but that mattered little to her. Women naturally hate each other, and are accustomed to live in an atmosphere of simulated affection. She wished greatly to secure the Bowdler for Sampson, so as to bring money into the family.

Mrs. Trampleasure was a harmless old woman, who sniffed about the house, being troubled with a perpetual cold in the head and a perpetual forgetfulness of the handkerchief in her pocket. Mrs. Trampleasure had got very few topics of conversation, for her limits of interest were few—little local tittle-tattle, and the delinquencies of Bella, the maid-of-all-work.

The horrible evening concerts were discontinued, and Mirelle ventured to sit at the piano and play for her own delectation, knowing that Orange was too wrapped up in her new gown, and Mrs. Trampleasure too absorbed in counting the stitches of her knitting, to give her a thought. Whenever the Captain appeared, Mirelle retired either to her room or to the summer-house. Whether in one or the other, she sat at the window, looking out but seeing nothing, her chin in her hand, steeped in thought.

Anyone who had watched Mirelle from her arrival in England would have noticed a change in her face. It was more transparent and thinner than before. But this was not that which constituted the principal change. The face had gained in expression. At first it was impassive; now it was stamped with the seal of passive suffering, a seal that can never be disguised or effaced. According to Catholic theology certain sacraments confer character, and these cannot be iterated. But the sacrament of suffering confers character likewise, and it can be repeated again and again, and ever deepens the character impressed. This stamp gave to Mirelle's face a sweetness and pathos it had not hitherto possessed. Before this time a cold and haughty soul had looked out of her eyes, now warmth had come to that frozen soul, and it was flowing with tears. She was still proud, but she was no longer self-reliant. Hitherto she had repelled sympathy because she had felt no need for it, now her spirit had become timorous, and though it still resented intrusion it pleaded for pity.

As she sat, evening after evening in the window, doing nothing, seeing nothing, her thoughts turned with painful iteration to all that had passed between herself and Captain Trecarrel since they had first met. For a few days after the ball she was resentful. She considered that he had treated her badly; he had attempted, and attempted successfully, to win her heart, and he had gained his end without making a return of his own. He had been cruel to her.

After a while, however, she saw the whole course of affairs in a different light. It struck her that in all probability he had been engaged to Orange—tacitly, may be, and not formally —for a very long while. Something that Orange had said led her to suppose this, and she remembered that the Captain had admitted as much in his answer at the ball when she congratulated him on his engagement. 'That is an old story,' he had said; 'I thought you had been admitted to the plot six months ago.' If he really had been engaged to Orange ever since she had known him, his conduct was explicable in a manner that cleared him of blame. He had looked on Mirelle as one about to become a cousin by marriage. Mirelle was much with Orange, and therefore it was his duty to be kind to her, and to act and speak to her as to a relation of her who was about to become his wife. Perhaps Orange had considered how unpleasant it would be for Mirelle to remain in Dolbeare after she had gone, and had proposed to the Captain that she should accompany them to Trecarrel. If that were so, and it was very probable, the Captain's solicitude to be on a friendly footing was explained, so was also the interest he took in her money affairs.

'If I had only known!' sighed Mirelle. 'If I had only guessed that they were engaged, I would never have been led to think of him in any other light than as a sort of brother or dear friend and adviser. Why did Orange not tell me?' But when she felt disposed to reproach Orange, she was conscious that she was unjust. She and Orange had not been more than superficially friendly. She had kept Miss Trampleasure at a distance, and had declined to open her heart to her. What right then had she to expect the confidence of Orange? Both the Captain and his betrothed no doubt supposed from the first that Mirelle was aware of the engagement, or at least suspected it; and he was friendly because he knew that his friendliness was incapable of misconstruction. The colour tinged Mirelle's brow and cheeks, and the tears of humiliation filled her eyes.

She endeavoured to undo the past by forcing herself to think of Captain Trecarrel as the betrothed of Orange, but it is not easy to tear a new passion out of the heart that is young and has never loved before. The heart of Mirelle was not shallow, and feelings once received struck deep root.

It was a comfort to her that Orange was too much occupied in her own concerns to notice that she was unhappy; it was at least a satisfaction to be able to bleed without vulgar eyes marking the blood, and rude fingers probing the wound.

At first, when she thought that Captain Trecarrel had trifled with her affections, she had felt some bitterness spring up in her soul towards him, but when she had changed her view of the situation, and his conduct was explicable without treachery, the idol that had tottered stood again upright, and, alas! remained an idol.

In reviewing the events of the ball, she saw now that she had acted very unwisely. She had offered an unpardonable insult to the family with which she was staying, and which was, in its clumsy way, kind to her. Young Sampson had found his way to the dining-room before supper, and had helped himself to the wine. She had seen him in the empty room engaged on the various decanters; she had seen him, for the room was on the ground-floor, with large French windows opening on to the terrace. After he had tried the wines, Sampson had come out to Mirelle, and, attracted by the sparkle of the diamonds, had demanded whether they were paste or real stones. She had refused to answer him, and he had put out his hand to take the chain, saying that he would soon ascertain by trying them on a window-pane. She was not justified in thinking that he intended to keep them. She was not justified in supposing that they would not be safe from his cupidity in her trunk. When she had said as much in her anger and excitement, she had offered him, and through him the whole family, a gross and unwarranted insult; and this insult she had accentuated in the most offensive manner by giving the jewels to a stranger to keep for her.

Mirelle put her hands over her face. She was ashamed of what she had done; she had acted unworthily of herself. If Sampson had insulted her with brutality, she had dealt him in return a mortal blow. Her only consolation was that neither Orange nor Mrs. Trampleasure knew of the incident, and she hoped that Sampson, for his own sake, would not tell his father.

She made what amends she was able, but it cost her proud spirit a struggle before she could bring herself to it. One Sunday that young Sampson was at home, when he was alone in the office, she went into the room and stood by the table at which he was writing. He looked up, but had not the grace to rise when he saw who stood before him. Her eyes seemed preternaturally large, and her lips trembled; she had her delicate fingers folded on her bosom.

'Mr. Sampson,' she said, in a voice that shook in spite of her effort to be firm, 'I apologise to you for what I said. You had offended me, but the punishment exceeded your deserts.'

'What did you say? And when?'

'I am speaking of the evening of the ball. You acted rudely in wrenching off my necklace, and I spoke hastily respecting your conduct. The language I used on that occasion was injudicious and wrong.'

He looked at her puzzled; then, with an ugly smirk, he said, 'So, as you have failed to catch the Captain, you want to be sweets with me!'

Is it ever worth while stooping to conciliate the base? The ignoble mind is unable to read the promptings of the generous spirit. Mirelle was learning a lesson, as John Herring was learning his, both in the same school—the school of life; and the lessons each learned were contrary to those they had been taught in childhood. They were finding out that those lessons were impracticable, at least in the modern world.

Mirelle recognised that she had made a mistake. The noble mind must fold its robes about it, and not soil them by contact with the unworthy. She withdrew with her cheek tingling as though it had been smitten.

Young Tramplara began to fawn on Miss Bowdler, and she to flirt with him, in the presence of Mirelle. This was meant on his part as a token to Mirelle that he was acceptable to other ladies, and that they had charms for him. The uncouthness of young Sampson, the squirms and languishings of the red-eyelashed heiress, his heavy jokes and her vapid repartees, were grotesque, and would have provoked laughter, had not Mirelle been too refined to find amusement in what is vulgar.

Mr. Sampson returned to the 'diggings,' and his absence brought relief to Mirelle.

Captain Trecarrel had been away for some days, staying in Exeter. On his way thither he visited Ophir, and got some of the gold-grains from the working. Ophir puzzled him; Ophir hung on his heart. It oppressed his mind; it was a constant source of uneasiness to him. He resolved on his return from Exeter to revisit it. But if he had his doubts, others had not; that was clear from the current of visitors setting that way, and the influx of applications for shares. Shares went up. Money came in, not in dribblets but in streams; it had not to be squeezed out, it exuded spontaneously.

In Exeter Captain Trecarrel had the gold tested. It was gold, not mundic; not absolutely pure gold, there was copper with it, but still it was gold. Trecarrel got rid of the gold grains to the jeweller in part payment for a ring to be presented to Miss Orange. He also purchased a handsome China mantelshelf ornament as a present for Mrs. Trampleasure; he got it cheap because the handle was broken off. He ordered it to be packed and sent to Launceston to the old lady. Then, when the box was opened, the handle would be found broken off, and the blame would be laid on the carrier. Unfortunately, however, the tradesman wrapped the handle as well as the ornamental jar in silver paper—each in a separate piece.

When the box arrived and was opened, a laugh was raised over the handle. Then it struck Mirelle that she ought to make a present to Orange on her marriage. But what could she give her? She had no money. Then she thought of her diamonds, and resolved to ask Mr. Herring to detach the pendant from her necklet and send it her. This she would give to Orange. She took out her desk and wrote the letter. It was a formal letter, but the ice was broken; she had begun to write to him, and cold though the communication was, the receipt of the letter filled Herring with delight. He at once complied with her request.

Orange was profuse in her thanks. She kissed Mirelle and admired the brooch. Miss Bowdler was at Dolbeare at the time, and both looked at it in the window, with many whispers and much raising of eyebrows.

That same afternoon Mirelle was with Orange and the Bowdlers. 'Thank you so very much,' said Orange. 'I shall value the pendant quite as much as though the stones were real diamonds.'

'They are real,' said Mirelle.

'The French make these things so wonderfully like nature that only experts can tell the difference,' said Miss Bowdler.

'I suppose these were some of your mother's stones,' said Orange.

'They were,' answered Mirelle.

'How generous, how kind of you to give them to me!' said Orange without a trace of sarcasm in her voice—(English can make paste imitations as well as the French)—'And though these are only paste, still, I dare say no one will know the difference.'

'They are real stones,' said Mirelle, haughtily.

'My dear,' answered Orange, 'do you know what a Cornish compliment is?—"Take this; it is of no more use to me." If these had been genuine diamonds you would have kept them for yourself; they would have been far too valuable to be parted with lightly. No one gives away anything but what is worthless. Look at Trecarrel's china jar. He got it cheap because it was faulty; he gave it to mother because he was bound to make her a present. If she had been worth money, he would not have sent her a worthless gift; but because she has nothing he sends her a nothing. That is the way of the world.'

'The stones form part of a set my father sent from Brazil to my mother in Paris.'

'Nevertheless they are imitations,' said Orange. 'I took them to the jeweller here, because, you see, my dear, if they had been diamonds, I could not have accepted such a costly present from you, but he unhesitatingly pronounced them to be paste. That, however, does not matter to me; it justifies my accepting and keeping the charming present, which will always be valued by me, not for the intrinsic worth, but as a memorial of your love.'

'Give me the pendant instantly,' said Mirelle, full of pride and anger. 'It is impossible that my father, a diamond merchant, could have offered my dear suffering mother such an insult as to send her a set of sham diamonds.'

She took the ornament, and went at once to the jeweller.

She came away resentful and humbled. 'That Mr. Strange should have dared!'

Not for a moment did it occur to her that perhaps her mother had sold the stones, and replaced them with paste.

CHAPTER XXIV.

THE OXENHAM ARMS.

As the time for his marriage approached, Captain Trecarrel's uneasiness increased. On his way back to Launceston from Exeter he got off the coach at Whiddon Down, determined to have another look at Ophir. He had heard a good deal about Ophir in Exeter, and not much in its favour. His lawyer whom he had consulted had a rich fund of reminiscences concerning Tramplara. Lawyers as a rule are not squeamish, but there was something about old Tramplara which was not to the taste of the solicitor Trecarrel employed. He had been engaged in a Cornish mining action in which his client had prosecuted Tramplara; a good deal had transpired on this occasion not encouraging to those about to transact business with Mr. Tramplara. Much had come out, but more had not come out, but was perfectly well known to those engaged in the case.

'My advice to you is, give a wide berth to the man.'

'I am going to marry his daughter,' answered Trecarrel, ruefully.

'Oh!'—a pause ensued. 'How about settlements?'

'I am all right there,' said the Captain; 'till five thousand pounds is paid down, I do not put my neck into the noose. They may bring me to the altar, but I will fold my arms and sit down on the steps. They cannot legally marry a man against his will.'

'How about the family——' began the lawyer.

'Thank God, I don't marry the family,' interrupted Trecarrel. 'When I have the money and the girl—she is not bad-looking, and will pass muster when clipped and currycombed—I kick the rest over.'

'Well, I wish you joy.'

Captain Trecarrel next consulted his banker, and found that the money world was shy of Ophir, and held Tramplara in much the same esteem as did the legal world.

'Who are the directors of the company?' asked the banker.

'There is a provisional list,' answered Trecarrel. 'Old Tramplara tried hard to get me on to it, but vainly is the trap set in the sight of the bird. Here is the prospectus. You see the names: Sampson Trampleasure, of Dolbeare, Launceston, Esq., Arundell Golitho of Trevorgan, Esq., the Rev. Israel Flamank, and some others of no greater importance. I have Tramplara's own copy, that is to say, one he favoured me with, and, as you see, he has pencilled in a few more names. Here is Mr. Battishill of West Wyke, the owner of the estate, but whether he is already a director, or only a possible director, I do not know.'

'Who is Arundell Golitho, Esq., and where is Trevorgan?'

'Never heard of the man, nor of the place.'

When Captain Trecarrel got off the coach, he saw Herring waiting for the coach, to intrust the diamond pendant to the coachman for transmission to Mirelle.

'Halloo! you here?' exclaimed the Captain; 'I thought you lived at the extremity of the known world, at Boscastle.'

'So I do; but I am here starting a mine.'

'Not a director of Ophir, eh?' asked Trecarrel, eagerly, his blue eyes lighting up.

'No, I am not so ambitious as to embark in gold, I content myself with lead; but if my lead mine promises less than Ophir, its performance, I trust, will be more sure.'

'Ah,' responded Trecarrel, dismally, 'you are bitten with the prevailing distrust. I presume you have not taken shares in Ophir.'

'No; have you?'

'I am going to take a big share in the concern. I marry the Queen of Sheba. Herring, I say, is there a public house near where I can get a chop? I am hungry and wretched. Come with me for charity's sake and let us have a talk together about this same Ophir. I want your opinion; and look here, I have old Tramplara's list of directors, and on it in pencil is the name of Squire Battishill of West Wyke. He is a respectable man, is he not? You know him.'

'Yes; I am staying with him'

'What sort of a man is he?'

'A gentleman every inch,—honourable and true.'

'Oh yes, I don't mean that. They be all honourable men, especially the Hon. Lawless Lascar, who figures on the list. Is he a man of fortune? If Ophir goes "scatt," as they say here, is there property on which the shareholders can come down?'

'Mr. Battishill is certainly not a director.'

'He is pencilled down as one, at all events, and pencilled by Tramplara himself. Tell me, is there a decent inn hereabouts?'

'There is a very tolerable inn in Zeal, if you do not mind descending a steep hill to reach it—the Oxenham Arms.'

'Come with me.'

Zeal is a quaint village of one street, that street being the high road from Exeter to Launceston. Since the time of which we treat the high road has been carried by a new line above the village, which has been left on one side forgotten, and has gone quietly to sleep. In the midst of the street stands a small chapel built of granite, and before it an old granite cross mounted on several steps. The houses are of 'cob,' that is, clay, whitewashed and thatched, with projecting chambers over the doorways resting on oak posts or granite pillars. Below the chapel stood the stately mansion of the Burgoynes facing the road, with vaulted porch, mullioned windows, and sculptured doorways. The Burgoyne family has gone, and now there swings over the entrance a board adorned with the arms of the Oxenham family. The manor-house has descended to become the village inn.

Into this inn, clean, but humble in its pretensions, Herring introduced the Captain.

'I say, girl,' called Trecarrel to the maid, 'throw on some logs; the turf only smoulders. And bring me some hot water and rum. I am cold and damp, and altogether dispirited and drooping. Let me have a steak as soon as you can.' Then to Herring: 'I am put out confoundedly. Ophir will not digest. Tell me candidly your opinion.'

'You are not treating me fairly,' said Herring. 'You have no right to ask me this question when you are about to become closely allied to Mr. Trampleasure——'

'Oh, confound Tramplara. I am not going to marry him, nor his sniffing wife, nor his cub of a son, heaven be praised! nor, better than all, Ophir. Nevertheless, I want to know something about Ophir, for though I am going to be allied to the family, I do not want to be linked by so ever small a link to a concern that may smash, least of all to one that is not exactly on the square. What do you make out about the gold mine?'

'It puzzles me. I have been over it and seen the gold dust washed out of the gozzen.'

'So have I.'

'And yet I am not satisfied.'

'Nor am I.'

'In the first place, I mistrust the way in which Ophir has been puffed and brought into the market.'

'I do not believe a word about the Phœnicians,' said the Captain.

'Again,' Herring went on, 'who have taken the mine in hand?'

'That I can tell you. There is Arundell Golitho, Esq., of Trevorgan. Do you know him. You are a Cornish man, bred in its deepest wilds. Does he hail from your parts?'

'Never heard of him.'

'Nor has anyone else, that I can learn. Then there is the Reverend Israel Flamank, but he counts for nothing. He is a crack-brained preacher, not worth a thousand pounds, and every penny he has he has sunk in Ophir.'

'Here is another: the Honourable Lawless Lascar. Who is he?'

'I have heard about him from my lawyer in Exeter,' said Trecarrel. 'Lends his name to rickety ventures for a consideration, and when wanted, not at home.'

'And Colonel Headlong Wiggles?'

'Colonel Headlong is a man who has not been happy in matrimonial matters—I mean, has been exceptionally unhappy; this would not concern us were it not that it has cost him a good deal of money. He has been endeavouring to recover moral tone lately by taking up vigorously with Temperance, and he has become rather a prominent orator on Total Abstinence platforms. He has lately edited a revised New Testament in which the miracle of Cana has been accommodated to Temperance views—the wine in his version is turned into water.'

'That is all.'

'Except those added in pencil. I do not like the looks of the board of directors. Tell me, Herring, have you any suspicion of trickery?'

Herring hesitated. He had, but he was without grounds to justify the open expression of his suspicion.

'By George!' exclaimed Captain Trecarrel, 'if I thought it were not on the square, I would break off my engagement. I inherit a respectable, I may say an honourable, name, and I do not choose that the name of Trecarrel should be trailed in the mire. The thing cannot last long without declaring its nature. If the gozzen that is crushed yields as much gold daily as I have seen extracted at one washing, then the dividends will begin to run. The working of the mine does not entail a heavy outlay. There are not many men on it.'

'Very few indeed.'

'And the machinery is not enormously expensive, I suppose.'

'No.'

'Then, why the deuce did Tramplara make a company of the concern, and call for shares? If he had been sanguine, he might have worked it himself, and made his fortune in a twelvemonth.'

'Another thing that makes me suspicious,' said Herring, 'is that the lease is only for a year.'

'For a year!' exclaimed the Captain, and whistled. 'Then be sure Tramplara will blow Ophir up before the twelvemonth has elapsed. If he had been sure of gold, he would have taken a lease for ninety-nine years. I will have nothing to do with the family. I will put off the marriage. Listen to this, Herring. I carried off all the bits of stone I could from the auriferous vein of quartz, and I crushed them myself. I borrowed a hammer from a roadmaker, for which I paid him fourpence, and I pounded them, and then washed the crumbled mass in my basin, and not a trace of gold could I discover.'

'That proves nothing. You could hardly expect to find the precious metal in a few nubbs you conveyed away in your coat pocket.'

'There ought to have been indications of gold. I should not have minded had I found as much as a pin's point. No! I believe Ophir to be a swindle, but how the swindling is done passes my comprehension.'

He sat looking into the fire, and kicking the logs with the toe of his boot. Then he threw himself back in his chair.

'I shall go to bed, Herring,' he said, 'and I shall stick there till there is a clearing in the air over Ophir. I am not going to be married whilst the cloud broods heavily. I shall go to bed.'

'Go to bed!' echoed Herring. 'It is early still.'

'I always go to bed when I want to get out of a difficulty. Old Tramplara is not far off, and he can come and see me. Young Sampson can come and see me also; but I defy both of them to get me out of my bed and into my breeches and blue coat against my pleasure. The marriage must be postponed.'

'Nonsense. You cannot do this.'

'I shall. I have got out of a score of difficulties by this means. There I stick till things have come round. My dear Herring, there is no power in the world equal to *non possumus.*'

'But what of the lady's feelings?'

'Oh, blow the lady's feelings!' said Trecarrel, coarsely. 'Ladies' feelings are superficial; that is why they are so sensitive about dress. Men's feelings lie deep; they line their pockets. Orange is a good girl; but she won't feel, or, if she does, she will rather like it. Women like to have their feelings fretted, just as cats like having their backs scratched. Orange can come and see me in bed, and nurse me if she chooses. Polly!' he called to the maid of the inn, 'get your best bedroom ready, and the sheets and blankets and feather-bed well aired. I am going to retire for a week or ten days between the sheets.'

Herring burst out laughing.

'This is no laughing matter,' said Trecarrel, testily. 'I would not go to bed unless I could help it; but, upon my life, I do not see any other mode of escape. You will come and see me sometimes, old fellow, for time will drag.'

'Certainly I will; but what will you say to the Tramplaras?—to Miss Orange?'

'Say—say? why, that I am indisposed. That will be strictly within the bounds of truth, and what is consistent with a gentleman to say. Indisposed—the word was coined for my case. I'll send to Tramplara himself, and get it over as soon as I am in bed.'

'You are joking.'

'I am perfectly serious. I have cause to be so. I am, or was, not so very far from my marriage day, and I do not relish the prospect. Bring old Tramplara here. When he sees me embedded and indisposed to rise, he will grow uneasy and the money will be forthcoming. I have no doubt in the world that he is meditating a trick upon me. He is wonderfully clever; but he met his equal in the matter of the Patagonians—I'll tell you all about them some day. Herring, by some infernal blunder I was pricked as sheriff of the county one year. It was supposed that I was worth about five times my actual income. I could not endure the cost of office, and I did not want to pay the fine for refusal, so I went to bed, and wrote to the Lord Lieutenant from bed. I said that I was confined to my couch, and could not rise from it, which was true, strictly true, under the circumstances, and that I could not say that I would live through the year, which was also true, strictly true; and I got off without fine. On another occasion my creditors were unreasonable and urgent. I took to my bed again, and after I had laid there a fortnight, they mellowed; at the end of a month they were ripe for a composition of eight shillings in the pound. I find that, in difficulties, if I take at once to my bed I constitute myself master of the situation. It is the Hougoumont of all my Waterloos.'

Herring was still laughing.

'You may laugh,' pursued Trecarrel, ' but my plan is superlative. Judge of it by the faces of Tramplara and his son when they visit me. You know the look that comes over a chess-player, when his adversary says "checkmate." I suspect you will see some very similar expression steal over the countenances of Tramplara and young Hopeful. The old man will coax, and the young one bluster. They can do nothing. Here I lie, and they bite their nails and rack their brains. They are powerless. They cannot bring Orange and a parson here and have me married in bed. I should bury my head under the clothes. They would not attempt it. It would hardly be decent. I do not think it would be legal.'

'You will write, I suppose, to Miss Orange?'

'No; I shall send for her father. I do not put hand to paper if I can help it. I never commit myself. *Litera scripta manet.* You have no idea, Herring, how successful my system is. Difficulties solve themselves; mountains melt into mole-hills; tangles unravel of their own accord. The perfectness of the system consists in its extreme simplicity. Polly! run the warming-pan through the sheets before I retire. Whilst I am upstairs, Herring, there is a good fellow, keep a sharp look-out on Ophir.'

CHAPTER XXV.

A LEVÉE.

IN France it was anciently the custom for the kings to hold *lits de justice*—that is to say, they lay in bed, and whilst reposing on their pillows, and the vapours of sleep rose and rolled from their exalted brows, heard appeals and pronounced judgments. The royal example found hosts of imitators. No one ever dreams of following a good example, but one that is mischievous has eager copyists. It was so in France under the ancient *régime*. Nobles received their clients, ladies their suitors, in bed. Magistrates heard cases in the morning, before rising, whilst sipping their coffee. So far down had this habit descended, that Scarron, in his 'Roman Comique,' describes a respectable actress receiving an abbé, a magistrate, and various ladies and gentlemen in her bedroom, whilst she lay between the sheets. In the Parisian world, the world of salt and culture, the bedroom—the very bed itself—of a distinguished lady was the centre round which the wit and gossip of the gay and literary world circled and sparkled.

The getting out of bed of a prince, and of those who imitated the prince, was as public as his lying in state. That was not the day of baths and Turkish towels, and therefore there was not the same reason against the admission of the public to a *levée* that would exist at present, at least in England.

Whilst the king drew on his stockings, he heard petitions; as he encased himself in his black satin breeches, he determined suits. 'When his shirt-frills were being drawn out, he dictated despatches; whilst his wig was being dusted, he granted concessions; and as he washed his fingers and face in a saucer, he conferred bishoprics and abbacies.

In like manner, the toilettes of ladies of rank and the queens of beauty and fashion were times for the reception of their favoured friends. Hogarth's picture of the toilette of the lady in the *Mariage à la mode* shows that this custom had extended to England. A *levée* was then, as the name implies, an assembly held during the process of getting out of bed.

Captain Trecarrel was not consciously copying the ancient *régime*. He lay in bed because it suited his convenience. He received visitors there because he did not choose to receive them elsewhere, till he had carried a point on which his heart was set.

'Why, bless my soul, Trecarrel! what ails you? Laid up in this wretched inn—caught cold on your way down? I hope nothing serious; not rheumatic fever, eh?'

'Severe indisposition,' said Trecarrel, looking at Mr. Trampleasure calmly out of his celestial blue eyes, innocent as those of a child, little spots of sky, pure and guileless.

'Good gracious!' blustered Tramplara, 'not anything gastric, is it? No congestion of any of the organs?'

'There is tightness in the chest,' said the Captain; 'that is normal.'

'Bless my soul! couldn't you push on to Launceston? Were you so bad that you broke down here?

> When a man's a little bit poorly,
> Makes a fuss, wants a nurse,
> Thinks he's going to die most surely,
> Sends for the doctor who makes him worse.

You know the lines, but whether by the Bard of Avon, or by Chalker in his "Canterbury Tales," I cannot recall. Poor Orange! What a state of mind she will be in!'

'I dare say,' said the Captain, composedly.

'The child will be half mad with alarm. What does the doctor say? What has he given you? Something stinging or routing, eh?'

'I have not sent for him.'

'Not sent for the doctor? By Grogs! and you seriously ill. How do you know but that it may interfere with your marriage on the eighth?'

'That is what I have been supposing.'

'You must get well, my dear boy; you positively must.'

'I hope so, but that does not altogether depend on me.'

'I insist on a doctor being sent for.'

'His coming will be of no use; I know my own constitution.'

'Have you sent word to Orange?'

'No; I left that for you. You see I am in bed, and I cannot write. I don't think the people of the inn would permit it, lest I should ink the sheets. Salts of lemon are not always satisfactory in removing stains.'

'Orange will be heartbroken.'

'The recuperative power of the female heart cannot be overestimated.'

'Mrs. Trampleasure will be in such distress, she will do nothing but cry——'

'And sniff. I say, father-in-law that want to be, how goes Ophir?'

'Oh, my dear boy, magnificently!'

'Like the Laira at Plymouth—eh, father-in-law elect?'

'What do you mean?'

'The rendezvous of all the gulls in the Western counties—

only, with this difference, the gulls go to Laira for what they can get, and they come to Ophir for what they can give.'

'I do not like these flippant jokes,' said Tramplara, puffing and waxing red.

'The joke is too near the truth. You see, father-in-law prospective, I have been in Exeter, and have talked Ophir over with lawyers, bankers, mining agents, and men of the world.'

'Well?'

'And I find that the general verdict on Ophir is, that it is a——swindle.'

Tramplara stamped, turned purple in face, and strode up and down the room.

'You insult me! Look at my white hairs. This is an outrage on my character—on my age. Do you dare to say that an old man like me, with one foot in eternity, would—would——'

'Reserve that for the Flamanks,' said the Captain. 'It is an argument without weight with me.'

'This is intolerable! You wish to break off connection with me.'

'Not at all,' said the Captain, smiling and twisting his fair moustache. 'I am only telling you what is said in Exeter about Ophir; my own opinion is inchoate. Sometimes I am inclined to believe in the genuineness of the article, but generally, I admit, what I admire most is not its genuineness, but the skill with which a spurious article is disposed of.'

'You have seen the gold?'

'But I have not found it.'

'You have dug out the quartz yourself, and followed the entire process to the last washing and sifting. Will not that content you?'

'I brought home with me some of the auriferous stone, and crushed it myself, and washed it myself, but not a particle of gold was there.'

'Simply because you took pieces in which there was no gold. Gold is not so common as hornblend.'

'Nor, apparently, as discernible in the stone. Look here, father-in-law that want to be.'

'I won't be spoken to in this style.'

'You want me to marry Orange, do you not?'

'I do not care a penny about you. All I care for is poor Orange and her feelings.'

'You are ready to pay me five thousand pounds for taking

Orange off your hands, are you not?' asked the imperturbable Captain.

'I am ready to pay you five thousand pounds as her jointure, because she is my daughter, whom I dearly love, and I wish to provide for her comfort and happiness in the future when I am dead and forgotten.'

'And you were thinking only of her comfort and happiness when you offered us those Patagonian bonds?' said Trecarrel. 'Fortunately, I was equally interested in the dear creature's comfort and happiness, and in her interest I declined them.'

'Have done with those Patagonian bonds!' said Tramplara, impatiently. 'You will bring my white hairs with exasperation to the grave. I shall go downstairs and leave you to soak in bed. Do you intend to lie here for a twelvemonth? I do not believe you are seriously ill.'

'Seriously indisposed is what I said,' answered the Captain.

'You have done this sort of thing before,' said old Tramplara, very hot and angry; 'I have heard of you. Ridiculous! not like a man.'

Trecarrel was wholly unmoved. He turned round in his bed with his face to the wall. The old man stamped about the room, swearing and uttering his opinions freely, without eliciting a word from the Captain. After a while he cooled down, finding that his wrath and remonstrances were ineffectual, and he seated himself on a chair by the bedside.

'Be reasonable, Captain,' he said. 'What is the drift of this farce?'

Trecarrel turned round in bed, and faced him with perfect equanimity in his handsome features.

'I say, Trampleasure, the second Solomon who draws gold out of Ophir, I give it up. How do you manage it?'

The fiery flush again came into the old man's face.

'There, there! I do not want to anger you,' said Trecarrel. 'I have a proposal to make to you, father-in-law *in nubibus*. Let me go with you into the mine. You shall indicate to me the auriferous vein, and I will pick out pieces and submit them to you. Those about which you are doubtful shall be cast aside; those you approve I will retain. I will pound them myself, and wash them myself.'

'Where? In our works?'

'By no means. Anywhere that suits my convenience and pleasure; at John Herring's lead mine, if I choose. Then, if I find gold, you shall have my name on your list of directors, and I will go heartily with you in the concern.'

'I do not care to have you as a director.'

'That is not true; you have several times urged me to be one. You want some respectable names on your list, which is sadly deficient in them. Will you oblige me with some partilars about Arundell Golitho, Esq., of Trevorgan? By some strange omission he has not been made a Justice of the Peace and a Deputy Lieutenant of the county of Cornwall.'

'I will answer no questions. You want to force a quarrel on me.'

'On the contrary, I want to dispel my doubts. I am, what I think you call in your chapel, an earnest inquirer. I can tell you one thing for certain, father-in-law that may, might, would, could, and should be; I am not going to be married to your Orange without the fulfilment of one of two conditions.'

'What are they?' asked Tramplara, sulkily.

'One is, that I may make the proposed investigation into the qualities of Ophir.'

'I refuse it,' said Trampleasure, hastily.

'You refuse to allow me fairly to test its value as a mine?'

'I do not say that. I refuse the proposed test, because it is unfair and insulting. You may come and extract as much quartz as you like from the rock, and crush and wash it on my floors, but you shall not carry it elsewhere.'

'What is your objection?'

'I say the proposal is insulting. Look at my white hairs. Do you suppose——'

'Leave the white hairs out of the matter. What is unfair in my proposal?'

'I will not consent. I will die before I permit it.'

The old man sprang from his seat. 'Good heavens! I shall have every visitor and applicant for shares pestering me to carry off specimens.'

'Why should they not?'

'Because it is against regulations. I have laid down a strict rule, to be relaxed to none, that every specimen raised is to be tested on the spot, and not elsewhere. I will have the trial take place where I can see that it is fairly conducted. How do I know but that behind my back the trial may be incorrectly, imperfectly, or dishonestly carried on?'

'I do not ask to do anything behind your back. You shall

select half a dozen specimens. We will bring them here. I will smash them up in the backyard with a paviour's hammer under your eye, and I will wash them in the water-trough there, with you looking on. Will that suffice?'

'What is your other alternative?' asked Trampleasure, sullenly.

'My second proposal is this. You have promised me five thousands pounds along with Orange.'

'I know I have, and I shall be ready to pay it when you are married.'

'My good father-in-law prospective, that does not quite satisfy me. Of course I do not question your honour and your intention to discharge what you propose. But speculation, above all, speculation in mines, superlatively such a speculation as Ophir, is risky. I do not wish to risk my chance of getting that five thousand pounds (and connubial felicity) on the continuance of the Ophirian gold yield.'

'You don't suppose I will pay you down the money now, before you are married.'

'No, I do not, and I do not want to run the chance of getting married, only to discover that the five thousand pounds has been sunk in Ophir, and is only available in the shape of paper on Ophir, or only to discover that Ophir has collapsed like a pricked bladder the day before.'

'What then do you want?' asked Trampleasure, very angrily, rubbing his knuckles with the palm of his hand in his irritation and impatience.

'What I want is, that you should lodge the money now in the hands of a third party, say of Mr. John Herring. If I fail to fulfil my part of the contract within a given time, say on the day already fixed for the wedding, or seven days after, I forfeit it and it returns to you. When I am married to Orange, then Herring is empowered to hand the money over to me.'

'Upon my word, Captain Trecarrel, of all audacious and exacting men I ever came across, you are the most audacious and exacting. And what if I refuse this condition also?'

'Then I remain in bed.'

'What is the advantage of that?'.

'I am engaged to be married on the eighth. If I am ill, my illness serves as an excuse for my absence from the hymeneal altar when expected there. The world can say nothing against that; and I am bound to maintain my character as a *chevalier sans reproche.*'

'Pray how long will this farce continue?'

'What farce?'

'Your lying in bed.'

'You will find a looking-glass yonder, father-in-law anticipative. Examine your countenance in it, and see if the expression is that of a spectator at a farce. It looks deuced more like that of a witness at a melodrama.'

'How long do you soak here?' exclaimed Trampleasure, sulkily.

'I shall await events from this commanding position. Ophir will blow up before long. It cannot continue, and will send you and yours head over heels into space, and where you will drop, heaven only knows. Then, of course, I shall be free.'

Trampleasure paced the room, his face blazing. He was very angry, he was also greatly perplexed. He was particularly anxious to get Orange married to the Captain. Presently he turned round, and said in a sullen tone, and with an angry lower on his brows, 'I will give you an answer shortly.'

'All right, I am in no hurry. The bed is not uncomfortable. Herring is coming here this evening to smoke a pipe with me, and I will ask him to hold the stakes.'

The next visitor was young Sampson. He came in fuming, and asked the Captain his intentions. He was Orange's brother. It was his duty to see that she was treated fairly, and, by God, he would do his duty. He was not going to let a militia captain play fast and loose with the poor girl's affections, and possibly blight her entire future by his heartless desertion. Trecarrel listened to him with the utmost coolness. He had expected this visit, and knew what its character would be.

'Sampson the little and weak,' he said, 'your father has sent you here to try what bluster will effect. May I trouble you to convey to him a message from me, and say that the effects are nil?'

'Are you going to desert Orange? If you are, I'll shoot you.'

'No, you won't,' said the Captain. 'In the first place, I am not going to desert Orange; and in the second place, if I were, the utmost you would do would be to try to get money compensation out of me, and that would be like squeezing a stone for milk. In one particular I am like Ophir. If you want to extract gold out of me, you must first put it into me.'

Sampson's face became mottled, and his eyes, with a startled expression in them, turned to the Captain, but, seeing his eyes fixed inquiringly on him, his fell. Trecarrel chuckled, and drew the sheets over his head. Presently he looked out again. Sampson was at the window killing flies. He had his back turned to the bed, and was stabbing at the flies with the pin of his stock.

'I have placed two alternatives before your father,' said the Captain: 'I will marry Orange to-morrow if he will comply with either. Either let him give me a fair chance of testing the ore of Ophir, and satisfy myself that the mine is genuine, or let him pay five thousand pounds into the hands of a third party, to be held till the marriage is concluded.'

'I refuse—I refuse each alternative, in his name and my own,' said young Sampson, stabbing at a fly with such fury that he broke a pane in the window.

'There goes eighteen pence,' said the Captain, 'beside letting a current of cold air in on me. Leave the room. I need repose. My indisposition gains upon me.'

The next to visit Captain Trecarrel was John Herring. Herring was not very willing to undertake the obligation the Captain was desirous of forcing upon him: however, he was good-natured, that is, easily imposed on, and in the end he consented to act as the third party, and receive the money into his keeping till the marriage took place.

On the morrow old Tramplara came back; he remained some time, and attempted to coax Trecarrel into good humour and the surrender of his ultimatum. Trecarrel especially urged the former of his alternatives, as he perceived that it was eminently distasteful to both the old man and his son. Tramplara went away, refusing both alternatives.

On the third day Tramplara did not come at all, but Trecarrel heard through the hostess that young Sampson had been there to inquire whether he was still confined to his bed.

On the fourth day the old man came, very sulky and rude, and gave way—not to the first alternative, but to the second. Herring was sent for, and the transaction was arranged to the satisfaction of the Captain.

'Now then,' said Trecarrel, 'my indisposition is better. Ring for shaving water. Clear everyone out of the room. I am going to rise.'

CHAPTER XXVI.

THE SHEKEL.

'Miss CICELY,' said John Herring.

'Yes, Mr. John,' answered Cicely, with a smile.

'Well—Cicely—if you wish it.'

'I do wish it; I dislike formality. You have stayed with us so long, and have been so good to us, and helped us so greatly, that I suspect a cousinship between us, if the respective Battishill and Herring pedigrees were worked. The West of England families are all united by marriage.'

'My family boasts of no dignity or antiquity,' said Herring. 'We have been humble yeomen down to my father, and never dreamed of calling ourselves gentlemen, certainly not of tacking an esquire after our names.'

'If your ancestors were humble yeomen, ours were very humble gentlemen. Do look at West Wyke. Did you ever see a gentleman's house elsewhere so small, and yet so full of self-consciousness? An embattled gateway in a wall that a boy could overleap, guarding a garden of hollyhocks. A front door with a huge beam to close it, running back into the wall, to protect the family plate, which consists of one silver caudle cup, and a whalebone-handled punch-ladle with a Queen Anne's shilling in the bowl. I believe our family stood barely above highwater mark, the line where the yeoman ended and the gentleman began; but so barely above it, that we were always liable to be submerged, and never able to lift ourselves wholly into a more exalted and secure position.'

'I dare say,' observed John Herring, 'that the smallness of your house has been the salvation of your family. You have not been expected to keep a large establishment; to entertain much, and to have a stable, and furniture, and a cellar.'

'I dare say you are right. By the way, how is the sick gentleman at the Oxenham Arms?'

'There is not much change in his condition. He is still indisposed.'

'Who is he?'

'A Cornish squire, Trecarrel by name, who is engaged to the daughter of Mr. Trampleasure.'

'No doubt Miss Mirelle will have had some of her airs taken out of her in the Trampleasure household.'

This was the first time that Cicely had voluntarily, and of her own prompting, spoken of Mirelle. Herring had mentioned her occasionally, but Cicely showed plainly that she retained no pleasant recollection of the Countess, and was uninterested in what had become of her. There was a spice of vindictiveness in her tone as she spoke. She was rejoicing that Mirelle should have her airs taken out of her.

'The poor Countess,' said Herring, 'has suffered much annoyance among those wretched people——'

'I have no patience with her,' interrupted Cicely, 'giving herself airs, and calling herself a Countess. Why, her father was only a merchant, and I cannot see how she can inherit her mother's title. The wife of an Earl is a Countess, and the daughters are Ladies, not Countesses.'

'It is different abroad.'

'You ought not to have humoured her. However, as you see no more of her now, no harm has been done by your falling in with her fancy. The Tramplaras are the last persons in the world to feed her vanity, and so by this time, it is to be hoped, she has learned to stand on the same level as those she is called to associate with.'

'Do you not think it must be intolerable for one so refined and sensitive?'

'Oh, there, there!' interrupted Cicely, again laughing. 'We have had enough of Mirelle; let us banish her from our conversation. The very thought of her gives me a shiver.'

'Cicely, tell me, has old Tramplara been pretty frequently to West Wyke of late?'

'He has been to see my father now and then.'

'Do you know that he has put down your father on his list as one of the directors of Ophir? His name is not yet printed, but Tramplara is counting on him.'

'Why should he require my father's name?'

'To give respectability to the concern.'

'I hope my father will not consent.'

'He *must* not. I am persuaded that Ophir is a fraud, and your father must be saved from being involved in what will cover with disgrace, and involve in ruin, all who are connected with it.'

'Good heavens! Do you think my father has already given his consent? Oh, please go in and see him, and stop him. I know he is becoming excited about Ophir. He laughed at it at first, but he has changed his tone of late.'

'I will go at once.'

Herring stepped into the hall to Mr. Battishill.

'Well, Herring!' exclaimed the old man, brightening up; 'back from Zeal! How goes the sick man—Captain Trecarrel? Dear me! he represents a fine old family, de Esse, alias Trecarrel, argent two chevronels sable, with a mullet for a difference. A Devonshire family—the Esse of Ashe, and the elder branch, died out in an heiress who carried Ashe to the Drakes; but the second son, a long way back, married the heiress of Trecarrel, and dropped the patronymic for the place name. How is the last limb of a splendid tree?'

'There is nothing more serious the matter with him than that he is going to marry the daughter of old Tramplara.'

'Good Lord! what a mésalliance! The Trampleasures are mushrooms—I had almost said toadstools. I suppose it is a case of money; the needy gentleman with centuries behind him takes the daughter of the wealthy founder of Ophir for the sake of the mountain of gold she brings. How is it that Trampleasure has not secured Trecarrel as a director? His name would carry weight.'

'Exactly,' answered Herring; 'that is what Tramplara wants—he has not got a name of importance on his list. Do you know anything of Arundell Golitho, Esq., of Trevorgan?'

'Never heard his name before.'

'Nor have I, nor has anyone else.'

'He must be some one of importance, or Tramplara would not have put him on the board?'

'I do not believe in his existence. You were asking why Captain Trecarrel has not become a director. For the best of reasons. He does not care to cover an honourable name with disgrace.'

Mr. Battishill's face changed colour.

'That is a strong expression, Herring, and ought to be justified.'

'Dear Mr. Battishill, you know what Polpluggan did for you.'

'Polpluggan was a disastrous venture, certainly.'

'You told me yourself it was a swindle.'

'Well, well, the word was too strong. I thought so at the time; but Tramplara has been frank with me about it. Since he has been here so much, engaged on Ophir, I have seen his books; he showed them me in the most open manner possible, he insists on my going over them myself. Polpluggan was a failure, not a swindle. I withdraw the expression.'

'And Ophir, I believe, is nothing less than a swindle, and will cover everyone who has to do with it with infamy. That is why Captain Trecarrel will not lend his name to the concern.'

'Why then does he marry the daughter of Ophir?'

'That is another affair. He has been engaged to her for some time, and cannot with honour break away.'

'What leads him to suppose that Ophir is a——a——'

'A swindle! Because he has been in Exeter consulting those who are likely to know; because he knows the antecedents of the man who has started it. I trust, sir, you have not given Tramplara grounds to hope that you will become a director?'

'Well, he has been pressing, very pressing, I may say, and I have not positively said I will not. You see, my dear Herring, the mine is sure to be a success. The applications for shares increase instead of falling off; that is a pretty good proof of public confidence.'

'That proves nothing, except that there are many fools in the world ready to part with their money.'

'They would hardly take shares unless they had convinced themselves that the speculation was sound. Nothing, I understand, can be more above board than the proceedings of Mr. Trampleasure. The gold ore is crushed and washed before the eyes of the public. I cannot see where the fraud can be.'

'There is roguery somewhere, I am convinced.'

'My dear Herring, that is your opinion. Others equally capable of forming opinions think differently. The mine is on my property, it is only reasonable that I should be a director and benefit by it. As Mr. Trampleasure put it to me—the world asks, Why is not the lord of the manor on the board of directors? The absence of his name from it damages the prospects of the mine. Other men of position and property hold back because I do not sanction the venture. It is necessary that I should lend my name.'

'You must on no account lend your name, sir,' said Herring, earnestly.

'You are very peremptory, Mr. Herring,' said the old man, nettled. 'The lead mine halts; nothing is being done there, no lead turned out, no machinery set up, no company got together to work it. And hard by is the auriferous quartz vein of Ophir——'

'Excuse my interrupting you,' said Herring, 'but may I

know whether you believe in Upayer having ever been Ophir?'

'That is a matter into which I do not enter. I put all these antiquarian theories aside. I look at the plain facts. Is gold found there, or is it not?'

'Gold is certainly washed there. How it comes there I do not pretend to say.'

'You mean to insinuate that it is not dug out of the mine.'

'I doubt it, because I mistrust old Tramplara, and I think the way in which the affair has been got up is suspicious. Did you ever hear the old people call Upaver Ophir?'

'No, but there is a similarity in the names. However, as I told you, I put all these antiquarian conceits on one side.'

'Mr. Battishill, we must consider them as an integral part of the swindle, if swindle it be. You do not, I presume, believe in the Jews and Phœnicians having worked this mine in remote ages?'

'I tell you I do not think of this at all; I am not qualified to enter into and examine this question. But when it comes to gravel containing gold dust, why, bless my soul! my eyes are the best judges. As for the Jews and Phœnicians, there is, at all events, this to be said for the theory of their having been here, that they dropped a shekel—a silver shekel—I saw it with my own eyes. I have an impression of it in my desk. Thus where a Jewish coin has been found, there, in all probability a Jew has been to drop it.'

'Who found the coin?'

'The Reverend Israel Flamank bought it of Grizzly Cobbledick, who had picked it up in his garden, or somewhere near the Giant's Table.'

'I beg you, sir, I entreat you, as you love your home and respect the name you bear, not to have anything to do with Ophir till I have followed this shekel up to its origin. It may serve as a clue by which the mystery will be unravelled. I will go and see Grizzly himself, and ascertain from his own lips where he found it, or rather, whether he found it at all.'

'You are a sceptic,' said Mr. Battishill, 'steeped in the spirit of the age.'

'Well,' asked Cicely, when Herring came out, 'what is the result?' She noticed that he was looking excited.

'Your father is bitten with Ophir,' he answered. 'He and I have nearly come to hard words. It is the first time we have had any difference, and we have been warm on both sides. I must find out about Ophir, if only to save him; for Tramplara has woven his web round him, and has so dusted his eyes with gold that he can neither free himself nor see clearly where he is. He will infallibly be brought to ruin again by that wretched old man, unless I get to the bottom of the mystery of this accursed Ophir.'

'Oh, Mr. Herring!' pleaded Cicely, putting her hands together; 'do—do help us.'

'Yes, *Miss* Cicely.'

'I beg your pardon,' she said, and the clouds cleared from her pleasant face. 'Cousin John, what should we—what should I do without you?'

'I have done nothing as yet. But I am determined to expose Ophir, and by so doing to save your father.'

'How will you set about it?'

'I have a clue—a shekel.'

John Herring went in search of Grizzly. The old savage was now generally to be found near Ophir. The mine exercised a strange attraction on the wild old man. The visitors spoke to him, and asked him questions about the Giant's Table, and the Jews, and the gold, and then made him presents. Some of the more intemperate among the Temperates had serious thought of setting him up as a representative of Jonadab the son of Rechab, and put leading questions to him, to elicit from him traditions of such descent. But further inquiries into the habits and peculiarities of his parent stock at Nymet damped their enthusiasm. The Nymet savages, even if temperate, which was doubtful, were not shining moral lights to hold up as examples in other particulars. Grizzly had become somewhat civilised by association with human beings. When he was tired of being questioned, he rambled off upon the moors, and disappeared up the stream in the direction of Rayborough Pool, but not for long. The stir of Ophir drew him back. He liked watching the stampers, and to stand on the bank above the washing floors, chuckling and sniggering at the people examining the sediment and picking out the glittering grains.

There Herring found him. He at once attacked him on the subject of the shekel.

'I found 'n in the airth just below the great stone to the head o' the Giant's Table. I found 'n about six foot vour inches below the surfass o' the ground. There was dree or vour more, all alike, but Loramussy! I didn't give mun (them) no heed. I thought they warn't worth nothing, and I gived mun to my little maid to play wi'. But her, I reckon, ha' lost the lot, all but thicky as I sold to the Reverend Israelite Flamank, and he sed it were an Israelitish shekel. I've a-heard the old volks used to call the Giant's Table a Gilgal, but they don't do that no more; and I can mind how this were always called Hophir, but the folks as is skollards took to naming 'n Upaver, and that be all I've a got to say. I can't say nothing about Jonadab the son o' Rechab, as were my great-granfer, cos a died when I was a baby. I'll thankee to remember a poor man as is nigh vour-score years old, and 'ud die afore he'd let a drop o' other liker down his throat but pure water, glory rallaluley, harmen.' And he held out his hand. 'Oh! I beg pardon; didn't think 'twere the young Squire. No offence.'

'Cobbledick,' said Herring, 'have you ever found any more silver shekels about the Table?'

'No, never; only once for all.'

'How deep down did you say they were?'

'What did I say? I found 'n in the airth just below the big stone to the head of the Giant's Table. I found 'n about six foot vour inches below the surfass o' the ground.'

'I have heard that already, word for word. Can you give me any idea of the depth, not in words, but by showing me about the depth that you call six foot four inches?'

Cobbledick looked blankly at him.

'What do you take your own height to be?'

Grizzly was posed.

'I suppose it took a deal of sinking to reach the depth where—you found the shekels?'

'Loramussy, maister!' exclaimed the old wretch, 'weeks and weeks; that shaft yonder were nothing to it.'

'That will do, Grizzly.'

Herring was convinced that the old man was repeating by rote a lesson that had been taught him. However much he was questioned and cross-questioned he returned to the same story, in the same words. Herring gave up the hope of getting anything more in this quarter. Cobbledick had degenerated into a beggar—a wretched, canting beggar, accommodating his whine to the craze of the persons who visited Ophir.

But Herring was not going to abandon the clue of the shekel because he could find out nothing from Grizzly. He went to the Giant's Table to catechise Joyce, but she was not there.

Joyce was now nearly well. The splints had been taken off her arms, and she could use her hands, and do light work; but the hands were stiff, and long inaction had weakened her arms.

Herring could not spare the time to wait for her return; he did not know where she was, and he was due at the Oxenham Arms for the final settlement of the arrangement between Trecarrel and Trampleasure, in which he was a party.

On the morrow, Captain Trecarrel left. In the evening Herring went in quest of Joyce and found her hoeing in the little field. He called, and she ran to him as a dog to its master, and with as marked demonstrations of delight at seeing him.

'Joyce, I came here yesterday to find you, and you were away.'

'Oh dear, oh dear, though!' she exclaimed; 'I were wiring a rabbit.'

'Joyce, I want a word with you.'

'You can have scores; as many as you wants.'

'I know. A woman is free of her words. You must tell me the truth now, my little maid, for a good deal depends on it.'

'Did I ever tell'y a lie, now?' asked Joyce, offended. 'You may cut me in pieces afore I'll say other than what be true to you.'

'What I want to know, Joyce, is, where did your father get that shekel?'

'I don't know what that be.'

'A silver coin. He says he found three or four here under one of the stones of the Table. There is a branch on one side, and on the other a cup with a flame rising out of it.'

'I never seed nothing of the sort, nowhere.'

'Your father says that he gave them to you, and that you lost all, except one which he retained and sold to Mr. Flamank.'

Joyce shook her head.

'You have never seen anything of the kind?'

'It be just one o' vaither's pack o' lies,' answered the candid Joyce; 'vaither hev been lying finely since Ophir began. He never showed me nothing like that; he never gived me no silver money. He never had none to give till Ophir began.'

'You are very positive.'

'If you doubt, I'll say, Blast me blue——'

'That will do,' interrupted Herring; 'your word will suffice without the blue blazes to colour it.'

The old man had lied about the shekel. He had not given it to the girl, he had therefore probably not found it at all, but it had been given him by those who had put the story into his mouth.

'I'll ax vaither if you likes,' said Joyce; 'he'll tell me, all right.'

'I do not think he will. That is all I wanted to know, my dear girl.'

'I say,' said Joyce, 'doant'y go off now right on end. Sit you down a mite here in the sun and have a chat. I never see nothing of you now, not as it used to be when I were ill and scatt to bits. I a'most wish my airms was broke again, that you could come and see me ivery day. That were beautiful.'

'Very well, Joyce, by all means. I have nothing particular to do, so I am quite at your service.' He sat down by the girl under the lee of the great stones. It was warm there and pleasant, leaning against the grey blocks of hoar antiquity and unknown use, stained orange and silvery white with lichen, and with white frosty moss like antlers of elfin deer filling the nooks in the stones. The ants were crawling over the moss in the sun; they were migrating and wore their wings for that one day. Turf was heaped up at the side of the cromlech, forming a rude bench. On this the two sat. As he took his place the thought came into Herring's head that far away in the dim prehistoric age, some such a savage as that which sat beside him had assisted when it was reared.

'It be lew (sheltered) here,' said Joyce; 'vaither hev took to sitting here mostly on a Sunday when he ain't wanted to the mine.'

'He leaves you very much alone now.'

'That he does. Vaither be much changed o' late. The vokes there ha' taught 'n to smoke, and they give 'n a bit o' backie now and then, and when he haven't got no backie, then he flips off this here moss, this black sort o' trade on the moorstones, and he smokes that.'

'A new sort of life for him,' said Herring.

'It amuses he,' answered the girl. 'He says he didn't know as Gorolmity had so many vules in the world. He says they be as plenty as stones on Dartmoor.'

'I dare say they are, and certainly those are fools who congregate about Ophir.'

'Vaither likes to hear mun talk, and go sifting and cradling and washing for the gold. It makes 'n laugh, it do.'

'Why, Joyce?'

'Why, because there bain't none of 'em knows where the gold comes from, and there bain't one of 'em as don't think himself as wise as Cosdon is big.'

'Where does the gold come from?' asked Herring, eagerly, so eagerly that Joyce turned sharply round and looked him hard in the face.

'Don't'y know neither?'

'Indeed I do not.'

'Vaither said as you didn't and nobody didn't. And larned and skolards as the volk be, vaither be too much for mun'

'Joyce, if you can tell me where the gold comes from I shall indeed be thankful.'

'Do you wish very much to know?'

Joyce was silent. She looked straight before her. Something was working in her mind.

'Well, Joyce?' asked Herring; he laid his hand on hers. 'If you will tell me this, you will repay me for all the little trouble I took to make your poor hands sound and strong again.'

'Then I'll tell you, come what may. It is just this that made me doubt to say. Vaither 'd kill me sure as vuzz blooms all the year, if he knowed as I had told you. Look here,' said Joyce; 'do'y see thicky ant there. Well, he took up a great moorstone, and sez he, " You, Joyce, be that ant, and I'll treat you the same," and down with the stone.'

'Yes,' said Herring, his blood curdling, 'I understand you.'

'And after that he sed, Glory rallaluley.'

'Joyce, your father shall never know that you told me.'

'Whether he knows or not I'll tell, because you wish it. If he does kill me, it don't matter much.' Then she looked him steadily in the eyes, and said: 'This be the way in which it be done. Vaither puts the gold dust in. When the bell rings, that's the signal for he to be ready up at the head o' the launder' (wooden channel) 'where the water runs along to go to the washing pans, and he just slips in some of the gold into the water. So the stream carries it down into the washing places where the pounded stone is ready to be washed.'

Herring almost laughed. The solution of the puzzle was simplicity itself—so simple that it had escaped everyone. Every eye had watched the stone, no one had thought that the water might be salted.

'I'll show you some of it,' said Joyce. 'There is a little bag hid away under the table. You understand vaither don't put none in when there be no vules to find it. Old Tramplara pulls a cord, and that lets the water on; and when the water is let on, vaither sprinkles the gold in it. He don't do it when there be no vules there, for Tramplara sez he ha'n't got much of the gold to waste. Then, after it has been washed and sorted out, he gives it back to vaither, and in it goes again for more vules to find. I've done it once or twice myself for vaither, when he couldn't go hisself. That be how I came to know about it.'

'I am lastingly indebted to you, Joyce, for telling me this.'

'You won't bring vaither to no harm because of this, will'y now? That 'ud be too cruel onkind o' you. But no—you'll never do no hurt to me nor vaither, I be sure.'

'Indeed I will not, dear Joyce. I shall never forget what I owe to you for having told me this; and I promise you your father shall not suffer for it.'

CHAPTER XXVII.

COBBLEDICK'S RHEUMATICS.

JOHN HERRING did not go at once to Mr. Battishill with the account of what he had heard. He waited till he had himself witnessed the transaction. Some time before the public were admitted to the mine, he went in that direction, making however a wide circuit, and secreted himself behind some of the rocks that commanded the head of the 'launder.' There he remained till Old Grizzly arrived, and, after having looked about him, laid down beside the stream close to the sluice that let the water into the wooden conduit for the washing floors.

Herring saw him strew the dust in the stream as it was admitted; he remained at his post of observation till some time after Cobbledick had departed, and then he went direct to West Wyke.

He told Mr. Battishill what he had learned from Joyce, and how he had verified the account with his own eyes. It was true he had not arrested Grizzly's hand and taken the gold dust out of it; but he had seen some of the gold supplied to the old man by Tramplara, and which he kept secreted under the Giant's Table, and there was no moral doubt that what the old man had strewn in the water was that gold powder which Tramplara intended should be found in the pans.

The revelation of the fraud made Mr. Battishill excited and angry.

'What,' he exclaimed, helpless in his agitation—'what is to be done? Good heavens! what can be done?'.

'That is what I have been considering. You are a justice of the peace, and you must sign a warrant for the arrest of Mr. Tramplara and his son. There can be no question that young Sampson is involved in the swindle equally with his father, who is the originator and mainspring of the whole concern.'

'I have not acted for many years. I had rather not.'

'But, sir, I think it most important that you should take this matter up. Remember, this fraud has been carried out on your property, under a lease granted by you, and that you come out of it without the loss of a penny. I think it possible—I only say possible—that some inconsiderate persons may cast reflections on you. Fortunately, your name is not on the list of directors, so that you will not be involved in the ruin this discovery will bring on many; but your abstention from becoming one may be commented on unfavouraby, unless you cut the occasion away. If you issue a warrant for the apprehension of the wretched swindlers, and become the main instrument of the break-up of the company and the exposure of the dishonest trick that has been played, no one can wag his tongue against you.'

'You are right,' said the old man. He held out his hand to Herring, and the tears came into his eyes. 'John, I cannot thank you sufficiently for having protected me against myself. I confess to you that old Tramplara had talked my suspicions down, and had raised in my breast the demon of cupidity. No, I will not say cupidity, but speculation. I do not care for money in itself, but I do delight in making it, or, what is the same thing, in scheming how to make it. I suspect I have been too overweening in my esteem of my own powers, and now you have given that conceit a fatal fall. Do you remember the wrestle in "As You Like it"? "Sir," I say with Rosalind, "you have wrestled well, and overthrown more than" Tramplara. I trust my self-esteem is dead as Charles. I shall never again venture to have an opinion contrary to yours.'

'But, Mr. Battishill, is not this a little wandering from the point? I want a warrant for the apprehension of father and son.'

'It is no wandering at all. I am explaining to you the reason of my submission. I tell you that you have but to propose a measure, and I carry it out as best I may. Go to Okehampton, and get a clerk to make out a warrant, and I will sign it.'

'One thing more. I do not wish Old Cobbledick to be arrested. He is too stupid and too ignorant to know what he has been doing, and it must be managed that he is allowed to escape. I have passed my word to Joyce that he shall not be brought into trouble. Poor Joyce is in terror of her life of him, and if he were to suspect that she had betrayed the secret it would go hard with her.'

'Oh, no,' said Mr. Battishill, hastily; 'Cobbledick is my tenant, that is, a squatter on my land, and I must protect him if I can.'

'It can be managed,' said Herring. 'I will go to him, and tell him plainly what I saw to-day, and threaten that I will have him apprehended, unless he absents himself to-morrow, and gets the Tramplaras to appoint a substitute. After that I will communicate with the constable, and we shall succeed in arresting gold-handed the fellow who salts the water.'

'Poor Cobbledick! I should be very sorry for trouble to come on him. He is a beast, not a man, and these Tramplaras have put him in shafts and driven him where they chose to go.'

'One thing more,' pursued Herring. 'Directly we have caught the man in the act, I must ride to Launceston at full speed. Old Tramplara is not here. He has gone home, because his daughter is about to be married; by the way, the marriage is to take place this week, I believe. If the news were to reach him before he is arrested, he would draw every penny of the shareholders' money from the bank, and make a bolt with it. Before we knew whether he were gone to Plymouth or Falmouth, he would be on the high seas, and those who have invested in Ophir would lose everything.'

'You are right, John, right again. You take everyone's interests under your protection. I suspect there will be wailing and wringing of hands when this scandal breaks on the religio-speculative world.'

Herring did not see Cobbledick till next morning. After the interview with Mr. Battishill, he rode into Okehampton and obtained the warrant. He did not wish to speak to Grizzly long before he dealt the stroke, lest he should give the alarm. When he did speak, he was straightforward with him.

'Cobbledick,' he said, 'I have long entertained suspicions of Ophir. I knew it was a swindle, but how the swindling was managed I did not know till yesterday. I had gone through every process of the mine attentively, except one, and I was satisfied that the trickery was not committed under my eyes in the mine itself. There was only one process I had not studied, and that was one which took place above the workings. I allude to the letting on of the water that washes the gozzen. Yesterday I watched that, hiding under a rock, and I saw you steal to the head of the launder, and I observed you salting the water with gold-dust. *Now* I know exactly how the fraud is carried out. Are you aware of the consequences? I have only to apply to a magistrate for a warrant, and you are arrested and committed to gaol, and there you will probably lie for many months.'

Cobbledick's face became livid.

'I do not want to throw you into prison, partly because I believe you have acted in ignorance of what you were doing, but chiefly because I wish to fix the noose round the right throats.'

'Cap'n [1] Tramplara set me on it,' said Cobbledick; 'he sed, if I didn't do 'zackly as he wanted, he'd tear down the Giant's Table, and be altogether the ruin o' me. He'd got that hold on Squire Battishill that *he* couldn't help me. And I did it to save myself.'

'I am quite aware that Mr. Tramplara made you his tool, and I do not want you to suffer, if it can be avoided, because you have been an ignorant and unwilling tool.'

'Unwilling,' echoed Grizzly, 'I'll swear; glory rallaluley.'

'I repeat that I wish to spare you because you were an ignorant tool, and also, and that especially, because of poor Joyce, who would be heart-broken were anything to happen to you, unnatural father though you be.'

'Ah! sure-ly it 'ud kill Joyce. Her be that tooked up wi' me, her can't abide as no harm should come to I. What 'ud her do without me, I'd like to know? Where'd her get meat, and clothes, and fire? If I were tooked and put in the lock-up, her'd die right on end wi' fright and hunger.'

The mean old man enforced this view of the case, thinking to deepen Herring's reluctance to compromise him.

'There may be two opinions about that,' said Herring: 'suffice it, however, that for the sake of Joyce I would spare you. Now the only way this can be done is for you to decline salting the water to-morrow, when I and other witnesses will be there to see the thing done, and I shall be prepared to arrest the doer.'

'If I don't do it, then it be Joyce who does.'

[1] The head of a mine bears the title of Captain.

'But Joyce must not do it. Who is in charge of the mine this week?'

'Young Sampson Tramplara.'

'Very well; tell him that you can't be there'

'Ow!' yelped the old man, 'I be took already cruel wi' the rheumatics. I reckon in another half a wink I shan't be able to stir neither voot nor hand.'

'So let it be. Your rheumatism incapacitates you from attending to your work, and Joyce is sent far off, on an errand. Then Mr. Sampson will employ another man.'

'He'll do it hisself. He don't let no one else into the dodge except me and Joyce.'

'So much the better. Then we shall catch the prime culprit in the act. Now, Cobbledick, you understand. Not one word of this must be repeated. If you let out what I have told you, then your chance of escape is gone. I shall have you arrested this evening, and you will spend the night in the lock-up. You comprehend this?'

The old man put his dirty finger to his eye and winked. 'My grandfer wasn't Jonadab the son o' Rechab. I arn't a vule, it be them as goes to Ophir as be the vules.'

Herring left him. Then Cobbledick's face changed. He was fairly frightened. He sought Joyce at once; no suspicion crossed him that she had betrayed the secret.

'Joyce,' he said in a hoarse whisper, 'the thing's a' busted blazes high.'

'What be, vaither?'

'Hophir, as they calls it. The young maister hev a found out all about 'n.'

Joyce was alarmed; she looked uneasily at her father, but there was no anger in his face.

'Joyce,' he went on, 'that old Cap'n Tramplara hev never gived me what he've a promised.'

'What hev he a promised'y?'

'He sed he'd a give me as many pounds o' backie as I worked days for he, a salting o' the water. He arn't paid me not these three weeks. See here, I ha' notched it on thicky stone. Now he don't know nothing o' this here bust-up. And when he do hear, then he'll not give me no backie more. And, I reckon, he won't pay me that he already owes me. So you cut along to Lanson so vast as your legs can carry you.'

'Vaither, I know nothing o' the road.'

'You cut right on end after the tip o' your nose,' he said,

'and you cut so vast as you can. You cannot miss 'n. And mind, you must get there afore the news of the bust-up do come to the Cap'n, and you tell n' this? "Give me the backie in pounds"—that's just so many pounds as you've fingers and toes on your body, and one over for your head. Now don't you be a jackass and forget that one over. A head is every mite as much consekance to a human cretur as his little toe. And you say to 'n; "Give me as much backie in pounds as I've fingers and toes, and a head;" and you hold'n out all straight afor'n that he may count mun hisself. And you mind you don't forget to reckon your head in. Then you go on and say, "I'll tell'y something mighty partickler about Ophir." Say as vaither sent me lopping all the way, so hard as I could lop. And if he gives you the backie, then you can tell 'n all— how the young maister hev found out all about n', and be agoing to lock up him and the young Cap'n Sampson in gaol. But if he don't give'y the backie, then you can just please yourself and tell 'n nothing. There now, don't'y bide about but cut away.'

'But you, vaither! Will you get into trouble?'

'I—I'm about to be took cruel bad wi' rheumatics, and what they calls the loinbagey. Now, afore you goes to Lanson, just you cut down to Ophir, and tell Cap'n Sampson I wants to see'n mighty partickler here to the Table.'

An hour later, young Sampson Tramplara was at the cromlech. As he approached, he heard moaning and cries issuing from the interior.

'What the devil is the matter here?' he asked, looking in. 'Who is that howling and groaning?'

'Oh, Cap'n, it be me; I be took cruel bad wi' rheumatics and the loinbagey.'

'Well, I'm not your doctor.'

'I sent to tell'y that I couldn't fulfil my duty to-day there to Ophir.'

'Then your daughter can do it.'

'Her's off to Lanson.'

'What the devil is she gone there for?'

'Sure, after my backie. Your vaither he promised me a pound a day for the work I did, and he arn't paid me for a long while. Look'y there, I ha' notched it all on the stone. There be as many days as you have fingers and toes, and your head chucked in as well.'

'You fool!' exclaimed young Tramplara, 'why did you not

o

apply to me, instead of sending all the way to Launceston for it?'

'Cos, if I'd ha' axed you, you'd ha' throwed a curse at me instead o' a pound o' backie.'

'You damned blockhead,' swore the young man, angrily.

'There—I sed as much. I'd rather hev the backie, though 'tother don't hurt, it only tickles.'

'Curse it,' exclaimed Sampson, in a violent rage; 'there is a particular reason to-day why I want the water well salted. Damn your rheumatism; you *must* be at your post.'

'I can't and I won't,' said Grizzly, sulkily.

'It is you won't, not you can't,' blustered Sampson; then he gathered his stick short in his hand, and catching the old man by the ragged collar of his coat, he beat him well, pouring forth at the same time a volley of curses.

'This is all sham; I don't believe in your rheumatism. This is idleness. You are a good-for-nothing scoundrel. I'll give you occasion to moan and cry out.'

'You leave me alone, Cap'n,' yelled Cobbledick. 'You forget, I reckon, that I have got the hanging of'y in my hands.'

'It may be so, but you forget that if I swing you swing also; one rope will do for both of us,' said Sampson. 'And for that reason I do not fear you in the least. Now then, will you do your work again to-day?'

'I can't.'

'I'll give you five pounds of backie.'

'I say what I sez; I can't do it.'

'Then,' said young Sampson, 'there is no help for it; I must manage the job myself.'

'You'd better,' assented Grizzly; 'if I was you, I wouldn't trust nobody else.'

'I don't mean to,' answered Sampson. He was panting after the thrashing he had administered, and as he cooled he began to question his discretion in giving way to his brutality. 'I say, Cobbledick, you mind this; you and I and my father are all in the same box, and you in the worst compartment of it, for it is you who have put the dust in. My father and I can always put on the look of innocence and throw the blame on you. You, if the rope has to be tasted, you will have the first bite.'

'I understand,' said the old man, putting his finger to his aye. 'Jonadab the son of Rechab weren't my father. I ain't a vule; it be they as goes to Ophir be the vules.'

'You won't take it ill that I thrashed you. You put me out, and I am naturally of a quick temper.'

'I say, Cap'n; I wouldn't let none else do the job to-day. I'd do it myself if I was you.'

'I intend to. I told you I did.'

'That be right. Do it yourself.'

Then young Sampson left the den. As he was turning away, he thought he heard loud laughter from within. He was of a suspicious nature, and he turned back.

'What are you laughing at, Cobbledick?'

'I bain't laughing; I be screeching wi' pain. What wi' the rheumatics, and the loinbagey, and the licking I ha' had, I hev cause to, I reckon; and I sez glory rallaluley between the twinges by way of easement.'

CHAPTER XXVIII.

CAUGHT IN THE ACT.

WHILST young Sampson was with Old Grizzly in his den, Herring was on his way down the Okehampton road to meet the constable at a spot already agreed upon. When he came to the point near the stream where the track to Ophir diverged from the high road, he found two post carriages drawn up in the way, from which were descending a party of grave-looking persons of a hard appearance of face, as if they were all in a spiritual and mental ironmongery trade. They were under the lead of the Rev. Israel Flamank, who was about to conduct them over the mine.

The way to it across the moor was rough, and not good travelling for a carriage. The chaises were ordered to go to Zeal, and the party, well supplied with comestibles, prepared to walk to Ophir, examine the washing of the gold, and then picnic in a serio-speculative mood on the moor.

Mr. Flamank was a veritable decoy-duck to the Tramplaras. Full of enthusiasm, earnest in belief, transparently sincere, he impressed even those who had cool judgments. He looked on Ophir as his own discovery, and was proud of it. To hear him talk, the Bible was written as a huge puff of Ophir, and the Christian ministry called into existence to tout for shares.

Herring was slightly acquainted with him. He had seen him several times at Ophir, and he knew that the man was sincere and honest. He pitied him because he saw him running headforemost to moral and pecuniary ruin. As he passed, he raised his hat to Mr. Flamank, who responded with a few words on the weather.

Herring observed him for a moment or two. Flamank was an excitable little man, and was specially excited on this occasion. On this occasion he had brought with him several men of means as well as piety, whom he particularly desired to secure for Ophir. Their faith was weak. They were ready enough to believe, with a thin kettle-broth faith, in any folly that would not cost them money, but when it came to embarking capital they asked to be established in their faith.

Herring was so kind at heart that, moved by a sudden impulse of pity, he resolved to give Flamank a chance of extricating himself from the wreck, unhurt in character if not in pocket. He called the pastor aside, and asked him to spare him a few moments.

'I am very busy,' said the minister, looking over his shoulder; 'I have a large party here, I cannot well be spared.'

'Sir, what I have to say to you is of the utmost importance. Send the party on with the promise of rejoining it. There is no possibility of their mistaking the way, which is well trampled like that which led to the den of the sick lion.'

'Very well, as you wish,' answered Israel, resignedly.

When all had departed, and Herring was quite alone with Mr. Flamank, he told him everything with complete frankness, and assured him of the total and irretrievable collapse of Ophir within a couple of hours. To say that the pastor was aghast is to understate the case; and yet he was unable at once to realise the completeness of the ruin with which he and Ophir were menaced.

'Nothing will shake my faith in the Phœnicians having been here,' he said. 'We are expressly told that Ophir lies between Meshaw and Sheepstor, and this place is exactly halfway between them as the crow flies.'

'But it is a long flight for the crow, and there are many other places where Ophir may be found besides this. Here we have distinct evidence of dishonesty.'

'There is evil always mixed with good, and falsehood is associated with truth,' sighed Mr. Flamank. 'It may be—of course, as you state you have seen it, it must be—that there is trickery here, but still Ophir *is* somewhere hereabouts.'

'That of course is possible. But we have not now to consider the whereabouts of Ophir, but the whereabouts of your reputation and your capital, both sunk in this swindle.' Then the full truth of Herring's words came home to the Reverend Israel. He sobbed and clasped his hands convulsively. 'Good Lord!' he moaned, 'avert this blow from me. I am prostrate! I do not so much mind the loss of all my little savings intrusted to Trampleasure for the purposes of the mine, as the loss of my character, the ruin of my influence, the destruction of my position. I have spoken and written about Ophir, and induced so many to embark their little means in it! Believing widows and Christian old maids have ventured their all in Ophir. I have urged them to it, assuring them it was a sound venture; I have shown them the sure word of prophecy speaking of Ophir; and now, what will become of them and of me?'

'My purpose is to ride to Launceston and have old Mr. Trampleasure arrested before he hears the news and can decamp with the money.'

'Oh, Mr. Herring, what is to be done? What can I do to put myself right?'

'I see one course open to you. You come with me and the constable and watch the process of salting, and help us to secure young Sampson Tramplara, or whoever does it. You will give evidence against those who are acting fraudulently. You will assist me in exposing the rascality. It will not then be possible for your good name to suffer, though your pocket may and probably will be lighter.'

'Thank you, thank you so much, Mr. Herring,' said the unfortunate man; 'I shall never be able to repay what you are doing for me save by my prayers. I accept your proposal. How is it to be carried out?'

'You must go after your friends, and make some excuse for deserting them. Then return to me, and I will take you with me. I must start the constable, who is going to the same spot by another route. Stay! you have a brown speckled shawl over your arm.'

'It belongs to a lady of my party.'

'Take it with you. Your black suit might be visible, but enveloped in the shawl you will be unobserved amidst the heather.'

The moor was clear. No one was visible on the flank of Cosdon or on the hill-side opposite, as Herring and his companion stole cautiously under cover to a place which commanded the sluice. Herring placed the pastor at some distance from himself; he wished the constable to be with him, so that they might make a rush together on the man they desired to take.

The constable had made a considerable détour; he had, in fact, worked round the hill from an opposite direction. Herring was on the look-out for him, and signed to him with a handkerchief fluttered behind a rock where to rejoin him.

The day was bright, but a cool wind blew from the northwest, rolling scattered masses of white cloud, like giant icebergs floating in a polar sea. Autumn was closing in. The days were shortening, the fern becoming russet, the heath had lost its bells; only a few sprigs of heather retained their harsh, dry blossoms. The gorse no longer bloomed throughout, though here and there one little gold flower still showed. 'When the furze is out of bloom, then sweet love is out of tune,' says a Devonshire proverb, which acquires its force from the fact that the gorse is in flower throughout the year. The whortleberry leaves were turned orange and crimson. Out of the peat the coral moss showed its scarlet incrustations.

'To my thinking,' said the constable, who found silence irksome, 'the worts' (whortleberries) 'of the wood ain't to compare with the worts of the moor. The wood worts is the bigger, but the moor worts is the sweeter. Do you like wort-pie with clotted cream on it as thick as the pastry?'

Herring nodded.

'He who don't like that don't know what good living is,' said the constable.

This functionary was a stout man, with a florid face and very pale blue eyes. He was silent for a while, and then he began again.

'I suppose I mightn't stand up and stretch my legs,' he asked: 'I'm in such a constrained and awkerd position sitting here on my 'aunches so long.'

'Certainly not,' said Herring, hastily. 'I entreat you to remain as you are.'

'There was a little fellow I knowed when I was a boy in Tawton—he's dead now. He had been to sea, but he warn't good for much, he were so small in size. He've a told me oft and oft the tale how he were tooked by pirates in the Mediterranean, and sold as a slave at Morocco, in one of them American States, I reckon. He said that the Moors couldn't make much of 'n, he were so small. He were no good to work in the mines, and he were no good to wheel weights. So, as they was determined to have their money's worth out of he, they made 'n sit day and night in one constrained and un-natteral position—hatching turkey eggs.'

Then he relapsed into silence, but not for long.

Presently he spoke again. ' I s'pose I mayn't light a pipe ? ' his faint mild eyes looked pleadingly at Herring.

'Certainly not.'

'I didn't s'pose I might. I axed because it be tedious waiting. No offence meant.'

After a further weary pause, he said in an undertone—' You don't think now, master, that he we be going to take will prove dangerous ? '

'I dare say he will show fight. If he be young Mr. Sampson Tramplara, he probably will.'

'Oh!' the rosy apple cheeks looked less cheery. 'Look here, sir; my body be as big as a rhinoceros, but my soul be no bigger than a nit. There seems a deal o' me looking at me cursorily, sir; but it ain't heart, sir, it be bacon.'

'Hush!' whispered Herring, 'look out. Here comes some one from the mine.'

'That be young Mr. Sampson Tramplara,' said the constable. 'From battle, murder, and sudden death, good Lord deliver us.' He spoke in an undertone. The wind blew up the valley, and there was not the remotest chance of his being heard. Then he added in a whisper, ' You'll mind what I said, in confidence, sir, about my courage. I'll back anyone up, sir, but don't'y thrust me forrard. There be divarsity of gifts, and I be famous at backing.'

' Herring held up his finger. He looked in the direction of Flamank, but could not distinguish him. He was among the tufts of brown heather, and the speckled cloak was over him, completely merging him in the bushes.

'Keep a sharp look-out,' whispered Herring, ' and when I touch you, spring up, and run with me down on Sampson Trampleasure. We must not let him slip away.'

They saw the young man come stealthily up the valley, looking right and left, evidently somewhat uneasy. The ' leat' or channel of water came to a grip in the moor-side, and was carried over it in a long wooden launder on daddy long-legs' supports. The stream was conveyed thence, still in wood, and covered, round an elbow of hill, and reached the washing-floors by a rapid incline. A wire conducted on poles from the mine to the sluice let the water on without the necessity of ascending to the launder head, which was invisible from the mine itself.

The stamping-mills were working, and the drum was revolving and grinding. A second leat carried the water to put these in motion. Herring and the constable could hear the thud, thud of the hammers and the monotonous crunching of the crusher.

Young Tramplara knelt down by the sluice, and took a packet from his breast pocket. Presently the poles supporting the wire creaked and swung in the direction of Ophir, and the sluice door was lifted. At once the water rushed down the wooden trough, and Sampson was seen, after a furtive glance round, to sprinkle the advancing stream with the contents of his packet.

Herring touched the constable, and both rose and advanced from behind the rock. Tramplara's back was towards them, and he was unaware of their approach. The wind was from him, and he did not hear their steps. At the same time the Reverend Israel Flamank rose and shook off his brown shawl. Herring and the constable were within a few paces of the young man, when he stood up, dusted his hands, and turned. Instantly he saw them, and uttered a cry of mingled rage and alarm. He turned sharply to run; then, thinking better of it, turned back again, and faced them, and, quick as thought, drew a pistol from his pocket and presented it at the head of John Herring. As he fixed him with his eye, Sampson recognised with whom he had to do, and Herring saw the flash of recognition in his evil eye. 'By God!' said Sampson between his teeth, 'I am not sorry for this. I'll settle old accounts with you this minute.'

Herring saw the finger twitch at the trigger, and instinctively bent his head. He heard the report at the same moment, followed by a cry and a heavy fall behind him.

He was himself unhurt, and his first impulse was to close with Sampson, but, turning his head, he saw the constable lying motionless, and, with a call to Mr. Flamank to run after Sampson, he stooped over the prostrate man.

The constable's face was mottled; all colour had deserted it but a dead purple in blotches in the cheeks. His eyes were closed, and he was motionless. Seeing the pistol produced, the worthy man had sprung behind John Herring, true to his word that he was good at backing. When Herring bent his head, the constable had received the charge which was designed to blow out Herring's brains.

John Herring scooped water out of the stream, and threw

it over the poor fellow's face. Then he tore off his neckcloth, and ripped open his waistcoat in search of the wound. The freshness of the water brought the man round. He opened his pale eyes, looked scaredly at Herring, and closed them again.

'Are you much hurt ? Where did the shot strike ?' asked John Herring.

Again the constable opened his eyes cautiously, and now he turned his head stiffly.

'Where is he?' he asked huskily.

'He has run away. Are you seriously hurt?'

'Very,' sighed the poor man.

'But where?'

'I can't speak yet. Wait a bit, and I will tell'y.'

In the meantime Sampson Trampleasure was running. He stopped his flight after he had gone some little distance, and looked back. He saw Herring bowed over the prostrate man, opening his waistcoat and uncovering his breast. With a curse, he turned and ran on.

Flamank, with tails flying, waving the brown shawl like a lasso over his head, ran after him, shouting, 'Heigh ! stop, Mr. Sampson ! stop ! You have killed the constable ! You must be hung ! Stay and let me catch you !'

'Try to stand,' said Herring to the constable. He lifted him to his feet.

'I be the father of fourteen, and another coming,' said the poor man. He was dreadfully frightened; he peered about him in all directions.

'And the eldest fifteen,' he murmured. 'Be you sure the murderous ruffian be out o' harm's way ?'

'Certain. Have you been hit?'

'Ay, I have.'

'Then where?'

'Here,' said the constable, holding up his hat.

The ball had gone clean through it.

Just then Mr. Flamank returned, panting and very hot.

'I can't catch him. I have run and shouted my best, but he would not wait to be caught.'

'He shall not escape me,' said Herring.

CHAPTER XXIX.

A RACE.

Sampson Trampleasure ran to the mine, burst through the assembled visitors, who tried to arrest him with inquiries after Mr. Flamank, and about the washings and cradlings and puddlings, and the whips and whims. He had an oath and a curse for all who stood in his way. He thrust to the stable, where he saddled and bridled his horse, and, in another moment, was galloping over the rough road.

The shocked visitors shook their heads, and concluded that there had been a breakage in the machinery. It did not occur to them that there had been a break-up of the entire concern. That fact was revealed to them later by the Rev. Israel Flamank.

Sampson Trampleasure reached the Okehampton road and sped along it in the Launceston direction. When he had crossed the bridge over the Taw at Sticklepath, and was ascending the hill on the other side, he looked back and saw some one on a grey in pursuit. He knew the grey mare—she belonged to Mr. Battishill, and he was certain that John Herring bestrode her.

'Ah!' said Sampson; 'a race between us which shall reach Launceston first.'

Mr. Battishill's mare had been a good horse once, but was now old. Sampson had a young and sound cob under him. The mare would be unable to endure so long a journey, she must be exchanged at one of the next stations. Sampson knew he could keep his distance and get first to Launceston, but that was not sufficient. He must delay Herring long enough to allow him to see his father, and, with or without his father, to leave Launceston before Herring rode through its gate. Believing that he had killed a man, he was in great fear for himself, and he would not have scrupled to fly without warning his father, but that he was unsupplied with money. He must make for a seaport that same night; an hour would suffice, if he could gain that.

The sun was setting as he rode over Sourton Down. There was a turnpike there. He called the man of the bar to him.

'You know me. I am Sampson Trampleasure, junior. I am riding a race with a gentleman for a wager; my horse is getting beat, and I must secure a fresh mount at Bridestowe.

Here is a guinea; I will give you four more if you will delay the gentleman a quarter of an hour.'

'All right, sir! We have to go some ways for our tea-water; I'll fasten the bar and go for mine.'

Sampson did not wait to hear how Herring was to be detained; he rode as hard as he could down the hill to Bridestowe, and drew up at the inn door.

'Here!' he shouted, 'give my horse some gruel; he is beat. Have you a horse I can hire, hostler? Mine won't carry me to Launceston.'

'He's not done yet,' said the hostler. 'Most of our osses be gone on wi' two chaises, but there be one in the stables that be fresh. But how about getting of her back again?'

'I'll leave mine if I take her,' said Sampson. 'I'm back again to-morrow, and I'll ride her here.'

'You can look at her,' said the hostler; 'her ain't a beauty to look at, but her can go brave enough.'

Sampson went into the stable. Presently he came out.

'No, Daniel, I don't like her looks. Be sharp with the gruel and put a quart of your strongest ale into it; my bay will carry me with that inside him.'

The hostler went leisurely about his work.

'Daniel, this won't do. There has been a breakage at Ophir, and I must be sharp amd tell my father. We must be back to-morrow before daybreak, or everything will be spoiled.'

'All right, sir; I'll look peart.'

Sampson was not satisfied with the man's undertaking to look alert. He went himself to the bar and gave his bay a quart of ale.

As he was galloping out of Bridestowe, he heard the clatter of horse's hoofs descending the hard road from Sourton Down, and he knew that Herring was at his heels.

Herring had reached the toll-gate, and found it barred. He had been unable to make the man hear. He found both the gate-house and bar locked. He was greatly annoyed, and, riding back, lashed his grey, and tried to make her leap the bar. But the mare was too old and tired to risk it, and she swerved. Then he tried to get round by a side lane, and through fields, but found this also impracticable. Full a quarter of an hour passed before he could get through. The man arrived at last, put down his water-can, and leisurely unfastened the bar. Herring was in too great haste to waste time in remonstrance.

The grey was failing; she tripped, and almost fell several

times in descending the hill to Bridestowe. He drew rein at the inn, and called, 'Hostler! here, I say!'

'All right, sir.'

'Have you a spare horse? I must ride on at once.'

'There've a been a gent here already inquiring,' said Daniel. 'Be you come from the same quarter?'

'I want a horse at once. I have no time for answering questions.'

'Because, if you be,' continued Daniel, composedly, 'there be no 'urry. The gent, that be young Mr. Tramplara, have a gone ahead already with the news. He says he must tell his father at once, and they'll be back early to-morrow morning.'

'Have you a horse, or not?'

'He sed, afore daybreak. Them was his very words.'

Herring was out of his saddle. 'The grey cannot go on. You must let me have a horse.'

'This grey ain't got the go in her like the bay Maister Tramplara rode. How old be her?'

'Never mind the age.' He drew the fellow's hand away as he was turning up the lips to examine the teeth. 'Is there a horse available?'

'There be one, sure,' answered Daniel; 'I offered her to the young Maister Tramplara, but he wouldn't have her. Her's not so bad to go, but the looks of her ain't nothing to boast of.'

'Off with the saddle and bridle, and bring her round.'

The hostler, a little man, with his toes turned in, very broad in body but short in stature, scuffled into the stable, and was a long time before he reappeared. Herring was impatient. He took a glass of cyder at the bar, and then went to the stable and met the little man coming out.

'There be summat the matter wi' the oss,' he said. 'Her's lame. Bide a wink, and I'll fetch a lantern.'

After having found a lantern, adjusted a tallow candle in the socket, and lighted it, Daniel went with Herring into the stable. The horse that was so good to go could not go a step. She was dead lame.

'Here,' said Herring; 'hold the light. Take the candle out of the lantern, and I'll turn up her hoofs. There it is!'

A knife-blade had been driven into the frog of the off front hoof, and snapped short in it.

'Is the Squire home at Lea Wood?' asked Herring. He set his teeth, and his brow contracted; his blood was up.

'I reckon he be, unless he be away,' answered Daniel.

Herring ran to his grey, re-saddled her, and rode out of the village to the house, situated a mile outside. He rang the bell, and asked to be allowed to see Mr. Hamlyn for a moment, and the Squire came to him in the hall. Herring told his story—that he was in pursuit of a man, with a warrant for his apprehension in his pocket. He drew it forth. He related how the horse had been wilfully lamed at the post-house to arrest him, and he begged to be allowed the use of one of the Squire's horses. His request was at once and readily granted. In a quarter of an hour he was well-mounted on a fine horse—Squire Hamlyn was noted for his good horses—a horse perfectly fresh, and was in full and fast pursuit. 'If I do not catch you now,' said Herring, laughing bitterly, 'it will not be my fault.'

But much time had been lost. It was already dusk. In another half-hour it would be dark. The heavy clouds that had rolled in broken masses through the sky all day had spread out over the entire surface, and obscured all light from the stars. Only to the west the declining day looked wanly over the ragged fringe of Cornish moorland heights. The road was no longer over open down, but ran between hedges, with trees on both sides. It lay in valleys with high hills well wooded folding round; the hills cut off the light, the dark foliage absorbed it. Sampson Tramplara was pushing on as well as he could, but his bay was feeling the length of the journey and the pace.

'Get out of the road, confound you!' shouted Sampson, as a dark figure was overtaken and made his horse swerve. 'What the devil do you mean by not standing aside?' Sampson had a hunting whip, his hand through the loop. He lashed at the foot-traveller, as he trotted by, with an oath. It was too dark for him to discern a face, but he saw that the person was a woman. It did not matter, the lash had curled round her. She must learn a lesson—so hard to teach women and pigs—that when a rider is in the road she must get on one side. He could not have hurt her, as she uttered no cry. Sampson was without spurs, but he dug his heels into the flanks of his bay and urged him on to a canter. Then he heard distinctly the clatter of horse-hoofs coming along the road at a good pace—at a gallop. Herring had got a fresh mount, and would be up with him in ten minutes. His bay could not get on faster—that was impossible. What was to be done?'

Sampson looked back along the road. He could no longer see the foot-passenger. She had doubtless gone down a side lane. There was light enough for him to see that the road was clear. He had come to a place where heavy oak woods closed in on the highway, and the trees overarched making it doubly obscure. If Herring was to be stayed, this was the place, now was the time; in another ten minutes it would be too late. Further on the road would be lighter and less solitary.

Quick as thought, Tramplara dismounted and led his horse along the road to a gate. He unfastened the gate, and took the bay through into the wood, where he tied him up behind the hedge. Then he unhinged the gate—it was a large five-barred gate—and with some little effort carried it into the road, and threw it down across it.

He looked at his legs; he wore light tight breeches—they would be seen if he stood aside in the hedge, waiting the result. So he went through the gateway and leaned his back against the post, standing inside with his arms folded. If there had been sufficient light, and anyone had been there to note his face, an ugly smile would have been seen covering it. 'By God,' he muttered, 'he escaped me once to-day: this time he shall not escape.'

He heard the tramp of the horse approach nearer; it was descending a hill, and muffled, then ascending the next. Herring's voice was audible, cheering on his horse. Not another sound but the rush of the Lew Water, a petty river, swirling over its stony bed, and breaking against snags of timber that had fallen from the banks.

Yes! a night-jar in the wood screeched; then was silent, then screeched again intermittently, as though signalling danger.

Late in the year though it was, close to Sampson, was a glow-worm. The light annoyed him. He could distinguish by it the crane's-bill leaf on which the insect sat. He put up his foot and broke down the earth, and then stamped it and the luminous little creature together. Through the interstices of the clouds one star was visible. He would have torn it out of the sky and stamped it to darkness in the mire, if he could have reached it.

Louder, more distinctly, came the clatter of hoofs. The road was level, and the pace of the horse accelerated. 'On, old fellow, we shall soon be up with him!'

Sampson heard Herring's voice almost in his ear. His heart gave a bound, and then—a cry, a crash, and, for a moment, silence.

'The gate has done it,' said Sampson Tramplara, stepping lightly into the road.

He was right; the gate had done it. The horse had been spurred on to a good speed, and neither he nor his rider had noticed the obstruction till the poor brute's legs were between the rails, and he was down and floundering. Herring was flung, and lay his length on the road. Sampson went up to him; he was unconscious. Then Sampson turned his attention to the horse.

'Where did Herring get this brute?' he asked. 'He'll do for me, if he has not hurt himself. Come up, old fellow, don't lie and go to sleep there.'

He took the reins, and brought the horse up on his haunches, but the poor animal was unable to stand. He had broken or severely injured one foot.

'No good to me,' said Sampson; 'lie as you are. I must force my bay to go on.'

He went back to Herring, and stood over him, a foot on each side. Then he drew the pistol out of his pocket.

'This time you shall not escape me,' he said with an oath; 'I'll take precious good care of that.' And he put the muzzle of his weapon to the ear of the unconscious man. 'Ah! you're deaf enough now, but I'll bark into your ear such a bark as will make you jump into eternity. I reckon I have done for one man to-day, and if I have to run at all, I may as well run for two as for one.'

He drew the trigger, but no report followed.

'Curse it!' he said, and flung the weapon on the road; 'I forgot I had already fired it off, and haven't had time to load again.' He paused, still astride over Herring. 'It is just as well,' he said; 'I can beat your brains out as well as blow them out, and then no one will know but what you smashed your skull in your fall. Where's that pistol?'

He turned to look for it where he had thrown it. It was too dark for him to see, so he groped in the road till he found it.

Then he came back to Herring, lying unconscious and without motion.

'I wonder is he dead already?' he said, and felt him, and put his hand to his heart.

'He's alive for the moment,' muttered Sampson, 'but not enjoying life now, nor like to have another and a sweeter taste of it. So, my boy—one for Ophir—one for me—and one for Mirelle! You threatened to break a ruler across my head, did you? I'll break something a deal harder over yours, or batter yours in.' He drew a long breath and raised his hand, holding the pistol by the muzzle. 'Ready,' he shouted; 'here goes!— one for——'

A scream of fury and fear combined, the scream of a beast rather than of a human being, and, in a moment, some one was on him, grasping his arm, and wrapping him round in rags rank with peat smoke. He could hardly make out who or what had grappled with him. He tried to disengage himself, but the hands, with long nails like claws, tore at him, and the rags entangled his arms, and the hoarse, discordant shrieks in his ear deafened, bewildered him.

Had a scarecrow assumed life, or leaped on him him from a field, to arrest his murderous hand, or had some spectre of the wood, some dead creature, risen out of the leaf-mould that had covered it to attack him? For a moment fear curdled his heart's blood and paralysed his arm: and the creature, whatever it was, took advantage of the moment to wrench the whip out of his hand.

'I'll kill you! I'll rip your heart and liver out wi' my nails. I'll bite my way through to 'em——'

Then Sampson recovered himself. He knew with whom he had to do.

'Keep off, Joyce, you fool!' he shouted, and thrust her from him with a blow. But like a tiger she leaped at him again, and bit at his hand and screamed. In her mad fury she could scarce form and utter words. Sampson Tramplara backed to the gate, defending himself with his pistol. He struck her repeatedly, but she felt nothing. If he had cut her with a knife she would not have known it, dominated as she was by her fury.

'You fool, Joyce, let me alone, or I will kill you!'

'You've killed the maister, you've killed 'n. I'll tear you to bits, I will.'

'Stand back! look to your master. If you want him to live, you must mind him at once.'

That answered; that alone could have answered.

She drew back.

'I'll see,' she said; 'if you've killed 'n, you'll niver escape me. I'll hunt you over airth and under water; I'll go after'y through the very fire. You'll not escape me. I'll see if he be alive or dead, but happen what may,' she said, and raised his whip over her head, 'you shall take that for a first taste.' Then she brought the lash down with all the weight of her arm, and the force her fury lent her, across his face. The lash cut it, and he staggered back and put his hands over his eyes, and cried out with pain. Then she stepped back to where Herring lay in the road. Young Tramplara stood for a moment, blinded with the blow and convulsed with rage. His first impulse was to rush after her and beat her down and stamp the life out of her. But prudence prevailed; he took the opportunity to unhitch his horse, mount, and ride away.

Joyce flung herself in the road beside Herring. All the rage and roughness went out of her instantly. She felt him, to find if his bones were broken. Then she drew him up and laid his head in her bosom, and listened for his breath.

'My maister! my dear, dear maister!' she cried, between fear and tears. 'My darling, my darling maister! speak now, speak, do'y?'

She rocked herself from side to side, moaning, swaying his head in her arms.

'Oh, maister, maister! what can I do?' She put her mouth to his, and breathed into his lungs the contents of her own. 'I'll give'y all the life that be in me, and welcome, if only I can make thee open your eyes again. You must not die. Speak, and let me know that you hear me: It be Joyce, your own poor Joyce, that has'y, and is a rocking of'y, and calling of'y to wake up. Maister, darling maister, do'y hear me? None shall touch you but me. I'll die afore I lets another near'y.' Then her tears broke forth; she felt her utter helplessness. 'They'll be coming for to take'y away, but they shall not do it.' She laid him back in the road, then stood up, removed the gate, and put it in its place; and then lifting Herring, she partly carried, partly drew him away, through the gate-opening into the wood; there she could hide both him and herself.

She took him again in her arms, swayed herself to and fro, moaning and then breaking into snatches of song. In the wood she resolved she would remain; no one should take him from her. If he were dead, there he should lie, dead, in her arms, on her lap, and she would sit over him watching and waiting patiently till she died also, and the leaves came down—copper-gold off the beech, and russet-brown off the oak—and buried them together.

But no! no!—he must not die! What could she do for him? He had known exactly what was right to do for her when 'she were all a broked in pieces.' He had known how

P

to mend her, so that now she was well and strong again. But then he was a 'skollard,' and she—she was but a poor ignorant savage. What should she do? Go to a cottage and ask that he might be taken in there? Her heart shrank from this. She could not breathe in a house. There, others would surround him, and she would be thrust out. No! she would nurse him there, under the sky and the green trees, where the wind blew, and the grass sprang up, and the birds sang. All at once a thought struck her. In her sense of loneliness, helplessness, misery, an unutterable yearning came over her for some help that she could not define, not even understand. It was a vague effort of the poor dumb soul within to articulate a cry for help to—she knew not whom. She threw herself on her knees beside the body, and stretched her arms from which depended the wretched rags torn to shreds, upwards towards the sky, and raised her face, quivering with agony, and cried hoarsely, again and again—'Our Vaither—kinkum-kum—kinkum-kum! Glory rallaluley!'

The star that Sampson Tramplara had seen and would have stamped out was shining aloft, and it smote through the leafy vault over her head, and sparkled in the tears that streamed over her cheeks.

So, throughout the night, she rocked her burden, and moaned, and pressed it to her bosom, and then knelt and wept, and cried—'Kinkum-kum! Kinkum-kum!'

CHAPTER XXX.

BETWEEN CUP AND LIP.

THAT same evening which had seen Herring flung senseless in the road was to decide the fate of Orange Tramplara. She was to be married that evening to Captain Trecarrel in the little chapel at his place. A dispensation had been obtained from the bishop (*in partibus*) to allow of the celebration out of canonical hours. The reason for this was that a priest was on his way to Plymouth from Camelford, and would arrive only in the afternoon—indeed, somewhat into the evening—by coach, and he would have to proceed very early next morning on his way to Plymouth. Consequently, the only manner in which it was convenient for the pair to receive the nuptial benediction from a Catholic priest was for the function to take place in the chapel at Trecarrel that evening somewhat late. On the morrow the Protestant ceremony was to be performed in Launceston parish church, followed by the wedding breakfast. Thus it happened that, about the time the accident—if accident it may be called—happened to John Herring, as related in the last chapter, Orange was dressing for the marriage ceremony that was to take place in the Catholic chapel at Trecarrel, and Mirelle was assisting her, at Orange's special request.

Mirelle was not to be a bridesmaid. Orange had asked her to be one; she could not well have failed to do so; but Mirelle had declined, and the request had not been urged. Mirelle was glad to escape thus. She would have to be present during the ceremony at Trecarrel, but she would kneel in some shady corner, where her face could not be seen and her tears noticed. Mirelle had passed a trying time. A weight lay on her heart which she was unable to shake off. Even Mrs. Trampleasure had observed the change in her appearance: the sunken eyes, and the transparency of her cheek; but Mirelle had explained this by the climate, which affected her. She had been accustomed to sun. Cloud and rain depressed her, and affected both her health and her spirits. Orange was elated; victory was all but achieved. In a few hours she would be Mrs. Trecarrel of Trecarrel, and be translated to another sphere from that in which circled her father and mother, Miss Bowdler, and the Reverend Flamank. Bah! her bridesmaids expected to be made much of after she was lady of Trecarrel, to be invited to her dances, to meet county people at her receptions, to be still 'Dear Jane,' and 'Darling Sophy,' and 'My sweet Rose.' They were very much mistaken. Once she had risen to her new perch she would peck at every presumptuous fowl that aspired to sit beside her.

'Mrs. Trecarrel of Trecarrel!' repeated Orange, as she surveyed herself in the glass. She would become her station, with her proud, handsome face and erect bearing. She had the figure and the dignity of a duchess. At least she supposed she had. That she was a fine woman could not be disputed, with a swelling bust, large and luscious eyes, a bright colour, ripe and sensuous lips, and magnificent dark, glossy, and abundant hair. A slight down, not enough to disfigure, showed on her upper lip—the badge of a warm and passionate nature.

'Father will be too much engaged to worry me,' she thought 'and mother's cold will keep her from wetting her feet at Tre carrel. That is a comfort. As for Sampson, he shall not cross my threshold, unless I invite him to shoot rabbits when I am sure no gentleman will be present.'

Mirelle was engaged on the rich but coarse hair of Orange. The delicate white fingers trembled, and were less skilful than usual.

'Really, Mirelle, you are clumsy this evening,' said Orange; 'you pull my hair and hurt me.' She looked before her into the glass.

'Are you crying, child?'

'No, Orange.'

'I thought I saw something glistening in your eye.'

Mirelle had the strength to repress her tears. She devoted her whole attention to that on which she was engaged.

'You will come occasionally and see me,' said Orange. 'I shall be so pleased to show you all I am doing; and I am certain the Captain will be delighted. Now, don't run the hairpins into my head! I tell you, you hurt me. Really, Mirelle, you are very clumsy. What ails you this evening?'

Mirelle made no reply.

'Try on the orange-wreath and the veil, child,' said Miss Trampleasure.

Mirelle took up the wreath and adjusted it.

'The Captain has always been partial towards you,' continued Orange. She was aware that what she said gave pain, but then, what triumph is complete without the infliction of wounds and agonies?

'Do you not think Harry is a handsome man? I do not believe I have ever seen, even in a woman, such beautiful and expressive eyes. There, Mirelle, is a pin with a large Cornish crystal in the head; put it in my hair and fasten my wreath with it.'

Mirelle did not, could not, speak. It was as much as she could do to maintain the mastery over her feelings.

'Do you know, you palefaced witch, I was at one time almost jealous of you. I thought the Captain was attentive to you—more attentive than he ought to be, and that you were trying to draw him away from me. Of course that was natural. Every girl begrudges another her lover, and would rob her of him if she could. It is a natural instinct. But Harry never really cared for you; he told me so; he was only playing—— Good heavens, Mirelle!' Orange sprang up, and the tears, tears of pain, started into her eyes. In a moment, in a flash of passion, she struck Mirelle on the cheek with her open hand.

'Do you know what you have done? You have run the pin into my head. Look—look!' She snatched off her veil. 'How can I wear this? There is a spot of blood on it.'

Then Mirelle burst into tears. She had an excuse for them —she had been struck.

'I am sorry,' said Orange; 'but really you hurt me. Look at the blood, and convince yourself. I did not mean to strike you; but the pain was sharp, and I forgot myself. Do control yourself. Hark! I hear horses' feet. The carriage will be here directly, and we shall start for Trecarrel. Dry your eyes and control your feelings. You must not let people see that you have been crying, or they will say '—her malice gained the mastery once more—'that you loved the Captain, and were envious of me.'

Mirelle covered her face.

'Of course,' said Orange, looking hard at her, with her red lips twitching, 'there is not a shadow of truth in this; still, tongues are sharp and venomous, and such things will be said if you give occasion for them.'

Mirelle stood up, proud, cold, and impassive. In a moment she had conquered her feelings. Her pride was touched, and that recovered her.

'No one shall dare to say such things of me,' she answered. 'Sit down, and I will finish your toilette.'

The hoofs on the gravel that Orange had heard were those of Sampson's bay, now utterly tired out, and scarce able to carry his master up the steep ascent from the valley of the Tamar.

He sprang out of his saddle, and burst into the hall as his mother descended the stairs in a stiff myrtle green satin dress, with a cap on her head adorned with rose-coloured bows.

'Where is my father?' asked Sampson, abruptly.

'He is dressed, Sampy darling, and in the parlour. I'm going in there too. We expect the carriage shortly. The bridesmaids will be picked up at their own doors, but our carriage is coming here.'

He did not wait to hear her, but rushed into the drawing-room.

'By Grogs! Sampy,' exclaimed Mr. Trampleasure, 'what brings you here? I thought you were to remain in charge at Ophir, and give us your visits, as the wisest of men said, like angel visits, few and far between. I want you there, and not here, boy.'

'Father, I must speak with you instantly, and alone,' he added, as he saw his mother come rustling and sniffing in at the door. 'Let us go into the office.'

'Nothing wrong with Ophir, lad, eh?' asked the old man, his colour changing.

'Everything,' answered Sampson. 'For heaven's sake lead on. Not a moment is to be lost.'

Mr. Trampleasure was arrayed in evening dress, with a very white tight neckcloth, and very stiff projecting frills to his shirt. He was in a fine black cloth dress coat. His hair was as white as his frills. He took up a plated branch candlestick, and led the way. His hand shook.

'Take care, Tram, darling,' said Mrs. Trampleasure, 'you be a joggling of the wax all over the carpet, and it do take a time getting of it out with a hiron and blotting paper.'

He opened the door of the office and went in. He had been working, and smoking, and drinking there that afternoon; there was a fire burning red on the hearth. The room reeked with rum and tobacco.

The old man put the candle down, and then stayed himself with one hand on the table. 'By Grogs!' he said, 'you've given me a turn, Sampy. What do you mean by saying that everything is wrong with Ophir?'

'I mean what I say,' answered the young man. 'Ophir is smashed up. That cursed fool Herring has found all out. Flamank knows also. They saw me salting the stream.'

The old man's face turned purple.

'That's not the worst—there's worse behind,' continued young Sampson. He hesitated a moment, and looked at his father. Mr. Trampleasure was feeling about him with the disengaged hand for his arm-chair. He gripped the table with the left. He tried to speak; he opened his mouth and shut it again. It was horrible to see him, like a fish, gasping, and nothing proceeding from his lips. 'It must come out. But first; father—we shall have to run for it. I especially. Where is the money?'

The old man pointed with a faltering hand in the direction of a strong box, let into the wall. Then he put his hand in his pocket and pulled out a bunch of keys. He tried to indicate a single key, but could not take his other hand from the table. The bunch fell on the floor.

All right, governor,' said Sampson. 'Now I will tell you the worst, and a cursed ugly worst it is. You may as well hear it from me as from another. I must be off to-night—at once; you suit your convenience. Do as you like. You have nothing to fear but the stone jug; I the wooden horse. I have shot one man dead to-day, the constable, and broken the neck of another, John Herring, so the two can keep each other company; and I must make off.'

Then old Trampleasure dropped like a stone on the floor. There came a sudden blow within his head, as from a hammer, and he saw nothing more.

Sampson stood over him for a moment. No time was to be lost. Every minute was important. Whatever happened to his father, he—Sampson—must get clear away. He saw in a moment what had occurred; his father had been struck down with an apoplectic fit, and could not escape. Time was too precious to be wasted in attending to him. He could not afford to call for assistance. He stooped and took up the bunch of keys, and went to the strong box. Without much difficulty he unlocked it, and fell to wondering over his father's wisdom.

Old Trampleasure had feared discovery, and was prepared for a sudden emergency. All the money that had come into his hands had been reduced to the most portable form possible, in hundred-pound, fifty-pound, and ten-pound notes. There they lay in thick packets: Sampson took them all. He left not one behind, and stowed them away in a travelling valise of his father's, which the old man took with him when he went to Ophir for a few days.

Then Sampson opened the private door of the office, and, without another look at the old man lying prostrate, darted forth.

'What a time them two are in there together!' grumbled Mrs. Trampleasure; 'and, oh dear! there comes the chaise to take us to Trecarrel.' She ran to the foot of the stairs, and called, 'Orange dear! Orange! the carriage be here!'

'I am ready, mother,' answered the bride, descending.

The hall was well lighted; and as she came down, followed by Mirelle, she looked radiant, proud, triumphant. She waved back Mirelle, lest she should step on her veil, with an angry, insolent gesture.

'My word, Orange; you are a beauty! I'll run and call your father.'

But he was beyond call.

CHAPTER XXXI.

JOYCE'S PATIENT.

Joyce and her patient could not remain concealed. Her cries had been heard when she fell—literally tooth and nail—on Sampson Tramplara, and those who heard them, being superstitious, thought best to keep away from the spot whence they had sounded.

Later in the evening the farmer of Coombow, coming home from a cattle fair, heard the moans and wailing in the wood, and was greatly scared by the injured horse, which had thrust itself into the hedge. So sincerely alarmed was he, and so thoroughly did his account of what he had heard and seen frighten his household, that not one of his sons—no, not all of them in phalanx, armed with pitchforks and lighted by lanthorns, would venture that night into the high road to ascertain the cause of the alarm.

With morning, however, courage came, and early, when the day began to break, nearly the entire househo'd, male and female, went out to see whether there was any natural explanation to be found for those things that had, in the darkness, so scared Farmer Facey.

The horse was found.

'Why, I'm blessed if this bain't Squire Hamlyn's roan!' said the farmer. 'I ought to know 'n, becos I reared 'n. Now this be reg'lar curious.'

Joyce had been unable to retire with her burden far into the wood. The hillside was steep, and she could not carry the unconscious load far up. She had attempted to do so, fearing lest she should be seen, but when she raised him he moaned with pain. She was like a cat playing with a dead bird, putting it down, then lifting it and carrying it away, then putting it down again.

It was not long before she was discovered and surrounded.

'Who is he? How comes he here? How did this happen? Why didn't you bring him to the farm?'

Questions were poured upon her. She looked about her angrily, suspiciously, as a cat would look when surrounded with those who, she thinks, will deprive her of her bird, or at least dispute her sole possession of it.

'He be mine. I found 'n; I saved 'n. Capt'n Sampson Tramplara would ha' killed 'n, but I prevented 'n.'

'But who is he?'

'He be the maister. He mended me when I were gone scatt. Nobody shan't so much as touch 'n. I've got 'n fast, and I'll care for 'n, that I will! There, you can go, and leave us alone here. What be you a bothering here for? I didn't call'y.'

'Nonsense! He must be taken into a house and put to bed,' said Mrs. Facey. 'Poor soul! Dear alive!'

'He shan't go under no house. If he goes anywhere, he shall go home.'

'Where is his home?'

'Where should it be but West Wyke?'

'What! West Wyke in South Tawton?'

'Sure-ly. Where else should it be. It don't jump about, now here, now there, I reckon.'

After much difficulty with Joyce, who was unreasonable in her jealousy and suspicion, it was decided that the farmer should send a waggon well bedded with straw, and that Joyce should be conveyed in this, with the still insensible man in her arms, to West Wyke.

There was no medical man nearer than Okehampton, and West Wyke was not as distant from Okehampton as Coombow, the place where they were.

'I arn't got no money,' said Joyce, 'but I'll pay you for the waggon, sure enough.'

'I do not expect payment,' said Farmer Facey, in a mildly deprecatory tone—a tone that implied he would yield the point if pressed. 'I dare say the gentleman, when he gets well, will remember me And if he don't, well—he'll be sure to have relations as will do what be proper and respectable.'

'It be I,' said Joyce, defiantly, 'it be I as has to pay, and blast me blue if I don't!'

'Where will the money come from?' asked Facey, surveying her rags.

'I'll pay wi' thicky arms,' said Joyce, thrusting forth her hands. 'See! is there a man among you can work as I can? When the young maister be well, then, sure, I'li come and work for'y two months by the moon, I will, for the loan of the waggon to-day; and I'll ax for no meat nor no housing. I'll feed myself, and I'll sleep where I can, in the open air.'

'Her must be one of the Nymet savages, sure-ly,' said the farmer, in an undertone, to his wife.

Joyce's ears were keen, and she heard him.

'What if I be a savage?' she asked. 'I bain't like mun [them] to Nymet. Them be proper savages. Vaither be a head above they. He hev a got what he may call his own.'

The waggon was brought to the place, and two men lifted Herring into it. Joyce climbed in, and, after having seated herself in the straw, took him again in her arms.

'If the cart go over rough stones, it shall joggle me,' she said; 'I'll hold'y, maister dear, that you shan't feel it.'

'I say, maiden,' said Farmer Facey, looking over the rail of the waggon as they were about to start, 'when the young gentleman gets better, just tell him he was took home in Farmer Facey's waggon, with his team and horseman, Farmer Facey, to Coombow. He might like to know, you see, and, being a gentleman, as I take it, he won't forget.'

Just as the cart was off, he called to the driver, 'Stay a bit, Jim! I think I'll take a lift, too, as far as to Bridestowe, and I'll just up and see the Squire. I'll tell him what has happened to poor Major; and, as it chances, I've another horse out of the same mare I can sell 'n—a tidy sort of a dark roan, you minds 'n, Jim. Mebbe we'll strike a bargain. I'll go wi' you now on the chance.'

At Bridestowe the waggon came to a long halt. Farmer Facey descended; the driver was thirsty. He had much to tell. A crowd gathered round the cart. Daniel, the hostler, climbed up the wheel to look into the face of Herring, and would have mounted the waggon, had not Joyce beat him off with Sampson's whip.

'Sure it be he, poor young man,' said Daniel. 'I know by token he forgot to chuck me a sixpence last night. 'Tis he as went after the Squire's horse. How came this about? Do'y say as Major hev a foreleg broke? Well, now, Loramussy! how can that have happened? The young gent may come round right enough, but the oss—he must be shot. 'Tis a thousand pities.'

'There be nothing happens but what be good for trade,' observed Farmer Facey.

'You're right there, maister!' answered Daniel. 'There's not a sparrer falls, nor an oss breaks his knees, nor gets spavined, but what it be good for them as is vetinaries, or has osses to sell. And it be the same wi' 'uman beings; them goes scatt at times, and it be for the good o' the doctors. So the Lord sends to every man his meat.'

'But how did it come about?' This was a question asked of Joyce repeatedly. But Joyce was uncommunicative. She kept her eyes fixed on the face of the injured man, and only now and then turned them with a sharp, defiant glance at anyone who approached too near.

The hostess kindly brought her a hunch of bread. She tore and ate it much as an animal devours its food. She returned no thanks for it. She could think of nothing but him whom she held to her bosom, watching every change in his face, or fearing lest he should die in her arms.

The journey was long, but Joyce did not relax her hold nor relinquish her place for one moment.

'Won't'y get down and hev a drop o' cyder?' asked the driver, at every public house they passed. 'It be a faint day for the horses, and they need refreshing.'

Joyce shook her head in reply. But if Joyce would not assist in cooling the horses by drinking herself, the driver was more considerate.

Between each of these refreshment stations, the man endeavoured to open conversation with her. He was a young fellow, fresh in colour, and not bad looking. He had a sufficiently observant eye to see that Joyce was a fine girl, though a very rough one. But she would not answer him; she did not even look at him, unless he ventured too near her charge.

She was patient at the stoppages, which were many. They rested Herring. She saw in his face that he suffered with the motion and was easy when the motion ceased. That sufficed her.

In the midst of Sourton Down stands a very humble tavern, backed by a few stunted trees, twisted and turning from the west; and by the roadside is to be seen a tall granite cross, once a burial monument of a British chief, and bearing an inscription that was cut into and rendered illegible in mediæval times, when the upright stone was converted into a wayside cross.

As the waggon halted before this little tavern, Joyce saw Herring's eyes open. He raised his arms and waved them in an unmeaning manner; then, looking intently upwards, as though he saw something far above him in the depths of the blue sky, he drew a deep sigh and murmured, 'Mirelle!'

Then his eyes closed again, and his hands dropped.

'Right, right, maister!' said Joyce; 'it be the Whiteface

you want and would seek. But why do'y look up there? Her be on earth, not in heaven. I be a nursing of'y, none for Joyce, nor for Miss Cicely, but for her you cries after and looks for up above.'

At Okehampton they met with no interruption, and were surrounded by no throng of inquisitive persons, and the reason was this. The parson of a neighbouring moorland parish had been summoned that day before the magistrates, on a charge of maltreating and starving a poor boy in his house, his wife's son by a former husband. The magistrates dismissed him with a reprimand and a caution; but the people were not disposed to treat the matter so lightly and the man so leniently. All the fluid portion of the populace had flowed out on the moor road after the retiring parson, with hoots, and clots of earth, and expressions of aversion. The rabble manifested an intimate acquaintance with his domestic arrangements, and taunted him with them. If the reverend gentleman could have commanded his temper, he might have speedily tired out his pursuers; but this he was unab e to do, and unwise enough not to attempt. He was a remarkably ugly man, ill-made, short in leg and long in arm, with large hands and feet, and a face with low brow and protruding jaws. He became mad with rage and humiliation, and turned savagely, whenever the crowd ventured near his heels, to charge them with his green gingham umbrella, and smite them furiously, uttering unclerical exclamations of abuse and contempt. His face was simian in its ugliness and malignity. The whalebones of his umbrella were dislocated, and the wires protruded. One boy was cut with the iron, and when this was perceived there rose a howl of indignation, and a moorstone whizzed through the air and knocked the parson's hat off his head. He was a poor man, and the injury done to his best hat and to his umbrella was more than he could endure. He ran as fast as his short legs could fly over the ground, and took refuge in a cottage, the door of which he barred; and then, escaping up the rude stair, he spat at his pursuers from the window.

Parson-baiting is not an every-day treat, and the luxury had emptied the streets of Okehampton. Consequently the waggon passed through almost unnoticed.

As the waggon crossed the bridge over the Taw, it encountered the two chaises with the party of serious speculators returning from Ophir. They had slept at Zeal. Mr. Flamank, as a director of the mine, had felt it incumbent on him to make a complete investigation into the method of working, and into the accounts. The men engaged on the mine had been examined by him, and he had overhauled the books in the office. Among these he had discovered a private book of the Tramplaras, which contained a register of the amount of gold expended in the salting, and the amount recovered after the washing. Those serious men whom the Reverend Israel had taken with him, in the hopes of inducing them to sink capital in Ophir, assisted him zealously in the detection of the imposture.

The transaction was humiliating to the little man, but he was a thoroughly conscientious person, and he did not shrink from that which he felt it was at once his duty and his interest to do, however galling it might be to his self-esteem. He carried away the books with him, and dismissed the workmen, warning them that they would be required to give evidence in the trial of the Tramplaras, which, as he supposed, would inevitably follow.

'I have been considering,' said Israel Flamank to those with him in the same carriage, 'that I have been very blind. Last night I was unable to sleep, and so I turned prophecy over in my head, and I saw clearly, at last, that the whole affair had been foretold. The name Trampleasure, if rightly estimated—that is, with a certain value given to each letter, and the capital letter *T* being reckoned as double a small *t*, and the *e a* in pleasure being turned into *i*, Tramplisure instead of Trampleasure, which is the way in which some persons would pronounce the name, and the *e* at the end of the name omitted as a mute—I say, thus valued, the name makes, when summed up, exactly six hundred and sixty-six, which is the number of the Beast, and which is also, we are distinctly told, the number of a man's name. Now this, I take it, is a very significant fact. The Beast, we are further informed, would deceive the very elect; and what else are we, I ask, but the very elect?'

'That is true,' responded all those in the chaise, and shook their heads affirmatively.

'And he spake great swelling words,' went on the Reverend Israel. 'Now old Mr. Trampleasure had a certain pomposity of manner about him that exactly tallies with the description given by the inspired penman.'

'Very true,' answered the carriage-load, and the heads all shook together again.

'It is remarkable also,' continued the minister, 'that in the sacred text the Beast Trampleasure is associated with the Woman, Babylon—that is, with Rome. For Babylon is Rome, as every schoolboy knows, ethnographically, entomologically, and enterically. Now, I ask you, is not a young Roman Catholic lady staying in Dolbeare with the family, and is not Miss Trampleasure about to be, or already, married to a Roman Catholic gentleman?'

'To be sure,' responded those in the chaise, and shook their heads knowingly.

'And, remember, the seer of Patmos saw two Beasts, and the little one derived his power from the elder, which was wounded, though not to death. That wound I take to be the failure of Polpluggan, from which old Trampleasure recovered. As to the little Beast, there can be no question about him—Sampson Trampleasure, junior.'

'That is certain!' exclaimed the chorus, and all the heads shook to the left.

'But, good heavens, what have we here!' cried Mr. Flamank.

The carriage stopped.

'What's the matter there?' inquired the driver of the chaise, as he drew up.

'Why, bless me!' said the minister, starting to his feet. 'As sure as I am alive that is Mr. John Herring. Stay, young man,' he called to the waggoner. 'How comes the gentleman in such a plight? Girl,' to Joyce, 'where did you find him? Is he alive? Is he badly hurt? How came this about?'

The little man jumped out of the carriage in a fever of excitement, and pity, and alarm. Joyce gave him no information, but he picked up something from the boy who drove, and learned that, in some way or other, Sampson Tramplara was involved.

'Bless my soul!' exclaimed Mr. Flamank. 'One cannot be too thankful for mercies. Actually John Herring made me —me run after this cut-throat murderer—and yet I remain unhurt; whereas John Herring, who takes up the chase, is killed. A really startling interposition of Providence.'

'He be not dead,' said Joyce, fiercely; 'I shan't let 'n die, I shan't.'

Then the waggon moved on.

'Where be West Wyke to?' asked the driver.

'I'll tell'y where to stop,' answered Joyce. 'Go right on till I shout Wo!'

She allowed him to proceed past the turning over the turf

leading to West Wyke, and then she suddenly gave the signal to halt.

'The road over the moor be too bad to travel wi' wheels,' said Joyce. 'You bide here, and I will fetch vaither, and he'll carry the maister home, along of I.'

Joyce was not long gone before she returned with old Cobbledick, carrying a hurdle. With the carter's help, Herring was lifted on to it; and then Joyce and her father departed over the moor, without another word to the man, conveying Herring between them.

'They be rum folk in these parts,' said Jim White, the waggoner, 'not to offer a fellow a glass of cyder, and the hosses all of a lather with the journey.'

CHAPTER XXXII.

DESTITUTE.

MR. TRAMPLEASURE'S death, through the bursting of a bloodvessel on the brain, and the escape of Sampson, left the three women at Dolbeare without a head. Captain Trecarrel did not appear, except to make a formal call of condolence, or to offer his services in a manner that implied that this offer was not to be accepted.

'Lucky dog that I am,' said he to himself; 'saved at the last moment in a manner melodramatic. There is a sweet little cherub that sits up aloft, and takes care of the fate of Trecarrel. By George! suppose I had been noosed and turned off before this terrible scandal came out, what should I have done? Now there lies before me one clear course of action. There is an opera company at this time performing in Exeter, and I am fond of music. I must positively go to the faithful city [1] by the next coach, and not return till the clouds have cleared somewhat. But before I go, there is one duty I must perform. I must let the directors of Ophir know of old Trampleasure's five thousand pounds lodged in the hands of John Herring.'

It is needless to say that the marriage had not taken place. It is needless also to say that Trecarrel did depart to Exeter to hear the opera company. It is also needless to say that he thoroughly enjoyed himself, liked the music, caught some of the airs, ate, drank, and smoked, and blessed his stars every day

[1] The motto of Exeter is 'Semper fidelis.'

that he was a free man. He not only blessed his luck, but he flattered himself that he had extricated himself by his own shrewdness. 'And now,' said he, 'here am I in Exeter, enjoying myself. Had I remained at Trecarrel, I must have gone to bed, and one may have too much even of a good thing.'

The affairs of the Ophir Gold Company were wound up. All the directors met, except Arundell Golitho, of Trevorgan, Esquire, who did not appear. But that was hardly wonderful, as no one knew who Arundell Golitho, Esq. was, and as the letter addressed to him, stating the circumstances of the company, the death of Mr. Trampleasure, and the disappearance of Mr. Sampson with the funds of the company, was returned unopened. The post-office was unable to discover Trevorgan. When the affairs were wound up, it was discovered that there were liabilities, but no assets except the five thousand pounds held by Mr. Herring. The shareholders had lost everything they had embarked in the concern, except what little would come to them out of the five thousand pounds after the liabilities had been discharged, and the lawyers had sweated the little sum to a cipher.

Then it was that the Reverend Ismel Flamank's character shone out. The man's vanity had received a crushing blow, he would never entirely recover from the ridicule that descended on him for his discovery of Ophir. He had lost his small capital sunk in the mine. He alone, however, had thought and compassion at this juncture for the orphan and the widow. He found that Orange and her mother were left absolutely destitute. The five thousand pounds known to be in Herring's hands would be absorbed and dissipated, and the furniture of Dolbeare sold. There was nothing, absolutely nothing, left, on which Mrs. Trampleasure and her daughter and Mirelle could live; for old Trampleasure had thrown Mirelle's money into the same venture, and it was gone past recovery.

Mr. Flamank exerted his powers of persuasion on the directors to induce them to propose to the shareholders a surrender of a small portion of the money that they were able to lay their hands on, for the maintenance of the widow and her daughter. But none are so remorseless as pious persons touched in pocket. He pleaded to deaf ears. The liabilities of the mine were considerable, and would eat into the little fund. The men's wages were in arrear. The builders had received only a trifle on account for the sheds they had erected. The company owed for the water-wheel, for the drum, for the stamping-mill, for the cradles, the buddles, and the whips and the whims. Nothing, in short, had been paid for. As for the receipts, they were nil, for nothing had been got out of Ophir but what had been put in. Old Tramplara, it was supposed, had sunk his own money in the concern, at least it appeared so; for he had drawn everything out of the bank, had sold all his investments except the Patagonians which were unsaleable. The gold employed in salting the mine had undoubtedly consumed a great deal, and what remained had gone, with the shareholders' money, into the pocket of Mr. Sampson. It was fortunate that only the first call had been made on the shareholders, and that few of the shares were fully paid up. Nevertheless the loss was considerable, so considerable as to sour the sincerest Christian among them, and make them indifferent to the woes of the arch scoundrel's widow and daughter.

When Mr. Flamank found that nothing was to be saved out of the wreck for the Trampleasures, he went about collecting contributions for them. But his credit was suffering eclipse, and exasperation against Tramplara too great for him to do much. He was unable to get together more than fifty pounds, given grudgingly, and not obtained without great personal effort and the endurance of many humiliations.

The five thousand pounds lodged with John Herring lay in the bank in his name. It was the only sum standing to his account. But when Herring was written to, no answer was returned. That was not greatly wondered at, for it was known that he had been found insensible on the road, and had been carried in the same condition to West Wyke.

The directors wrote him to the effect that the affairs of Mr. Trampleasure, deceased, were so involved in those of the Ophir Mining Company that it was necessary to settle both together. Mr. Trampleasure had died insolvent. His chief creditors were the directors of the company, and the administration of his effects had been granted to them. They were, therefore, empowered to call in all moneys due to the deceased, and, as such, they claimed the five thousand pounds which were to be repaid to Mr. Trampleasure in the event of the marriage of his daughter with Captain Trecarrel not taking place on a certain day. That marriage had not been solemnized at the time specified, nor was it probable that it would be within a reasonable period, therefore the money was due to them as a debt to the late Mr. Trampleasure.

The cheque did reach them after a time, written with a

shaking hand, and the money was drawn. Herring could not have refused it. With the cheque came a letter offering to purchase the entire plant of Ophir, wheel, and stampers, and crushers, everything in fact, at a moderate valuation. The offer was too good to be refused. The directors closed with it by return of post. There was, consequently, no sale by auction at Ophir, but everything in Dolbeare was condemned to go by the hammer, except the personal effects of Mrs. and Miss Trampleasure, and of Mirelle. The house was to be cleared of everything, except the clock on the stairs, the crayon portraits, and the walking-sticks. The ladies could not remain for the auction. They would have had no home to go to, had not the Reverend Israel Flamank intervened and opened his doors to them. He did this in a gush of benevolence, and, unhappily, without first consulting Mrs. Flamank, who, when told what he had done, went into 'tantrums,' and made the house so unpleasant for the Reverend Israel that he spent the rest of the day in making pastoral calls and eating pastoral meals with his sheep.

By evening Mrs. Flamank became calmer, and, when her husband returned late, was so far subdued that she yielded a reluctant consent to giving the Trampleasures shelter for a month.

'You know, Betsy Delilah, dear saint,' said Israel, 'if we do not take them in, the poor creatures will be turned into the street, and that your tender heart would be unable to bear, sweet angel!'

'I'm sure, Izzy, we have lost enough by the Trampleasures already. However, I will not say nay, because it will look well, and people will say we practise what we preach. Only —I warn you, Izzy!' she held up her finger; 'mind yourself.'

What Mrs. Betsy Delilah meant by this warning, he understood perfectly. With his many excellent qualities, Mr. Flamank had a weakness: he was given to caress his female devotees.

In the Established Church there are two schools differing in their tendencies. The tendency of the extreme of the High Church is towards plunging into pecuniary difficulties; the tendency of the extreme of the Low Church is towards lapses into amatory difficulties. If this be the case in the Established Church—if this be done in the green tree, what goes on in the dry?—in the nonconformist churches, where the ministers are not independent of their congregations—where the mercury of their salary rises and falls with their popularity. It is natural that in such circumstances there should be developed a tendency towards fawning on and fondling of pious ladies with money. A little coaxing retains a sheep that inclines to err into another fold. The pressing of the hand changes a shilling subscription into a guinea, and an arm round the waist elevates it to five pounds. When the habit has been acquired of showing these tendernesses to the well-to-do, old and ugly ladies, it sometimes extends also to those who are good-looking and young, and becomes at last wholly indiscriminate.

Now the Reverend Israel Flamank was a sincere and good man, and he drew the line, with singular moderation, at kisses. These were scriptural—the Apostle Paul had a fancy for them, and recommended them wholesale. But the arm round the waist he did not allow. He found no warranty for it in Holy Writ. But he would take a lady's hand in one of his, and stroke it with the other, and read and expound to her the Song of Solomon. There was no harm in that; and it was really remarkable how these innocent attentions told on his income and his acceptableness to his congregation.

Mrs. Flamank did not like these familiarities. Though she knew they were as harmless as the love-making of actors and actresses on the stage, and were inseparable from the position of a minister in an Unestablished Church, she objected to them. She was very determined, if she received Mrs. Trampleasure, Orange, and Mirelle into her house, she would permit none of these Pauline caressings under her eyes. But it is easier for a resolution to be taken than to enforce it. Mr. Flamank was very discreet for a week or ten days, but after that he began to soften towards the ladies. Mirelle kept him at a distance from the outset. He had been highly pleased at the prospect of getting a daughter of the Scarlet Woman into his house. He looked on her as an erring sheep, one who erred through ignorance; and he hoped to enlighten her, and lead her into the paths of truth. He was, however, somewhat puzzled how to set about it. Mirelle withdrew from family devotion, and declined to assist at his scriptural readings. She would not attend his chapel. She allowed him no opportunity of opening a conversation with her on religious topics. She was cold, reserved, and silent. Mrs. Flamank rather liked her: there was no fear of Israel patting her hand.

The pastor attempted to dazzle her with his evangelical talk, much in the same way that young Sampson had attempted to impress her with his brag of feats performed with dogs and horses. On one or two occasions he had the temerity to attack her, but he came off with falls which damped his ardour. Once, when he assailed her on the subject of belief, she cut him short with the observation, 'We do not speak the same language. When I say, I believe, I mean that I hold as certain, but I notice that you use the word differently, as synonymous with I suppose. We look at different objects and through different instruments; I through a telescope at constant verities, you through a kaleidoscope at vari-coloured and ever-varying opinions.'

With Orange it was not the same. She was in trouble. Mortified pride and wounded love brought frequent tears into her eyes. She looked very handsome in her mourning suit. What is the first duty of a pastor, but to comfort the sorrowful, to soothe the ruffled soul, to apply the balm of Gilead to open wounds? So Mr. Israel Flamank was assiduous in his comforting and soothing, and dabbing on of balm,—more assiduous than Betsy Delilah liked. Orange was coarse of grit, and did not object to the little attentions of the pastor which would have been insufferable to Mirelle. She accepted them with indifference; she was without religious instincts, and the words of the shepherd fell empty on her ear. But there was something flattering in his efforts to console her, and at the present time, when her pride was hurt, any flattery was pleasing. Captain Trecarrel was not there to staunch her tears, to cheer her and give her assurance of a future; anyone who could afford her some alleviation to her humiliation, and encourage her with a hope of better things, was acceptable, even though he were a dissenting minister.

Flamank was perfectly sincere. His heart was full of kindness and devoid of guile. He was troubled at her distress, and unhappy at his inability to help her. It was unfortunate that his mode of expressing these justifiable feelings did not meet with the approval of Betsy Delilah. They irritated her, and she determined to shake herself free of her guests at the first opportunity.

Captain Trecarrel had returned to the neighbourhood. Orange heard of it, and waited several days in expectation of a visit. But he neither called nor sent to inquire after her and her mother. She brooded over this neglect. Did he really mean to desert her? He could not behave so cruelly, so unworthily. Her hot blood raced through her veins. She resolved that she would go herself to Trecarrel. She would go alone; no one should know of the visit. She would speak to Harry face to face. When he had her before him, and saw her in her black, her face—her beautiful face, wet with tears, his love would blaze up, his manly pity and generosity would force him to assert his right to protect her.

He was staying away only because of the scandal about Ophir. He was waiting for that to blow away, and then he would return to her. She felt sure of that; she measured his love by her own. Would she have forsaken him had ruin overtaken him? A thousand times no—no—no! She must know his intentions for certain. Her future depended on knowing this. She was unable to endure the thought that she should be seen going to seek him, and therefore she resolved to go by herself after dark. She would not tell Mrs. or Mr. Flamank, nor her mother, nor, of course, Mirelle. The thing could be done with ease. The drawing-room had French windows, through which the little garden could be entered. The drawing-room was rarely sat in; it was used for company occasions. The family occupied the dining-room, in which they had their meals, and in which they worked and talked afterwards, amidst the fumes of meat, cabbage, and cheese. This was economical; it saved carpets and furniture, and an extra fire.

Orange waited till all had gone to bed. They were early risers, and retired early in that house. Then she softly descended the stairs, her shoes in her hand, and entered the drawing-room. She easily unclosed the shutters, without making any noise, unlocked and unbolted the French window, opened it, put on her shoes, and stepped forth on the gravel.

The street was deserted; only a low tavern at the end had the door open, and a light shone forth into the road. In that gleam, a young woman, adorned with gay ribands, was laughing and romping with two nearly tipsy young men. The language, the gestures, were gross and disgusting.

'Have another nip of gin, Polly.'

'No, you shan't have none of his, Polly; I'll give you some, my duck. You be my sweetheart, and not his.'

'Who goes there?' screamed the girl, and made a rush at Orange. 'Here's a girl for you, Tom, and then you let me alone with Joe.'

Orange flung her off with scorn, and ran along the road. A burst of laughter and jeers followed her.

'She be going after her young man down to the lane end,' cried the girl.

Orange's cheek burned. That was true—hatefully true. She was going to seek her lover, but only because he did not come to see her. After this incident she was unmolested. She met no one else on her long walk to Trecarrel.

Would she find the Captain up? She hoped so—she supposed so, for she knew that he sat up late; he had often told her as much. It was as she had conjectured and hoped. When she reached the house, she saw a light from his smoking room—a comfortable room, where he kept his whips and guns; a room ornamented with stuffed foxes' heads and their tails, and with the antlers of red deer. A door from this little room opened on to the lawn. Orange went to the window, but the blind was down and she could not see in; but she heard Trecarrel within whistling an air. It was an operatic air he had recently heard in Exeter, and which had caught his fancy. How splendidly La Fontana had sung! What schooling her voice had gone through, and what quality was in it! How graceful she was, and what passionate action she showed! 'You never get that sort of a thing out of an Englishwoman,' he mused. 'Our countrywomen cannot act; they have no fire, no passion; they are dolls and move mechanically. Their voices, moreover—— Good heavens! who is that?'

He started up. The door opened, and Orange came in. He had been seated over his fire, with his cravat off, a bottle of claret and a glass on the table at his side; he had just finished a pipe.

'No fire, no passion in an English girl!' There were both before him, flaming in Orange's eyes, and heaving in her bosom.

'Bless my soul, Orange! what on earth has brought you here?'

'You, Harry, you!' She was out of breath and choking with emotion. 'Oh, Harry, dear Harry, why have you not been to see me?'

'Come over to the fire; you must be cold.'

'I—I cold!' she laughed bitterly. 'I am burning; feel my hand. I have run; but it is not that—the flame is here.' She touched her heart. 'It is eating its way, it is consuming me. Oh, Harry, why have you not been to see me? You do not know what I have suffered!'

'We have both suffered,' he answered; but there was not much token of pain in his blue eyes, nor tone in his voice. 'Come over here; I am sure you must be damp with the night air. This is most indiscreet of you, Orange. I hope you have come attended.'

'I am alone.'

'You ought not to have come. It is wrong—it is indelicate.' He was fitting on his cravat as he spoke. 'Good heavens! what would be said had you been seen?'

'No one has seen me; no one knows where I am.'

'This is madness!' he said. He twirled his moustache; he was greatly discomposed. 'I wish you had been more reasonable, Orange.' Then to himself, 'I wish I had remained in Exeter, or gone to bed.'

'I dare say it is madness and unreasonable,' she said; 'I am mad. Do you know, Harry, all that has happened? Do you know that my mother and I are beggars? We have nothing left to us.'

'My good Orange, I have been myself on the verge of that same condition all my life, and so can sympathise with you.'

'You have a house of your own; we have none. You have land that no man can take from you, and you can at least dig that and live on its produce. But my mother and I have nothing—no house, no land, no money! We eat the bread of charity, and how long is it to last? Harry, I ask you.'

He was silent, engaged on his cravat. It offended his delicacy to be seen and to converse with a lady without his cravat.

'You do not answer me, Harry; you are not going to desert me now I am down. If you had been poor and an outcast, would not I have taken you, though I were wealthy?'

'But there is the rub,' said the Captain, interrupting her. 'If I were rich I would share it with you and welcome; but I am not rich—I am miserably poor; hardly able to keep my head out of a debtors' prison.'

'Harry, I do not mind that. You are bound to me; you cannot desert me in my misery. No, I know you too well; you are too good, too noble, too true a gentleman. I cannot—I will not believe it! Take me as I am—we can but be poor together—and I will work as your slave. With love labour is light, and poverty is made rich.'

'That is rather a pretty sentiment, Orange, but it is impracticable.'

'It is not impracticable; try me.'

'That is absurd. I cannot try you, and, if the experiment fails, dissolve the partnership.'

She was silent, and looked him full in the face. Then her feelings overcame her; she stretched out her arms to him. 'Harry!' she gasped, 'Harry, I love you!'

He did not put out his arms to encircle her, to take her to his heart; but he put his hand to his pipe, and began to scrape out the ashes with a bit of stick—a toothpick that was on the mantelpiece.

'Be reasonable, Orange; it is impossible for us to marry now. There is this terrible scandal about Ophir barring it for one thing; there is my poverty for another. We must wait.'

'I knew it,' she said, relieved; 'I knew the delay was for a time only. But, Harry, in the meanwhile I have no home. Where am I to live? What roof is to cover me from the rain and the snow? Where am I to get food to put in my mouth— whence the clothes to cover me? Whilst you are waiting for Ophir to be forgotten, I am starving.'

'This calls for consideration,' he said, still cleaning his pipe. And now he blew through it, to assure himself that the passage was clear.

'Harry, you have an aunt at Penzance; take me to her. I will live with her a few years, till this trouble about Ophir is passed, and then you shall marry me from her house.'

'That is not possible, Orange. My aunt strongly disapproved of my engagement. She is a most bigoted Catholic, and could not endure the thought of my taking a Protestant to wife.'

'I will be a Catholic; I do not care.'

'But,' said he, coldly, 'that is not all. Our families are so wide apart in the social scale. My aunt is very proud of her race, and you know your stock is not—well, neither ancient nor gentle. You may change your creed, but not your blood. I think nothing of this; if I had considered it, I would not have sought to marry you. But my aunt—you see we are speaking of her, and you propose that I should take you to her—my aunt is very stiff in these matters. I cannot force you into her house; so you see this scheme is impracticable also.'

'Where am I to go?' asked Orange, desperately. 'I must live somewhere. You are my proper protector, to whom I fly. I ask you, find me, give me a home. See, Harry, I am poor now, but it may not always be so. The directors of Ophir have left us some thousands of pounds in Patagonian bonds.'

'Oh, I know them; they were left because worthless.'

'They are worthless now, but they may become valuable hereafter. Let us wait till then; I will be patient, and in time you will marry me.'

'Oh, certainly, when the Patagonians are at par.'

'But in the meantime, Harry, what is to become of me?'

'Really, I am at a loss to know. I am at my wits' end what to propose.'

Then her cheek and brow became crimson.

'Harry, I am sunk so low that I care not what the world says, and what becomes of me. I will stay here; you shall not send me away. I have no pride left. Let me be a poor serving maid, a kitchen-wench in the house, and work for you. If the world talks, let it—I defy it!'

Trecarrel sprang back. This was indeed madness; she must be cured.

'Orange,' he said, 'I am too honourable to listen to such words with composure. Go back whence you came. Here! I will accompany you; you must not be alone.'

'No, I came alone, and I can go alone. But—what is to become of me?'

'You think only of yourself, Orange; you are selfish. Poor Mirelle! how she must suffer also. What is to become of that sweet and fragile flower?'

Orange looked him full in the eyes. A light flickered and flashed in hers—a terrible light. She stood as a statue before him for a moment. Fierce thoughts—wild, dark like smoke from the bottomless pit—rose, and rolled over and obscured her brain.

'Poor Mirelle! Sweet and fragile flower!' At that moment, with her, Orange, pleading before him, with her in an agony and in abasement before him, he could think of Mirelle, and throw Mirelle in her teeth.

Then she turned to the door. All hope was gone.

'Let me attend you home,' he said.

'I have no home,' she answered hoarsely.

'Let me go with you to where you are lodging.'

'I came alone, I will return alone,' she said, and left the room.

She hurried into the road. When there, however, she stood and waited. Would he come after her? She waited on; the light in his smoking-room disappeared, it reappeared at another window, and travelled upwards, then shone out of an upstair room. Captain Trecarrel was going to bed.

Then Orange ran back to Launceston.

As she passed the low public-house, she stumbled over something. It was the young woman, drunk, lying in the road. She reached the house of the Flamanks, and thrust open the drawing-room window and went in.

'Hah!' exclaimed Mrs. Flamank, standing there, with Mrs. Trampleasure trembling and sniffing behind her; 'this is fine goings on in my house. Out to one o'clock in the morning, cutting about, heaven knows where, and with whom. This is a Christian habitation. Out of my house you go to-morrow.'

'Betsy Delilah!' remonstrated Mr. Flamank from the door, 'the poor souls have no house to go to.'

'She,' exclaimed Mrs. Flamank, indicating Orange—'she don't want one. She likes the street at night, apparently.'

'Madam,' said Mirelle, stepping forward, and speaking with composure, 'give us but two days' shelter, and then we will trouble you no more, I undertake. I have a friend to whom I will appeal.'

Then she went upstairs, and wrote:—

'Mr. Herring!—Come to us. Help us!—MIRELLE.'

CHAPTER XXXIII.

TRANSFORMATION.

GRIZZLY COBBLEDICK and Joyce carried John Herring to the Giant's Table. Joyce had not the smallest intention of surrendering her charge to Cicely. She had feared lest the farmer should accompany the waggon, and insist on the injured man being conveyed to West Wyke House. Fortunately, the chance of making a bargain with the Squire had arrested him at Bridestowe, and the young lout who acted as driver was easily managed.

Grizzly consented to receive Herring into his den, not because he felt gratitude to him for having saved him from imprisonment, and for having cured Joyce of her injuries, but because he thought that 'backie' might be extracted from him.

Gratitude is not a savage virtue; but then, is gratitude to be found anywhere? It is a figment of the poet and moralist, like the unicorn and the mermaid. A simulation of this ideal virtue is assumed by those who are cultured, but the genuine plant grows on no human soil and under no known climate.

Grizzly bore Herring no ill-will, and he thought it possible that the tobacco which was lost to him through the insolvency of Tramplara might be made up to him by the indebtedness of Herring. He would see to that; he would hold Herring in captivity till as much 'backie' was produced as could be counted on the toes and fingers, with the head thrown in. If he died, he died. Speculations succeed or fail; there are blanks and prizes in the lottery, disappointments and luck in life.

'Cut off,' said Grizzly to his daughter, 'and go and wire a rabbit. The young maister, if he comes round, will want some'ut to eat, sure.'

'But what if he wakes up whilst I be gone?'

'Then he wakes—that be all.'

'You'll be good and kind to 'n, vaither,' entreated Joyce.

'Why not? He ain't done me no hurt,' answered Grizzly.

It took a little persuading and threatening on Grizzly's part before Joyce could be induced to relinquish her place. She would not have gone, but have sat on in unreasoning jealousy and fear of losing Herring, unless her father had insisted on her giving him proper food.

'What'll the like's o' he say to turnips, eh? He ain't one to eat mun. The quality eat nort but meat. You may give a horse the best beef-steak, and you may set before a man the choicest hay, and neither will begin to bite. You must give mun what them likes, not what you think best. So wi' the maister; he be quality, and, when you offers 'n your turnip and cabbidge, that be there a biling over the turves, he'll turn his head away. It be all the same to he as giving 'n hay or a horse beef. You must give to ivery creeter its proper food.'

When Joyce was gone, old Cobbledick surveyed Herring carefully and examined his bones. No bones were broken. His head was suffering from concussion, not from fracture. The old fellow had wit enough to ascertain this. Then he proceeded to partly undress him. It was not the custom of the Cobbledick tribe to unclothe themselves when they retired to rest; but then they were hardly clothed when about by day. If Cobbledick now stripped Herring it was not in the interest of the patient, but in his own. Having removed a portion of the garments of the still unconscious man, he proceeded to vest himself in them. Inexperience made him put on the clothes clumsily, and neither in their traditional order nor in their proper manner. Still, the general effect was one of transformation. He tried on Herring's boots, but was unable to compress his great flat feet into them; so he flung them aside; but he laboriously removed the spurs, and buckled them on his own heels. The stockings he left on Herring's legs; he knew he would be unable to wear them. His own limbs, from the knees downwards, were swathed in hay-bands. He assumed the waistcoat, but not the shirt, and was careful to set the watch in the pocket—the wrong pocket, of course—and let the seals dangle from the fob. The waistcoat was open, and his brown, dirty skin showed dark against the nankin. The coat was rather tight, high-collared, with a roll; Cobbledick was mightily pleased with it. He jumped and swung the tails from side to side, and ran after them, round and round, like a kitten pursuing its own tail. He sallied forth to a pond and contemplated himself in it. The effect was not perfect. He went back and deprived Herring of his cravat, which till now he had left about his neck. This he wrapped about his own throat, making it very stiff, and holding his chin high in the air. Herring's hat was there; it had not been left in the road; Farmer Facey had picked it up and tossed it into the waggon as it departed. Cobbledick put the beaver on, somewhat on one side, as he had seen Sampson Tramplara cock his hat when tipsy; and he took up the hunting-whip Joyce had brought with her, and, so accoutred, he lounged in the door of his den. But Grizzly was not satisfied with himself. His hay-swathings were not in character. He proceeded to divest himself of these. Then his bare legs looked incongruous with the remainder of his equipment. Now Herring had worn cloth gaiters over his stockings. Grizzly had unbuttoned these with much difficulty. Indeed, it can hardly be said that he had unbuttoned them; he had rather torn them off, sending the buttons flying. To button them on his own calves was a feat beyond his powers. His fingers were incapable of performing such work as passing a button through a hole. He tried, and abandoned the attempt in despair.

He flung his own rags over Herring, and went forth to examine himself again in the pool. The brown shins and calves did not please him. He sat down and thought.

Then he remembered that the masons engaged at Ophir had been mixing lime for whitewashing. What if he stole down there and whitewashed his legs! That would complete his transformation. The old man was as conceited as a young buck newly accoutred by a fashionable tailor.

So Cobbledick started for the mine, walking with difficulty. The constraint of the garments encasing his nether limbs was to him as great as that caused by Saul's armour to David. David, finding he could not go in this, put it off him. Grizzly was less wise; he waddled on in suffering and constraint, and was caught and thrown occasionally by the spurs that dangled at his bare heels. The gorse scratched his shins, usually protected by hay-bands; but he heeded not these inconveniences. With his head in the air, one arm akimbo, and the hand holding the riding-whip resting on his hip, he strutted on, wishing, and yet fearing to be seen—desirous of admiration, and yet shy of the reception he might meet with from those accustomed to see him half-naked.

He mounted a flat slab of granite, and, taking off his hat, bowed and waved it, as he had seen old Tramplara salute distinguished and wealthy visitors to Ophir. Imitation is strong in the savage and in the idiot. By the help of this faculty the social world gets on without jars, for there are savages and idiots in all ranks of life, and the deeper their savagery and their idiocy the more pronounced is the development of their imitative powers. They copy the manners of those around them, simulate their breeding and virtues, and so disguise their nature and pass muster. Social education consists in the training of neophytes what to copy and what to disregard in the bearing and manners of those with whom they associate. But such as are left without instructors pick up and imitate all that they ought to avoid, and overlook what they should copy. Thus it is that servant maids reproduce in themselves the pretences and follies of their mistresses, and not their thrift and good sense; and the butler apes his master's vices and eschews his virtues.

Left alone in the den, lying on the fern, with the smoke of the peat fire and the reek of stewing vegetables filling it, Herring opened his eyes and looked about him.

It was some time before he recognised where he was, and then he was unable to account for his being there. The evening was stealing on, the sun was setting; there was a glow of golden light outside the door, and a streak of yellow glory came from a notch in the stone at the back of the table, unfilled with moss. Herring's head was painful, and all his limbs ached. He could scarce move his arms; they were sprained and bruised. He tried to stand up, but the effort gave him torture, and he was forced to lie down again. He was, however, satisfied that he was sound in limb, though sprained and bruised. He could

close his hands and move his feet. Then he thought of the
events that had recently taken place. He could follow the
thread to one point—after that it was broken off. He had
borrowed a horse at Bridestowe, he had ridden hard in pursuit
of Sampson Tramplara—and then ensued darkness and a
blank.

Had Sampson shot him? He tore open his shirt and felt;
there was no wound. He felt his head; it was not bandaged.

How came he in the den of the Cobbledicks? As he was
puzzling over this question, the entrance was darkened, and
Joyce entered, carrying a fowl by the legs. The moment she
saw that he was conscious, she uttered a cry of joy, and was at
his side, on her knees, grasping his hands, with tears and flashes
of delight in her eyes.

'Oh, maister! the dear maister! you be alive and not
going to sleep away dead! You can see who be here—your
own poor Joyce. Right glad I be to see the life in your eyes
and the blood in your cheeks again. Oh, glory rallaluley! I
be joyful! I could sing my heart up over my lips, and away
through this great covering stone.'

'Joyce!' said Herring, 'I do not understand. What is the
meaning of this? How came I here?'

'Sure, my maister, it were I as brought you here. The
young Cap'n Sampson Tramplara would ha' killed'y, but I
fought 'n for'y, and I were too much for 'n. You mended my
arms and made them strong, and they were strong enough to
keep 'n off from killing of you. He'd ha' done it. He had
that in his hand would ha' scatted your head all to smash, and
he were about to do it, but I were too strong for he, thanks be
to you for mending of me up. Glory rallaluley!'

'But how came I here, Joyce?'

'Sure enough, because I brought'y in a waggon as grand as
a king. Sure,' she said, laughing and crying in one breath, ' I
never went on nothing but my own bare feet afore, and but for
the grandness, I'd rather walk any day. But I could not ha'
carried you thus far. That were why I were forced to hire a
waggon. Not but as though I wouldn't ha' done it. I'd ha'
carried you the world over in my airms, if I could, and never
let you drop till I died. But—Loramussy! what have become
of your clothes? By the blue blazes! this be vaither's doing.'

'Joyce, how did this take place? I cannot understand.'

'The horse were throwed and you with him. Cap'n Sampson had put a gate across the road; and you rode quite innocent

like right on to it. After you were down, he came out from behind the hedge, and would ha' killed you, but your own poor Joyce were there, and her fought 'n, and her tore at 'n. He might ha' cut her flesh off her bones, and scat her bones, but her'd not hev let 'n hurt you no more.'

Then she seized his hands in a paroxysm of joy and covered them with kisses, and pressed them to her beating heart. 'It were I, your own Joyce, as saved'y.'

See what self-respect will do—how it lifts out of the slough! Once Joyce had licked his hand like a dog. Now she had learned her own worth, she had battled for and saved his dear life; and her pride had heaved her from the low estate of bestiality to the level of a human being. She kissed his hand, she no longer licked it. That marked a distinct stride in civilisation.

'But,' she added, as she knelt over him, still holding his hand to her bosom, and looked out of her wet and burning eyes into his face, 'it were none for Joyce, nor for Miss Cicely, I did all this—it were for you and the Whiteface.'

Joyce loved him; her love for him filled her whole dim soul with light. She was perfectly humble; she knew she was a poor savage, and as widely removed from him on one side as she was from the fox or badger on the other. There was no self-seeking in her love. It was in this simple, pure, unselfish devotion that the human soul broke into flame and transformed Joyce. She looked up to Herring as she might to a star; she had no thought of attaining to either. It was enough for her to look up and be led by the light each shed on her way.

Her father was also transformed externally, but remained the same low brute at heart. There was no outer change in the girl, the same foul rags, only more ragged than before, the same dishevelled wretchedness of aspect; but within, all was different. God spake, and there was light.

Herring looked up at her, wondering, but still much confused; his head could not endure much thought. She was swaying herself from side to side, still holding his hand between hers in her bosom; and the tears ran down her tanned cheeks and fell over him—a soft and soothing rain, a rain bearing balm and blessing. She had raised her eyes, and her lips moved.

'What are you saying, Joyce?' he asked, thinking she was speaking to him, but that he could not hear.

'I were saying nort to you,' she said; 'I do not know

hardly what I were saying, but my heart were that nigh to bursting wi' joy, that I felt I must speak—but not to you—sure I didn't know to whom I were speaking and saying that I were so happy as I never was afore and never will be again. And I tried to say glory rallaluley turned backsyforemost, but the words wouldn't out, and I just cried for gladness, and looked up—that were all.'

'What is that noise?' asked Herring.

'What?' she asked, dropping his hand and listening.

There were shouts and cries approaching. Then the crash of a stone against the supporters of the table. Next moment in dashed old Grizzly, without the hat, wild with alarm, and threw himself on the ground, where he tore off his coat and neckcloth, waistcoat and breeches, and, screaming with rage and terror, threw each article, as it came off, in the faces of the men that peered in at the entrance.

'Take mun! take mun! I will none of 'em! I will never have none o' the sort again.'

His legs were torn and bleeding. One was smeared with white to the knee, the other was of its natural tan.

Some of the miners had seen Cobbledick engaged in adorning his shins with whitewash, dressed out in his borrowed garb, and had set upon him with jeers. He had fled and been pursued.

'I'll hev none of it never more,' he cried, and swore horribly. 'Give me my rags again.'

That was the end of the transformation of Grizzly. But the transformation of Joyce, which was from within, was more enduring.

CHAPTER XXXIV.

HERRING'S STOCKINGS.

JOYCE was unable to retain Herring. Those who had pursued her father saw him lying in the old cromlech, and the secret was out. Moreover, she herself began to see that it was not possible for her to keep him in the den. Her father's behaviour, when left in charge of the patient, had shown her how utterly untrustworthy he was, and Joyce could not always be there.

Ophir had exerted a deteriorating effect on Grizzly. He had become idle; he had learned to beg; he had acquired a taste for rum. He expected Joyce to do everything for him, that he might lounge away his time about the mine, repeating his parrot story to the visitors, putting the dust into the water, and watching them find it.

Old Tramplara and young Sampson had given him money, and the workmen, supposed all to be sworn abstainers, had indulged him from their bottles of cold alcoholic tea. Like a savage brought suddenly into association with civilised man, he learned their vices, and unlearned none of his own brutality.

When it was known at West Wyke that John Herring was lying ill under the Giant's Table, Mr. Battishill and Cicely sent to have him removed to their house, and poor Joyce offered only a faint, though sullen, resistance. She knew she could not keep him, but she was reluctant to lose him. She knew that it was good for him to go, and she did violence to her own heart in suffering him to be carried away. She followed him to the doorway of West Wyke, holding his hand, and without taking her eyes off him.

'Come, Joyce,' said Cicely, 'you have been so good and devoted hitherto, that you had best remain as nurse. Come in and attend to Mr. Herring till he is well.'

But Joyce shook her head.

'I'll not go under no hellens [slates], or I should smother,' she said. 'Where be you a-going to take 'n to?'

'We shall put him in that room,' answered Cicely, indicating the window.

'There'll be a light there of nights, I reckon. I shall see 'n. And of day, when vaither don't want nort a-doing, I'll just hop over and sit down outside, in thicky corner o' the garden wall.' Then Joyce grasped Herring's hand in both hers, and the tears filled her eyes. 'It were I, your poor Joyce, as saved you. You'll not forget that, will'y now?'

Then she turned away, and wiped her eyes with the back of her hand. Cicely looked after her. Joyce did not turn back; she walked on with her peculiar free stride, her head down, and her arm across her face.

Herring had been jarred and contused by his fall, and he suffered greatly for a few days. Every movement caused pain. The doctor visited him, and insisted on quiet, and that his head should be kept cool and his mind unoccupied.

The news of Mr. Trampleasure's death and of Sampson's evasion were not communicated to him till it was seen that he troubled his mind about the result of the exposure of Ophir. Nothing could be done, at least by him, in the matter.

Every day Joyce came and sat in a nook of the garden against the wall, looking up at the window. Her hands were unoccupied; she could neither knit nor sew. She platted her fingers about one knee and remained in the corner as still as though carved out of stone, almost as rugged as though cut out of granite. Herring's bed was near the window, and he went to the casement, and leaning on the sill looked forth and spoke to her. Then her eyes, in which a strange wistfulness had risen up, lighted, and she smiled. She had brought him something, a little bunch of late wild flowers, some coral lichen daintily folded in green moss, a cluster of blackberries, old and inedible, but the sole cluster she could find. These little gifts she would intrust to no one to convey to Herring. No other hand should touch them and divert from him the something which went out from her with them. When he came to the window and looked out, she threw them up at him with so sure an aim that the bunch of borage and crane's-bill, the sprig of heather, or the blackberries, always reached his open hand.

This devotion of Joyce was embarrassing to Herring. As he lay in his bed he thought about her, whether something could not be done to bring her out of her rude life. He spoke his thoughts to Cicely, and she promised co-operation.

Next day, Cicely took a chair into the garden, and seated herself beside Joyce. The poor girl did not seem pleased with the visit. She had rather be alone.

'I do not think you will see Mr. Herring to-day, Joyce. His head is worse, and he will not be able to rise and speak to you from the window.'

'Why don't he get well faster?' asked Joyce. 'He'd ha' been right by this time wi' me.'

'Well, certainly you treated him very well. He tells me you gave him capital boiled chicken. How did you manage to get that?'

'I took her,' answered Joyce.

'You stole it!' exclaimed Cicely. 'From whom!'

'From you. I know'd the young maister must have 'n, and so I took 'n. If he'd hev chanced to want milk, I'd ha' milked anybody's cow for 'n. If he'd ha' wanted your head, I'd ha' cut 'n off for him—my own likewise, for that matter. Would you?'

'I do not think I would, Joyce.'

'Then he ought to hev been with us out to the Giant's Table, not here.'

'You profess great readiness to do anything for him, Joyce. He was speaking to me about you yesterday, and wishing I could teach you something.'

'I don't want no teaching of nort,' said Joyce, sullenly.

'But would you not like to learn to knit?'

'No,' answered Joyce, 'I don't want to larn nort. What do'y knit with them long sticking pins?'

'Stockings, Joyce.'

'Vaither don't wear none; I don't, neither. Them's no good to us.'

Then the upper casement opened and Herring leaned out.

'What, Joyce!' he called; 'is Miss Cicely teaching you to knit? That's right. You are going to knit my stockings for me in future. I promise you I will wear none but those of your knitting.'

'Give me the pins,' said Joyce, vehemently. 'I'll larn.'

'Go back, Mr. John,' said Cicely; 'you know you are forbidden to rise to-day. Go back, or you will be worse to-morrow.'

'Is the maister not getting better?' asked Joyce, anxiously.

'He is; but his recovery is slow. His head has been injured, and we must take care that there be no relapse. We can pray to God for him, Joyce.'

The girl looked round full in her face inquiringly.

'Will that make 'n well?'

'I trust so.'

'Better than the doctor's medicine?'

'It helps the doctor to cure him.'

'I know nothing about it,' said Joyce. 'Did the maister pray for me when I were scat?'

Cicely could not take on herself to answer.

'I be sure he did,' said Joyce, confidently. 'Why did I ax you about it? If that would hev made me well, he'd ha' done it. You don't know the maister as I do.'

'Do you know about God?' asked Cicely.

'See there, now!' exclaimed Joyce, with animation, 'that be 'zackly what the maister once axed of I; and I sed, Sure I do, I see 'n every day when it bain't raining and there be no clouds. I reckon I thought he meant the sun. But I know better now, and I'll tell'y how I comed to know. Thicky night as the maister were thrown down and hurted by Cap'n Sampson, I thought he were sure to die in my airms. And I felt then that I must say something and ax some one for help—some one as wouldn't want to take 'n away from me. It weren't the sun as I spoke to, for the sun had gone down. I don't know 'zackly what and where he was I called to, but I knowed very well he were up where the sun be by daytime, but he as I mean were there o' night time ekally well. Then, after that, when the young maister were able to open his eyes and speak, I were that lifted up with gladness that my heart were nigh to starting, and I could do nort but cry tears, and tell he as I mean—but I don't know a mite who he be—how glad I were. I know very well he weren't the sun, for, you sees, the sun were then a-sinking, and I never gave 'n a thought for a minute to look at 'n. I looked right up, up, up; and there were over me the great covering table stone, and I seemed to go right through thicky and see above the clouds as well, and the stars, and I'm blessed if I know where to. I be no skollard; I can say nort but glory rallaluley and kinkum-kum.'

'Kinkum-kum!' repeated Cicely, with a puzzled look.

'Sure—what else? I reckon he begins with Our Vaither, and he goes on to kinkum-kum; but I know nort more nor that. I ha' heard the Methody vellers a say it at their meetings on the moor.'

Cicely laughed; she could not help it—she was tickled.

'You have made a comical muddle of it,' she said, and turned her head to conceal her amusement.

'I don't know, and I don't care,' said Joyce, doggedly. 'He heard it, up there, when I said it, that I knows, sure-ly; and he didn't laugh, that I knows also.'

'Shall I teach you what it really is?'

'No,' said Joyce, resentfully; 'you laugh. If it be good for me, I'll ax the young maister to larn me when he be well. I sed them same words to he once—what make you giggle—and he didn't laugh; he didn't even smile, but I saw that in his eyes was more like tears. However, the words be good as they be, and I sez them scores and scores of times by day and by night, thinking of him as is sick, and he up there;' she pointed with her finger—not to the window, but far, far above it. 'He as I knows nort about, don't laugh, but listens, just as the maister listened when I said them to he at first; and he takes off his hat, as did the maister.'

'I wish I could persuade you to come indoors, Joyce. It is cold out here, the wind blows keenly over the garden wall, and I cannot remain here.'

'I bain't cold,' said Joyce; 'you can go in, I don't want'y here. I'll bide here alone a bit. But I'll larn the knitting and make the maister his stockings. I will, sure. He sed he'd never wear none but what I made, and what he sez he sticks to.'

A few days later Herring came down. He was now much better, though still stiff and bruised; his mind was perfectly clear, and he was impatient of his confinement.

'Mr. Battishill,' said he, 'now is our opportunity; Ophir is done, and Upaver begins. I will make a bid for the plant of Ophir, and remove it to the silver lead. I will rent Upaver of you, and mine there on my own account.'

'Very well,' answered Mr. Battishill; 'I can say with the shepherd in the "Winter's Tale," "Now, bless thyself, I meet with things dying; thou with things new-born." I was set on Ophir; you never doubted in Upaver.'

'You forget, sir, you were the finder of the silver lead.'

'Ah, yes; but I was drawn aside by the glitter of the gold of Ophir. I am sorry for Ophir, too; it was a dream of splendour. But again, with Paulina, "To the noble heart, what's gone and what's past help, should be past grief."'

'You have been at your Shakespeare, sir, whilst I have been upstairs.'

'To whom else should I go, John? "For I do love that man," said rare Ben Jonson of him; and who that has mind and heart does not say the same? Shakespeare is the common and personal friend of humanity. By the way, John, there are some letters for you. We would not let you have them before now, as, no doubt, they are on business. They come from Launceston.'

Herring looked at them. Their purport is already known; they were from the directors of Ophir.

'If Miss Cicely will write for me a letter about the machinery at Ophir, I will sign it,' he said. 'We had better secure it at once. I knew that Ophir would fail, and that was the reason why I did not hurry to get machinery for the silver lead. Now we shall secure the entire plant under half-price.'

'Oh, John, how far further ahead you see than do I! But you are calculating on working the mine yourself; how can you combine a mineralogical captaincy with military duties?'

'I have sold out,' said Herring, slightly colouring.

'Sold out, my boy! sold out after having been in the army only a few years! That is a very rash and inconsiderate proceeding.'

'I could hardly help myself,' he answered; 'I got into trouble. When the accident to Mr. Strange and his daughter took place I was on my way to Exeter to rejoin my regiment. I had been summoned back. I could not desert the Countess Mirelle, with her father dead and without a protector; and so I wrote to my Colonel for a short extension of leave. He refused it, but addressed his reply to Welltown, my little place in Cornwall, to which he had written before. At Welltown my presence here was unknown, and the letter was forwarded to Exeter, and it lay at my quarters till I went there, which, as you know, was not for some time. When I got to Exeter at last I found that my neglect had got me into a serious scrape. Not only so, but the regiment was at Portsmouth, under immediate orders to sail for Honduras. I had difficulty in exchanging. Moreover, I felt that I must be here to superintend the working of the silver lead mine; so I sold out.'

'John,' exclaimed Mr. Battishill, 'it is all very fine your pretending that interest in the icy Countess and enthusiasm over a mine detained you. Nothing of the sort. You found us in trouble and unable to help ourselves, and so you sacrificed your own prospects for the sake of pulling us through.' He pressed the young man's hand. 'I owe you a debt I can never repay!'

Mr. Battishill did not know all. He knew nothing of Mirelle's diamonds consigned to Herring's trust. He entertained no suspicion of the interest Herring felt in that cold and haughty girl. He little dreamed that Herring had taken on himself the double office of guardian angel to Mirelle as well as to the house of Battishill. He did not suppose that even care for that poor savage, Joyce, had mingled with the other motives in deciding the young man on abandoning his military career.

When Herring came out of doors for the first time, he found Joyce in the garden awaiting him. She was crying and laughing for joy.

'Maister,' she said, 'you will keep your word about them stockings.'

'Certainly,' he replied with a smile. 'I give you three months in which to learn to knit, and after that I will wear no stockings but those of your knitting.'

'Good-bye,' she said abruptly.

'Whither are you going?'

'To larn to knit,' she answered.

CHAPTER XXXV.

BEGGARY.

HOPE is hard to kill. One last desperate effort Orange made to recover the Captain. That same night, whilst Mirelle was writing to John Herring, Orange wrote to Trecarrel, but her letter was not as brief as that of Mirelle.

'Harry,—Now the last shelter is refused us. We must leave this house the day after to-morrow. That is, the day when the sale at Dolbeare takes place. We cannot go thither, we cannot stay here. We have none to look to for advice but you. You *must* give it us; you are bound to assist us. Remember, had the disclosure and death of my father taken place one hour later, everything would have been changed, and I should have been your wife; then I would have opened Trecarrel to my poor mother. You cannot take advantage of an accident which intervened to break off our marriage. I do not ask you now to renew that contract; I ask you only to come to the aid of a widow and an orphan, and to help them to find shelter for their heads.'

She sent this note to Trecarrel by a boy next morning. He brought answer that the reply would arrive later. Then Orange went out. She was not sanguine of success with the Captain, for she had failed in a personal interview, and it is easier to refuse by letter than by word of mouth. Still, some sort of hope fluttered in her heart. She could not believe that the Captain would be so mean as wholly to desert them, and deny them his advice. She had not asked in her letter for more than that. Perhaps she had been too exacting when she forced her presence upon him last night.

She went to visit her friend Miss Bowdler. If the Captain had failed her, Miss Bowdler would not. Miss Bowdler was a well-to-do young lady, who lived with her 'Pa' in a large, handsome, red-brick house of Queen Anne's period, a house rich within with plaster-work of exquisite design and wood-carving by Grinling Gibbons. The house was one of many rooms, and it was solely tenanted by the young lady with the red eyelashes and her 'Pa.' They were rich, but were not received into county society; a source of vexation to Miss Bowdler, though her 'Pa' was indifferent so long as his creature comforts were attended to. Surely Miss Bowdler would give her friends shelter for a few days. Orange was not aware that Miss Bowdler had reckoned on using her (Orange) when Mrs. Trecarrel as her door into society of a superior class; and that now the marriage was broken off and this door was shut, the disappointment was bitter.

Orange rang the bell, and the summons was answered by the footman, working himself into his coat, with unbuttoned waistcoat. He looked at Miss Trampleasure superciliously, and proceeded leisurely to button his waistcoat.

'Is Miss Bowdler at home?'

'I don't know.' Then, with a jerk, he brought a red hand through the sleeve.

'I asked if your mistress were in,' said Orange, with indignation.

'I ain't deaf—I heard,' replied the footman. 'I don't think she is what is called "At Home."'

'She is to be seen?'

'I can't take on myself to say that. You can stop in the 'all, and I'll go and inquire.'

Slowly, still buttoning himself, the serving man stalked away.

Orange's cheek flamed, and the tears mounted. This man had been all obsequiousness before the crash.

Suddenly a loud voice in her ear startled her.

'You're a beggar, you're a beggar! Oh, shock-ing, shocking! Not a penny. Cluck, cluck, cluck!'

Orange recovered herself at once. Near the door on a perch sat a white cockatoo with pink feathers on her face, and cold, hard, unsympathetic eyes, staring at her.

'Polly,' said Orange, bitterly, 'what you say is too true.'

'Oh, shock-ing! Does your mother know you are out? What o'clock, you beggar? Oh, oh! Not a pen-ny! Hot cockles! Cluck, cluck!'

'Polly, Polly, don't make such a noise! Pa!—oh!'

A door opened, and a red-haired head appeared. It was that of Miss Bowdler. The moment she saw Orange she started back. The footman had gone to the greenhouse in quest of her.

'Oh, Sophy! dear Sophy!' exclaimed Orange, springing forward.

Miss Bowdler recoiled from the outstretched hands.

'Good gracious, Miss Trampleasure, what a time of day for a call! My dear Pa does not like to be interrupted at this time; I read to him his newspaper of a morning. You will not, I know, detain me. Yes, Pa! coming, Pa! coming in an instant! There have been disturbances in the North among the cotton-spinners. Pa is in a fever to hear the particulars.'

'Hot cockles!' said the parrot, sentimentally, putting her head on one side and winking.

'Oh, Sophie, do listen to me. I want so much to see you. I have a favour I wish to ask you.'

'Pa, Pa! I'm coming.'

'Tol-de-rol-de-rol!' said the parrot. Then, swinging herself round on her perch, she went into convulsions of laughter.

'I pray you excuse me,' said Miss Bowdler; 'I told John Thomas expressly to say I was not at home in the morning, because Pa is so particular.'

'Do you hear?' asked the footman, who had appeared on the scene, now in full condition, every button in its place. 'Miss Bowdler is NOT AT 'OME.' Then he opened the door pompously. The red-haired lady took the opportunity to dart back into her room.

'You're a beggar!' shouted the cockatoo, with a look of devilry in her eye; 'you're a beggar! Not a penny! Shocking, shock-ing! Oh, oh!' and then screamed and ran round and round her perch, laughing.

The door shut with a slam behind Orange. She set her teeth and stamped her foot.

'Would that I were Mrs. Trecarrel for one day only,' she said, 'that I might insult this wretched girl before county people.'

Her mother had a friend in the town, a very intimate confidante, a stout old lady, Mrs. Trelake, widow of a mayor of Launceston, a brewer. Mrs. Trampleasure had insisted on her daughter going to this old lady, and asking her to receive them for a week. Orange went thither, with her heart on fire from the humiliations she had undergone at Miss Bowdler's house. Orange was received at once with cordiality by Mrs. Trelake. She was a lady of moderate stature, with an immense throat. The throat was not a column supporting the head, but the face was sculptured out of the column. There was something good-natured in the face. Possibly she may have been good-looking when young; but it was now impossible, on seeing her, to observe anything but the solid trunk of throat. The old lady was stout, but neither her stoutness nor her throat incommoded her; she moved with nimbleness. She was, moreover, robust in health. Mrs. Trelake was a woman destitute of vanity.

She had a neat hand, and was ignorant of it. She was aware that her neck was ugly, but she took no pains to hide it. She was one of those persons who make no effort to please, and are themselves easily pleased. She liked every one with whom she was brought in contact, but she loved nobody. She was the same genial person with every one, rich and poor, with her servants and with her guests. All she asked of her acquaintances was that they should amuse her, and of her servants that they should give her no trouble. Her sympathy was superficial. If an acquaintance spoke to her of trouble or good fortune, of embarrassment or great expectations, she entered into the situation from the outside, and without the smallest internal appreciation. If she cried with a companion, it was not because her friend had occasion for tears, but because her friend was in tears. If she laughed, it was not at a joke which she made no effort to understand, but because the joker laughed.

If you who knew her so well had told her your wife was dead with inexpressive voice, she would have received the information with indifference; if you had told her the same news with broken utterance, she would have sobbed; if you had told her the same fact with a smile on your lips, she would have sniggered. And your wife, remember, was her intimate friend.

People of this description are more common than is generally supposed. We have occupied some time over the portrait of Mrs. Trelake, not because she acts a prominent part in this story, but because we desire to inform our readers what to expect from the Mrs. Trelakes of their acquaintance when they appeal to them for help in their troubles.

Mrs. Trelake received Orange with warmth and pity. She saw that the girl was in trouble. The heart of Orange was full of her reception at Miss Bowdler's, and she recounted it to the old lady. Mrs. Trelake was shocked: she held up her hands, she blessed her stars, she vowed she could never look on Miss Bowdler again with regard; she undertook to cut her in the streets. (Mrs. Trelake dined with Miss Bowdler the same evening, and, when Miss Sophy told her version of the story, Mrs. Trelake was indignant over the dinner table at the audacity of Orange in presuming to thrust herself upon the Bowdlerian privacy.)

'To-morrow is the sale at Dolbeare,' said Orange.

'The sale, my dear! How dreadful!' Mrs. Trelake looked round the room at her pretty china and her case of stuffed humming-birds. 'I could not bear to part with my things. Every article sold, I suppose. Will those pretty china jars go, with the dragons on them? I wonder whether I could get them cheap?'

'Even to the beds and chairs. The house still belongs to us. That is, we have the lease, but we shall have to let it, so as to pay the rent.'

'Not able to let the house nor pay the rent! Oh, my dear, how dreadful!'

'I said that we should have to let it.'

'I understood perfectly, my sweet child.'

'We cannot go into the house stripped of everything. We cannot stay longer at Mr. Flamank's. It was very good of him to take us in, but we are unable to trespass further on his kindness.'

'Certainly, my poor child, it would not do.'

'Then—to-morrow, whither are we to go?'

'Really, my dear, I don't know. I have a bad head at guessing conundrums. Is it a conundrum, though?' asked Mrs. Trelake, doubtfully. She had not been listening. She was calculating her chance of securing the dragon vases at the sale.

'You knew and loved my mother. I am sure you love her now.'

'Ardently, tenderly,' said Mrs. Trelake, effusively.

'Will you take it ill if I ask a favour of you?'

'Not at all.'

'Would you receive us for a week? I do not ask for more. In a week we shall have had time to settle something as to our future.'

'Oh, Orange! don't say a week; say a month. My house is at your disposal. I really have a fair cook; and now tell me, what does your mother like? For breakfast, now? Is it grilled kidneys? You must put me up to all her little fancies, and I will instruct my cook to meet them. She is a good soul and does what I desire. When will you come? To-morrow? Oh, try to come this evening. Well—if not, at what o'clock? Tell me the time and I will have a dainty meal ready. Orange! I have a pheasant in the larder. I hope you like pheasant.'

'We shall be with you at noon. How good and kind you are, Mrs. Trelake!'

'Not at all. I am delighted.'

Then Orange left. Ten minutes later Mrs. Trelake wrote an elaborate note of apology, to say that her servants objected to receiving so large a party at once. The cook would not stay, and how could she replace so valuable and obliging a servant? The housemaid said that three persons extra would throw too much work upon her, and she would go. So, she, Mrs. Trelake, was very sorry, but for peace and quietness sake, she had to yield, and must withdraw the promise to receive the Trampleasure party. She herself had nothing to do with this, but servants were becoming so masterful that the only way in which she, an elderly lady, could get on was to yield to them in every point.

'We live in the world, we didn't make it,' concluded Mrs. Trelake; 'we must shape ourselves to the world, not force the world to fit us.'

Whilst Orange was standing at the window, reading this letter to her mother, she saw a woman whom she knew coming to the back door. This was a rough girl who did the scullery work at Trecarrel. She brought the answer from the Captain.

Orange at once darted into the garden and intercepted the girl on her way to the kitchen.

'You bear a letter for me.'

'Yes, miss.'

She handed her a letter. Orange turned it in her hands. The address was badly written by some uneducated person.

'Who gave you this?'

'Mrs. Kneebone, the housekeeper.'

'Is there nothing from Captain Trecarrel?'

The girl hesitated.

Orange tore the note open. It was written in the same hand as the address.

'Please, miss, the Captain be very serius indispodged, and heve a took to his bed. He carnt rite, according hev axed me to say so. Your's full of respex, JOANNA KNEEBONE.'

Orange looked up, angry, her heart beating violently. The girl was still there, but moving towards the kitchen.

'What do you want in the house?' asked Orange.

'There be another letter, miss, I hev to deliver.'

'Well, give it to me.'

'It be for the other young lady,' answered the girl; 'and I hev to give it only into her hand.'

'You cannot do that,' said Orange; 'she is gone out.'

'Please, miss, will she be gone for long?'

'She will not return till late at night. Give it me.'

'But, miss, I were told by the Cap'n particular not to let

nobody hev it but the young lady herself; it were very partickler.'

'Then you must wait here till night. This is not my house. I cannot ask you into the kitchen to sit down; you must wait about in the road. It is raining, and you will be wet through. I cannot help it; it must be so unless you let me have the letter.'

'You'll be sure to give it, miss?'

'Of course I will. Do you mistrust me?'

'There it be, miss; but I doubt if the Captain will be best pleased I haven't waited and let the lady have it herself.'

The letter was delivered. The address was in the Captain's handwriting. The seal was large, in red wax, stamped with the Trecarrel arms; Orange knew them well—two chevronels, a crescent for a difference. The girl turned to go away.

'Good afternoon, miss.'

Orange took no notice of the salutation. She was looking at the letter. As the girl departed, she glanced back. Orange was turning the letter, and examining, first the superscription, then the seal. There was an expression in her face which made the girl say, 'I doubt if I have done right now in giving her thicky letter.'

Orange went in. She ascended the stairs to her own room, or rather, to the room she shared with Mirelle. Mirelle was there. That which Orange had told the girl was not true; Orange had told an untruth deliberately, knowing it was an untruth. Orange stood in the doorway and looked at Mirelle, and a flash shot from her dark eyes. Mirelle had not raised her head to see who entered, and she did not therefore encounter and observe the glance of hatred and jealousy flung at her.

Orange quickly shut the door and descended the stairs again. She took her bonnet and went out,—went out into the rain. What cared she for rain? She went into a lane where she saw no one, and would be unobserved. Then she tore the letter open. It was written in Captain Trecarrel's best hand, and ran as follows:—

'My dear Mirelle,—Indisposition prevents my calling and paying my respects to you as I should have desired. I am in profound distress to learn the predicament in which you have been placed by the unscrupulousness of a man whom I will not designate as he deserves, because he is dead. *De mortuis nil nisi bonum.* Observe this maxim strictly, and Mr. Trampleasure will never be heard of again. I write now to entreat you to accept the asylum of my aunt's house. She lives at Penzance, and is both a charming old lady and a strict Catholic. I have written to her to-day, stating your case, and by the middle of the week will have her reply. I make no question but that she will open her house and her heart to you. One little bit of advice I know you will excuse my offering. I saw, on the night of the ball at Dolbeare, that you wore a very valuable set of diamonds, worth, I dare say, over a thousand pounds. On no account allow the vultures—you know to whom I allude—to set their claws in them. Mrs. T. and Miss O. are at the present moment impecunious, and impecuniosity is a temptation to unscrupulousness,—an infirmity that runs in the blood of a family that I will not name. You do not know the value of these stones, and might be sorely taken in if you disposed of them to a country jeweller. Moreover, I presume they belonged to your dear mother, and it would be unjust to her memory to get rid of them to relieve the present pressing necessities of persons in whom she could feel no possible interest. If you doubt being able to keep them safely—I feel convinced that you will be besieged with entreaties to sell them—trust them to my aunt or to me. I remain, my dear Mirelle, yours very faithfully, 'HARRY TRECARREL.'

Mirelle never saw that letter. Orange tore it with her teeth, and then trampled the fragments into the mire. She walked up and down that lane in a fever, regardless of the rain that fell and drenched her.

Her faith in Trecarrel was gone. She was a girl who had been brought up to believe in nothing; neither in truth, nor honesty, nor sincerity. But she had believed in Trecarrel, and now that one faith was in fragments. She saw him as he really was, in all his despicable meanness. She scorned him, she hated him, but with that hate was mingled love, or rather that hate was but wounded, writhing, anguished love. During the night she rose from her bed. Mirelle slept with her. The rain had ceased, the clouds had broken, and the moon shone into the room. She left her bed because she could not endure the silver glare over her face. As she stood by the bed she looked down on the face of the sleeping Mirelle. It was like the face of a dead woman sculptured in the purest Carrara marble, and lovely as the noblest chisel could cut.

Orange drew the pillow from the bed, and held it up, that the pillow might shadow the white face. The heart of Orange beat furiously. She hated Mirelle. She had but to put that pillow over her mouth, throw herself upon it, and with her strong arms hold down the tossing figure,—that figure so frail and feeble, and then she could laugh at the schemes of Captain Trecarrel.

But no. Orange put the pillow back with a curl of the lip. She could not do that, easy as it was to do. But as she stood over Mirelle she vowed never to permit Captain Trecarrel to take that pale girl to the hearth from which he had cast Orange Tramplara.

'You're a beggar! you're a beggar!' that terrible screech of the parrot came back in her ear at that moment. 'True, true!' said Orange, between her teeth, 'I am a beggar. I have asked for love! I have begged for help! I have begged for sympathy! I have implored advice! I have been refused everything, and given rebuffs and insults. I have but one thing remaining to me, a hold on Mirelle, beggar though I be, and never shall he who has refused me all I asked, give to her what he has denied to me, his betrothed.'

The sleeping girl turned her head away. The fierce eyes of Orange stabbed her and distressed her, even in sleep.

Orange put her hands over her heart. It was bounding noisily, the moonlight throbbed in her eyes, the thoughts beat in her brain. That horrible idea of the pillow, and Mirelle under it, came over her again. She saw the feet beating in the bed in rhythm with the pulsation of her heart, and her hands clenched as though gripping the delicate wrists. As one at the edge of a precipice turns giddy and feels impelled to throw himself where he fears to fall, so was it now with Orange. A dread—a dread was on her lest this horrible thought might in a moment become a fact. She turned away. She paced the room; she could not rest in a bed. She was like a wild beast in a cage.

'Orange!'

She started. Mirelle was sitting up.

'What do you want?' asked Orange hoarsely, and stood between Mirelle and the moonlight, that her face might not be seen and betray her heart.

'He is coming.'

'Who is coming?' asked Orange, fiercely.

'I knew he would.'

'Who? who? who?' Orange clutched the pillow convulsively.

'John Herring. I wrote to him. I have been dreaming, and I saw him open my letter, and he started up and cried, "I am coming to you, Mirelle. I am coming to you with help."'

CHAPTER XXXVI.

MIRELLE'S GUESTS.

A TRUCE was concluded between the Reverend Israel and his wife. He undertook to depart on a missionary circuit during the remainder of the time that the ladies were in her house. Mrs. Flamank very unreasonably charged her husband with encouraging Orange in disorderly ways, the encouragement consisting in privately combating his wife's attack on Orange's character, and finding a charitable explanation for her leaving the house at night. Mr. Flamank departed early in the morning as a deputation for the parent missionary society of the religious community to which he belonged, to advocate the claims of a very promising mission to the heathen in the Imaginary Islands.

Hitherto this station had been promising rather than performing, but now it had real cause for congratulation and for appealing to the charitable. A native chieftain, with his entire family, consisting of several wives and a tail of children like the tail of a comet, had become a convert.

Ho-hum was the capital of the Imaginary Isles, situated in the largest of them, with a good port at which vessels from England called with gowns and novels for the missionaries' wives and daughters. At Ho-hum there were four rival missionary churches. The Imaginary group formed an archipelago, but as Ho-hum was most considerable of all the islands, not one of the churches would be content with evangelising a smaller island, and thereby confess itself inferior in pretensions to those communities which occupied the major island. Penelope by night unravelled her embroidery of the day. The work of Christian missions is like that of Penelope, with this difference, that each is engaged in unravelling the work of all the others.

In the island of Ho-ha, a chieflet of indifferent character, Hokee-Pokee-Wankee-Fum by name, had proved himself such a nuisance to the heathen society that he was expelled the island with his family and took refuge in that of Ho-hum, where, however, he met with a chilling reception from his native friends. Finding himself destitute of means, and cold-shouldered by his own people, he lent a ready ear to the solicitations of the One-and-Only-Christian missionary to receive instructions in his catechetical school. As this instruction was supplemented with mealies, he listened and ate. He liked the chapel of the station, because it was adorned with pictures and gilding and much frippery. Then the Reverend the Superior of the establishment wrote home to the 'Annals of the Faith' a letter in the most remarkable English ever penned. It was to this effect, 'that Ho-kee, a chieftain of the island of Ho-ha, having heard the verities which were at this time now inculcated at the mission of the Immaculate Joseph in Ho-hum, had left, like Abraham, his home, and had come to seek the verity. This aborigine, passionated with a vivid desire to apprehend, had commenced to receive the holy instructions into a heart truly recognisant,' &c.

But, presently, the rival station of the Pure and Reformed Christians drew away the 'recognisant aborigine,' having offered him meat as well as mealies with its instructions. At this station the missionary laboured to divest his catechumen of the unprimitive and erroneous teaching in which his mind had been enveloped by the One-and-Onlies. And he wrote home, in good English, an account of the enlightened 'native chief Pokee, who had been unable to digest the erroneous doctrines of the sister Church of the One-and-Onlies, and whose soul was refreshed by the pure and primitive truths (divested of human accretions); but as some expense had been incurred,' &c. &c.

Hokee-Pokee-Wankee-Fum was, however, before long shaken in his attachment to the Pure and Reformed, by the missionary insisting on his limiting himself to one wife. This was more than he could endure, and he opened his ears to the ministrations of the pastor of the Universal Christians. By him also he was told that he must have but one wife, but a concession was made that the rest might be retained under the designation of domestics. With the Universals, the name, not the thing, was essential. The Universal teacher set vigorously to work to strip the mind of Wankee of all the unevangelical instructions he had received from the Pure and Reformed, and he wrote home concerning his convert, to the 'Universal Missionary Reporter,' that Wankee in testimony of his sincerity had retained but one wife out of the three score; but he added, as wives were valuable commodities, this was much like a farmer voluntarily abandoning his flock of sheep and limiting himself to one ewe lamb. Under these circumstances, it became the duty of Christians to indemnify this zealous Wankee, therefore he must solicit subscriptions, &c. &c.

Unfortunately, this missionary was strict on the subject of temperance, and forbade the use of spirits. Now Wankee was fond of grog, and when he had been reprimanded and put on short commons of food, for yielding to his passions, he grew sulky and deserted to the Particular Christians, who allowed grog and had no sharp and defined belief or code of morals, but a very decided disbelief in everything taught in the other churches. Accordingly the missioner proceeded still further to divest Wankee-Fum of his acquired faith, and he was brought to that condition in which he protested against everything and professed nothing. To his bewildered mind, Christianity seemed a bird of paradise on which the sectaries had fallen with the object of restoring it to its primitive condition as it emerged from the egg. One pulled out the gorgeous tail, another stripped off the coronal of plumes, a third reft off the wing feathers, and the last, after having plucked and singed it, held up a naked and expiring monster as typical primitive Christianity.

The Particular pastor wrote home to say that he had converted a native prince of the name of Fum, with his entire family, consisting of one hundred and six souls; that a great door was open for the advance of vague and vapid Christianity. He was resolved (D.V.) to send Prince Fum to his own island of Ho-ha, as native teacher and founder of a church. To do this effectually, money was needed, &c. &c.

This was the glad news received by Mr. Flamank, and he hastened to divulge it in missionary meetings of the Particular Christians in Cornwall, and to collect money for establishing Hokee-Pokee-Wankee-Fum in the island of Ho-ha as an evangelist.

On the one condition that the Rev. Israel Flamank should absent himself from home did his 'sweet soul' Betsy Delilah consent to allow Mrs. Trampleasure, her daughter, and Mirelle to remain a couple of days longer in the house.

Mrs. Flamank was a kind woman in her way, but that way was a hard one. She felt pity for the widow, and as much tenderness as it was possible for her to feel for Mirelle; but she detested Orange. And the reason why she liked Mirelle was because Mirelle had snubbed her husband, and if there was one thing in the world that Mrs. Flamank delighted in it was in seeing Israel suffer rebuff.

Thus it was that Mrs. Trampleasure and Orange were left

without even the minister to advise them what to do and whither to go.

The day had come on which they must depart. It was the day announced for the auction at Dolbeare. Whenever Orange went into the town and passed under the old gateway she saw plastered against the wall an announcement of the sale, and details of the desirable lots into which the Trampleasure furniture had been assorted.

Mrs. Trampleasure was all day in tears. She was thinking of mats and cushions, worked with her own hands, which would go to the hammer. The cruet-stand, also; O woe! woe! There was, moreover, a set of Blair's 'Sermons' she had been wont to read on rainy Sundays—sermons devoid of ideas, and therefore adapted to a mind incapable of receiving ideas. She lamented, likewise, a Rollin's 'Ancient History,' which she had attempted ineffectually to read for the last thirty years. Though she had not read Rollin, the sight of his back on her shelf, in many volumes, gave her a sensation of solidity and well-grounding. But the thought that especially troubled her was that she had left behind in Dolbeare two pillow pincushions fastened to the back of the best bed. In her hurry and distress at leaving she had forgotten these treasures, and they would be sold with the furniture. The pincushions were of white satin, ornamented with figures and flowers in coloured beads. They were heart-shaped—of the size of a bullock's heart, heavily stuffed. They depended, by white satin ribands, from mother-of-pearl buttons. These pincushions had been given to Mrs. Trampleasure on her marriage by a great-aunt. They would hold, on a moderate computation, a thousand pins apiece. What anyone in bed could want two thousand pins for did not enter into the consideration of the artist who constructed them. For some years these pincushions had adorned the head of the bed occupied by Mr. and Mrs. Trampleasure. But they exhibited a tendency to fall down on the sleepers in an unprovoked and startling manner. Mrs. Trampleasure had sewn them up repeatedly, passing the stitches through the mother-of-pearl buttons; but whether spiders ate the threads, or the damask bed back was unable to support the burden, down one or other would come, till at length Mr. Trampleasure, upon whose nose one had pounded whilst enjoying a refreshing slumber, woke with an oath, and flung both the guilty and the innocent pincushion across the room, vowing not to suffer their re-erection above his head any more. After this they were banished to the spare bedroom, and, though not under Mrs. Trampleasure's daily observation, they did not cease to be dear to her soul. These precious pincushions, through inadvertence, were doomed to fall into strange, perhaps inappreciative, hands. The thought made her weep and sniff.

'Mother,' said Orange, 'everything is packed. All is ready for us to start. We must decide now whither we will go.'

'There was Charity on one, with a feeding-bottle in her hand—I believe a Florence flask, and a backie-pipe stem stuck through the cork—as nat'ral as nat'ral; and on the other was Hope with her anchor, and a serpent twined round it, as I thought; but your dear father would insist it was a rope. "But," said I, "look: it has an eye." However, your father maintained that was only a loop in the cord.' Mrs. Trampleasure was thinking of the pincushions.

'Whither are we to go, mother?' asked Orange.

'I am sure I don't know,' answered Mrs. Trampleasure, 'without my Blair, and my Rollin, and my pinkies.' Mirelle was sitting at the window. The day was passing, and no signs were seen of John Herring.

'I wonder how them pinkies have sold,' mused the old woman; 'I shouldn't wonder if they've fetched a lot of money. I should say they were cheap at five pounds. If I get a chance I'll buy them back at that figure.'

'We have no money,' said Orange, 'except a trifle which will be consumed in inn expenses; we must go to one, as we have seen nothing about lodgings. Mirelle, are you awake?'

'Yes, Orange.'

'You will have to give French lessons, and I will do the housework at home and take in sewing. So perhaps we shall be able to keep body and soul together.'

'I am waiting,' answered Mirelle.

'What nonsense!' said Orange, impatiently. 'Do you suppose that Mr. Herring will trouble himself about us?'

'I am sure he will.'

'He has not come, and he must have received your letter.'

'Please, ma'am'—it was the servant who spoke from the doorway—'the mistress hev sent to say, shall I go and fetch a coach?'

Orange looked at her mother. Mrs. Trampleasure wept.

'Yes,' said Orange; 'we will go at once. Yes, girl: go and fetch one.'

'It is unnecessary,' said Mirelle, rising. 'A coach has come. John Herring is here.'

A rap at the door, and in another moment John Herring was ushered into the room.

'Thank you! thank you for coming,' said Mirelle, advancing to meet him, and holding out both her hands.

Herring was not looking strong. His fall, and a hard ride during the night from West Wyke to Launceston, had made him look pale and worn and unwell. But Orange, her mother, and Mirelle were too engaged in their own troubles to notice the change in him.

'You have come to take us away from this house?' asked Mirelle.

'Yes, I have. You called me.'

He held her hands, and looked into her eyes, and was lost in wonder at their depth and beauty, and in a dream of love. She met his gaze frankly, but, as it was prolonged, her eyes fell.

'Whither are you going to take us?' asked Orange.

But Herring had ears for one voice only; he had thoughts at that moment for one person only, who stood before him.

'Oh, Mr. Herring,' said Mirelle—and she looked up timidly again, but, again encountering his eyes, lowered her dark lashes —'take us away—anywhere. We cannot remain here any longer. We are turned out of the house. We trust you perfectly; take us where you will.'

'Let me lead you to the coach.'

Then Orange said to Mrs. Trampleasure, 'Mother, you must go and thank Mrs. Flamank before leaving.' But at that moment this good lady appeared, relieved by the sight of the carriage standing at the house door. Her visitors were departing.

She received the thanks given her for her hospitality with graciousness. She even kissed Mirelle on the brow. 'I hope,' she said, condescendingly, 'that you will find a comfortable and happy home, my child. Aha!'—she looked at Herring, and then at Mirelle—'I have my suspicions. Well, well! Time will show if they are justified.'

Herring saw the ladies into the coach, and mounted the box beside the driver.

The carriage drew up at the door of Dolbeare. Herring descended, opened the coach door, let down the steps, and presented his arm to Mrs. Trampleasure.

'Mr. Herring,' exclaimed Orange, turning white, 'what is the meaning of this? Do you not know that this is no longer our home? You have not heard. You have made a mistake.'

'Pray step inside, ladies,' said he, smiling.

Bewildered, not knowing what to say, all three descended. No; Mirelle was not bewildered; she was perfectly collected. What Mr. Herring did was right. Where he led she followed with confidence; she had entire reliance on him.

They entered the hall. Everything was as it had been: the clock on the stairs was ticking; the door of the dining-room was open; a fire burned in the grate; on the table lay a bundle of old walking-sticks, tied together. Herring took up this bundle.

'But, Mr. Herring,' said Orange, passing her hand across her eyes, 'what is the meaning of this? Are we walking in a dream?'

'This is no dream,' answered Herring. 'Countess, I make over this bundle of old sticks to you; the house goes with them; the rent has been paid for the current year, in your name; the lease is made over to you. Everything the house contains is yours. Everything has been bought as it stands, in your name.'

Orange and Mirelle stood silent. Neither could comprehend the situation.

Herring did not speak to them for some minutes, he could understand their perplexity. Orange looked round for her mother, but Mrs. Trampleasure had not entered the room.

Presently Herring went on: 'You will find, Countess, that a sum sufficient for the maintenance of the house, and for your comfort, is lodged in the bank, in your name, and that the same sum will be paid quarterly. You can draw as you require. This house, with all its contents, is yours. Everything has been purchased and paid for in your name.'

'Mr. Herring,' put in Orange, speaking with a flushed cheek and a quivering lip, 'what are we here?'

'You have been kind to her when she needed a home, you have done your best to make her comfortable, now you are the guests in this house of the Countess Mirelle Garcia.'

A cry of joy from the upper story, and down the flight and into the room rushed Mrs. Trampleasure, laughing and crying. 'They are there, they are there, my Orange! Oh, joy!'

'What are there, mother?'

'My own satin pinkies.'

'They are not yours,' said Orange, with a curl of the lip and a hard look settling into her eyes. 'They, like everything else, have been purchased in the name of the Countess Mirelle Garcia de Cantalejo.' She stood and looked at Mirelle from head to foot. A battle was raging in her heart. Should the rage and hate boiling there overflow her lips? She caught Herring's eye fixed inquiringly, suspiciously, on her. Then she dropped a profound curtsey to Mirelle, and said, 'We are not your guests, gracious Countess, but your most humble and obliged servants.'

Then Mirelle threw her arms round Orange, and kissed her cheeks and brow and mouth.

'Dear, dear Orange!' she said, and her tears flowed, 'do not speak thus. You are nothing other to me than a sister.'

Then she looked round to thank Herring, but he was gone.

CHAPTER XXXVII.

A SECOND SUMMONS.

HERRING was gone. He did not remain to explain how it was that everything had fallen to Mirelle; he went because he did not desire to explain anything. In his own mind he had debated what was best to be done. Should he inform her that she had a fortune, part of which he had invested in the West Wyke mortgages, and part he was about to sink in the Upaver lead mine, and part still remained in uncut diamonds, not disposed of? Should he make over everything to her, and free himself of further responsibility?

He hesitated about doing this, and throwing off a charge he had laid on himself. Mirelle was unable of herself to manage what was properly hers; her ignorance of the world would place her at the mercy of anyone who offered to conduct her affairs for her. Orange was engaged to Captain Trecarrel, and would probably marry him when the trouble about Ophir, and the time of mourning for her father, was over; and, though Trecarrel was a gentleman and, no doubt, of unimpeachable integrity, still he was a needy man, and might not be a discreet adviser. So Herring resolved to retain his hold over the property, at all events for a while, till the Captain had married Orange, and he had time to decide whether Trecarrel was a man to be trusted to act as guardian to Mirelle.

In a small town everyone holds his nose over his neighbour's chimney-top, and knows exactly what is cooking below. In Launceston it was a matter of general conversation that the Countess Mirelle Garcia had come to the aid of the Trampleasures, that she had arranged with the creditors, and had made such an offer before the sale took place that the auction had been abandoned. Everyone knew this—the mayor, the chimney-sweep, the barber, the milliner, and Polly Skittles behind the bar of the Pig and Whistle. Everyone knew that Mirelle had money in the bank, and multiplied the sum by four. Now everyone believed that her diamonds were real, and that they were the outward sign of a magnificent fortune behind. Everyone, we say, for after the ball at Dolbeare the entire town knew of the diamonds, but the mayor, the chimney-sweep, the barber, the milliner, and Polly Skittles of the Pig and Whistle concluded they were paste. The one jeweller had tested them and found them paste, and the one jeweller had a wife, and the wife had a tongue. Now, also everyone began to regret that more attention had not been shown her. Those mothers who were burdened with cubs were especially regretful, and resolute to make amends, and bring the Countess to their little parties, and hitch their cubs on to her. Now, also, Miss Bowdler began to regret having been inhospitable to Orange Trampleasure. Mirelle was a countess—a foreign countess, it is true; but still, where titles are rare a foreign title is better than none. Hitherto she, as well as the rest of Launceston, down to Polly Skittles, had delighted to talk of her as Miss Strange, because they supposed her poor—a sort of hanger-on to the Tramplaras; but now that the conditions were reversed Launceston society reconsidered the question of her treatment. If foreign titles do descend through the female line—well, this was a foreign title, and the young lady had a legitimate right to bear it. So Launceston, from the mayoress, the chimney-sweeperess, the barber's wife, the milliner, to Polly Skittles behind the bar of the Pig and Whistle, began to speak of her as the Countess, and Polly went so far as to call the Tramplaras Trampleasures, because of their kinship to Mirelle.

Miss Bowdler speedily convinced herself that she had made a mistake. There were no baronets and their ladies near the capital of Cornwall, and if there had been they would have moved in a sphere unapproachable by Sophy. There was not even a retired oil and colourman who, as mayor, had been knighted on a royal visit; for royalty never did visit Launceston, not even the Duke of Cornwall, though the city was the capital of the county from which he drew his title, and in which he owned estates. It would be something for Sophy Bowdler to be able to talk of her friend the Countess, and to describe her diamonds, when visiting her relatives in Redruth and Bodmin.

She had made a mistake, and she hastened to repair it. She was the first to visit Dolbeare after the return of the Trampleasures. She did more; she offered a holocaust to secure a renewal of friendship, and the holocaust she offered was John Thomas the footman, who found himself summarily dismissed for the impertinence of his manner to Miss Trampleasure.

Sophy Bowdler pushed her way into Dolbeare, past the maid who appeared at the door. She herself opened that of the sitting-room in the old familiar style, and rushed to Orange to take her to her heart.

Orange hesitated a moment, and then received her overtures with simulated pleasure. It was not her interest to quarrel with old friends.

'You must excuse me, darling Orange, if I was abrupt with you the other day. My Pa, my dear Pa, is, you know, rather short in temper, and I had begun to read to him an account of the riots in the north, when I heard the parrot screaming, and she disturbed him. He swore he would wring Polly's neck. You know I dote on that bird; and I was so frightened. Pa is a man of his word. So I ran out, and then he called me back, and I was distracted between my desire to see you, and my fears for Poll, and my duty to Pa.'

'Pray do not mention this.'

'But I must, Orange. That impudent John Thomas made me so angry with his want of manner that I had to dismiss him, and now we are on the look-out for another footman. Can you —or can the Countess—recommend me one?'

The next to come was Mrs. Trelake, very pleased to see her dear old friend, Mrs. Trampleasure, back in Dolbeare again. She was provoked at not having been able to receive her. 'But, my dear, put yourself in my place; what else could I do? However, all is well that ends well. Hah! the china vases with the dragons were not sold after all! We shall have our game of cribbage together as of old.'

Then came Mr. Flamank. His excursion among the Particular Christians on behalf of the mission to Ho-ha, under the ministry of the native prince, Hokee-Pokee-Wankee-Fum, had not been crowned with success. Ophir was too fresh in the memories of men. Some of the Christian auditors had suffered through it; all knew how Flamank had helped to launch the concern, and, although he had taken an active part in exposing the fraud, it was surmised that he had pocketed something by the transaction. Some rudely asserted that the Ho-ha mission was but another Ophir, and that Wankee-Fum was as mythical as Arundell Golitho of Trevorgan, Esq. Mr. Flamank returned from his round much disappointed and depressed. He heard from his wife what had occurred. Then he went to Dolbeare to offer his congratulations. He was surprised and puzzled. If Mirelle were rich and willing to rescue her kinsfolk from their difficulties, why had she said nothing of her intention before? Why had she allowed him to invite the party to his house and embroil himself with his wife about them?

Perhaps her remittance had not arrived. Perhaps—— But why form conjectures? He did not understand her. Her ways were radically different from the ways of plain Christians. Where these went straight, those went crooked. There are persons mentally shaped liked boomerangs. They go out of the hand in one direction, make a sweep half round the horizon, and return to the hand whence they started.

It was possible, as the Countess was rich, that she might interest herself in Ho-ha, and Flamank thought that, by dwelling on the social and moral aspects of the case, and not pressing the religious, she might be induced to help Wankee-Fum liberally.

Mirelle received Mr. Flamank civilly. She felt that he had acted with kindness and unselfishness towards her and the Trampleasures, and she respected his goodness, though she did not like its fashions.

After some desultory conversation, Mr. Flamank broached the subject of the Ho-ha mission. Mirelle at once became chilly. When he asked her for a donation she declined to subscribe.

'You forget, I am a Catholic.'

'Not at all, my dear young friend, not at all. But this is distinctly a case of enlightenment, where all around is dark; and although Hokee-Pokee-Wankee-Fum may have embraced the tenets of the Particular Christians, still you must remember he is a Christian, and we are all travelling in the same direction.'

'Sir,' said Mirelle, 'as I was walking along the Bodmin road, I saw three children going along the same way and in the same direction as myself—only they were walking backwards. One tumbled into a furzebush on the right, another fell over the bank into a ditch on the left, and the third went under the hoofs of carthorses in the middle of the road. It would have been better for all those children not to have travelled along the road at all, than to have attempted it with perverted views.' Then she rose, bowed, and left the minister with Orange and her mother.

The next caller was Captain Trecarrel. Orange had been expecting him, and had given instructions to the servant on no account to admit him. Accordingly, when he called, neither the Countess nor the Trampleasures were 'at home,' and the Captain was forced to depart, leaving three cards.

Orange took possession of the cards, tore them in half, and put them in an envelope.

'Dear Mirelle,' she said, 'I have been writing to Harry, poor fellow. He has been so troubled about our affairs that he has taken to his bed. He is seriously unwell. I have been writing full particulars to him of all that has taken place, but since my letter was finished I have sprained my hand, and cannot hold a pen. Would you mind directing the letter for me, dear?'

So the address was in Mirelle's handwriting. The letter was posted, and reached the Captain on the morrow.

'Now,' said Orange, 'he will be forced to keep his distance for a while, till I have time to look round.'

Orange was not satisfied. Mirelle was certain to go to Trecarrel for mass, when next the priest came that way, and then an explanation would follow. Orange did not understand how it was that Herring had bought in all the furniture in Mirelle's name, and had placed a sum in the bank to her account. She questioned Mirelle thereon.

'My dear, how comes it that you have so much money? that you are able to do so much, and to live independently?'

'I do not know.'

'What has become of your diamond necklace and tiara? Have you sold them?'

'No, Mr. Herring keeps them for me. I do not want them now. I mean—for wear.'

'Mr. Herring has them!'

'Yes; I asked him to take care of them—that was before I knew they were paste.'

'But, perhaps they are not paste, but real diamonds, Mirelle.'

'What I gave you formed part of the set, and that was certainly paste.'

'Yes, that is true; but it is possible that the rest may have been genuine stones, in which case the value must be great.'

'I do not know, Orange.'

'But, my dear, whence comes the money lodged in the bank? Whence the money that bought all this furniture?'

'I do not know. I have not asked.'

'You ought to know. It is imperative on you to ascertain. Do you think that Mr. Herring has sold your diamonds for this purpose?'

'I am certain he has not. He would not dare to dispose of my mother's jewels without consulting me. I gave them to him to keep for me. I did not authorise him to sell them.'

'Have you any means of which we know nothing?—money not given to my father which you trusted to Mr. Herring along with the diamonds?'

'No, Orange.'

'Has nothing been forwarded to you of his property from Brazil?'

'No, Orange.'

'Then, whence comes this money? I suppose Mr. Herring has spent a hundred and fifty pounds on the furniture. He has lodged a hundred pounds in the bank, and promises you as much quarterly.'

'Yes, it is so.'

'But, Mirelle, do you not see that, in this case, you are living on Mr. Herring's alms! He is not a rich man. I have heard from my father about him. I do not believe he is worth more than six to seven hundred pounds a year, and he is giving you four out of the six or seven—nay, he has given you more.'

Mirelle looked before her. She had not thought of this before. Brought up without care of money, everything she had being paid for by her father, it had not struck her that she was now living on the bounty of one who was no relative.

'It is very good of Mr. Herring,' she said.

'My dear Mirelle, this must not go on.'

'Why not?'

'What right have you to accept and spend the money of Mr. Herring? He is no relative. You have no claim on him.'

Mirelle was uneasy. 'Why, then, has he done so much for me?'

'That is what I ask. Realise what this means. He is impoverishing himself to support you? What will the world say? What must it say? That which Mr. Herring is doing for you he has no right to do for any woman except a *wife*.'

Then Mirelle sprang to her feet trembling; she could not colour over brow and bosom like Orange, but two rosy tinges came into her cheeks. Her whole delicate frame quivered, and her eyes became dull. She placed her hands over her heart, and looked at Orange speechlessly.

'Yes,' said the latter, 'you cannot; what is more, you must not receive all this from a young man without having a shadow of claim upon him. The only claim you can have to justify the receiving of so much is the legitimate claim of a wife.'

'Have done!' gasped Mirelle, holding out her hand entreatingly.

'No, Mirelle, I must be plain with you. In this town it will soon be known that you are being supported in comfort by a young officer, who is neither a brother nor even a cousin. What conclusion will be drawn?'

'Orange,' said the girl, pleadingly, 'I pray you to be silent.'

'I will not be silent,' answered Orange. 'One of two things must be done; must, I say. Do you hear me, MUST. Either you give Mr. Herring a legitimate right to maintain you, or my mother and I leave this place and do not speak to you again.'

'I do not understand you,' said Mirelle. 'Why should you cast me off?'

Orange looked at her, and a scornful smile played over her lips. She was unable to believe in the purity and guilelessness of the soul before her. She thought Mirelle a hypocrite, and as a hypocrite she despised her.

'Oh! you want further explanation, do you? Learn then that it is not the custom in England for a woman of character to live on the generosity of a gentleman who is neither a husband nor a kinsman.'

'I see that I have no right to expect this of Mr. Herring. But he is so good, so generous, and so thoughtful, that he has not considered himself, in his pity and solicitude for me. However, it shall not remain so. I will tell him that I cannot accept his liberality.'

'Or—that you can only accept it when he has given you legitimate claims on him.'

'I will not accept his liberality.'

'What is to become of us—of you—if he hears this from your lips? Remember, we have nothing. We must starve. You—what will you do?'

'I do not know.'

'Listen to me, Mirelle. There is only one thing that you can do. Next time Mr. Herring comes here, if he tells you that he loves you, and asks you to be his wife—accept him.'

'I cannot. Oh, I cannot!'

'You must do it. It is the only salvation for us and for you. Then, no one can say anything to his furnishing you with every penny of his income.'

Mirelle put her hands over her eyes. Orange watched her contemptuously. The girl was very still, but the tears oozed between her slender fingers and dripped on her lap.

'Have you been so blind as not to see that his heart is bound up in you? He has loved you from the beginning, and, you little fool, you have not known it. He has done so much for you because he loves you. He cares nothing for us—my mother and me. He is a good and worthy man. Make him happy. Repay him for what he has done for you. You are not likely to find another who would make as trustworthy a husband. Do not sigh after the man in the moon; he will not come down to you. Mr. Herring is a gentleman, an officer in His Majesty's army; has a private fortune, not large, but enough to support a wife in comfort; and he is honourable, truthful—and soft.'

Mirelle made no response.

'Now, suppose that you refuse him, and tell him, as you are bound to do, that because you refuse him you will no longer burden him for your support. What then? Why, you and we are placed in precisely the same predicament we were in before. We shall have a sale here after all; have to leave this house, and be adrift in the world. Will you hire yourself to be cook to Mrs. Trelake, or shall I recommend you as parlour-maid to Miss Bowdler, for her John Thomas to flirt with in the pantry? This is not all. After everything that Mr. Herring has done for you, you cannot refuse him without being guilty of black ingratitude. Now, what do you say? There seems to me no option as to what your choice should be. But some persons do not know on which side their bread is buttered. Are you prepared to go into service? Shall I write you a character to Sophy Bowdler?—clean, obliging, and steady; understands glass and china. There is really no alternative. Remember, also, that my mother and I depend on your election likewise. Reject Mr. Herring, and when you go to Miss Bowdler as parlour-maid, my mother becomes cook, and I barmaid at an inn.'

Mirelle rose. She did not speak, but left the room with tottering feet, and her eyes so full that, to find her way, she felt about her with trembling hands. When she was gone, Orange laughed.

'Now,' said she, 'the next thing to be done is to bring that other fool here.' Then she wrote a note to Herring, requesting him to come to Launceston, as her mother and she wished to consult him on important business. She added in a postscript, 'Mirelle will be most happy to see you.'

CHAPTER XXXVIII.

A VIRGIN MARTYR.

IN the privacy of her own room, by night, in the little garden-house, her favourite refuge by day, Mirelle considered what Orange had said to her. She was hurt and offended by the manner in which Orange had spoken, without quite understanding why. Her refined nature winced before the rough touch of one coarse as Orange, not only because the touch was rude, but because it sullied.

Mirelle believed that Orange was her friend—a rude friend, but sincere. What had she done to convert her into an enemy? She was not a friend to whom she could open her heart, and she had no desire to receive the outpourings of that of Orange. They were friends so far as this went, that each wished well to the other, and would do her utmost to promote each other's happiness.

Orange was the interpreter of the world's voice to Mirelle, the guide through its mazes. That voice was odious to her; nevertheless she must hear it. Its ways were distasteful; nevertheless she must tread them. She knew nothing of the world, except what she had been taught in the convent. She believed it to be wicked and ungodly. The virgin martyrs had been cast to wild beasts, some had been devoured by leopards, others hugged by bears. The world was an arena in which she was exposed, and Orange the rough but kindly executioner who offered her a choice of martyrdom. An angel, a captain of the heavenly militia, with eyes blue as the skies of paradise, had been sent to stand by, and guard many a virgin; but she, Mirelle, must endure her agony undefended, and see the angel stand by one who seemed rude and dauntless enough to fight the battle unaided.

King Alphonso X. of Castile said that, if he had been consulted at the creation of the universe, he would have made it much better; the sisters of the Sacred Heart had intimated as much in their instructions. In the first place, they would have made a world without men, and that world would have remained a paradise. Men are the cankers that corrode the roses, the thorns that strangle the lilies in the garden of the Church, the moths that fret the garments of the saints, the incarnation of the destructive principle.

Mirelle remembered how her mother had suffered through union with Mr. Strange. She thought of Mr. Trampleasure, of Sampson—she really knew very few men, and those she knew were not of the best type. There was the Captain, indeed, but he was unattainable, and Herring was at least inoffensive and well-meaning. If she must be thrown to beasts, let her be cast to such a gentle beast as this. Hereafter, only, will there be no marrying nor giving in marriage, and women will be at peace; there, into that blessed country, the men, if admitted at all, will be like priests, wear petticoats and be shaven; above all, will be in such a minority that they will be obliged to keep their distance and adopt a submissive manner. Mirelle had a good deal of natural shrewdness, but no experience of life. Brought up in a convent, the only world she knew was the little world within four walls, in which the wildest hurricane that raged was occasioned by a junior appropriating the chair properly belonging to a senior, and the fiercest jealousies blazed when a father director addressed four words to Sister Magdalen of S. Paul, and only three to Sister Rose of the Cross. When she had gone out, it was on visits to her mother, and there she had met very artificial old gentlemen, and still more artificial old ladies, persons who looked like pictures in illustrated story books, and talked like the people she read of in the same books. She supposed that her board and education were paid for at the Sacré Cœur. She supposed so, she took it for granted. She considered it probable that those pupils who could afford paid, and those who could not afford, were received gratuitously. The sisters never mentioned such matters, her mother never alluded to them, and Mirelle had scarce accorded such sordid cares a passing thought. Bread and instruction came to her as food and light to the birds; the birds take what is sent, and do not trouble their feathery heads about the how and whence. Now she was driven to consider how she might live, and whether it was right for her to subsist on alms, and those the alms of a gentleman who was no relation, and how, if these means were withdrawn or rejected, she was to live at all.

After much thought, little sleep, and many tears, she decided that she would accept John Herring.

She had made up her mind. Now she must obtain command of herself to go through the approaching ordeal with dignity.

As Orange had anticipated, her letter brought Herring to Launceston. He had gone to Welltown, his house in Cornwall on the coast, to look after his business there. He had let the farm, but he had a slate quarry in the cliffs overhanging the sea, and he liked to keep an eye on it. This slate-quarry had been worked in a desultory manner, chiefly to supply local requirements, but Herring's ideas had expanded since he had seen the rise and fall of Ophir, and since he had embarked in silver lead, and he saw his way to an extension of the business. He knew that Bristol was a port where he could dispose of any amount of slate, if he were able to convey it thither. Below Welltown the cliffs rose sheer from the beach; that beach was a thin strip of sand, only to be reached by a dangerous path cut in the face of the rock. Welltown cove was to some extent sheltered from the roll of the Atlantic by a reef from Willapark, as a headland was called, which started out of the mainland into the ocean, and was gnawed into on both sides by the waves, threatening to convert it into an island.

Herring had a scheme in his head; he thought to construct a breakwater on a continuation of the reef. Then he would be able to bring boats under the face of his slate-quarries, and lower the roofing stone upon their decks. The idea had not occurred to him before, because he had been poor and unable to command a few thousand pounds. But now he had Mirelle's diamonds to draw upon. He could invest her capital in his own slate-quarry as well as in Upaver lead mine, and benefit himself as well as Mr. Battishill. He would look after both investments himself. He would hold both the slate and the lead in his own

T

hands. Mirelle's money would not only be safe, but would bring in rich dividends. Was he justified in acting thus—in speculating with the fortune of another without her knowledge and consent? He asked himself this question, and answered it in the affirmative. Without his seeking, Providence had thrust on him the charge of Mirelle's fortune, and he must do the best he could with it. Her father had done what he thought best, and every penny that had been intrusted to her guardians had been lost. Then Providence had overruled matters so as to constitute him her guardian. He would act justly by her. He was not self-seeking. It was true that the development of the Welltown slate-quarry would improve his own fortune, but this thought influenced him far less than consideration how best to dispose of Mirelle's money. He would sink her diamonds in his slate, not because it was his slate, but because he knew the security and value of the investment. He was working for her, not for himself, to increase her fortune, not his own, to insure her a future, not himself. Thus it was for Mirelle that he was erecting machinery at Upaver and planning a breakwater at Welltown. In the midst of his schemes he received the letter of Orange, and the postscript made his heart leap. He had been too humble-minded to hope. Mirelle stood aloof from him, high above his sphere. She was to him the ideal of pure, beautiful, and saintly maidenhood, to be dreamed of, not aspired to, to be venerated, not sought. She had of late received him with more kindliness than heretofore, had put away her early disdain, and had treated him as an equal. There had transpired through face and manner something even of appeal to him. Was it possible that she had begun to regard him with liking, perhaps even with love? He was so modest in his estimation of himself that he blushed at the thought—the audacious thought—that this was possible.

Herring posted to Launceston, and went at once to Dolbeare. Mirelle was in the little garden house as he passed. She saw him, and knew that the crisis in her life was come. He was admitted to Dolbeare, and sat with Mrs. Trampleasure and Orange for half an hour. The latter had discovered some important business requiring advice, and this was discussed; yet Herring saw plainly enough that this was not of sufficient importance to have made Orange summon him. Mr. Flamank could have advised her equally well. There was something behind. What that was Orange let him understand.

'And now,' said she, 'we must detain you no longer.

Mirelle is in the summer-house. She likes to be alone, dear girl, and she wants to see you. You slipped away, on the occasion of our return hither, without awaiting her thanks. She has been troubled at this; she knows she owes you some return. Go and see her; she is expecting you, and angry with us for keeping you from her so long over our own poor affairs.'

Herring coloured. Orange had not a delicate way of putting things. He knew that Mirelle had not asked Orange to act as intermediary between them, yet this was what the words and manner of Orange implied.

He bowed and withdrew.

Mirelle was awaiting him. She had been given time to school herself for the trial. Twilight had set in, and but for the fire that glowed on the hearth it would have been dark in the little room. The fire was of peat, without flame, colouring the whole room very red.

Mirelle rose from her seat and stepped forward to meet Herring. He looked her in the face. She was very pale; the colour had deserted even her lips, but the light of the burning turf disguised her death-like whiteness. As he took her hand he felt how cold it was; it trembled, and was timorously withdrawn the moment it had touched his fingers. His heart was beating tumultuously. Hers seemed scarce to pulsate; it was iced by her great fear and misery, and the strong compulsion she exerted to keep herself calm.

'I am glad to see you, Mr. Herring,' she said. She spoke first, and she spoke, as on a former occasion, like one repeating a lesson learned by heart. 'I was told that you were coming, and I have prepared myself to speak to you, and say what has to be said. You have been good to me, very good. You have done more for me than I had any right to expect. I have no claim on you, save the claim which appeals to every Christian heart, the claim of the friendless and helpless. That is a great claim, I have been taught, the greatest and most sacred of all. But the world does not recognise it; it does not allow you permission to pour on me so many benefits. You have bought everything the house contains with your own money—for me. You have taken the lease of the house, and paid the rent out of your own purse—for me. You have undertaken to find me an income on which I can live in comfort; you rob yourself— for me.'

She paused a moment.

A conflict woke up in the mind of John Herring. Should

he tell her all? Should he say that this was not true—he had used her money, not his own? If at that moment he had done so, that event which was to trouble and darken both their futures would not have occurred. Herring was young; he was without strength of character to decide in a moment what to do. He let the occasion slip. He would wait; the revelation could be made later. He did not understand the supreme importance of the moment. He did not realise to what Mirelle's words led.

'Countess,' he said——

'No,' she interrupted hastily, 'do not speak. You must let me say what I want. Il me faut me décharger le cœur. If I had been a nun at the head of an orphanage, I would have said Give all, and God on high will repay you. Give; no one will deny you the right, and I will accept with joy. I will be your almoner to the little ones of Christ. But, alas! it is not so. I can spend what you provide only on myself, and I do not find that this is right. In the world is one fashion, in religion is another fashion. You see well yourself it cannot be.'

'Countess, will you allow me to explain?'

'No; I need no explanation. One only question I ask, for there is one thing I desire greatly to know. That neckchain and that coronet of diamonds, have you sold them?'

'No; I have them yet. You intrusted them to me.'

'They are false. Do you know the brooch you sent me for Orange was all of false stones—of paste? I doubt not the rest of the set is the same. Did you know this?'

'Certainly not. I have not examined and proved the stones. I had no suspicion that they were not genuine.'

'My father sent the set as a present to my mother,' said Mirelle, 'and they were of paste.'

Herring was surprised.

'This cannot be, Countess; your father was a diamond merchant, and knew perfectly the false from the true. He could not have sent your mother what was worthless. The stones must have been changed later.'

'They were in my mother's keeping,' said Mirelle.

That was answer enough. Her father might be guilty of a mean act; her mother, never.

Herring had his own opinion, but he had the prudence not to express it.

'But enough about this,' Mirelle went on. 'I only asked for this reason. If you had sold my stones, supposing them to be real, and had used them to relieve me and the Trampleasures in the moment of our need, when we had not a house to cover our heads, I should have been very, very thankful.'

She said this with an involuntary sigh, and with such an intense expression of earnestness that Herring caught the words up, and said eagerly:—

'Do you mean this? Do you mean that you would have thanked me if I had sold your diamonds and used the proceeds to relieve your necessities?'

'Yes, I do mean this.'

'Why did you not ask me to do this?'

'Because I supposed the stones were paste, and worthless.'

'Tell me, dear Countess Mirelle, if you had confided diamonds to me, knowing them to be diamonds, you would not be angry with me for selling them for this very purpose—to provide you with the means of living yourself, and of returning the kindness shown you by Mrs. Trampleasure and her daughter?'

'I would go down on my knees to thank you. I would be full of gratitude to you.'

He breathed freely; he had received his absolution. He had been justified in acting as he had done; Mirelle had approved of his conduct with her own lips. He had carried out her wishes. It was unnecessary for him to tell her all, now that he was certain that he acted as she would have him act.

But he did not read her heart. He did not understand the real significance of her words. She would indeed have been thankful to know that she had received her own money, so as to be free from all obligations to him—so as not to be forced to take the step the thought of which killed the life out of her heart. That hope was gone—a poor hope, but still a hope. Nothing remained for her but the surrender; she must become a sacrifice.

'It was not so,' she went on sadly, 'I knew it was not so, for you would not have parted with my mother's set of stones without consulting me. No, Mr. Herring, I have not the poor pride of knowing I am my own mistress, and independent of every one. You have been to me a generous friend and a guardian when I needed assistance and protection.'

'Dear Countess Mirelle, I am ready still to act as your friend, your guardian, and your protector.'

'I know it, Mr. Herring, and I frankly accept your offer. I am willing that you should continue such for the rest of my life.'

'Countess!' Herring's voice shook; 'how happy, how proud you make me!'

'Let me speak,' she said. Then her heart failed her. She went to the fire, and rested her hands on the mantelpiece, folded as in prayer, and leaned her brow for a moment on them. The red glow of the fire smote upwards and illumined and warmed the face. She was praying. Her strength was ebbing away; the dreaded moment had come. 'O holy and innocent Agnes, pure lamb! Thou who didst bow thy neck to the sword, intercede for me! O Cicely, thou whose heart was filled with heavenly music, making thee deaf to the voice of an earthly bridegroom, pray for me! O Dorothy, thou who didst pine for the lilies and roses of Paradise, plead for me!'

She raised her white brow from its momentary resting-place. The strength had come. The moment of agony had arrived, and she was nerved to pass through.

'Mr. Herring,' she spoke slowly, leisurely, 'I have no right to accept your offer, unless you confer on me the right—the only right——'

She could speak no more. Her white, quivering face, her sunken eyes, and uplifted hands that shook as with a palsy, showed her powerlessness to proceed.

Herring took a step forward. She drew back, shrinking before him as perhaps the martyr shrinks before the executioner.

'Stand there, I pray—oh, do not come nearer!' she pleaded, with pain in her voice.

'Mirelle, dear Mirelle!' he said; and then the pent-up love of his heart broke forth. He told her how he had loved her from the moment that he first saw her, how, hopeless of ever winning her, he had battled with his love, how vain his efforts had been, and how his highest ambition was to live for her and make her happy. He spoke in plain, simple words, with the rough eloquence of passion and sincerity.

She listened to him, with her hands again on the mantelpiece, looking at him, with her dark eyes wide open, and the red glow of the fire in them. She did not follow his words, she heard them without comprehending them. She was full of her own grief and could think of nothing else.

She woke out of abstraction when he asked her, 'Mirelle, may I think myself so happy as to be able to count on your being mine?'

'I will be your wife,' she said.

'Oh, dear, dear Mirelle! My whole life shall be devoted to you. This is the happiest day I have ever known.'

'One thing I must say,' said she; 'you know I am a Catholic. I will never give up my faith. You will assure me perfect freedom to follow my own dear religion. I could live without everything, but not without that.'

He gave her the requisite assurance.

'You and I,' she said sadly, 'have not the same faith—that is, as far as I can see, you disbelieve in more than half of the verities which are the very life of my soul. We cannot be united in the holiest and most beautiful of all bonds, which has eternity before it, to which both press on together. That cannot be. You go one way, I another. But as far as can be, I will be all that you will require.'

'You are everything I desire now. I have but to look at you, and I think I see a saint or angel from heaven.'

She put up her hand, and brushed his words away. They offended her. But they were sincere; there was no flattery in them. Mirelle was an ideal to Herring. Again he stepped forward. He would take her hands, he would kiss colour and heat into those cold and faded lips. He had a right to do this. Was she not about to become his wife?

But again she drew back, and in a tone of mingled terror and entreaty said, 'Oh, Mr. Herring, I pray you do not come nearer to me. I am so frightened and bewildered. The thoughts that rise up beat my temples and contract my heart. I have gone through a great deal to-day. I have said that I will be your wife. Do not exact of me more than I can bear. Do not press the advantage you have gained over me, I entreat you. You are kind and considerate. I am not very strong, and I think not very well. Leave me to myself, I pray you; go away now. If I have made you happy, I am glad of it; let my promise suffice. Come here to-morrow, if you will. No, no'— again with her fear overmastering her, she grasped at a respite— 'not to-morrow. I shall not be sufficiently myself to receive you. The day after will do. Then I shall have more strength to speak to you about the future. Not now. I pray you leave me alone now.'

'Will you not even give me your hand?'

She hesitated, then timidly drew near, with her large eyes on him full of anxiety, and she held out the long shaking white fingers. He kissed them. They were cold as the fingers of the dead.

'I shall return the day after to-morrow,' he said.

'I shall be ready then to receive you,' she replied.

He went out. Then, when she knew that she was alone, at once all her strength gave way, and she fell on her knees, clasping her hands together, swaying her body in the agony of her pain, and broke into a storm of tears.

Mirelle did not keep her word to Herring. She was unable to do so. That night she was attacked by a nervous fever, and became delirious. The strain had been too great for her delicate system.

Herring called, and heard how ill she was. He did not leave Launceston; he remained till the crisis was past.

The doctors were uncertain what turn her illness would take, and how to treat one constituted so differently from their run of patients. In this uncertainty they did nothing, and, because they did nothing, Mirelle recovered.

There was a natural elasticity in her youth which triumphed over the disease.

Orange sat up with her, night after night. She would allow no one else to share the burden with her till Mirelle's delirium was over.

During the height of the fever, Mirelle talked. Orange stayed with her, not out of love for her cousin, but out of fear lest others should discover, from the rambling talk of Mirelle, the secret which she alone possessed. The name of Trecarrel was often on the lips of Mirelle; she prayed, and broke off in the midst of a prayer to speak of Trecarrel. At the same time she seemed oppressed by a great terror, and she cried out to be saved from what was coming. Not once did the name of John Herring pass her lips.

When, at length, Mirelle was well enough to be moved downstairs, then Herring was admitted to see her. He had repeatedly sat before, by the hour, with Mrs. Trampleasure or with Orange, talking of the poor girl lying ill upstairs.

'She has been delirious,' said Orange, 'and, if it were not unfair, I could tell you how often your name——'

'It is unfair,' interrupted Herring, 'and I decline to listen.'

'As you like,' said Orange, shrugging her shoulders; and, as she left the room, she sneered.

When John Herring saw Mirelle at last, he could hardly command his tears, she looked so thin and transparent; her eyes were very large and bright, her face like ivory. She held out her hand to him. He scarce ventured to touch it. She seemed to him like the ghost-moth which, when grasped by the hand, vanishes, leaving only silvery plumes sprinkled over the fingers.

He kissed the wasted hand with reverence and love, not with passion, and Mirelle smiled.

'Mr. Herring,' she said, 'I have had a long time to myself, whilst I have been ill, in which to prepare my thoughts. What must be—must be, and may be soon. It is now Advent, a season in which it is forbidden by the Church to marry; but I will be yours as soon after Christmas as you like. Do not doubt. When I am your wife I will do my duty.'

CHAPTER XXXIX.

WELLTOWN.

JOHN HERRING returned to Welltown. There was much to occupy him there. He must prepare the house to receive its mistress. He must get what he could ready for the extension of the slate-quarry. The breakwater could not be begun in winter, but the stone could be quarried for it among the granite of Row-tor, and the head taken off where the slate was to be worked.

Welltown was a bleak spot. It stood against a hill, only a little way in from the head of the cliffs. The hill had been quarried for the stone of which the house was built, and then the end of the house had been thrust into the hole thus scooped. The hill rose rapidly, and its drip fell over the eaves of the old quarry about the walls of the house. If the hill had been to seaward it would have afforded some shelter, but it was on the inland side, and the house was therefore exposed to the raging blasts, salt with Atlantic spray, that roared over the bare surface of the land. Not a tree could stand against it, not a shrub, except privet and the so-called teaplant. Larches shot up a few feet and lost their leaders; even the ash died away at the head, and bore leaves only near the ground. A few beech-trees were like broken-backed beggars bent double.

Day and night the roar of the ocean filled the air, the roar of an ocean that rolled in unbroken swell from Labrador, and dashed itself against the ironbound coast in surprise and fury at being arrested; beneath its stormy blows the very mainland quivered.

Welltown was an old house, built at the end of the sixteenth century by a certain Baldwin Tink, who cut his initials on the dripstone terminations of the main entrance. The Tinks had owned the place for several generations, yeomen aspiring to become gentlemen, without arms, but hoping to acquire a grant. Baldwin had built one wing and a porch, and proposed in time to erect another wing, but his ability to build was exhausted, and none of his successors were able to complete the house; so it remained a queer lopsided erection, the earnest of a handsome mansion unfulfilled. Baldwin Tink was an ambitious man; he expected to be able to form a quadrangle, and pierced his porch with gateways opposite each other, so that the visitor might pass through into the courtyard, and there dismount in shelter. But as he was unable to add a second wing to the front, so was he also unable to complete his quadrangle; and the porch served as a gathering place for the winds, whence they rushed upstairs and through chambers, piping at keyholes, whizzing under doors, extinguishing candles, fluttering arras. The windows were mullioned and cut in granite, the mullions heavy and the lights narrow. The porch was handsomely proportioned and deeply moulded, but as want of funds had prevented Baldwin Tink from completing his exterior, so had it prevented him from properly furnishing the house inside. The staircase was mean, provisional, rudely erected out of wreck timber, and the unpanelled walls were plastered white. As the rain drove against the house, fierce, pointed as lances, it smote between the joints of the stones, and, though the walls were thick, penetrated to the interior and blotched the white inward face with green and black stains. There was no keeping it out. When the house was built, nothing was known of brick linings, and the only way in which the builders of those days treated defects was to conceal them behind oak panelling. Poverty forbade this at Welltown, and so the walls remained with their infirmities undisguised. Our readers may have seen a grey ass on a moor in a storm of hail. The poor brute is unable to face the gale, and therefore presents his hinder quarters to it, and if there be a rock or a tree near, the ass sets his nose against it, and stands motionless with drooping ears, patiently allowing his rear to bear the brunt. Welltown presented much this appearance—a dead wall was towards the sea, and the head of the house was against the hill. The furiousness of the gales from the south and west prevented Baldwin Tink facing his house so as to catch the sun in his windows, and the only casement in the entire house through which a golden streak fell was that of the back kitchen.

What the house would have been when completed can only be conjectured; as it was, it was picturesque, but dreary to the last degree.

The Tinks had long since passed away from Welltown. The final representative of the family, unable to complete the house, sold the estate. With the proceeds he started a drapery shop at Camelford, and died a rich man. Political economists lament the extinction of the old race of English yeomen, and advocate the creation of a race of peasant proprietors. A natural law has fought against the yeoman, and will forbid the spread of peasant proprietorships. The capital that is sunk in land produces two and a half per cent., that sunk in trade brings in ten, twenty, twenty-five per cent. The young yeoman had rather sell his paternal acres to the squire and invest the purchase-money in business, than struggle on upon the farm all his life, without the prospect of becoming, in the end, more wealthy than when he started.

Welltown passed through one or two hands, and then came to the Herrings, who occupied it for three generations, and, having married women with a little money, had got on some little way, not far, in the social scale. The slate-quarry had brought in money, not much, for the demand was limited. The neighbourhood was thinly populated, and little building was done. But the equinoctial gales came to the assistance of the Herrings, for after every gale carts came for slates to repair the devastation done to roofs by the wind. The sale of slates enabled the Herrings to enlarge their dairy by the purchase of additional cows. They salted their butter, and sent it in firkins to Bristol by the little boats that plied up the Channel from the port of Boscastle.

John Herring had let the farm, on his father's death, to an old hind, Hender[1] Benoke, who had married John's nurse, Genefer; and this couple lived in the house, and when he was there attended to him.

Now that Herring was interested in the slate-quarry, he built himself an office near it, on the cliff above a deep gulf called Blackapit, gnawed by the waves in the headland of Willapark. In this office were a fireplace and a bed.

Welltown had to be done up to receive the bride, and whilst

[1] Hender is the modern Cornish form of Enoder. There was a Cornish saint of the name. Genefer is Gwenever.

it was in the hands of plasterers, carpenters, and painters, Herring lived in his office by the slate-quarry. He was comfortable and independent there. Genefer came there every day to attend to his wants; but he dined at Welltown in the evening, after the quarrymen had left work.

One morning, after Genefer had made his breakfast, she stood beside the table, with her hands folded, watching him.

Genefer Benoke was a handsome woman still, though over fifty. She had very thick brown hair, high cheekbones, a dark complexion, and large, wild, pale grey eyes. She was a tall, well-built woman, abrupt in manner and capricious in temper. Hender, her husband, was a gloomy, sour man, always nursing a grievance and grumbling against some one; a man who considered himself wronged by every one with whom he dealt; by his master, who treated him liberally; by his wife, whom, however, he feared; by his workmen, because they were idle. He was dragged by his wife to chapel, and he grumbled because he was obliged to pay for his pew, and he was angry with the minister because he was making a good thing out of the credulity of his congregation. He was jealous of the storekeepers at Boscastle, because they were making unfair profit on their goods. He was sulky with his pigs because they ran to bone rather than to fat, and with his poultry because they laid their eggs where they were not readily found. He growled at his Bible because the printing was too small for his eyes, and was bitter against his clothes because they wore out.

Genefer was a strange woman. The Keltic blood in her veins was pure. A wild, dreamy woman, who had acted as white witch till she thought the profession sinful and had given it up, to throw herself with all the vehemence of her nature into one of those fantastic forms of dissent that thrive so vigorously on Keltic soil. She prophesied, she saw visions, and dreamed. None hunted the devil with more vehemence and pertinacity than Genefer Benoke—the devil-hunting with her was no pretence; she saw him, she smelt him, and she pursued him, now with a broom, then with her bare hands.[1] She went into fits, she had the 'jerks,' she foamed at the mouth, she rolled on the floor and shrieked, and exhibited all the outward signs of a regenerate and converted person.

There was no hypocrisy in her. If there had been the least

[1] Devil-hunting is a favourite feature among some of the wilder sects in Cornwall. Very extraordinary scenes may be witnessed at one of these chases.

tinge of unreality, her husband would have fastened on it, and her power over him would have been at an end. But her trances and fits and visions were real, and he regarded her as a person of superior spiritual powers, almost inspired, gifted with supernatural clearness of vision.

'Master John,' said Genefer, 'you've a told me sure enough why there be all that havage (disturbance) in the old house, fit to worry a saint of God out of life, what with the smeech (smell) of paint, and the hammerings, and the sawings, and the plasterings. You've a-told me, right enough, that there be a new mistress coming, and I be not that footy to go against it. The Lord said, "It is not good for man to be alone," and that settles the matter; but I want to know what she be like.'

'Oh, dear Jenny, she is everything that she ought to be. You may take my word for that.'

'Ah! all fowl be good fowl till you come to pluck 'em. There be maidens and maidens, and you must not take 'em by what they purfess, but by what they be. When the Lord were by the Sea of Tiberias, He seed a poor man coming out of the tombs, exceeding fierce, and He axed, What be thy name? Then he answered, Legion, which means six thousand. But the Lord knowed better than that, and He sed, sed He, "Come out of him thou one unclean spirit, and go into the swine." Ah! if you listen to what they sez of themselves, they be Legion—six thousand. Loramussy! with their airs and their graces, and their good looks, and their fortune, and their learning, and their pianny-playing, and their flower-painting, and this and that— they'd make you believe they was possessed with a legion of graces, but when you come to get hold and look close, there be naught there but one mean and selfish spirit, bad enough to make a pig mazed.'

'My dear Jenny, I hope and trust your future mistress will please you, but you don't expect that I should put the choosing into your hands.'

'I don't that 'xactly, Master John. No, I don't go so far as that. But you might have done worse. There be none but a woman as can see into a woman. It be just the same as with the Freemasons. They knows one another wherever they be, and in the midst of a crowd; but you as bain't in the secret have no idea how. It be just the same with women. Us knows one another fast enough, and what is hid from you men be clear to we. There were a battle against Ephraim, and the men of Gilead took the passages of Jordan, and when the

Ephraimites were a-flying, then said the Gileadites to 'em, "Say Shibboleth!" and they said Sibboleth, for they could not frame to pronounce it right. So they took them and slew them there. I tell you, Master John, there don't at no time meet two women wi'out one putting the Shibboleth to the other and finding out whether her belongs to Ephraim or Gilead. I'd like to know of the missis as be coming what her be like, but I know very well it be no good my axing of you. You've not took her down to the passages of Jordan and tried her there.'

'Ask me what I can tell you, and I will satisfy you to the best of my power.'

'Master John, it be a false beginning papering the porch room with white and gold. The bare whitewash were good enough for your mother and your grandmother, and it would be good enough for your wife, I reckon, if her were of the proper sort. And if her be not, let her take herself off from Welltown. Will you tell me this, Master John; be she a Cornish woman?'

'No, Jenny, I do not think she is.'

'Be she strong and hearty, wi' brave red rosy cheeks and a pair of strong arms?'

'She is slender and pale, Jenny.'

'A fine wife that for Welltown! Pale and weak: that be as I dreamed. But it were no dream—it were a revelation. What sort be her as to her religion? Be her a Churchwoman, or one of God's elect?'

'That is an unfair way of putting it,' laughed Herring.

'I put it the way it be written in the Book of Light,' answered Genefer, doggedly.

'She is a Roman Catholic,' said Herring. 'I hope now you are satisfied.'

'See there!' exclaimed Genefer. 'What sez the Scriptur?—"Thou shalt not plough with the ox and the ass together." What do that mean but that two of a sort should run together under the same yoke of matrimony? If you be Church, take a Church wife; if you be a Cornishman, don't fetch an ass out of Devon to plough the lands of Welltown wi' you. What sez the prophet?—" Can two walk together except they be agreed?" Here be you two arn't agreed about what be chiefest of all, and how will you walk together along the way of life?'

'My dear Jenny, you have had the management so long that you presume. I am not any longer a boy to be ordered about, and I must insist on no more of this sort of interference with my affairs. You acted as a mother to me when I was deprived as an infant of my own natural mother, and I shall ever love you dearly for all you have done for me. But, Jenny, there are limits to forbearance, and you transgress.'

'Ah, sure!' exclaimed Genefer Benoke, 'it were I as made you what you 'm be. I didn't spoil you as some would have done. You 'm a good and proper squire, because I trained the sapling. "Spare the rod, spoil the child," said the wise king. Master John, when the old miners were seeking a lode they took a hazel-rod in their hands, and they went over the ground a holding of thicky. And when they passed above a lode the rod turned in their hands. It were all the same wi' hidden treasure. I've a heard of a Trevalga man, as he went over the mounds of Bosinney wi' such a divining-rod, and it turned, and he dug and found King Arthur's golden crown and table. It be all the same with mortal earth. If you want to bring to light the pure ore, the hidden treasure, you must go over it wi' a stick. There be good metal in you, Master John, and you may thank your old nurse that her didn't spare the rod. Her explored you pretty freely with the divining-wand.'

'I am thankful, Genefer,' said Herring, laughing; 'I recall many of these same explorations, and they have left on me an ineffaceable respect for you, and some fear is mingled with the love I bear you.'

'It is right it should be so. What 'ud you have been without me? Your mother died when you was a baby. Your father couldn't be a nursing of you by night and day. It were I as did all that. I'd had a chance child,'—in a self-exculpatory tone, 'the lambs o' the Lord must play;' then louder: 'and I'd a lost it. I did everything for you, I were a proper mother to you, and so it be that I love you as my own child; and as the Lord has not seen fit to give me none of my own body, saving that chance child as died—and I reckon the stock of Hender be too crabbed and sour to be worth perpetuating—what have I to live for, and care for, and provide for, but you? And see this, Master John. King David said as the Lord rained snares out of heaven: snares be ropes with nooses at the end; and King David sez the Lord hangs these out of every cloud, whereby them as walks unawares may hang themselves. What be them hangman's ropes dangling about, thick as rain-streaks, but all those things God has made, and with which He surrounds us, by which we may lift ourselves above the earth if we be prudent; but if we be fools, then we shall strangle ourselves therein. I reckon the new mistress be one of the Lord's snares hanging down out of heaven. If you use a wife properly, and lay hold of her, and pull yourself up by her, then you will mount to heaven; but if you let her get round your throat, her'll sure to throttle you. That be what makes me badwaddled' (troubled) 'about you, now I see you wi' such a rope before you. Keep your feet and hands a working up her, and don't you never let her knot herself round you.'

Such was the house and such were the persons destined to receive Mirelle. John Herring loved Welltown; he had been born there and bred there. Every stone was dear to him. The dreary scenery was full of romance and beauty because associated with early memories. Old Genefer he loved; she had been his nurse, his guide, his friend. She was masterful, and exercised the authority of a mistress; but this had grown with years, and was at first endured, at last disregarded. It had become a part of Welltown, and was sacred accordingly. Herring was too full of content with his own home, of admiration for the barren coast scenery, to suppose that the same would not equally delight Mirelle. He would explain to Mirelle the good points in Genefer's character, the greatness of the debt due to her, and for the sake of these she would overlook her faults.

Alas! the place and the persons that were to receive Mirelle were the most uncongenial to her nature that could have been selected.

But to return to the office on Willapark, and Genefer standing at the table before her foster child.

'I told you,' said the old woman, 'that I had dreamed; but it weren't a dream, but a vision, falling into a trance, but having my eyes open. I thought, Master John, that it were a wisht' (wild) 'night, and the wind were a tearing and a ramping over the hills and driving of the snow before it in clouds. And I saw how that, in the whirl of the wind, the snow heaped herself up like the pillar of salt between Zoar and Sodom. And I saw how you, Master John, thought it were wonderful and beautiful, that you stood before it mazed. And when the night were gone, and the sun came out, and it glittered like a pillar of diamonds, then you cast your arms round it, to hold it to your heart; and you looked up to it for all the world as though expecting something as never came and never could come. And you laid your heart against that pillar of snow, and when I would have drayed you away you sed, "See, Jenny, how fair and pure she be!" But I could not take you away; and still you looked up into the snow, asking wi' your eyes for something that never came, and in nature never could come. But wi' the warmth of your heart it all began to melt away; and still you looked; and it ran between your fingers, and dripped in streams from your heart, and trickled down your face like tears; and so it thawed slowly away, and still you held to the snow, and looked, and nothing came. That be the way the heat went out of your heart, and the colour died from your cheek, and your lips grew dead, and your hands stiff, and the tears on your cheeks were frosted to icicles, and your hair waxed white as wool; and when all had melted clean away still you was the same, wi' your arms stretched out and your eyes uplifted—not now to the snow bride, for that were gone, but to a star that twinkled aloft over where she had been, and I touched you, for I were troubled, but could not move you—you were hard ice.'

CHAPTER XL.

NOEL! NOEL!

CHRISTMAS had come, not a day of frost or snow, but of warm south breezes charged with rain; no sun shining, but grey light struggling through piles of vapour. Mirelle was so much better that she was able to go in a coach to Trecarrel to mass. A priest was staying there for a few days.

The mass was early, and she left before dawn, but the day broke while she was at Trecarrel, and there was as much light in the sky, when she prepared to leave, as there would be throughout the day.

Captain Trecarrel came to her, to insist on her coming into the house and having some breakfast. It would not do for her, in her delicate condition, recovering from illness, to remain so long without food. She declined gently, and the utmost he could bring her to accept was a cup of coffee and some bread, brought to the carriage in which she had seated herself, wrapped in shawls, for her return journey.

Captain Trecarrel, standing at the coach-door, thought her lovelier than he had ever seen her. There was none of the proud self-reliance in her face now that had marked her when she first came to Launceston. She was thin, tremulous, and frail as a white harebell, with a frightened, entreating look in her large dark eyes—a look that seemed to confess weakness, and entreat that she might be left to herself.

Captain Trecarrel knew nothing about her engagement to John Herring. If it had been known in Launceston, it would have come to his ears, for the Captain was a great gossip. The secret had been well kept; it was not only not known, it was unsuspected. Orange had not spoken of it, and her mother had been restrained from cackling by sharing in the general ignorance.

'In case I do not see you before the new year, I must wish you a happy one,' said Mirelle, holding out her hand. 'Now, please tell the coachman to drive on.'

'The year can hardly be happy for me,' said the Captain, and sighed. 'Dear Countess Mirelle, suffer me to take a place beside you. I want to go into Launceston on business, and I shall be grateful for a lift.'

'Business to-day! Do not these English keep the feast? I have heard Orange and her mother anticipate Christmas, but almost wholly because of the plum-pudding.'

'The bells are ringing,' answered Trecarrel. And on the warm air came a merry peal of village bells. Captain Trecarrel saw the supplicating look in her eyes, a look entreating him not to take advantage of her weakness; but he was too selfish to regard it; he accepted her silence as consent, jumped into the chaise, and told the coachman to drive on.

There was no sign in the manner of either that a thought was given to the return of the visiting cards. That was Christmas Day, a day of joy and reconciliation, of peace on earth, and general goodwill. Why rip up a sore? Let the past be forgotten, at least for a day. Captain Trecarrel was puzzled about those cards. Were they Mirelle's answer to the letter he had written to her? His offer of protection under the wing of his aunt at Penzance had been unnecessary, because Mirelle was not penniless; she had means at her disposal of which he knew nothing. Probably her father's money in Brazil had been forwarded to her, and reached her, fortunately, after the death of her trustee.

Trecarrel was not a man to love deeply anyone but himself. His feelings for Orange had never been strong; if he cared for anyone beside himself, it was for Mirelle. Had he offended her by his letter? Was it really she who had sent the cards back to him? He was determined to find out.

'You directed a letter to me some weeks ago,' he said.

'Yes; Orange had sprained her wrist, and she asked me to address the letter for her.'

'I was disappointed on opening it. I knew your handwriting at once; it was so unlike that of an Englishwoman, so French in its neatness. An Englishwoman scrawls; a Frenchwoman writes.'

'I have noticed that.'

'I was disappointed on opening the cover; I thought it might contain your reply to my letter.'

'What letter?'

'That which I wrote to you when you were at Mr. Flamank's house.'

'I did not receive it.'

'The loss is not great. It was sent to inform you that I was confined to my bed, and that I was too gravely indisposed to follow the dictates of my heart and fly to your succour.'

'Orange, I am sure, felt your absence greatly.'

'You, also, would have been thankful for my assistance, surely?'

'Yes; but I had no right to expect it. Orange had a right to exact it.'

Trecarrel bit his lip.

'You seem, dear Countess, to have been very ill. You look terribly fragile and white.'

'I have been unwell——'

'More than unwell—ill; dangerously ill?'

'Yes; my head was bad. I did not know anything or any person for several days.'

'I fear these wretched troubles have been the cause. O that I could have been near to give advice and protection; but important business—military, of course—called me to Exeter, and when I returned to Trecarrel, I was prostrated by a nervous attack for a week. I fear you have been embarrassed for money, but now, I understand, matters are settled agreeably.'

'We are not troubled about money matters any more.'

'Nor likely to be so?'

'I trust not.'

'Because, if you were, I would say, command me. I am not a rich man, but still, bless my soul, I can help a friend at a pinch, and am proud to do so.'

'There is no occasion, Captain Trecarrel. All fear of pecuniary embarrassment is at an end.'

'I hear everything at Dolbeare was bought by you.'

'All was bought in my name.'

'And the Trampleasures, *mère et fille*, are your guests. How long will this continue?'

'I do not know.'

'It is not pleasant to be sponged on, especially——'

'I beg your pardon. I feel it a duty and a pleasure to do everything I can for them. They have been kind to me.'

'Then you saddle yourself with them indefinitely. I hope the load will not crush you.'

Mirelle made no reply. She did not like the contemptuous tone in which he spoke of the Trampleasures, and Orange was to be his wife. She looked out of the coach window on her side.

'Old Tramplara's death was, of course, a great shock to me,' continued Trecarrel; 'so sudden, too, arresting me on the threshold of my marriage. It was a trial to my nervous system. But I am frank to confess, it was to some extent a relief.'

Mirelle looked round with surprise.

'I may as well tell you the whole truth,' said the Captain. 'You are in the midst of cross purposes, and do not understand the game. It is only fair that I should give you your orientation. I always admired Orange; she is a handsome, genial girl, somewhat brusque and wanting in polish, but good-hearted. I called a good deal at Dolbeare, not only to see her, but to keep Mr. Trampleasure in good humour. I am a man of very small income and with good position in the county, which I am expected to live up to. I have been pinched for money, and I wanted Mr. Trampleasure to advance me a loan. So I got on intimate terms with the family, and, somehow, he made my prospects contingent on my taking Orange as wife. Then the sum I wanted would be given as her dower. You understand. Well, being a light-hearted, giddy young fellow, I fell into the arrangement, and all went smoothly enough till you came.'

Mirelle gasped for breath. She put her hand to the window.

'You want air,' said the Captain. 'I will let down the glasses.'

Mirelle thanked him with a bend of the head; she could not speak. A great terror had come over her.

'When you came,' continued Trecarrel, 'then I woke to the fact that I had never loved Orange. I had admired her beauty as I might admire a well-built horse or spaniel, but my heart had not been touched.'

'Oh, Mr. Trecarrel!' exclaimed Mirelle, putting her white fingers together, 'let me out of the carriage. I must walk; I shall faint; I feel very ill.'

'Dear Mirelle—you will let me call you Mirelle?—you must not walk; you are not strong enough.'

'I pray you! I pray you!'

Then he stopped the coach, opened the door, and had the steps lowered.

'The lady is faint. Go slowly, coachman. She wishes to walk a little way.'

Then he helped Mirelle to alight, and pressed her fingers as he did so, and looked at her tenderly out of his beautiful blue eyes.

'No,' she said, as he offered her his arm, 'I must walk alone. The road is rough. I shall be better presently. The carriage jolts.'

'You cannot walk,' answered the Captain; 'I see that you have not the strength. I insist on your taking my arm, or stepping back into the carriage. I am very thankful that I came with you. You are not in a fit state to be alone.'

She turned and looked at him. 'Oh, Mr. Trecarrel, I should have been far better alone.'

'Why so, Mirelle?'

'I cannot say. I need not have talked.'

'Do not talk now; listen, whilst I speak to you.'

'Speak then of something else—not of Orange.'

'I do not wish to speak of Orange. I will speak only of yourself.'

She held up her hands again, in that same entreating manner. 'I am too weak,' she whispered.

Her ankle turned as she stepped on the loose stones. A mist drifted across her eyes, so that she could not see the road. The air was rich with the music of church bells, the merry Christmas peal of Launceston tower and the village churches round, calling and crying, Noel! Noel! Noel! Glad tidings of great joy! Roast beef and plum-pudding and mince-pies! Good Christian men rejoice! Pudding sprigged with holly, and over the pudding brandy sauce, blazing blue! Noel! Roast beef garnished with horse-radish! Noel! Mince-pies piping hot. Turn again, Whittington, to your Christmas dinner. Noel! Noel! Noel!

Mirelle did not hear the bells.

'No, I cannot walk,' she said.

Then Captain Trecarrel helped her back into the coach.

'I shall be better alone,' she said.

'You must not be left alone,' he replied. 'I cannot in conscience allow you to go on without me to look after you. As you are so weak after your illness, it was madness to come out this Christmas morning.'

She sighed and submitted. He stepped in beside her and closed the door.

'Mirelle,' he said, 'I will not be interrupted in what I was saying, because I have determined to throw my mind and heart open to you. I dare say you have wondered how my engagement to Orange hung fire. I was bound to her, but my heart was elsewhere. You cannot understand the distressing situation in which I found myself, bound in honour to hold to an engagement which I detested, when all my hopes of happiness lay in another direction. You do not know what it is to be tied to one person and to love another. It is now many months since I first saw you, and the more I have seen of you the deeper, the more intense has been my love for you, and my repugnance towards a marriage with Orange. You and I are one in sympathies, in rank, and in faith. We understand each other; we are, as it were, made to constitute each other's happiness.'

Mirelle put her hand on the Captain's arm, and tried to speak—to avert what he was saying; but the words died on her tongue. She trembled helplessly. Then she clasped her hands, and wrung them on her lap, despairingly. Speak she could not; but if Trecarrel had looked into her face, he would have seen the agony of her soul, and how she implored him, with her terrified eyes and her quivering lips, to forbear. He did not look. If he had, and read that appeal, it would not have stayed him.

'I did not venture to declare to you—no, not even to allow you to suspect—what was passing within me. I am a gentleman of high and honourable feelings. I knew that I had allowed myself, through inadvertence, to become entangled in an engagement to a person whom I could regard, but could not love. All at once I became aware that my heart was elsewhere. I proceeded, however, as an honourable man, to fulfil that which I had undertaken. What my misery was, you can ill conceive. I saw the fatal day approach with feelings of disgust and despair. That day would bind me for life to an uncongenial companion, and separate me for ever from her whom I felt, whom I knew, to be essential to my happiness. Is it a marvel that, when circumstances occurred which arrested the marriage, I felt relief? Is it to be wondered at that now I feel a doubt whether I ought to go further in this matter? Ask yourself, am I further tied—in duty—in honour? Can I conscientiously marry a girl whom I do not love, whom I have even come to regard with repugnance, with whom I can never be happy, and whose whole life will be embittered by the knowledge that though she has my name and my hand, she has not gained my heart? No, Mirelle; dear, dearest Mirelle, no!'

'Stay—in heaven's name, stay!' gasped Mirelle. 'You must not speak to me thus.'

'Why not?'

'I must ask you a question,' she said, and wiped the cold dew from her lips and brow. 'I must ask of you a favour.'

'Ask me anything; it is yours.'

'Captain Trecarrel, this is Christmas Day. After eight days I shall belong to another. I ask you—allow me to be married in Trecarrel Chapel.'

Her heart beat so fast that it took away her breath. She was unable to proceed.

Captain Trecarrel's blue eyes opened with amazement. He could not believe his ears.

'I shall be married to—John Herring.'

Then she sank back in the coach, and threw her handkerchief over her face. The wheels rattled over the pavement of the street.

'Stop!' shouted the Captain. 'Damnation! stop!'

He got out. 'Drive on hard to Dolbeare, coachman; the young lady has fainted.'

So the coach rattled through the market-place and along the High Street, whilst the bells rang merrily, merrily, Glad tidings of great joy! Roast beef and plum-pudding and mince-pies to those who can afford it; to the poor—nothing.

CHAPTER XLI.

WHITE FAVOURS.

The weather had changed abruptly. The wind had turned north-east, had become rough and frozen, and whirled snow before it over a white world.

Eight days had elapsed, and the marriage ceremony had been performed in the chapel of Trecarrel. The Captain was not present at the ceremony: he was in bed, indisposed.

The carriage was at the door of Dolbeare to convey the bride and bridegroom to Welltown. A hasty breakfast had been taken. No friends had been invited. The journey was long, and the horses must be rested midway for an hour. The days were short, and there was no chance of reaching Welltown before dark. It was bad travelling over fresh snow, and along an exposed road swept by the furious gale. The horses stamped and pawed the snow, the post-boys were impatient. Herring was anxious to start. Mirelle was upstairs in her room alone. All the boxes were corded and in place. Then Orange, who was in the hall, called her cousin.

Mirelle appeared, slowly and uncertainly descending the stairs. Orange uttered an exclamation of surprise. 'My dear, you are still in white! You have not put on your travelling dress.'

'I did not know.'

'But what in the world have you been doing?'

She had been weeping and praying. Her eyes were red and full of tears, and there was that exalted, luminous look in the white face of one whose soul has just descended from heaven, as there was in the face of Moses when he came down from the Mount. In her white dress, with her white veil over her dark hair, and a bunch of snowdrops in her bosom, just as she had stood at the altar, so she was going forth into the stormy world—as white as one of the snow-flakes, as fragile, altogether as pure.

Her travelling dress was in the box, and the box was on the carriage. There was no help for it; the box could not be taken down and unpacked. She must go as she was, wrapped round with many cloaks.

She was reluctant to depart. She had not spent happy days

in Dolbeare; but, nevertheless, she did not like to leave it for the unknown. The future was strange and feared. Orange and her mother had not been congenial friends, but they were of her own sex. What would become of the Trampleasures now? They were without money. She turned to her husband.

'Mr. Herring,' she said timidly, 'my mother and my sister, what of them?'

'Dearest Mirelle, that is as you like.'

'Oh, Orange, and you, Mrs. Trampleasure! Will you come and live with me where I am going? I entreat you to do so. Make my home your own. I do not think you will be happy here, where you have met with so many sorrows. And I—I shall miss you.'

She looked at Herring, asking with her eyes if she had done right.

This was not what he wished. Orange was not the sort of companion he relished for his wife. There was an indescribable something about her which he disliked. Then an idea struck him. He called Orange and Mirelle aside into the little drawing-room.

'Mirelle, everything I have is yours. You may dispose of all at your pleasure. I know what has happened here. Orange is engaged to be married to Captain Trecarrel; but, through the sad disaster that has taken place, her little fortune is lost. Is it your wish, Mirelle, that this sum should be made up to her? The loss of this fortune stands in the way of her happiness and that of Captain Trecarrel.'

Mirelle trembled, looked down for a moment, and then said, 'Yes, dear Orange, it shall be so. All that sum which was to have been yours, but which was lost, shall be given to you. Be happy with Captain Trecarrel.'

Then Orange flamed up. Her eyes sparkled, her cheeks flushed, and she clenched her hands.

'Never, never!' she exclaimed. 'He deserted and insulted me. Never, never, will I take him.'

'Well, Orange,' said Herring, 'you do as you think best. The same sum that was lodged by your father in my hands in trust for you, to be paid over on your marriage, shall be placed in the bank in your name. If you can forgive the Captain, well, so be it. None will be better pleased to hear it than Mirelle and I; but if not, you will find a welcome at Welltown. I must not delay longer. We have a lengthy drive before us, and cannot reach our destination while there is light in the sky.'

He handed Mirelle into the carriage, and stepped in himself.

The post-boys wiped their lips—they had been given a tumbler each of spiced wine—they cracked their whips, and away whirled the carriage.

'Orange, Orange! throw rice,' called Mrs. Trampleasure.

Orange stooped, picked up a handful of snow, and flung it after them, in at the carriage window, and it fell over Herring and Mirelle, a cold shower.

But the maid was more vehement and strict in her adhesion to traditional usage. 'First one slipper—a red one, then another—black, whirled through the snowy air, and fell in their track.

'What are you about, Bella!' exclaimed Mrs. Trampleasure. 'That's my dear 'usband's slipper—that red one is, and the other is Sampson's.'

'Look!' said Orange. The red slipper and the black had fallen with the toes pointing in the direction taken by the carriage, and lay between the wheel-marks.

'Mother, it looks just as though the dead father and the runaway son were after them.'

Hark! what is that? A faint, low music, scarcely audible, and when heard at once caught and puffed away by the frozen blast. Was that the wind, playing a weird æolian strain through the spines of the Scotch fir? But if so, strange that the vibrations should frame themselves into a strain like that of Ford's old glee:—

>   Since first I saw your face, I resolv'd
>   To honour and renown you!

'Come in, mother, the wind is cold. It freezes to the marrow.'

CHAPTER XLII.

THE SNOW BRIDE.

A WILD road that which leads from Launceston to Boscastle, up hill continuously, for miles after miles, across barren moor unrelieved by rocks, studded at intervals by cairns under which dead primæval warriors lie. In summertime the road is rendered tolerable by the distant views; the rugged range of Cornish tors, Brown Willy and Row Tor on the left; far away south the dome of Hengistdun, where the Britons made their last stand against Athelstan, and which to the present day is studded with the cairns that cover their dead, To the southeast the grand distant range of Dartmoor lost in cobalt blue.

But that road, on such a day as this, was unendurable. There was no shelter whatever; not a hedge, not a tree; not a village was passed through. Llaneast, Tresmeer, Treneglos, Egloskerry, lie buried in valleys where trees grow and the sun sleeps on smooth greenswards. The road seemed to be slowly mounting into the skies, into the bosoms of the snowclouds which shed their cold contents over it. White favours! The horses were plastered with them, the post-boys were patched with them, the carriage encrusted with them, the windows frosted over with them. Mirelle sat on the east side; she tried to look through the glasses, but could see nothing but snow crystals.

Herring spoke to her, but conversation was impossible; the wind howled and beat at the windows, as with icy hands, striving to smash them in. There was no keeping the wind out: it drove in between the frames and the glass, it worked its way through below and chilled the feet on the matting.

The horses went slowly; the snow balled under their hoofs, and the post-boys had to descend repeatedly to clear their shoes. The road was no post-road, and no change of horses was to be had half-way. There was no choice, therefore, but to rest the jaded beasts at the wretched little tavern on the heath, called 'Drunkards all.' There is a legend to account for the name. A traveller came one Sunday to the pothouse, with its little cluster of cottages around, and saw the people reeling from the tavern to their homes in the morning. 'What!' he asked. 'Does no one go to church here?' 'No,' was the hiccuped reply. 'Sundays we drinks and drinks—here we be drunkards all.' He passed the same way one weekday, and found the cottagers staggering from the tavern to the fields. 'What!' he asked. 'Is no work done here weekdays?' 'No,' was the answer. 'We drinks and we drinks—here we be drunkards all.' Once again he passed that way, and it was midnight; but the road was encumbered with tipsy men and women. 'Does nobody sleep here?' 'Sleep!' was the reply. 'No, we drinks and we drinks—we be drunkards all.' And as he went through the churchyard of Davidstow, he saw tombstones inscribed 'D. o. D.—D. A.'; and when he asked the meaning, the sexton said, with his thumb over his shoulder, 'Them from where you came from; Died o' drink—Drunkards all.' So the hamlet got its name, and has kept it to the present day.

Herring begged that a great fire might be made up, and some smouldering turf was put on the hearth in the little guest room. Firewood was an unattainable luxury in this treeless waste; the only fuel was peat. The walls were whitewashed, the floor was slate, on which milk had been spilled, and was frozen. The turf had not taken the chill out of the air in the room when the hour for resting the horses was passed. Herring had ordered dinner, but nothing was to be had to eat, save fried ham and eggs, nothing to drink but hard cyder and muddy beer. Mirelle had no appetite. She sat in her white dress by the low fire, deadly pale, with dark rings about her eyes, shivering. She held her hands to the dull ashes, and thought of the sunny garden of the Sacré Cœur. How the bees hummed there, and the hyacinths, blue and pink, bloomed early and filled the air with fragrance, and against the wall gold-green glistening flies preened their wings, loving the sun, and happy basking in it.

'It is time for us to move on, dear Mirelle,' said Herring; 'we have only made half of our way, but the worst half is done. The rest is, for a part at least, down hill.' She rose mechanically. He wrapped the shawls well round her, but there was no warmth in the slender white form to be wrapped in. There was no colour in her lips, none in the transparent cheek, only the blue icelike veins in her temples.

He led her to the carriage; again the post-boys wiped their lips, this time of sour cyder, and cracked their whips. The wheels went round noiselessly, and the carriage was lost to sight in the driving snow. Not only did the wheels revolve noiselessly, but the footfalls of the horses produced no sound; the postillions were silent, and those within the carriage did not speak. Verily that might have been taken for a bleached phantom coach drawn by phantom horses, conveying phantom bride and bridegroom from the grave of one at Launceston to the grave of another at Boscastle.

Herring took Mirelle's hand. She made no resistance. He held it in his, hoping that his warmth might thaw those frozen fingers. He pressed them, but met with no answering pressure; the hand was possibly too numbed to feel.

Now ensued hedges. They saw a woman, head down against the snow, stalking along the top of one—the usual footpath in these parts, where the lanes are often deep in water.

Here and there came walls, and here and there ragged thorns; then moor again, and then the carriage began to descend.

Mirelle held her breath. Darkness had set in already; the post-boys lit their lamps at a cottage that was passed, and through the windows could be seen the snowflakes falling as flashes of white fire in the radius of light cast by the lamps. The steam of the horses was blown back and formed haloes.

Mirelle's hand trembled in that of Herring. She looked round at him. He saw, by the reflection of the lamp-lights, that her eyes were wide with fear

'What is the matter, dear Mirelle?'

'That noise—that terrible noise!'

'What! the roar of the ocean?'

The thunder of the Atlantic filled the air. Driven before the gale, the mighty billows dashed themselves to dust upon the adamantine cliffs and flung their shivers high into the air. The roar was continuous, but with pulsations in it, as the wind rose and fell. It seemed to Mirelle as if she and Herring were drifting in the vast void where there was no earth, no creation, no planets, no light, no life, no God; in chaos filled with howling winds and thundering unseen forces that clashed purposeless and self-destructive. But worse still, to the outer answered an inner desolation. There also, chaos was. She was drifting in spirit in a void, without a hope, without an interest, without a purpose, with heart and brain dead.

The carriage whirled down a rapid descent, and the roar waxed louder, more hungry, more terrible. No rocks could withstand the weight of water hurled against them. The iron walls must yield before those Titanic blows, and all the world dissolve and sink beneath the angry, inky ocean.

'Will that not cease?' asked Mirelle, timidly.

'The waves can always be heard here,' answered John Herring, 'but, of course, only as a pleasant mutter in still weather.'

'At night—does it go on all night?'

'To be sure; the sea never sleeps. In time you will come to love the sound. It will be a lullaby, soothing my darling to sleep.'

Mirelle shuddered.

Lights were visible, twinkling below.

'There is a little town, Boscastle, lying in that glen,' said he; 'we shall pass above it on our way home.'

Home! the word conveyed no warmth to the heart of Mirelle.

Home is a quiet nook in the sun, among roses and mignonette, with a kitten purring at your feet, and a blackbird singing out of a syringa hard by, and the white cap of Josephine seen through the kitchen window, and her pleasant voice singing a *cantique* of the Mois de Marie whilst she shells peas. Home! A cold house in a void world, without a bush or tree, without stillness, in the midst of blackness and storm, and with salt spray and the boom of breaking billows filling the air with bitterness and thunder.

A scream over the carriage. Mirelle cried out in an agony of fear at that Banshee note.

'Do not be frightened,' said Herring. 'That was a gull driven in by the storm. Poor Mirelle! you will be glad when we reach home. This has been a trying day for you.'

She could not answer. She did not think she would be g'ad to reach Welltown; she was indifferent whether she got there or not. It was all one to her whether she alighted in a cold home or went on for ever and ever thus in storm and snow. Would it not be best of all to be allowed to descend and lie down on the white bank, and wrap the white fleeces round her, and so go to sleep? Then, indeed, she would go home—to a home she knew, to a home peopled with dear friends, saints and angels, with whom she had spoken from early childhood.

The longest day has its ending. The carriage drew up at last at the porch door of Welltown. Herring sprang out; no lights were in the windows. He looked along the front of the house; all was dark. No cheering welcome of twinkling candles, of ruddy fireflash through the panes. He knocked loudly. Then Genefer came to the door with a stable lanthorn.

'What! Master John! Well, to be sure. I never thought it. The day were so wisht and wild.'

'Jenny,' said Herring, impatiently, 'open at once. Let me in; you knew that we were to arrive this evening.'

'The storm raged so bad, I thought sure you'd put it off.'

'Come in, dear Mirelle,' said Herring, greatly incensed, and led his bride into the porch out of the wind.

'Have you no fires lighted? Nothing ready?' he asked, angrily, of Genefer.

'No, Master John. It be bad luck to wed in snow and storm: snow cools love and wind blows it away. I reckoned you knew that well enough, and would have put it off till the sun shone.'

A cold reception. The hall dark; only a little turf

smouldering on the hearth, giving out neither light nor heat.

Mirelle came in; she did not look round; she was stupefied. It was all one to her. She had not expected much, and was not disappointed.

Genefer put the lanthorn on the table and proceeded to light a couple of wax candles. Herring divested Mirelle of her dark wraps.

Then the old woman looked at her. In the large gloomy hall Mirelle stood like a spectral figure, illumined by the candles, the white veil hanging over her shoulders and back.

'Lord of mercy bless us!' exclaimed Genefer, starting back. 'It be the same—the same! O God!—the same I dreamed! The Snow Bride.'

She looked at her with dismay, then raised her hands and said, 'That ever I should have seen the day! O Master John! Master John! But the Lord sends strong delusions on them whom He will bring to naught!'

'Go at once, Jenny, and get supper ready. Heap up wood on the hearth. Is there a fire upstairs?'

'I don't know whether there *be*—there *was*, to dry the rooms; but there be nothing ready. It be a thousand pities you cannot get it all undone, and, if it must be done, do it another day, when the sun shines and the air be plum' (warm).

'This is intolerable,' said Herring, now thoroughly roused. 'You are determined, Jenny, to drive me beyond the limits of forbearance.'

'The Lord ordains,' answered Genefer: 'what will be will be. There! I'll have the fire up directly. Now, Hender'—aloud, and with her head through the kitchen door—'look spry, and bring in a faggot, and clap it on the turves. Take the bellows,' she said to Mirelle; 'blow away at them turves, and they'll glow. I'll be off, and get something warm directly.' But, instead of going directly, she stood in the door, and looked at Herring, and said: 'The sheep always goes before the wind. You may put them in a loo place, but they won't bide there: they go with the wind to where they will freeze and die. It be all the same wi' men. When the Lord blows, they goes before His breath to their destruction, and not all the wisdom of the wise will avail to keep them loo.'

'Would you like to go upstairs, Mirelle, to your room?' asked Herring.

She lifted her sad eyes to his face and nodded. He took a

candle and led the way. The boards creaked as they went up
the uncarpeted stairs, and the wind wailed through the staircase window, clinking the little diamond panes; the draught
was so great that the candle was nearly blown out. Against
the glass the snow was patched in masses, as though the window
had been pelted with snowballs, and the white patches reflected
back the candle-light.

Upstairs was a bedroom, above the hall, and adjoining it a
small boudoir over the porch. There was a fire on the hearth,
and the bedding was ranged as a wall round it, to be well aired.
Some billets of wood were heaped up beside the chimney-piece,
and these Herring put on. He plied the bellows, and soon a
yellow flame danced up. The room began to look more cheery.
It was a pretty room; Herring had thought much about making
it pleasant. The paper was bright, with roses in sprigs over
the walls, and over the window were sprigged curtains lined
with forget-me-not blue.

'There, dear Mirelle,' he said, 'I will have the boxes
brought up; and I hope, in half an hour, Jenny will have
dinner ready for us. I am sorry for her neglect. She is a tire-
some, self-opinionated old woman, but you will come in time
to value her. She is a Cornish crystal—and rough.'

He did not leave the room at once, but stood and looked
round it; he had not seen it before, since it had been done up,
with firelight flickering and candles lighted. He was pleased,
and said, 'It is pretty—is it not, Mirelle?'

She looked up wonderingly at him. What was pretty?
What could be pretty in such a place?

He had lighted candles on the dressing-table and on the
mantelpiece. Over that hung a picture of his mother—a sweet
young face, with a pleasant smile on it.

'That is my mother,' he said; 'she is looking down on you
out of heaven. This was her room: I was born in it, and she
died here.'

In a corner, near the fire, was a little *prie-dieu*, and over it
a crucifix. Herring had procured that, because he made sure
it would please Mirelle; but she did not observe it. She was
cold, and crept near to the fire.

'I should like to show you the boudoir. I have done it up
very nicely for you.'

'Oh, not now! another time.'

'Very well, Mirelle, I will go and hasten Genefer.'

He left the room, a little disappointed that no expression of pleasure had escaped her on seeing how he had thought and prepared for her. Then he descended to the hall to stimulate Genefer to activity, and to see to his wife being given her boxes immediately.

More than half an hour passed before dinner was ready; when it was on the table, and the room was bright with candles, and a dancing fire was gambolling through a faggot of dry sticks, Herring went upstairs to call Mirelle. He found her sitting, still dressed in white, by the fire, looking into it, lost in a dream, with her hands folded in her lap, and tears on her cheeks. A little colour had returned to her lips, and the flickering firelight, reflected in her large dark eyes, gave them a fictitious life. She did not hear Herring enter, and when he spoke she started and shivered, as though frightened. She speedily recovered herself, and descended with him. She had removed her veil, but was otherwise unchanged in dress. The snowdrops in her bosom were crushed, and their bruised heads hung despondingly. Herring removed the bunch and put it in his button-hole. Mirelle could not eat much; she did not speak, except in brief answers to his questions. She was apparently thinking, and it was with an effort that she attended to what her husband said.

Genefer watched her intently. The old woman's face was grim and dissatisfied. She was respectful, and attended to her, but without the alacrity and cordiality in her manner that might have been looked for in an old family servant when welcoming to her home her master's bride.

When dinner was over, and Genefer had withdrawn, Herring said to Mirelle, 'Now, dearest, come into the ingle-nook, and sit on the settle. The great back will cut off every draught, and you will become warm there. I will bring my chair beside you.'

She rose, without answering, and took the place he indicated. The settle was of oak, dark and well polished, with the four cardinal virtues carved in panels above the heads of those who sat in it. It had stamped and gilt leather at the back, a little way up, and a crimson cushion on the seat. Herring thrust a footstool under Mirelle's feet, and, taking a chair, drew it near her.

'Dear Mirelle,' he said, 'welcome to your future home.'

'Thank you, Mr. Herring.'

'You must not call me *Mr.* Herring.'

'No, I know I must not. I will do my duty. I will call you by your Christian name. But you must not be angry with me; it will not come at once. I will do my best, if you will have patience.'

'Mirelle!—nothing could make me angry with you.'

'Nothing?' Then she sighed and looked into the fire

'Is there something troubling your mind?' he asked, unable to understand her manner.

'Yes,' she said, and looked up timidly at him, then withdrew her glance before his eyes; 'I will do my duty. You are my husband, and I must let you see all my heart. It is proper that you should. I will do what I know in my conscience to be right.'

'I will gladly look into that dear heart, and all I ask and hope is that I may find there a little sparkle of love for me.'

She shivered, and was silent again, still looking into the flames broodingly.

'Dear, dear Mirelle,' he said, 'although you are now my wife, bound to me for ever, you have not yet given me, or received from me, a kiss. You have not once told me that you love me.'

Then she looked round full at him, with her large, sad, dark eyes, and rested them on him for full a minute without a word; but he saw that something was stirring in her heart. Then she said gravely, 'I respect you very much, John Herring.'

'Respect will not do for me. I want love,' he said with vehemence.

'I esteem you above all men.'

'That is insufficient. I will be satisfied with nothing short of love.'

'I do not love you.'

Those few words went like a bullet through his heart. He could not speak.

She saw that she had pained him unutterably. She went on. 'I am bound to speak the truth. I cannot lie; I cannot dissemble. What I say is true. I give you everything that is in my power to give. I am yours. I believe you to be the best, the noblest, the truest of men. But love——'

She slowly shook her head and sighed, and relapsed into looking into the burning wood.

His power of speech was gone from him.

'You must not expect too much from me,' she said; 'I will do my duty.'

'Duty!' he cried, and sprang to his feet. 'Duty is not

what I ask for. I know you will do your duty—as an angel of God will do his duty. But I ask for, and must have—love.'

'I cannot, I cannot,' she said, in a desolate, despairing tone, and again shook her head.

'Why not? Is it so impossible to love a man whose whole heart is yours, who thinks of and cares only for you?'

'I would love you if I could! It is not my fault. I am willing, but I have not the power. I *cannot*.'

'Why can you not?'

She raised her large, dark eyes and looked at him, with a dull despair in them, and her lips quivered, as she answered, 'Because I love another.'

That went like a second bullet through his heart, and rendered him speechless again.

'You are my husband. I know my duty. I am bound to conceal nothing from you. I am bound to tell you all that is on my heart. My love is for another. I cannot help it; you have nothing to fear. None can suffer from this as I do. I will try from day to day to deaden it. I will be true to you in thought as in deed. What I have promised, I will perform. But there it is—in my heart, burning, consuming. You could not put out that roaring fire on the hearth; it must blaze till it has eaten itself away. In time the fire here,' she touched her bosom, 'that fire, will have consumed itself and be white ashes, and the hearth cold. Then you may light another fire on it, but not till then.'

Herring had been standing looking at her, with one hand on his brow. Now he turned away.

'Are you angry?' she asked piteously. 'I felt in my conscience that I ought to conceal nothing from my husband; I knew that I was bound to tell you all. Are you angry?'

'I am in pain,' he said. His hand was on his heart. 'I am in deadly pain.'

'And I—I too,' she whispered, and her head drooped towards her lap, like one of her broken snowdrops.

Herring walked through the hall to the main door. There he turned.

'Mirelle!' His face was almost as white as hers.

'Yes, John.'

'God be with you. Good-bye.'

He opened the door. The wind tore in, and brought snow with it, and the thunder of the mad sea mad that it had found a barrier which it could not demolish nor overleap, and in its madness tearing itself to spray.

Then the door shut, and Mirelle was alone.

CHAPTER XLIII.

HUNTING THE DEVIL.

MIRELLE sat over the fire, looking into it. Had she done right in telling John Herring all her mind? She supposed that she had, and yet she was not quite sure. Her nature was so entirely frank, she had such a horror of concealment, that it had seemed to her a duty, an imperative duty, to lay bare her heart before her husband. She spoke out everything, without disguise, to her confessor, and the husband stood to her, she supposed, in much the same light. She would be guilty of a fraud, an impiety, if she allowed him to live with her without knowing the true state of her affections. She had thought this over a great deal, and she had satisfied her conscience that she was bound to tell him all. But now that the confession was made, she was frightened at the results. She had driven Herring from her. Whither was he gone? Would he return? Was it always right to speak the truth? Was not perfect openness the most refined form of cruelty?

Mirelle began dimly to see that she had acted unwisely; that she had been selfish in her desire to do her duty, and keep her own conscience clear. She owed a duty to her husband, a paramount duty, and the duty she owed him was to make him happy. In her effort to do her duty to herself she had run counter to her duty to him.

So she sat over the fire, in her white bridal dress, with her white face, and cold tears distilled slowly from her eyes.

Without, the wind raged, and splashes of snow were thrown, like mortar from a trowel, against the window panes. There was a red carpet on the hall floor, but the wind got under it, and it rolled like a sea of blood. She could see the first roller begin by the door and travel the whole length of the room. The curtains over the window swayed as though some one were in the embrasure stirring from side to side and pulling at the curtains to keep himself covered, and yet was seeking a place through which he might peep unperceived at the Snow Bride by the fire, melting away in tears.

The hall door creaked, and the latch, to her fancy, was tried; but no hand was there. It was the wind that thrust against the oaken boards and rattled the latch.

How the ocean roared! No doors nor windows could exclude that terrible all-pervading thunder. The sound was not in the wind alone, it was in the solid earth. It was not heard through the ear alone, it was felt by every nerve, for the foundations and the walls vibrated. In one of the hall windows was a cracked pane, and through it the wind screamed, and sobbed, and wailed. Were there ships at sea, this awful night? Were they near the coast? If so, there was no hope for the vessels, none for the crew. The stoutest ships must be broken against the iron cliffs, and the sailors dashed out of human shape.

There were souls drifting in that fierce wind and bitter cold —souls of drowned men on their way to purgatory and hell. What was that piping, and sighing, and crying at the window? Poor drowned souls peering in, and pleading to be admitted; poor souls still wet with the brine, shivering with cold, feeling their desolation, their nakedness, torn from the bodies they had so long and so happily tenanted; poor souls wailing and gnashing their teeth, because cast into the outer darkness and eternal cold.

A dog outside began to bark savagely. Had it seen the wan train of weeping souls sweep by? Then he lapsed into an occasional bark of distress, then was silent, then barked again.

What ailed the dog? The snow was drifting into his kennel, and he was cold and could not sleep.

There were rats in the old house. The cold had driven them in, and they were racing through the walls in quest of warm corners and of food. In one place glass had been put down to block a run; but the rats had broken their way through. Every rat that passed over the glass made it clink. They were between the ceiling and the floor overhead. One— two—three, one—two—three. One of the rats was three-legged, he had lost a foot in a gin. His footfalls could be distinguished from those of the other rats. He went slower than the rest, that old cripple; one—two—three, one two—three.

Where was John Herring? What had become of him? Was he still walking in the snow and wind? Would he press on, thinking only of his misery, till, numbed with frost and weary of battling with the wind, he fell in the snow and slept his life away?

Whither would he go? What would he seek? Rest, and the lulling of the terrible pain from the wound she had dealt him. How could rest be got? Only in one way.

Then Mirelle sprang up, terrified at her own thoughts, and clasped her hands over her face to hide from her the horrible picture that rose before her fancy. She fell on her knees, faint with fear.

The three-legged rat had found a bit of tallow-candle end that had been thrust by a child through a knot in the flooring, and he skipped about on three paws, uncouthly, in an ecstasy of delight. But a rat with four legs came by and lusted after the candle end, and fell on the cripple, and bit him. He screamed with pain and for aid. Then other rats, sound in limb, ran to the scene, and finding the cripple getting the worst of it, took sides against him, and bit and mangled him, he screaming with rage and pain all the while; and, after that, they divided the candle end between themselves, as their perquisite for having come to the aid of their four-legged brother, and left him the rush-wick, which he could not digest.

On the stairs was a clock—a very noisy clock, that ticked loud, and made a great whir before it struck the hours. This clock had dropped its weight, which fell with a crash the night John's mother died. The weight came down but once again, when Jago Herring, his father, died. A quaint old clock, with a figured face representing a drooping flower and a winged hourglass, and underneath the inscription—

> The flower fadeth,
> The hour runneth.
> Sic transit gloria mundi.

Twelve o'clock! Midnight had come, the hour when the dead are abroad.

Against the wall was a mirror. Mirelle was afraid to look in it. She knew that dead men peered over the shoulders of the living when they looked incautiously into the glass after twelve at night. What face might she see there? She took her handkerchief to put over it; the handkerchief was too small, and was, moreover, wet with her tears. She had a little shawl; she took that up—a black shawl—and went with it to the mirror, with head averted.

As she was engaged in hitching the ends of the shawl over the glass she suddenly heard piercing cries, then howls and loud words shouted shrilly.

The shawl fell at her feet: she stood frozen to the floor; her heart stood still. The cries continued, waxing louder, more agonising; she heard feet racing along the passage upstairs, and then a man's voice, in gruff tones, raised in remonstrance. Then the door of her room was shaken, and again the man spoke. She could distinguish now what he said.

'Genefer! stand off. You may not go in and scare them wi' your screeching and devil visions.'

But the door was beaten open in spite of his protest, and the feet were audible rushing over the floor of the room. Then again a cry, a wail, and loud exclamations in shrill tones; and in another moment down the stairs came the feet, with sobs and moans, and Genefer Benoke burst into the hall, with a great cloak cast over her, her hair loose and flowing wildly about her shoulders, her large grey eyes wide open, and staring blankly before her, and both her hands extended in front of her, now scrabbling in the air, then expanded wide, with every finger apart. Her feet were bare.

'I see un! I see un! Look where he goes! Ah! thou foul devil! thou spirit of the bottomless pit! See, see! where he goes, the accursed one, with the smoke of the everlasting torment swaling round and round him!'

She stooped and picked up the black shawl, and lashed with it before her.

'Where goest thou? Do'y see un, Hender? Do'y see un? He be like a black shadow with no sartain shape, stealing along, and now I sees a bit clear and then another bit. There be one fiery eye peer out, and now it be gone, and there shoots out another. Look in thicky corner, where he stands, and gapes and mows and tosses his arms. The Lord is my light and my salvation, whom then shall I fear? See, Hender! he has his fingers in his mouth and is drawing out the corners, out—wide—wider—like gum elastic, the whole width o' the room, and the fire comes out—it be the mouth of hell! Hender, Hender! see where he be writing on the wall, and the letters be letters of fire?'

Then she uttered a piercing shriek, and clasped her hands over her eyes, and buried her face in the black shawl.

Hender Benoke followed his wife.

'Come, come back to bed, Genefer. What do the devil mean by walking o' nights like this when it be freezing hard, and folks wants to be warm between the blankets? Come back, and if you must run arter 'un, run o' a summer night, ondeacent though it be—in your smock.'

'My boy! my John! O master, dear Master John! O the day, the day!'

'Come back to bed; you're frightening the young lady.'

'Her! her! the Snow Maiden that'll freeze the blood in the heart of un! Where be she? I cannot stay, it will be too late. I've a read the writing in fire. Let go, Hender; do not hold me back! I see the devil; he be making for the door, and I must after him, and smite him, with the Lord's word. Come on, you—you!' She grasped Mirelle by the arm. 'It were you as brought the devil here to tempt us, and you must strive along of me to drive un, or he will carry the dear maister away.'

She made for the porch door, drawing Mirelle after her. Hender again interposed.

'Genny,' he said, 'you cannot; you must not.'

'Very well then—no!' exclaimed the woman, letting go her hold of Mirelle. 'No, no, it be none o' you can drive the devil, for you be an idolater, and idolaters has their portion in the lake that burneth wi' fire for ever and ever. I must drive un with the Word of God. Run, Hender! bring me the great black Bible; quick, man. The devil be gone out at the porch door.'

She dashed to the window, tore aside the curtains, and cried: 'I see un, I see un on the snow, going like a puff o' smoke, and at every step he takes the snow glints white as a flash of moon. Bring me my black Bible, that I may pursue un, and catch un up, and smite un atcross the horns, and fell un like an ox.' Then she came into the midst of the room, and stood before Mirelle, and fixed her eyes sternly on her.

'Down on your knees, maiden,' she said, and pointed to the floor. 'Down on your knees if you know how to pray, and pray to the Lord for a soul, a poor, despairing, human soul as is brought to great temptation, and heaven or hell stands on the turn o' a hair. The Lord hath revealed to me that this night he fought the battle of Armageddon, and Apollyon and I must wrestle together for a human soul. Jacob wrestled with an angel till the break of day, and he would not let him go till he had blessed him. And I be called to wrestle, not wi' an angel but wi' a devil, and I will not let un go till I have tooked the soul that he be seeking out o' his hands. Down on your knees and help me if you can. Give me the Book.'

Hender had come in with the Bible. She snatched it out of his hands, and in another moment had slammed the door behind her, and was flying through the snow, with bare feet, and her black hair lashed by the wind, regardless of the cold and storm, holding the great Bible above her head with both hands, and crying after the black shadow that went like a puff of smoke before her, in whose treadings the snow glinted like flakes of moonlight.

Hender stood in the porch looking after her and muttering. But Mirelle was kneeling on the red carpet in the midst of the room, and the wind got in beneath and lifted and rolled this carpet about her so that she seemed to be kneeling on a red sea.

All at once, Genefer stood still, threw up the Bible, caught it, and clasped it to her bosom. Both she and Hender heard a shot. A gun had been discharged; the report entered the room where Mirelle knelt, and she heard it.

'Glory be to God!' cried Genefer; 'he be driven back, but not by me. Sisera were slain by the hand of a woman, and it were revealed to Deborah that so it should be. So she went wi' Barak to the battle, for she reckoned that the woman into whose hand the Lord would sell Sisera were herself. But it were not so. Glory be to God! The devil be driven back, though not by me! I saw Satan as a stream o' smoking pitch run down Willapark and fall into Blackapit.'

Then she came quickly back, all her excitement over.

CHAPTER XLIV.

WILLAPARK.

Forth into the storm John Herring had gone. That day so desired had ended thus! He had gained her whom he loved —whom he had long loved, but only to know that her heart could never be his. He had taken the Snow Bride to him, and, as Genefer had warned him, she was about to chill him to death. No light would rise in those eyes for him; no smile come on those cheeks for him. Those lips would not meet his; that heart not beat for him. She respected him, but she feared him. Now he understood her conduct towards him through their engagement and that day. She stood in terror of him; she shrank from his love, because she had no love to give in return for it.

Herring could think of nothing continuously. The gnawing pain at his heart was too intense to suffer him to think connectedly. He was like one walking in semi-consciousness, staggering after a stunning blow, seeing nothing clearly, thinking no thought out. He did not know whither he was going.

He was without hat, he was without great-coat. He had gone forth in his despair, without a thought of himself, what he should do, whither he should go. Did it matter whither he went? Wherever he went he must carry this pain with him. What should he do? He could do nothing, he could not staunch the wound that had been dealt him; the wound had cut too deep and had severed the main artery of life. There was no balm in Gilead for such a wound as that; it must bleed, bleed hope, energy, desire out of him. He cared nothing for life now. Life was a torture chamber, and the poor sufferer on the rack turns and cries out, 'Put an end to my agonies. Use the dagger, *la miséricorde*!' What is life, if granted, worth? After the rack, what is life with disjointed limbs and riven heart-strings? Who would receive as a boon so worthless a gift? No; in the torture chamber none ask for life, there but one desire is harboured, and that for death.

Herring had gone unconsciously towards Willapark, the headland that starts into the sea, gnawed half through by vast gulfs, in which the waves boil as in a cauldron. Willapark, white with snow, shelved up towards the sky; beyond was the void whence came thunderings and roarings, where nothing could be seen. So hitherto had he been going contentedly up his white way that led to heaven, expecting felicity at the top, and all at once he found himself at the edge of an unfathomed gulf, and a loved hand touched and thrust him over, and now he was falling into the awful void; whither he knew not, how it would end he only guessed.

By Blackapit was his little office, a small wooden erection; he could see it rising out of the snow. He had lived so much there of late, had slept there so frequently, that on leaving Welltown he instinctively took this direction.

He drew the key from his pocket and unlocked the door. Inside all was dark, and the smell was musty; the office had not been opened for some days. He shut the door, and went directly to his chair near the fireplace. There was, of course, no fire there, but that did not matter; he preferred sitting in the dark. How the gulls screamed around the house. The storm frightened them, even them, accustomed to wind and waves, and they cried and wailed as they fluttered disconsolately over the mainland. Perhaps they thought that in such a raging sea no fish would live, that all would be beaten to pulp, and their hope of food destroyed.

Herring seated himself in the chair : it was an arm-chair. He placed his elbow on the arm, and rested his throbbing temples in his hand.

This was the end. She did not love him, she loved another. Who was that other? That he did not know; she had not told him, and it did not concern him. All that concerned him was the one fact that she was not his. He had purchased to himself a precious heart, and when he knocked to be admitted he was told to abide outside, the key had been given to another.

He sat on in his wretchedness, not knowing how the time passed. He was becoming dead and cold in his chair, as Genefer had foreseen.

He stood up at last and struck a light. He kept tinder-box and candles in the Willapark office—tallow-candles they were —and he lighted one and placed it on his table.

Then he opened his desk and took paper, and a pen. His hand was so cold that he could not write. He tried to warm it with his breath, but in vain. He must write to Mirelle. If she had told him her secret, he must no longer conceal his— he must let her know that he had taken care of her fortune, and that it was now her own to do with it what she liked. Had she known that she was wealthy, she would never have accepted him, John Herring, now in purgatory, suffering for the wrong he had done her—a wrong done unconsciously and in good faith. She had taken him only because she believed herself to be destitute and dependent on his bounty. He had acted wrongly from the first. Light came to him, as to others, when too late to walk by it. Now he saw what the proper course would have been. If he mistrusted Tramplara, he should have confided all to Mirelle, and allowed her to choose her own trustee. But no! that would not have done; for, had the secret of the diamonds come out, old Tramplara would have claimed them as the legal guardian. He was bewildered; he did not know in what way he had acted wrongly, and yet what he had done, conscientiously believing he was doing right, had led to disaster—had landed him in a position from which there was but one escape. He had been to Mirelle a worse enemy than Tramplara. The trustee of her father's appointment had robbed her of the money intrusted to him; he, John Herring, the trustee of his own nomination, had robbed her of her life's happiness. Could he doubt for a moment that had she been free she would have refused him and have given her hand and fortune to the man of her choice? Now there lay before him no remedy save one. He had chained her to him, and whilst that chain remained she must suffer. Till it was broken, happiness was impossible to her. 'Oh, Mirelle! Mirelle!' the cry broke from his heart. Here was bitterness past enduring, to be on the threshold of happiness, and to be thrust back; to have the cup at his lips, and to have it snatched from him and spilled on the ground.

He lit the fire in his grate and warmed his fingers; he did not care for the comfort of the fire, he sought only to thaw his hand, to enable it to write. In his despair it seemed that there was but one course open to him—to restore to Mirelle the liberty of which he had deprived her. When able to write, he took the pen and ink, and slowly, with many pauses, gave her in full the story of the diamonds stolen by Grizzly Cobbledick from Mr. Strange's trunk, then given to him by Joyce. He assured Mirelle that he had acted as he supposed best, with no thought of reaping advantage to himself, certainly with none of gaining her by means of her own fortune. She would do him this justice. He confessed his mistake, and made the only amends in his power by restoring her the freedom of which he had deprived her. He did not date the account, but he signed it, and folded it. Then he made an abstract of all her money. He stated where the remainder of the uncut diamonds might be found, and what the amount of money was which he had received for those he had sold, and how he had disposed of this money. The room was his office, and his books were in it. He consulted them; and as he went over the accounts he recovered, to some extent, his composure; but his purpose never swerved.

When he had finished his task, he put the account with the letter, inclosed both in one wrapper, and sealed it. J. H. was his stamp; no arms, for he had no right to bear any.

Then he rose and went out, closing his door after him. He walked through the snow, which was thin on the headland, for the gale carried it away, and shook it into the sea or heaped it in the valleys. He could see, or he thought he could see, the distant lights of Welltown. Mirelle was not gone to bed yet; the light was red, shining through the hall curtains. What was Mirelle doing?

The snow had ceased to fall, and the air was clear of everything save spray, which was driven over the land in scuds. The headland shook under the blows of the ocean. On the left hand was that awful gulf, Blackapit, an almost circular well with sheer cliffs descending three hundred feet into the boiling foam and fury. He approached it; there was no rail, nothing to prevent anyone from falling over. On a dark night, when no snow covered the ground, anyone stepping astray would, in a moment, plunge into that horrible abyss never penetrated by the sun. At low water there was an inky tarn below, but now, through the narrow entrance, mountains of water beat their way, and when within tore themselves to froth in their agony to escape, and rolled back to the entrance, there to clash against another intruding billow. Then there rushed up into the air a white pillar of whirling foam that fell back again upon the contending surf below, unable to escape upwards. The roar of the raging water in this abyss was as the roar from the mouth of hell. There came upon Herring the thought of himself falling down that chasm, the hands extended, clutching at the rocks, and the nails torn to the quick in frantic effort to cling; kittiwakes, gulls, and skuas shrieking and dashing about him as he went down into that raging, ravening, thundering void. Rest there!—there—there! in that frantic turmoil, the very thought of which made a whirlpool in the brain! Herring sprang back with convulsive shrinking before such an end. No, he could not plunge down Blackapit!

He returned to his wooden house. It was warm and bright, and the sight of the fire and of the candle composed his nerves after that horrible dream of Blackapit. Over the fireplace was his gun—he had shot gulls with it from his window. On a summer day he had taken a boat and rowed about Blackapit and Welltown cove, and with a bullet killed porpoises. There were seals also in these bays. How horrible was the head of a seal, so human, rising straight out of the waves. He had never been able to kill one, the human eyes had unnerved him when he took aim.

He resumed his seat; his candle had a thief in it, a fungus, and burned dull. He snuffed the candle. Then he put some fuel on the fire, and looked musingly into it. He thought of how he had first known Mirelle, of her coldness towards him, how she had thrown away, or lost, his sprig of white heath. He remembered the very tones of her voice when she laughed at his name, Herring. He recalled her manner, as she scorned the idea of his being other than bourgeois. He recollected how she had cast reproach on the memory of her dead father, because he, being bourgeois, had dared to mate with her noble mother. And he had done the same thing—had taken advantage of her distress to tie her to him,—her the ideal of nobility, purity, beauty, to himself a humble yeoman's son, of no merit, and with few qualifications to attach any woman to him. His breathing was short; the pain at his heart was very real and physical. His head had been clear whilst he was working at the accounts, but now his brain began again to cloud over.

Then he stood up, and took down his gun. It was loaded with swanshot for the gulls. He had bullets in his drawer—for porpoises.

He drew the shot and went to his drawer; the bullets were not there. He turned over papers, and fishing tackle, and sundry odds and ends. He came upon a little book of sketches—how came they there? They were drawings he had made as a child of six and seven, very rude, and gaily painted with gamboge and carmine and Prussian blue. There was Noah's Ark, and the most marvellous beasts of all kaleidoscopic colours, marching up a plank into it. There was the Burning Fiery Furnace, and the three men being cast in at the top, comical little figures, with very little bodies, and very big hands and feet, all the toes and fingers extended. Herring remembered painting these pictures, at a table in a window, whilst Genefer was sewing, and his father was in the hall below, practising on his violin. He had painted these daubs in the little porch room, now done up in white and gold for Mirelle. No, the bullets were not in the drawer. He could not think where he had put them; his head was confused. He sat down again, with the gun across his knees. When had he last gone out porpoise-shooting? He could not remember. Not last summer, for he had been too fully engaged then at Upaver, and only making flying visits to Welltown, and then busy with the slate-quarry. As he sat thinking, the bunch of snowdrops Mirelle had worn fell at his feet. He had put them in his button-hole when he removed them from her bosom, and now that he stooped they dropped.

He picked up the little bunch. Poor, bruised, broken flowers, crushed and withered like his hopes; pure flowers, white as Mirelle. They had rested all day in her bosom. He put them to his lips, and a great trembling like an ague attack came over him. If he had asked her to give him the flowers, would she have given them to him? Yes, but with a needle in them to pierce his hand. She had given him herself, but with herself his death-wound.

Now, all at once, he remembered where the bullets were—on a shelf in a sort of recess or cupboard at the foot of the bed. He went to the place and found them. He took one, dropped it down the barrel, and rammed it home.

'God forgive me,' he said, 'but there is no help for it. So alone can I undo the wrong I have done; so alone restore to Mirelle the liberty and the happiness of which I have defrauded her.'

He leaned his head on the barrel; the steel was cold to his hot and heavy brow. He rested it there some moments, thinking. Then he raised it, and the round red ring marked his forehead.

The gnawing pain was not there; there was trouble there, but the pain was in his heart. Then he lowered the butt end of the musket on the floor, and, leaning forward, placed the mouth of the barrel against his heart, and slid his hand down it towards the trigger. A sense of alleviation of pain, a foretaste of rest, came to him, from the pressure of the gun on his heart.

'God pardon me, it cannot be otherwise! May He be with her and bless her! Mirelle! Mirelle!'

He touched the trigger.

At that moment the door flew open.

'Maister! dear maister!'

With the start, the gun was discharged, but not through his heart; the bullet whizzed past his ear, and penetrated the roof.

Then ensued silence for a minute. Herring was leaning back, hardly knowing what had happened, and whether he were alive or dead.

The smoke filled the little room. As it cleared away, his eyes saw Joyce.

'Maister! sure you have frightened of me dreadful; but—I've a brought'y the stockings.'

He did not speak. He understood nothing.

'Dear maister! what be thicky gun for? Did'y think I were a robber, and you fired at me? No, no! I be no robber,

I be come a long way. See! I ha' done it all myself. I sed as I would. I've a brought'y a pair o' stockings all of my own knitting.'

He remained speechless.

'Look!' she persisted; 'put thicky gashly gun away. There be no robbers here; I be your Joyce, your own poor Joyce. Look! the stockings be warm, of lambswool, and vitty, and I did knit mun every bit and croom myself.'

CHAPTER XLV.

'KINKUM-KUM.'

'It be warm and comfortable in here,' said Joyce, looking round her. 'Surely, I used to think it snug under the Table when the winds were loud; but there us had always a door open for the smoke to go out at. There were no chimney there, and there couldn't be none, for because of the great stone overhead.'

Herring put his hands to his brow. He was dazed. He could not understand Joyce's presence there and then.

'What a mighty long time you've a been away from West Wyke, maister! But, sure, I have been away a bit too. I've a been with Farmer Facey to Coombow. I sed I'd go to 'n, and work out the hire of the waggon as brought you home after you were nigh upon killed by Cap'n Sampson Tramplara, and I did it. I went there, and I were there two whole months by the moon. Both Farmer Facey and his wife sed I did more work than two men. But, sure, this fire be beautiful. I've a been out in the snow and wind all day, and the most of the night too.'

Herring looked inquiringly at her.

'Where have you come from, Joyce?'

'Where have I come from? Where else, sure, but from West Wyke. I be come to look for you, and to bring'y the stockings I've a knitted. I sed I would, and I've a done it.'

'I do not understand, Joyce. From West Wyke?'

'Sure-ly.'

'Not to-day, and in this storm?'

'I've not done this all in a day once for all, but I've been a foot all to-day, I can tell'y. It were hard walking. But see ⸺' she held out her feet; they were stockinged and shod.

'Bain't that vitty' (tidy), 'and bain't I peart' (smart)? 'You should ha' seen mun, though, when they was new and beautiful; but I've a been so stogged in snow that they be now wetted through and through, and all their beauty washed out of 'em.'

'You have walked here?' Herring was coming out of his dazed condition into one of wonder at Joyce.

'Sure I have. I'll tell'y all about it, but I must sit me down by the fire; I be that stiff and tired I can scarce stand.'

'Joyce, what is the meaning of your coming?'

'I'll tell'y all right on end from beginning till now. I sed I'd a been working for Farmer Facey to Coombow.'

'What for?'

'Did you not hear me say it? He lent his waggon to dray you home to West Wyke, after you was nigh upon killed.'

'Well, what then?'

'Sure he wanted to be paid for it. There were a waggon and two horses for a day, and there were that boy, Jim White, along of them.'

'Why did you not tell me? I would have paid.'

'No,' answered Joyce, 'it were I as had the care of you. I sed I would do that, and I did it. I went and worked out the hire of the waggon and of Jim White myself.'

Herring looked at her with amazement.

'I cannot allow this,' he said.

'It be done,' she said, with an air of triumph. 'It be paid and all; I paid with my arms, by work; and the farmer sed I worked better than two able-bodied men, he did. And Farmer Facey's wife, her were a good un; her larned me to knit. It came about so. When as first I went there, I were that shy of going under the hellens, I thought I'd smother; so I sed I'd lie in the linney, and I did lie there a night or two. It were comfortable in the straw. But at last I seed the woman knitting stockings, and I sed I wished her'd larn me that; and her sed her would if I'd come inside of the evenings—it were late in the fall and the nights were long. Well, I were that set on larning that I did; I went in. I sed to you as I'd knit your stockings, and I've a done so. See, there they be. That Jim White were a worrit. If he'd a let me along I'd have larned a deal faster; but I larned at last, I did. It weren't so bad and spifflicating after all in the house by the great fire. The smoke didn't fill the room; her went right on end up the chimney. Maister! when I were larning to knit stockings, I were that set up I

Y

thought I wern't like a savage no more as I used to be, but were dacent like other folk, and I found like that I could abide and breathe under hellens. Miss Cicely would hev taught me to knit, but I couldn't wait. I had to go to Coombow and work out the waggon and Jim White. I worked mun all out, and the farmer sed I were better to he than two labouring men. When I comed away at last, Mistress Facey her gived me thicky stockings, her'd a knit mun herself, and thicky shoes, they be brave and beautiful. Her gived them to me, and would take nothing for 'em. I didn't reckon much of 'em at fust, but I sees now I couldn't have walked here with bare feet in the snow. So they be good for more than to look to.'

'Why have you come here?'

'I've brought you the stockings I've knitted. I sed I would, and I've done it. You never came nigh to West Wyke for a long time, and Miss Cicely were lost to know what had become of you, and the old Squire be took worse; and I'd done the stockings, and I thought as you'd never come to see 'em. One day when the Squire were very bad, Miss Cicely comed to I, and said as how her wondered why you never came, and as how her wished you could know how the Squire were, and that he were axing every day after you. Then I sed, the stockings were done, and as you didn't come for mun, I'd carry mun to you. Her told me where you lived. I were to go right forward to Launceston, and there to ax my way to Boscastle. So I sed I'd go, and I'd take your stockings. The wind were up and there were going to be ice and snow, and you'd be wanting them to keep your feet warm. So I came.'

'But, Joyce, how did you find your way here, to this house?'

'I came about dark to Boscastle, and I went about and inquired after you, and some sed they didn't think you was here, and some sed, if I wanted to find you, I must go to the office, you were there mostly, and always of nights; and they gave me directions, and so I came.'

'But, Joyce, it is now past midnight.'

'I dare say it be. I couldn't get in at the door when first I found the little house, and tried, and there was no light in the windows, and I thought you might not be come yet, and I'd wait about a bit. So I waited on the lew side, but the wind were so wild, and the snow drifted, and I were forced to go away. But I came again after a while, and still the door were fast. So then I thought I'd go and find a haystack or a linney, where I might sleep, and I'd come again in the morning. But I rambled about for miles, and never found nothing of a place where I might lie. I got to one house, where there were lights in the windows, but a dog began to bark, and I were feared he might bite me as Farmer Freeze's dog had bitten and tore me—you mind that time as I hearkened to the wood-doo,—so I didn't venture into the shippon but comed away, and then I don't know exactly where and for how long I wandered about, but at last I saw a light here, and I found my way back to the office, but I had rare tumbles and climbings over walls and into ditches. However, I have found you here to last, dear maister, and I be glad, I be glad.'

'Good heavens, Joyce! is all this true?'

'Sure-ly. Did I ever tell you a lie?'

'Since when have you been afoot?'

'I started afore light, I reckon about five o'clock.'

'My poor, poor Joyce!'

'I be none so poor now. See my stockings and shoes! And do'y look here what a sight o' brave clothes I have, as Miss Cicely gave me.'

'Have you had anything to eat?'

'Sure. A woman at a cottage gave me some bread and a bowl of skimmed milk.'

'When?'

'I reckon at noon.'

'Twelve hours ago. Have you had nothing since?'

'No; I couldn't wait when I comed to Boscastle, I were that longing to get on and find you.'

'Joyce, you must be starving.' He sprang up and went to the cupboard, the same whence he had taken the bullet. A week ago he had a loaf and some cheese there. The bread was stale, but still it was edible. He brought it out, with the cheese and a knife.

'Joyce, off with these soaking shoes and stockings. Sit down at the table and eat what you can. I will get you something warmed over the fire to drink as quickly as I can.'

The thought of what Joyce had gone through distracted his attention from his own misery. There were others in the world beside Mirelle, others demanding his consideration and sympathy.

'The Squire be took cruel bad,' said Joyce, 'and Miss Cicely be very desirous to see you, and that you should come to the Squire. There be Upaver mine. Squire have a looked after things so long as he could, but there be nobody to do that now.'

'What is the matter with Mr. Battishill?'

'I dun know, but he be cruel bad; and the mistress were looking along the Okehampton road every day, and hoping as you would come. You've been such a long, long time away, and us can't get on without you no ways, that you knows very well.'

He was a help to some. His presence was desired by some. Only to Mirelle he was unwelcome.

'Be this house yours?' asked Joyce, looking round. 'I won't say but her's comfortable wi' fire and can'l and all sorts; but her's none so big as West Wyke, and not such a wonderful sight bigger than the Giant's Table. I know when I gets back, Miss Cicely will be asking of me about it; what sort of a place her be, and whether her be big or small, and built of stone. Her's all of board, just like some of them places they runned up to Ophir, where the gold was. But that be all tore abroad now.'

Poor girl, she was hungry. The bread was hard as biscuit, but she ate it eagerly. Herring gave her some hot wine and water.

'The old Squire be axing after you the first thing in the morning. And he do fret wonderful for you. Miss Cicely do say it be like a child wanting his nurse. He be gone a " bit tottle" (foolish), 'I reckon.'

'I shall go back to West Wyke to-morrow, Joyce.'

'O glory rallaluley! I be glad. I'll have a wink of sleep, and then I'll be fresh as a buttercup to go wi' you. I may go along of you, mayn't I now, maister dear?'

'Yes, Joyce. You shall not walk, you shall ride.'

'I rided once afore wi' you,' she answered, 'but you know nort about that. It were when you were nigh upon dead, and I held your head in my arms all the way, and you never waked but once, and that were on Sourton Down, and then you held out your hands, entreating like, and cried something, and that were all, and never spoke no more.'

'What did I cry out?'

She looked steadily into his eyes, and said in a low tone, 'Mirelle.'

He covered his face, as a spasm contracted his heart. Joyce had touched too recent a wound for him to endure the touch without shrinking. Joyce saw that he was in pain. She went to him, and, kneeling at his feet, drew his hands away from his face, and looked into it; then shook her head.

'Her don't belong to you yet then?'

'No, and never will.' He spoke with bitterness.

'You be changed, maister dear. I never seed you afore like as you be now. You look just about a score of years older than what you was once. Is it the Whiteface has done it, or what be it, maister darling? Tell your own Joyce, and see if her won't go through ice and snow to serve you any day, if her can.'

'You can do nothing for me.'

Still she looked at him, holding his hands, trying to read his secret in his face, with eyes full of earnestness. Then, suddenly, there came a revulsion in his thoughts.

'God forgive me for what I have said! *You* do nothing for me!—Joyce, dear Joyce, you have done for me this night more than you are aware of. You saved my life once before, you have saved my life again to-night, and something more than my life.'

She did not understand him. How could she?

'Maister,' she said, 'put thicky gashly old gun away; it frightens me.'

He rose at once and obeyed, putting the gun back in its old place on the crooks.

'You be coming back to West Wyke?' she asked.

'Yes, to-morrow.'

'You'll be better there. There the old Squire be fond of you, and you be so kind to me; and there be Miss Cicely, too, her's a pining likewise, acause you be so long away; and there be I,' she looked down at his feet, 'knitting stockings as fast as I can knit for you. If I can do nothing more, I can do that.'

'Oh, Joyce! Joyce!' He could say no more, his heart was full. Here at Welltown—wretchedness, coldness, repulsion; there at West Wyke—not happiness indeed, but rest, warmth, and love.

'And, maister dear, you'll larn me the kinkum-kum. I wouldn't let Miss Cicely larn me. Her began to laugh when I said kinkum-kum. But when I were bad wi' my broken arms, and I asked you to say it, you didn't laugh, but you tooked off your hat and said it as good as a Methody. And now, I'll tell'y, that night when I drayed you out of the road into the wood, and thought you was going to die, and I didn't know what ever to do, I got such a pain here,' she put her hand to her heart, 'as I could scarce abear it. And then I went down on my knees, just the same as I be now, and I put up my hands over where you lay, and I cried that same kinkum-kum, and him as I knows nort about, he heard me, and he did what he could, I reckon. He made you better, and he set my pain and trouble at rest. There, maister darling, I can see you be in pain and trouble now. Just you do the same; go down on your knees, and say the same right on end, and the rest from pain and trouble will come sure-ly.'

'Joyce!'

She was still looking in his face, desiring something, with a great distress in her eyes. Now, a smile broke in her eyes.

'O rallaluley!' she exclaimed. 'Your face were at first like Cosdon when hard frozen, but now the springs be breaking.'

The lines in his face had softened, his lips quivered, and his eyes filled. Then, all at once, he fell on his knees beside Joyce, and held up his hands as she had taught him, and said in broken tones and slowly, 'Our Father.' Joyce repeated the words.

'Which art in heaven—hallowed be thy name.'

Joyce still followed. 'Thy kingdom come.'

The storm had passed away, almost suddenly. The clouds had broken; in the west the moon hung unveiled, and cast a ray of purest silver into the little room, and bathed in her stainless light the poor savage and the young soldier, kneeling and praying together.

CHAPTER XLVI.

A BAR OF ICE.

NEXT morning John Herring returned to Welltown. He was a changed man. His lightheartedness, his simplicity of character, were gone for ever. Hitherto he had been a big boy, with buoyant spirits and with a belief that the world was a paradise. He was a man now, seeing life before him as a sad desert that must be tramped over, where he must meet with suffering, and count himself happy if, at long intervals, he reached and could rest by a brackish pool. The world is no paradise, it is a vale of Sodom, where the pits are bitterness and the rivers brine. It is no playground, it is a convict establishment. It is a theatre in which all act tragedies, and the lookers-on mistake them for farces.

Herring had spent the remainder of the night by his fire, revolving in his mind what must be done. Joyce slept soundly on his bed in the corner, tired out with her trudge through the snow. Herring had made her take off her gown, and had thrown an old fishing coat of his over her. Though he sat over the fire thinking of his own future and Mirelle's, he cared also for Joyce's boots and gown and stockings, that were drying by the stove, and turned them, and took thought that they were not burnt.

In the morning he sent Joyce into the village of Boscastle to detain the chaise in which he had come to Welltown the previous evening. Then he went to see Mirelle once more.

He was, as Joyce had observed, greatly oldened and altered. One night had worked the change in the outer as well as in the inner man. There comes a time to all when the rose-coloured spectacles must be laid aside for those of blue glass. The time comes sooner to some than to others. It had come now to John Herring, and the aspect of everything was changed to him.

Mirelle was unaltered. She was pale, indeed, but that was her usual complexion, and her eyes were red, but they had been red the day of her marriage. She was more collected than on the previous evening, and Herring was more composed.

He entered the house without Genefer perceiving him, and went upstairs to the little porch-room. Whilst he was in the hall he heard Mirelle's steps above, and knew she was there.

She did not seem surprised to see him. She received him with ease and gentle kindness, not as a husband, but as a friend. There was in her heart a sense of relief; she could speak with him on an understood footing, and she would not be subjected to demonstrative affection. Herring was prepared for this. She saw that he was looking worn and ill, but she made no remark. She was the cause of the change in his appearance, and she knew it. She regretted it, but it was inevitable.

Mirelle was dressed in a sober dark gown. Every trace of bridal white had been put away. When he entered, she was engaged on her trunks.

'Your jewels are here,' he said, showing her a secret drawer in a large old cabinet. 'I give you the key. Do not leave it about; though nothing is to be feared from Genefer or Hender, yet it is wise to keep articles of value under lock and key, and not to trust the key to any one.'

'They are of no value. They are paste.'

'I beg your pardon, they are not. I took them to a jeweller, who examined them. Some of the stones had been abstracted at some time, and replaced by artificial diamonds, by whom and when, I cannot, of course, say. I have had all these taken out, and true stones of good quality put in their places. The necklet and diadem are now perfect as at first.'

Mirelle was surprised.

'You think the set of diamonds was originally complete.'

'I am convinced it was so.'

'And that the stones had been removed and paste substitutes put instead into the sockets.'

'I believe so.'

'Then you do not think my father gave what was worthless to my mother?'

'I cannot suppose so. It is not likely. The pendant was tampered with more thoroughly than the rest of the set, because it was removable. Probably after that had been altered, one by one the stones of the necklace were removed. Some person in need of money disposed of the stones as the need came.'

Mirelle thought.

'Yes,' she said, 'I have no doubt it was done by Antoinette.'

'Who was Antoinette?'

'My mother's maid, who did everything for her. I am glad to think that my father was not guilty of a mean act. I thank you for clearing his memory from such a stain. Henceforth I shall believe that Antoinette was guilty.'

'So be it; and from henceforth I hope you will realise the necessity of keeping precious stones under lock and key. Show them to nobody unnecessarily, and, above all, show nobody where they are kept.'

They spoke to each other with perfect coolness and self-possession. Pyramus and Thisbe met and conversed with a wall between; John Herring and Mirelle were separated by an invisible wall, but it was one of ice.

'I have brought you, as well, the key of my office on Willapark. I keep there my accounts of the slate-quarry. Should anything from the office be required, the foreman will come to you. If not asking too much, I would wish him not to be given free run over it, and that you should be present

when he wants anything. There are things there which I do
not care for him to turn over, papers and accounts among
which I do not wish him to rummage. You will do me this
favour?'

'Certainly. Are you going away?'

'I am going away for awhile. You know that I am
working a valuable silver lead mine on the borders of
Dartmoor, and it must be looked after.'

Why did he not say where it was—'near West Wyke?
where you and I first met, where your father died?' He did
not say this, because it would be painful for him to say it,
and for her to hear it. The name would call up recollections
they must endeavour to crush out of their minds.

'You will return again?'

'I will come back to see how the slate-quarry progresses.
I had purposed building a breakwater, but I shall not now
carry out this purpose.'

'Why not?'

'The lead mine is sure to engross my time and attention.
I shall be here but little. My interests will be centred in the
silver lead.'

'Very well.'

'I shall provide for your comfort. You will have, as
before, your own account in the bank, under the same name,
Mirelle Garcia de Cantalejo. You will draw from the bank
what you require.'

'I thank you, Mr. Herring. You are very kind.'

'You will do with the money what you like; you are
entire mistress of it. You will pay for the expenses of the
house from it, and keep what company you like. There are
not many neighbours, but such as there are will call, and they
will be hospitable to you, and glad to receive hospitality from
you. I dare say you will require additional servants.
Genefer——'

'I beg your pardon, I do not wish to have that woman in
the house. She frightens me.'

'She is a worthy, devoted soul. You are sure to like her
when once you have learned her value.'

'She frightens me; I thought I should have died of fear
last night.'

'I cannot consent to her dismissal. She was my nurse,
she has been with me from my birth, and loves me as if I were
her own child. When I look back I see how her life has been

devoted to me. Besides, the home farm is let to Hender, and he and she must live here: there is no other house for them, and the outbuildings are included in the lease. It is unavoidable. If I could have gratified you in this particular I would have done so, but I cannot.'

Mirelle became, if possible, colder. She bowed her head stiffly.

'Very well,' she said, after a pause, awkward to both: 'if it cannot be, I must endure this cross also. But I entreat you, do not say me nay to my next petition.'

'I will not. I would refuse you nothing, you may be very confident, but the impossible.'

'It will not be impossible for Orange and her mother to come here and reside with me.'

Herring took a hasty turn up and down the room. The request vexed him greatly. There was something in Orange he did not like, something in her manner towards Mirelle which made him mistrust her professions of affection, something—a coarseness of mind which he suspected rather than perceived, which he shrank from voluntarily bringing into contact with the unsullied purity and delicacy of Mirelle's soul.

'Is this also refused me?' asked Mirelle. Then her coldness giving way, the assumed stiffness yielding to her natural emotion, 'Oh, John Herring, do not be unkind to me! You have been so good, so much better to me than I deserve.'

'I—I unkind to you, Mirelle!' In a moment also his assumed coldness cracked, and the warm suffering heart showed its blood through the rent, as the black crust of lava that descends Vesuvius breaks, and the fire of the core is seen glowing between the rough edges.

'I tell you the truth, my friend,' she said. 'I will call you my friend; that you have been ever since we have known each other—that you are still.'

'Yes,' said Herring, regaining his composure, 'what I have been, that I am and shall be, your friend—nothing more.'

'I tell you the truth, that woman Genefer nearly killed me last night. I was sitting over the fire till late, after——' she hesitated.

'After I left you; yes, go on.'

'After you left me, after I had driven you away, my friend, my poor friend!' She looked up into his eyes piteously. He turned his away; he could not bear to look into the soul that was not his, that never could be his. She went on:

'After you were gone, I sat on till very late, thinking. I was unhappy, and I cried. I sat by the fire; you can understand, I was in trouble about myself and about you. After midnight I was roused by hearing the most dreadful shrieks and the rushing of feet along the passage overhead.'

'That was nothing,' said Herring, forcing a smile. 'My good Genefer has strange fancies that take her perversely at unsuitable seasons. She was only driving the devil.'

'But I cannot bear hearing the devil driven in the depth of the night, in a lonely house, in the midst of a raging storm. It will kill me. I have been very ill, you must remember, with a nervous fever, and it has left me weak and liable to be shaken by strange events. I fear that I cannot bear such an event again. I cannot stand much.' She looked now full of entreaty and helplessness—a frightened, feeble girl, in dread of strange things, she knew not what.

'That is true. I will see and speak to Genefer before I leave. I must give some explanation of, and excuse for, my hurried departure, and at the same time I will be peremptory with her on this point. She must not do such a thing again. If she wants to drive the devil, she must drive him in her own chapel.'

'This house is so lonely and cold. I must have some one always with me, some one whose presence will be a protection against fears, some one whom I can consult about matters that concern the house. I am wholly ignorant about these; I am only a girl just come from school, and come into a strange land. When I was at Dolbeare I slept with Orange, and I should like to have her here to sleep with me again. Then, if I heard noises in the night, I would cling to her, and she is so strong and so brave that she would protect me and revive my courage.'

'I do not like Orange.'

'May I not have her here? I must have some one, and I had rather have her than any one else.'

Herring again paced the room. A great repugnance to this proposal rose up in his heart: he had no real and reasonable grounds for it, but he had an instinctive dread of the plan.

'You will not refuse me this,' pleaded Mirelle. 'See! I did not ask you for all those generous and kind things you have devised for me. But a man does not understand the feelings of a woman. You are strong and unable to comprehend my terrors. To you they are childish and absurd, but they are very real and serious to me. I only ask you this one thing—if Genefer must remain, let Orange come.'

He could not resolve to give his consent.

'Would it not be better if I were to find you a suitable companion, some lady, young, and, if you desired it, of your own faith?'

'How can I tell that she would suit me? There were many girls, my schoolfellows, at the Sacré Cœur. They were of my own age, and all were good Catholics, but with several of them I could not live, and with some I should not care to live. How can I tell that you would find me just the very girl that I should like? No, I know Orange. We do not think alike. She has not faith. She is older than I am, and though companions we are not intimates; but I know her, and she loves me; she has good sense and she can advise That is all I want.'

'Was there no girl at your old school whom you would like to ask to come to you? You must have had some dear friend there.'

'Yes, there was la Princesse Marie de la Meillerie; we were close friends. But conceive! I could not invite her to this place of banishment, where there is not a tree nor a flower. This world here is not nature in flesh and clothing, it is the skeleton of nature, and it demands the enthusiasm of a geologist to admire such a country. My companions, again, were of the *haute noblesse*, and were not of the sort to become *gouvernantes* to young unprotected ladies.'

'No, I see that.'

'Moreover, who would come here, where you have a church picked bare to the bones of all that surrounds and sweetens religion? My friends are Catholics, and love a living church, not one which is only bones, though the smallest of bones be preserved and *in situ*, and the entire skeleton be well set up.'

'I dare say it is so.'

'Then you will allow Orange Trampleasure and her mother to come to me. See you! they are at Launceston, and are left without money.'

'I promised in your name to place five thousand pounds to the account of Miss Orange.'

'Yes, I do wish that. But that is not sufficient. They are not comfortable at Launceston. It was there that they met with their great reverse. It was in that house that Mr. Trampleasure died. The people of Launceston suffered by the failure of the gold mine, and they will not forgive Mrs. Trampleasure and Orange, though only the old man and Mr. Sampson were guilty of wrong towards them. I know that Orange and her mother would like to leave the town, and go elsewhere, where they are not known. That also is a reason why I wish them to come to me.'

'Very well,' said Herring: 'if it must be so, let it be so. It is a compromise, and a compromise is never satisfactory. I retain Genefer and you Orange. Ask them to come here to you on a visit of a couple or three months—temporarily—not as a permanence, and only till they have made up their minds where they will finally settle.'

'I must accept this,' said Mirelle, with a sigh: 'you were so very, very kind to me *before*—now that we are married, you are only half as kind.'

'Do not speak like this,' said Herring, hastily. 'I am what I was before, a friend, nothing further—I can be nothing further.'

'You will be always my friend?'

'Always.'

He drew a long breath. His heart was swelling and likely again to rend the crust and show its fires. He conquered himself and held out his hand.

'You will find that one drawer of my desk in the office is locked; I keep the key to that. Everything else is open to you. Good-bye!'

'What, so soon?'

'I am going away in the carriage that brought us to this place yesterday.'

'Ah, well!—to the silver lead mine.'

'Yes.'

'What will be your address?'

'You will not need it.'

'Shall you soon return?'

'I do not know. Good-bye.'

They shook hands. Mirelle's lips trembled and her eyes filled. She bore Herring a sincere regard; she felt her deep indebtedness to him. She had treated him with great cruelty, and had caused him unspeakable suffering. This was a chilly separation. She felt inclined to say something better than 'good-bye'—that is, to say 'Stay.' But she could not do this.

They touched hands through the walls of ice that intervened, and that froze the word on her tongue.

CHAPTER XLVII.

WELCOME HOME!

The weather changed with the capriciousness proverbial in the West of England. There a week of continuous frost and east winds is almost unknown. No sooner has the snow been shaken over the hills than the sky repents of its cruelty, and brings a warm breath over the face of the land, before which the white mantle vanishes as if by magic, and the grass comes forth greener than before.

It was so now. The wind had changed after midnight, and a rapid thaw had set in. Herring returned to Launceston in the carriage in which he had left the day before. The post-boys had removed their favours, and the earth was putting off hers as well. Herring took poor Joyce back with him. When she came to Launceston, she desired to push on. She wished, she said, to go to Coombow and see Mistress Facey. Herring was obliged to remain the night in Launceston; he had to make the arrangements with the bank that he had undertaken.

He did not go to Dolbeare. He saw no one but the banker; and then he went on his way by coach. He did not pick up Joyce. Perhaps he overtook and passed her on the road without noticing her; his mind was full of his own troubles, and he had no attention to bestow on the road and those who were on it.

When he passed Okehampton his thoughts took a turn. The grand bulk of Cosdon rose before him. The soft glory of the evening sun was on it; the snow had not thawed off the mighty head, though it had gone from the valleys, except where drifted and screened from the wind and sun. The rooks were wheeling and cawing; they anticipated fine weather, and were thinking of overhauling their last year's nests. Valentine's Day, for birds as well as for maids and men, was only a month off. The rooks blackened a field; the worms had come out after the frost to enjoy the sun and soft breeze, and the rooks were enjoying the worms. 'Caw, caw!'

Then the guard blew his horn, and away they went, a rush of black wings, but to no great distance. They settled in a couple of oak trees, and waited till the coach had gone by. The coachman cracked his whip. That alarmed them more than the horn; it resembled the report of a gun, and they sprang into the air with loud remonstrances against a repetition of the St. Bartholomew's Day of last rook-shooting. 'Caw, caw!' They danced a minuet against the blue sky overhead—a minuet of incomparable intricacy. There be three things, said the wise king, too wonderful for me—the way of a bird in the air, the way of a ship in the sea, and the way of men and maids. The ship darts from side to side, tacking against adverse winds, aiming at a port which she seems to avoid; and the way of maids with men sweethearting, in the Valentine days, in sweet spring, is much the same, full of tricks and evasions, disguises and cross purposes, wonderful as the way of a ship, wonderful as the mystic dances of the rooks overhead.

The air was warm, the sounds were spring-like, the beautiful moor was glorified by the sun, setting in a web of golden vapour. The scene was familiar to Herring, associated with pleasant days. He got off the coach at the bridge over the Taw, that he might walk quietly up the hill and over the downs to West Wyke. Windows were glittering in the sun like gold leaf. There was one that was open and swinging in the light air. It flashed across the valley shafts of fire, welcoming flashes to the broken-hearted man toiling up the hill. In a thorn-bush the sparrows were chattering—hundreds holding parliament, all their little voices going together, and none attending to what the other sang or said. Lo! in the hedge, already, a celandine, the glossy petals as glorious as those flickering windows. A sense of rest after long trouble came upon Herring. He stooped and picked the celandine—January, and these bright heralds of sunshine out already, come forth to welcome him home to West Wyke.

How soothing in his ear sounded the murmur of the Taw, rushing over the old grey granite boulders, breaking from the moor to run a quiet course through rich meadows and among pleasant groves. The gentle rush had a lullaby effect on the troubled heart of the walker. A very different sound this from the boom of the Atlantic against Willapark and the churning of the imprisoned billows in Blackapit.

A track led off the road to Upaver. How was the mine getting on? The track was well trampled and the wheel marks many; that was a cheering sign. Hard by stood a post which Tramplara had set up, painted white, with a board on it and a hand pointing moorwards, 'To the Gold Mines of Ophir.' Some-one had scrambled up the post, scratched out the 'To,' and written in its place 'Damn,' giving thereby coarse but emphatic expression to the general sentiment. Herring smiled bitterly as he noticed this. Next he came to the cottages.

'Good evening, sir! Glad to see you home again.'

The speaker was a labourer returning to his fireside, his day's work over. Herring did not remember him, but the man knew him, and his tone showed pleasure.

Home! Was this home?

'How is all going on with you?' asked Herring.

'Well, sir, my missus hev given me another little maiden. That makes fourteen childer. Eight maidens and six boys, but we've a buried three.'

'You have your quiver full.'

'They bring their love wi' them, sir; and that, I reckon, you'll find when you've a home of your own, and a wife, and the little uns coming every year.'

Herring sighed.

'Good evening, sir. Here be my nest.'

'Good-night.' Then Herring went on—home? Before him was West Wyke, and the last glimpse of the sun was on it. The window of West Wyke it was that had flashed the welcome to him.

The old ash trees, the old gateway with the grey owls, the old chimneys, the old ivy-mantled porch, the old firelight flickering through the hall window. A moment more, and the old welcome.

With an exclamation of delight, Cicely sprang from a stool by the fire to meet him, as he entered without knocking: entered as he would to his home. He was no stranger, to knock and ask for admission. He went straight in, and in a moment felt that he ought to have more hands than two to give to those who grasped them.

The old Squire and Cicely held him.

'Oh, John, dear Cousin John, you have come at last!'

'John, John, I am so glad to see you again.'

But who was that, also, on her knees, insisting on having his hand to cover it with kisses, sobbing and laughing, with tears and joy in eyes and voice? 'Oh, rallaluley! the maister be come back from that whist place!' Yes—Joyce; the true, devoted Joyce, who had only stayed an hour at Coombow with Mrs. Facey, and then had walked on, all night, and had come in—nay, burst in, on the Battishills in the morning, with the tidings that the master was on his way back to West Wyke.

Over the chimney-piece, about the pictures, wherever it could be stuck, was bright holly with red berries. And see! hanging from the black beam, a bunch of mistletoe.

Herring's heart was full. He could not speak, but he took Cicely's head between his hands and kissed her; he stooped and lifted Joyce, and pressed his lips to her cheek; and the old Squire's arm encircled him, and drew the young head down beside the old grey one.

The tongues of all failed. Herring raised his eyes, over which a mist was forming, and saw above the doorway an inscription in red holly berries—

Welcome Home!

By degrees only did the flush and fever of joy in these good, simple souls subside, and Herring was able to recover his composure.

Then the young man stood by the Squire's chair and looked at him; his heart reproached him for having deserted him for so long a time.

'We hoped you would have dropped in and eaten your Christmas dinner with us, John,' said Mr. Battishill. 'We set your chair at the table, and a sprig of holly by your plate, in hopes you would arrive.'

'I am very sorry, sir, that I was not here. I should have been far happier here among such dear, kind friends.'

'It is you, John, who have been a kind friend to us,' said the old man. 'Just consider. If you had not rescued the mortgages out of Tramplara's hands when you did, they would have fallen to the creditors, the directors of Ophir, and we should have been turned into the cold.'

'You repay what little I have done for you a thousand fold,' answered Herring.

There was a flush on the old man's cheek, caused by excitement.

'Now we have you here again,' he said, 'you must remain with us, at all events, for some time. Consider this as your home.'

'Yes,' answered Herring, 'I have no home elsewhere.' He spoke sadly. Cicely looked hard at him. He went on, 'I will stay on with you till I tire you out with my society.'

'That can never be. There is Upaver crying out for you; I am past attending to that. I am not what I was a few months ago. The wheels are becoming rusty and the gear breaks.'

z

Cicely looked from her father to Herring questioningly. Did John note the change in the old man? A change there was; he was failing in many ways. Just now the delight of seeing Herring again had revived him; nevertheless the change was observable enough. The eager look had gone out of the eyes, and the lips had become more tremulous than ever.

As Cicely turned her eyes from one to the other, there dawned on her the truth that a change had come over John Herring—a change greater than that which had passed upon her father. She had not been apprised of this by Joyce, and was unprepared for it. She noticed it first with incredulity, then with perplexity, and she resolved to speak with him on the subject. The man was not the same. The same in outward feature, in colour of hair and eyes, but he was not the same in expression. He was aged. A wave had passed over his head, and he had come forth half drowned. The elasticity was gone from his tread, the sparkle from his eye, the dimple from his cheek, the laugh from his lips. The eye had become more steady, lines had formed on his brow and in his cheeks; the lips had lost their flexibility, they were closed and firm. He no longer held his head erect with strong self-consciousness; he seemed to have acquired a slight stoop, the head was somewhat bowed.

It was clear to Cicely that Herring had undergone some grievous trial, of what sort she could not guess, and that he had emerged from it with a strengthened character, though with a saddened heart. Cicely did not indeed take this in all at once. Her curiosity was roused and her attention fixed, and by degrees the greatness and significance of the change forced themselves upon her.

The old man observed nothing. But now Joyce, who had been thrust into the background, insisted on asserting herself.

'See, dear maister, what be come to your Joyce. Do'y look here!'

She stood forward in the light—the light of several candles, lit to welcome Herring home. She wore a dark-blue serge gown, and a white kerchief round her neck, and crossed over her bosom. Her luxuriant dark hair was combed and pruned, and fastened up under a white cap. The gown was short, and showed white stockings and black shoes. Her wild face was subdued and softened, the rudeness had gone out of it, and a strange tinge of sweetness and modesty had come in place of the savagery. She was really a handsome girl, of splendid physique, easy in every motion.

'Did'y ever see wonder like this?' asked Joyce, holding out her skirts and apron, and showing her white stockings. 'And see how grand my hair be. What do'y say to this, maister dear?'

'Why, Joyce, I congratulate you with all my heart. This is what I have been wishing for, but never hoped to see.'

'You have wished for it—you! O glory and blazes! I be glad.'

'I told you as much, Joyce,' said Cicely Battishill.

'I know you did, miss, but I couldn't believe it. I thought you sed it just to persuade me on.'

'Cousin John, we have enlarged our household to-day. We have taken Joyce in. Her dread of going under the "hellens" has given way. She will learn to make herself useful. Now, Joyce, you may go back to the kitchen, and help Charity to get supper ready.'

'What has become of the old man—Grizzly?'

'We allow him to sleep in one of the linneys, and he is given broken meat once a day. He has fallen into bad ways of late. Ophir injured him as much as it injured his superiors, only in a different way. He learned from the workmen to drink, and now he loafs about the country trying to get something given him by inconsiderate persons to keep his throat wet. He is at Upaver a good deal; there the miners make game of him, and treat him. He has taken to smoking. I have threatened that if he carries his pipe into the shippon, I shall refuse him the linney as a bedroom, and he will have to return to the Giant's Table.'

'I am glad that he and his daughter are parted.'

'There was no chance for her as long as she remained under his thraldom. Fortunately she had set her head on going for two months to a place called Coombow, and that opened the way to her leaving Grizzly altogether. He is a hopeless savage. We did believe at one time that he was capable of improvement. He worked hard on his patch of land. But Ophir diverted him from the upward path, and since then he has been going down hill nearly as fast as his barrel when it broke from its tether.'

'Well, John,' said Mr. Battishill, 'I must not let Cicely engross you. Come and talk to me. I will tell you what we have been doing at Upaver. We have got the leat cut, and the wheel and crushers in place, and a smelting house run up. I have not been able to go there myself, but the foreman, a very worthy, sensible fellow, comes up every other day and reports progress. I have seen to the accounts as you desired; but I am not what I was. My head has become confused, and I have had to ask Cicely to help me out with the accounts. I hope you will not find them in a great muddle, but I was never very precise, and ladies do not understand the difference between debit and credit sides of a balance sheet. The table of work is left with me, and I pretend to look it over, but have not the means of verifying it. I do not think much has come out of the mine yet. I cannot say the profits are large. Indeed, the credit side of the book is blank.'

'I do not expect anything yet. I am content that the machinery should be in place and in working order. Now I am here, we will attack the lode.'

'There is the rub, John; the machinery is up, but not in working order; the leat is cut, but the water won't run along it.'

'That will soon be rectified, and then the profits will come in freely.'

'I hope so, John.'

'I am sure of it, sir. Do not you lose heart.'

'I have made such a failure of life, John, that I have ceased to be sanguine. I can see nothing in the retrospect but blunders and losses.'

'No, sir, you have made mistakes, but all must do that before reaching success. Upaver was your own discovery.'

'That is true, very true. I think we will christen this mine Wheal Battishill.'

'Do you not think Wheal Cicely would sound better?' asked John Herring.

'My suggestion is the best,' said Cicely, colouring. 'Let it be Wheal Friendship.'

A bright and cosy supper. The great fireplace full of crackling flame. A white cloth on the black oak table near the fire, and silver and glass upon it sparkling in the candlelight, and the flicker of the flames embracing a huge faggot.

'Good luck never comes alone,' said the Squire. 'What do you think! My dear old friend, John Northmore, has sent me a couple of pheasants. I have not seen him for many years, and I do not know how he comes to remember me now; however that may be, he has, and most opportunely. Here comes one of his pheasants to table. I thought I was forgotten of all the world, but—I hope it is an omen of coming success to Wheal Friendship—old friends are beginning to remember that there is such a man as Richard Battishill, J.P.'

'Shall we sit down?' asked Cicely. 'Everything is ready.'

'Although my cates be poor, take it in good part;
Better cheer may you have, but not with better heart,'

quoted the Squire. 'You are godfather to the wine, John. It is some of the case you ordered down from Exeter. We will drink in it success to Wheal Friendship.'

The old man was garrulous and cheerful during supper. The family plate was brought out in honour of John Herring, and the Spode china, red with burnished gold in leaf and scroll. How bright and comfortable the table was! how warm and cheery the room! What kindly, happy faces were round the table! This was something like home.

The pain did not leave John Herring's heart, the cloud did not remove from his brain, but, under the influences now brought to bear upon him, the pain lost its first poignancy, and the cloud hung less deep. At the conclusion of supper, Cicely persuaded her father to go to bed. The old man was obstinate at first. 'He liked to be with John, and to chat with him over the fire. He had just begun to enjoy his wine. The room had only now become warm—why should he be banished to his cold chamber upstairs? He had not seen John for months; he had business to discuss with him. There was a good story he remembered, which he wished to tell him;' and so on, a string of reasons why he should not go to bed. But he was weak, and, though he was obstinate for a few minutes, yielded to his daughter's perseverance, and she helped him upstairs. John Herring remained by the fire. He was glad to be alone; he stood with his back to the fire, thinking. Two nights ago—forty-eight hours only—had passed since he had gone home to Welltown with his bride. Home!—was that home? The house half buried in snow was cold within, the reception was cheerless, no fire, no table spread, and, worst of all, no love from her whom he had taken to be his wife. He had been driven from that home with despair in his heart. He returned to West Wyke: the sun was shining, the birds singing, the flowers opening, the house was decked to receive him, and the kind hearts therein bounded to meet him.

Which was his real home? He raised his eyes to the door

as it opened to readmit Cicely Battishill, and read over it, in scarlet letters, 'Welcome home!'

Cicely seated herself opposite him in the ingle nook, and the soft firelight played over her pleasant face and glowing auburn hair. She was a thrifty body, and she had put out all the candles save two on the great table. These were not really needed—the firelight filled the room.

'How do you think my father is looking?' she asked.

'He is greatly altered. I fear that his anxiety about both Ophir and Upaver has been too much for him.'

'Ophir did upset him greatly, but Upaver—Wheal Friendship, I mean—has done him good; it has occupied him, and taken his thoughts from his own infirmities. He thinks he is deep in business, and that amuses him. He schemes all sorts of things and suggests them to the foreman, who is too civil to say that they are impracticable. No, Upaver has been to him not a care but a distraction. That which ails him is general failure of power. The doctor has visited him and is very kind, and he can do nothing. The new parson at Tawton, Mr. Harmless Simpleton, has also called, and seen my father. He is a very admirable and agreeable gentleman.'

'Your father seemed cheerful this evening.'

'Yes, he was excited by your return. It has given him the greatest pleasure to see you here again. You do not know how he clings to you. Cousin John, I cannot express myself as I ought, but I feel very deeply thankful to you for having relieved and brightened the closing days of my father's life. We were threatened with disaster, and it seemed at one time as if he would sink, and utter ruin would cover and blot us both out. You have saved us, and now the dear old man's evening is like one which succeeds a day of cloud, when suddenly all the vapours roll away, and a blaze of golden sun glorifies the landscape. I believe that my father is as happy as he possibly can be now that he has you here.'

Herring made some commonplace remark in reply.

'Yes, we owe a great deal to you—more than we can ever repay,' said Cicely.

'You are going to make my fortune at Upaver,' said he, half jestingly.

'Oh, John! that is nothing to you. You do not care about that.' She paused for a couple of minutes, with her eyes on the fire, rocking her foot, her hands clasped over her knee. Presently she turned towards him, with sympathy in her honest eyes and in her trembling mouth. 'Do not be offended if I tell you what I have observed. There is a great change in you. I am sure you have gone through a time of great trouble. We were selfish, and vexed, and impatient, because you did not come to us. We thought you were amusing yourself elsewhere, and had forgotten us, and how much we depended on you. We had no suspicion that you were unhappy. I can see that you have had your cup of bitterness. Neither my father nor I have asked you any questions about yourself at any time, and we really know nothing about yourself and your belongings. I do not want to know anything now that you do not wish to tell me. Indeed, indeed, I would do or say my best to comfort you, if I thought that I were capable of making you happier by my interference. There was something you said just now to my father—it was only one sentence, but I saw that it contained in it the kernel of much trouble. My father bade you look on this house as your home. Then you answered that this was the only home you had. Did you really mean what you said?'

'Yes, Cicely. I have no home anywhere, except this that you offer me.'

'You have lost Welltown?'

He hesitated. Then he said in a low tone, 'I have lost it in one sense. It has ceased to be a home to me; the acres remain—that is all.'

'Oh, John, I am so sorry for you. I know you loved the place. I know what an ache it would give me to lose West Wyke.' She did not in the least understand what his loss really was. He did not enlighten her—indeed, it was not possible for him to do so.

Presently she returned to the charge.

'Have you any brothers or sisters?'

'None.'

'And your father and mother are dead?'

'Yes. My mother died when I was born, and I was reared by a nurse. I know her only by her picture.'

'John, tell me,'—she looked at him very earnestly, and with her expressive and sweet face full of compassion—'tell me—have you no one, then, to love you?'

He shook his head. 'No one.'

'At Welltown—no one?'

'My nurse. No one else.'

'How lonely in the world you must be!'

'Utterly,' he answered.

Then she brightened up, and, dashing some tears from her eyes, held out her hands to him laughingly across the glowing hearth. 'There, there, poor boy! We have been talking of Cornwall. There you may be alone and unloved, but here, in old Devon, under the shadow of Cosdon, you have a home, and hearts that care a great deal for you; there is my father, here am I, then there is Joyce, and lastly my white cat! See; he is up on your knee this moment. There! never again say that you are solitary and unloved. It is not true, it is utterly false. Good night, Cousin John! sweet sleep, happy dreams, and a glad awaking to you!'

CHAPTER XLVIII.

TWO BEQUESTS.

NEXT morning John Herring went early to Upaver. The wheel was up, and the leat had been cut. But the wall supporting the axle of the wheel was improperly built, and the leat was improperly levelled. Much that the contractor had undertaken to do had been left undone, and most that he had done was done so badly that it had to be done over again.

Herring called for the day-books, and soon saw that the men working for day wage had taken three days to do what might have been done in one, and that was work which need not have been done at all.

Ophir had demoralised the entire neighbourhood. The object aimed at there had been to make a great display of activity, but to produce nothing. What had been begun at Ophir, the workmen supposed was to continue at Upaver.

Herring rang the bell of the mine, and called the men together. He dismissed the foreman on the spot—that civil and intelligent foreman whom Mr. Battishill esteemed so highly. He told the men that henceforth he would be their captain; he would be at Upaver every day, and would set every man his work, and what he set each man he expected him to execute. A fair day's work for a fair wage, and no payment for idle hours. Those who disliked his terms might go elsewhere in quest of new Ophirs. There was one subsidiary matter he wished to speak of. Old Grizzly Cobbledick was much at the mine, and was treated by the men. He disapproved of this. He would not have the old man given drink and made sport of there. If he would work, he should be given work; if he were determined to get drunk, he must get his drink elsewhere.

Then Herring examined the adit.

Much the same story there as outside. The work had been gone on with anyhow, the ore thrown out with the cable.

He did not return to West Wyke to dinner in the middle of the day; he was too busy. He remained in the mine, and made the men dig whilst he was present. The vein 'bunched,' and the bunch of nearly pure metal was before him. A rich profit was a certainty.

When the men knocked off work, he turned to go to West Wyke. He was covered with dirt, but he was in good spirits. He had not been mistaken. Upaver mine would clear the property of its incumbrances, and repay every penny that had been sunk in it. Mirelle's money had been invested in the mortgages; Mirelle's money had been spent on the mine. Her money was not only safe; it was where it would yield excellent interest.

As Herring came away, he found Grizzly awaiting the men leaving work, to beg of them tobacco, a draught of cyder or spirits, or some coppers.

'I want to speak to you,' said Herring. 'Come along with me.'

Grizzly trudged at his side. There had been a rude savagery in the man when Herring had first known him which was not without its dignity. Old Cobbledick had then worked on his own land, grown his own potatoes, lived in his own house, and thrashed his own child. The consciousness of independence had given him an upright carriage and an open and haughty look. All this was gone. Ophir had robbed him of the one redeeming element in his nature. He had found it easier to beg than to work. He had abandoned all attempt at labour for a livelihood, and with that had lost independence. Formerly he had been defiant in his sense of freedom, he was now cringing in his submission. He had been a temperate man, drinking only water; now he drank whenever he could find anyone to treat him, and whatever was given to him. Association with men higher than himself in civilisation had lowered, not lifted, him. It is so with all savages when brought in contact with civilisation; some seize the moment, and mount, others are cast into deeper degradation than they knew before. It is so with ourselves when set within the orbit of higher and nobler forces than we knew before. They exercise on us a centripetal or a centrifugal energy. Cobbledick was debased. His rags of old had become him, they now made him repulsive; he had ceased to be a man, and had become a scarecrow.

'I want to speak to you, Cobbledick,' said Herring, walking on his way, the old man at his side.

'Your honour! I be all ears. It be the backie sure-ly has a come into your head.'

'It is the drink, Grizzly; the drink.'

'Oh!' exclaimed Cobbledick, 'to think I lived these scores and scores of years without a knowing what it were. But now—glory rallaluley! Praises be! I can get drunk when I meets a real gemman.'

'Grizzly, I have forbidden the men at the mine to give you anything. If you choose to come there and work, I will find you work that you can do, but if I discover that the men give you drink, and encourage you in your idle, vagabond ways, I shall dismiss them, and find others who will obey me. Mark this, Grizzly, not another drop of anything, in treat or otherwise, do you get at Upaver. Go back to the Giant's Table, and dig your fields there like a man, instead of slouching about, picking up halfpence and sips of gin, a wretched beggar.'

'I ain't to get nothing to Upaver?' asked Cobbledick incredulously.

'Do you not understand plain words? Not a drop. I will not have Upaver a curse to you and others, such as Ophir was. If you will work, I will give you tasks equal to your powers.'

'Ekal to my powers!' roared Grizzly; 'look at my hands. See, they be two, three times as big as yours. I could break every bone in your body with mun. I be strong; I reckon stronger than most of they fellows down to Upaver.'

'Very well, then, work.'

'I won't work. I ain't forced.'

'No, I am sorry for it. It is a mistake that you are given broken scraps from West Wyke. That keeps you from famishing, and emancipates you from the necessity of working.'

'You'd cut me off that next, I reckon.'

'Yes, I would.'

'You would!' repeated the old man malevolently. 'You takes away my liquor, and my meat, and my daughter as ought to work and keep me in my old age, and—' he turned and looked up in Herring's face—'you took the box from under the hearthstone.'

Herring started. The old man observed his advantage and chuckled.

'Grizzly, it is quite true that I took the box. You had no right to it; you had stolen it from the carriage that was upset. I took it that I might return it——'

'Oh, in coorse, in coorse, you returned the box at once, and all that was in it, to the young lady with the white face.'

Herring could not answer. The old man, with his natural shrewdness, saw that he had gained an advantage. Of the value of the contents of the box he had no idea. He determined to improve his advantage.

'You took thicky box, as you take to plundering me of everything I has. I reckon you'd like to take from me the chance of sleeping in the linney.'

'Yes, I would, Grizzly. Whatever I deprive you of is for your own advantage. It is not safe for you to lie in the straw of the linney. I know that you have gone in there more than once, tipsy, and smoking your pipe.'

'Well, what then?'

'Why, you may be setting fire to the linney, and burn that and the house, and yourself as well. However, to return to the box. If that box had been found in your possession by anyone but myself, you would have been sent to prison. The box was not yours. It was stolen. If I desire now to deprive you of drink, it is because drink is degrading you. I want to force you to work.'

'I won't work no more,' said Cobbledick angrily. 'There be the backie, also. You've never paid me that.'

'What tobacco?'

'Ah! when you was sick, and my Joyce nussed you under the Table, you got in debt to me a score pounds and one more; that be as many as you've a got fingers and toes, and your head throwed in to make another. That be what you've owed me a long while, and never paid yet. There were that old Tramplara, he owed me scores and scores of backie, but he never paid me none at all. He went scatt. I did think you were a gemman, and would serve a poor man better.'

'I do not understand about the tobacco.'

'Loramussy! it be easy enough to understand, sure-ly. You was brought here in a waggon; well, that waggon had to be paid for, and my Joyce paid with her work, and then she was a neglecting of me. You were brought to my house, and I had to clear out and go elsewhere, and after that Joyce did nothing more for me. You expect me and my Joyce to work for'y, and you never pay a brass farthing! No gemman be like that. I call that a proper blaggard trick, I do.'

'Good heavens, Grizzly! If you want to be paid for the use of your house because it served as my hospital, by all means name the price. I will pay you in tobacco if you desire it. How much do you require?'

'As many pounds as you've fingers and toes, and your head chucked in.'

'You shall have them.'

'And then,' pursued Grizzly, 'there be Joyce. What hev you gone and tooked 'er away from me for? Oh, ah, you've not? That be fine. Her worked peaceable enough for her poor old vaither till you come by and turn 'er head with your talking and sweethearting——'

'Grizzly!' exclaimed Herring angrily, 'hold that villainous tongue of yours at once.'

'Ah, you don't want to be told of all the wrongs you've a done to me. Oh dear! the deal of pains and expense as her hev a put me to, what with her rearing, and her feeding, and her clothing, and—that is to be all for nort. When her be good full growed and able bodied, and might work for her old vaither, then you draws 'er away for reasons of your own, and leaves me without a child. Now her can't think of me nor work for me, nor light a fire for me, nor cook a biling of turnips, nor wire a rabbit—all becos you've a turned her head so as her can think, and talk, and work, only for the young maister, and I'm to bide content with a score and one of backie. That ain't in reason. That ain't how a gemman would act. Why, there were a man t'other day to Okehampton market, brought his wife there with a halter round her neck and sold 'er there for half-a-crown—not for backie, but for a real half-crown in silver.[1] Her were oldish, and not like my Joyce. If I be to part wi' Joyce, I'll take nort but silver for her, and I won't be content wi' less nor four half-crowns. I've got to make my own fire now, and do everything myself. Not you, nor Miss Cicely, nor the old Squire shall stay me. I won't sell 'er not a penny under four half-crowns and some'ut over to wet the bargain with. If you don't accept my terms I'll have her back, and if her sez her won't come back I'll do by her as I did afore—I'll

---

[1] The author knew the woman thus purchased, and the man who bought her, and with whom she lived till her death. The transaction took place about forty years ago, as described.

just scatt all the bones she has to her body. Her got her bones o' me, and I've a right to do what I will wi' my own. I can scatt mun or I can sell mun. And I won't sell mun a penny under five half-crowns, that be my figure, and blast me blue if I takes a shilling off. I'd rather break her bones first and dung my pertaty ground wi' 'em. Feel my hands, how strong they be.'

He suddenly laid hold of Herring's wrists, and his grasp was as an iron vice. Herring was a strong man, but he was unprepared to meet and resist such strength as the old savage exhibited.

'Did her give you the shining stones in the box? I reckon it were so, and her knows what to expect for doing that, and I'll do it. Did I go and take the box from the carriage? And can the constable come and carry me off to gaol for that? Then surely, if I say to un, there be the young Squire to West Wyke have a been to the Giant's Table and have a took away my daughter, then if there be justice for one there be justice for another, and the constable will come and carry you to gaol also.'

Herring walked on quicker. He was alarmed for Joyce. It would be wrong to send her back to her father. She had risen to a higher level than he; she could not associate with him longer. Moreover, he was uneasy at his threats, for the wretched old man, as he knew, would execute them without compunction.

'Six half-crowns I sed, and if you won't buy her of me for yourself, and give me the money in silver, I'll fetch her home to the Table, and I'll scatt every bone in her body. I will, glory rallaluley! You ain't a going to take everything from me, and give nothing in return.'

'There!' exclaimed Herring angrily; 'take that.' He drew his purse from his pocket, and dashed it at the old man. It struck him on the chest, and Grizzly had his hand on it in a moment.

'I can catch,' said he. 'The men chucks me bits of their pasties, and I can snap like a dog. I never lets mun drop.'

'Take that and torment Joyce no more. You will find ample in that purse to supply you with tobacco, and drink too, if you will have it. Take it, you despicable scoundrel, and leave the poor girl alone.'

'A sale be a sale,' said Grizzly. 'If you've a bought her, you have her and I've nort more to say to her. I sed seven half-crowns. Dash my brains out if I sed a penny less.' Cobbledick opened the purse and peeped in. 'Oh, rallaluley! them be guineas! golden guineas! they be worth more than eight half-crowns, the price I axed for Joyce, I reckon. Shan't I only smoke backie and get drunk. Glory! glory!'

'Do as you will. Some men cannot be helped. One must let them go to the devil their own way. You are one, and the sooner you go the better.'

'I be going. I be going as fast as I can!' exclaimed the old man, misunderstanding him.

'Then go, and do not trouble Joyce any more.'

'Oh no. I've a sold her to you. Don't'y come and try to cry off the bargain, and want your guineas back. This be scores better deal than that of the man with his wife in Okehampton market. Now, what about the linney?'

'You may not sleep there, not on any account, if you are bent on getting drunk and smoking. I'll send you down some straw with which to litter the Giant's Table.'

'Oh, rallaluley! this be fine games.' And the old savage dashed off over the moor.

Thus ended Herring's attempt at reformation of Grizzly Cobbledick. He had gone forth that morning resolved to check the old man in his downward career by cutting off the occasion of drinking, and he had supplied the man with the means of drinking himself to death.

However, he went his way, relieved in mind, to West Wyke. He had saved Joyce from further unpleasantness from her father.

Cicely met him in the porch.

'You have been a long time out,' she said. 'My father has been calling for you all day. He is very feeble; you will notice how different he is from what you saw him last night. The excitement of your return stimulated him, and now has come the relapse. Hark! I hear him calling.'

Herring went in with her.

'Papa has only come down this afternoon. I persuaded him to lie in bed during the morning, but when he thought you would be returning from Upaver, he insisted on being dressed and descending to meet you.'

'John, is that you?' called the old Squire from his chair by the fire.

'Yes, sir. I have been all day at Upaver. I have got news to tell you. We have come on a bunch of metal which I hope will clear you of all care.'

Mr. Battishill nodded. 'Yes, yes!'

The news did not seem to interest him greatly. Herring

saw with concern that he was looking feeble and old. He had fallen back sadly after the flicker of last night.

'I am not strong,' said the Squire; 'I cannot speak loud or long to-day. Come here.' He took John Herring by the hand. 'Come, Sissy.' He beckoned Cicely to draw near. 'John, I fear my time is coming to an end. I have been trying to-day to become interested in Upaver, but I cannot. I can only fix my mind on one thing. Perhaps, when that is settled, then I may be able to hear about Upaver, but not till then.'

'Do not lose heart, Mr. Battishill, now that you are on the threshold of success.'

'It is this, John. Should I have another stroke, or be unable to attend to matters, what is to become of Cicely? What is to become of West Wyke? I want your promise that you will stand by her and the old place.'

'I will do all I can for her, and for West Wyke. You may rely on me, sir.'

'I felt convinced in my own mind that I might do so, and yet I desired your promise. I became troubled, and clouds came over my spirits. As Sebastian says, "My determinate voyage is mere extravagancy." It always has been so with me. I have set my mind on the wrong things, and gone the wrong ways to work when I took anything in hand. But it is not so now. Owls can see in the dark, and so can I. If I have made blunders hitherto, I will hit straight this time. I have your promise, have I not, John?'

'Yes, Mr. Battishill.'

'You will not desert poor Sissy. She has no relations, and I have positively no one in the world to look to except yourself, whom, upon my word, I have come to love and regard as a son.' The old man patted Herring affectionately on the shoulder.

'I give you my promise, sir.'

'There! that makes me content,' said the old man. He had taken Cicely's hand in his left, he held John by the right. All at once he put their hands together. 'There!' he said, and chuckled, 'as Hamlet says, "There is a kind of confession in your looks, which your modesties have not craft enough to colour." I know you love each other. I give Cicely to you, John, and my blessing. You will take care of her—and, you will quarter the owls.'

He leaned back and his eyes closed. He was satisfied that at last he had done the right thing at the right time. The fatal faculty of making muddle and mischief followed him to the end.

Herring turned to Cicely and released his hand. She was trembling.

'You, Cicely, insisted that we were cousins. You have heard your father: he has made the relationship closer. We are henceforth brother and sister.'

She looked up, then her eyes fell, and the colour rose and sank in her face.

'Yes,' she said faintly; 'I understand perfectly, *brother John*.'

CHAPTER XLIX.

CAST UP.

'IT be good for the soul to see men die,' said Genefer, entering Mirelle's room. 'Come along of me, mistress.'

'What is it, Genefer? Do not frighten me.'

'In the midst of life we are in death. It teaches us how frail and uncertain our life be. Come and see 'em die afore your naked eyes.'

'Genefer, I will not!' Mirelle held back in alarm.

'You must come. The wreck is drifted right into Welltown cove, and it will be your own rocks as will break the ribs of the vessel and cut the flesh off the bones of the drownded. If there be a chance to save any of the poor creatures on board of her, then you must be there to direct what is to be done. You be mistress here now. I know my duty; so do Hender. When the master weren't here, and afore you comed, it were different. But now, it be not Hender nor me as be answerable. It be you as is put in authority, and have to say to this man, Come, and he cometh, and to another, Go, and he goeth. If you bide at home and do nothing, then let 'em be drownded, and them as has done good shall enter into life, and them as has done evil shall go into everlasting death, and the blood of the souls that be lost shall rest on your head.'

'But what is it?'

'I tell you there be a vessel drove by the storm right in, and her be drifting into Welltown cove. It be no good her trying to get into Boscastle Harbour, with the white horses galloping. Her comes side on upon the reef, and will go scatt afore your eyes.'

'Can nothing be done?'

'You must be there and see,' answered Genefer Benoke; 'if there be lives to be saved, they will be saved, but you must be there to see to it.'

Mirelle put on her cloak and hat, and went forth. This was a duty, and Mirelle had a strong sense of obligation to do her duty, whenever it was presented before her.

The storm of last night had subsided, and the wind had shifted. A thaw had set in, and the sun was streaming over the melting snow. The blue sea was strewn with foam streaks. Though the wind had abated, the sea was still churning. The passion of the night could not abate at once; the pulses of the Atlantic were throbbing. The sight was magnificent. The billows that rolled upon the headland were at once shattered, and sent up columns of foam white as the snow upon the ground. Earlier, the morning sun had painted rainbows in the salt drift, but now the sun hung over the sea, and, if he painted them still, did so unseen by those on land. The whole coast was fringed with a deep border of fluttering white lace. The air was salt, and the lips of all who faced it became briny. Out at sea stood the Meachard, an islet of inaccessible black rock, capped with turf. On this no snow rested. The waves besieged the Meachard on all sides, like the rabble of Paris attacking the Bastille; they appeared to explode on touching the rock into volumes of white steam, that rushed up whirling, and swept the crown. The reflection of the sun in the sea was shivered into countless, ever-changing flakes of fire. Over the surface of the water the gulls were fluttering in vast numbers —they seemed like sea foam vivified.

This was the sea after the storm, already exhausted, and with relaxed power. What must it have been in the height of its rage, during the night?

'Where is the ship?' asked Mirelle, looking in vain for a vessel on the uneasy surface.

'Look!' old Genefer pointed.

'What, that? It is so small.'

'There be men aboard, living and calling on God now, and in ten minutes they'll be standing afore their Judge. They can look out of their eyes now, and see you up here on the cliff in your black gown, and in ten minutes their eyes will be full of salt water, and able to see nothing. They can cry aloud for mercy now, and in ten minutes the time of mercy will be over for each, and the time of retribution will be begun!'

Mirelle could hardly believe that the little cockleshell drifting on the rocks before her could contain men in jeopardy of their lives. It was but a cockleshell, a child's ship made of a walnut. But there were men and women on the headland watching intently and with interest the fate of that petty boat, and an excise officer stood there with his telescope to his eye.

'She is the "Susanna" of Bristol,' said he.

'Her's never been in our harbour,' observed a Boscastle man. 'I reckon there be about four aboard. Her be about the size to carry four.'

'What be the lading, Pentecost?'

'That don't matter to you or I, Gerans,' answered Pentecost. 'Times be altered when an honest man might profit by what the Lord sent us.'

'It do seem a deadly shame that a man may not accept the good gifts Providence showers upon him, but the Government must interfere.'

'Ah!' put in Genefer, 'that be the way of things. The sower sows his seed, and the fowls come and carry it away. The Lord sows His word, and the Church passons come and take it away that it can bring forth no fruit, and leave nort in its place. It is the same when He sends a storm and casts a ship ashore. A Christian man may not stoop and take up a keg of brandy the Lord has rolled to his feet, but the 'xisemen must come and take it away, so to speak, out of his mouth.'

'There be five shillings for every corpse as be picked up and brought to burial,' said another. 'But I'd rather have a keg of spirits than a corpse any day. Besides, who's to earn a crown like that? They may do it on the shores of Essex that be mud and sand. But here! old Uncle Zacky goes about after a storm with a sack, and picks up what gobbets of human flesh he can find on the shore, but the parish won't give un more than half a crown for as much as he can carry up the cliffs, and that takes a sight more picking up than would a whole corpse. These bain't times in which honest men may live.'

'I say, maister!' called Pentecost to the preventive man; 'spose her be laden with sea coal, and the coal come ashore. Do'y put your foot down on that and say nobody ain't to shovel that up, it belongs to his Majesty, God bless him? And next tide the coal be all licked down into the belly of the ocean, and is no good to none.'

'What be the good of us keeping donkeys?' asked Gerans; 'I reckon they cost us something for hay in winter. Us don't keep donkeys for nort; us keep 'em to bring up the cliffs whatever comes ashore. And us is to have the expense of keeping donkeys and not to put 'em to no use! We are to keep the donkeys for the delight of our eyes, as beautiful objecks of nature,'

'I reckon her be laden with cloam' (earthenware) 'ovens,' said Pentecost. 'I wish his Majesty joy of them when they comes ashore. If Job were here and wanted a shard to scratch himself withal, and ventured to pick up a bit of scattered cloam off the beach, you'd be down on him in a jiffy, wouldn't you now, maister?'

The preventive officer took no notice of the gibes cast at him; he kept his telescope on the vessel.

'Her be on the breakers now,' said one of the men.

'What be the good of staying here?' asked another. 'There be no chance of getting nothing unless us was to chuck this chap over the cliffs first.'

'Don't say that, Pascho; there'll be five shillings for every corpse we can bring up the cliffs. And if we manage to save one alive, surely the young lady here will give us a trifle and a drop of cyder to drink her health and the corpse's. I seez it in her eye.'

'I will give you ten guineas for every man you save,' said Mirelle, vehemently, 'and as much as you can eat and drink.'

'Didn't I tell you so?' exclaimed Pentecost. 'Look alive, boys! There be the ship gone scatt! Down the cliffs with you all, and see if we cannot earn a few gold guineas and drink long life to the lady and the corpse as we brings up alive.'

The ship had struck. The waves and foam swept over her, and in a few moments she went to pieces. Some figures were discernible battling with the water. It seemed to Mirelle impossible that these tiny ants were sufferers, that they were of human flesh and feelings like herself—they seemed so small. There was nothing horrible in the sight; it was not so shocking as the drowning of mice turned out of a trap into a bucket. When Gulliver cried with pain in Brobdingnag, the giants laughed. In a microscopic creature the agony of death must be microscopically small.

Mirelle looked on the drowning pigmies, quite unable to realise the awfulness of the event, her sympathy stirred by her reason, not by her heart, for the appeal was not such as could move the sympathy save through the brain.

The first to sink was the mate. We will fly over the water

with the gulls, instead of straining our eyes from the cliffs. Are the gulls about us screaming or laughing? The first to sink was the mate. He was an old seaman, a godfearing man, honest of heart, who had left the sea because he had earned enough to maintain himself on land in his old age. But he had lent his money to a younger brother, to enable him to set up a small shop in Bristol. The brother failed and ran away, leaving a wife and four little children wholly unprovided for. So the old man went to sea again to earn enough to support his brother's deserted wife and children. He sank. The gulls are cynics—they laughed.

The second that sank was the captain; a fine man, upright, rough in exterior, but soft-hearted. He had been an unlucky man. Engaged to a girl he had long loved, after many years of waiting, in which both turned the corner of life, he was now making his last voyage before he married her. She was at Bristol, preparing the little house they had taken. She had put flower-pots in the window, and was this morning setting a geranium there, to make the place look bright for the return of William and her own marriage. Then he sank. She would not see him again. The gulls laughed.

The third who sank was a boy, the only son of a widow. The boy had wanted much to go to sea, but he was the darling of his mother, and she would not suffer him to go with any but our captain, whom she knew and could trust with the only being on earth she loved. Now he was gone, and the widow must weep. The gulls laughed.

The fourth who went down was a sailor, a careless fellow, drinking and heeding neither angel nor devil; but there was a vein of gold in his heart waiting to be brought to the surface. It is said that on midsummer night all buried treasures rise and shine. Midsummer night had not come to him yet. Another year, and he would be a better man, but this other year was denied him. He sank, and the gulls laughed.

These were all who sank, but there was one who came ashore. He and the boy were clinging to the same piece of timber. Then this man kicked the boy on the chest and so he fell off and went down, and this man had the balk to himself. The waves went over him, and he lost consciousness, but not his hold. He was saved, and the gulls, wheeling above, laughed and scoffed more loudly than before.

Up the narrow track cut in the face of the cliff this man was carried.

'By goll!' said Pascho, 'I hope the chap ain't dead, but he looks cruel bad. It makes all the difference to us between five shillings and ten guineas.'

'Now look here, you niggers!' exclaimed Pentecost, angrily. 'What be all you a coming up and making believe you are helping? You've had nort to do with the saving of this chap, and so don't you come putting in your claims for a share. Go back and see if you can't pick up a corpse or two as will find you in liquor or backie for a week or a fortnight. The ten guineas is to share between five of us, and that will be four too many. I lugged un out of the water.'

'Ah, but I squeedged the water out of his chest,' said Pascho.

'And if I hadn't held the rope,' said Gerans, 'you'd have all been swept into the water and become crowners' sittings.'

'There!' said Pentecost, 'chuck him across a barrel, and let the water run out of him.'

'There be no barrel here; lay him flat.'

'Yes, in the snow indeed. Do you think I want to risk my honest earnings that way? He must be took to bed and hot bricks be put to his feet.'

'Where is he to go to?' asked Pascho.

'To Welltown, of course; where else? There ain't no other house nigh.'

'Let the young lady see un,' said Genefer. 'It be a rare fine sight for the soul to see a man hanging atween life and death. Let her see un.'

The men laid their unconscious burden at the feet of Mirelle.

She looked into the face with mingled sympathy and terror. The figure seen battling with the waves had grown big—human size now, it was no longer an ant. She could feel pity.

As she looked, she started and shrank away, holding up her hands to shut out what she saw.

'There!' said Genefer, 'it be a brave and improving sight. I reckon it do as much good to the soul as a lump of sugar with a drop of peppermint on it does to the stomick when out of sorts. It warms and strengthens and gives tone. He be a young man. Well, the Lord, I reckon, has got a work in store for he, as He has called him out of the deep, and has given him the life back as were trembling at the door of his heart to leave. As for the rest, they be cut off in their sins. Take him to Welltown.'

'Stay, stay!' exclaimed Mirelle, interposing with vehemence. 'He shall not—he shall never go thither. Never, so long as I am mistress there.'

'Is he to lie here on the snow?' asked Genefer. 'You will have to give an account of it if he do, and die in consequence.'

'He shall not be taken to Welltown.'

The men looked at each other.

'Where be we to carry un to, then?' asked Pentecost.

'If he die, I'm danged if it be fair if you deny us the ten guineas. He has life in him now, and if he lose it, it will be your fault, young lady. We've done our parts and earned our money.'

'Take him where you will, but not to Welltown.'

'There is no other house near.'

'Here,' said Mirelle, her hand trembling; 'here is the key; take him into the slate-quarry office. There is a bed there.'

'Ay, let him go there,' said Genefer; 'he can be cared for there just as well as at Welltown.'

The men stooped and raised the unconscious man again. Mirelle covered her eyes—the man saved was Sampson Tramplara.

She had promised ten guineas—and that ten guineas had saved his worthless life. Well for her had she at this juncture offered fifty to have him tossed back into the sea. The men would not have done it for twenty—there were too many present; they would have hesitated for thirty. But for fifty, he would have troubled her no more.

CHAPTER L.

TWO DISOBEDIENCES.

NEXT day Orange arrived. Mirelle had sent for her; she could not remain longer alone at Welltown, especially now that young Sampson was so near. She did not go to the office on Willapark to see him; she did not inquire after him. But she told Genefer that he was to be supplied with whatever he needed, and was to remain where he was till he was well enough to leave, and then he was to go his way.

As soon as Orange arrived Mirelle told her that Sampson had been saved from drowning after shipwreck, and was at the office; and Orange went immediately to see him.

Sampson was now quite recovered from his submersion. The fire was lighted in the stove, and the room was warm.

'Oh! you have come, have you?' he asked, when Orange entered. 'Not wise, I reckon, unless you are bent on bringing observation on me. What is this I hear? I am on Herring's land and in his office! This is a queer state of affairs; but the wheel of fate in its revolutions lands one in strange places, and places where one would least like to be. How came you here?'

Orange explained to him what had taken place since his disappearance; how Mirelle had been married to John Herring, and she had been brought to Welltown.

'That's queer. I haven't seen either him or her.'

'I am told that he has been called away on business—military, I suppose—and you cannot be surprised if she has not chosen to see you. She knows well enough who you are. But now, Sampson, about yourself. How came you here? And—are you safe, quite safe, here?'

'No, I arn't, that's the cussedness of it all. I can't stay here, especially now the Countess Candlesticks knows of my presence and has got a tongue in her head. If I stay here I shall be taken, and I can't go, because I have no money to go with.'

'How came you here?'

'Cast up by the sea, I reckon,' answered Sampson.

'But how came you to be wrecked?' asked Orange.

'Why, because I was aboard ship.'

'You may as well answer me civilly,' said his sister. 'If you get away from this place, it will be by my help, and I must know all about you, and whither you want to go.'

'Curse it,' said Sampson, 'if you want to know whence I have come I will tell you—from Bristol, and if you want to know why I left, it is because Polly Skittles has blown on me. If you want to know where I am going, you must be content to remain in ignorance, for I don't know myself.'

'But, Sampson, how came you to be in Bristol?'

'Because it was not my intention to run to France, or any place where I could not speak a word of their damned parleyvous. I don't see why a fellow should not lie snug in England instead of going into exile abroad. So, when I had to leave Launceston, I cut off first to Plymouth; but there I became funky, that was too near home, and so I made for Bristol, and there I've been enjoying myself ever since, and might have been living at ease like a fighting cock but for Polly Skittles.'

'You behaved abominably, Sampy. You carried off all the money that was in the house, and left mother and me absolutely destitute.'

'Oh, ah! I was not such a fool as to leave anything. Everyone for himself is my maxim. But be reasonable; if I had left money you would not have had it, the creditors would have been down on you and have carried off everything. By George! I have had many a laugh over that Ophir since I have washed my hands of it. That was a rare plant, better than Polpluggan. And father did come out splendid in it. The way in which he beat old Flamank's covers and bagged his game was superlative. Well, he died like Wolfe at Quebec. "They run! Who run?" "The Ophirites." And didn't they run?'

Sampson clapped his knees and roared.

'It strikes me that it was you who ran,' said Orange, sullenly. 'Now, tell me, what are you going to do?'

'I'll tell you one thing I have learned, and I had to go to Bristol to learn it. Orange, never trust a woman. I might have been all right now but for Polly Skittles. I was an ass, I allow that. I sent word to her at the Pig and Whistle where I was, and asked her to come to me and share my fortune with me. Well, she couldn't keep her tongue in her head, but was bragging about the rich man she was going to marry, and so from hint to circumstance, and all was blown. The beaks were on the scent and after me, and I had to make a run for it. I got on board the "Susanna" for Port Isaac. I thought if I managed to get there, I might give them the slip again. And now, damn it all, here am I stranded at Boscastle, and when the news reaches Bristol that the "Susanna" has been lost, it will be known also that I am saved, and the beaks will be after me again.'

'What has become of the money, Sampson?'

'Oh, blast it! there is the mischief. I brought away all I had with me, and it has gone down in the "Susanna." I did have some trifle about me when I came ashore, but those who saved my life relieved me of my purse. That was natural, and I cannot complain; I'd have done the same. But I am mad to think that all the gold of Ophir lies at the bottom of the Atlantic.'

'What is to be done now?'

'You must provide me with money.'

'Nonsense, Sampy. I—I have nothing. You know that well enough.'

'I don't know anything about it. You're clever enough to get what you want. You hooked Captain Trecarrel fast enough when you had set your mind on having him.'

Orange became scarlet. 'You are cruel, Sampson; you are worse, you are brutal. I will have nothing more to say to you.'

'Yes, you will,' said he, insolently. 'If you don't, I'll go myself to Welltown, and force that pale-faced fool to give me money.'

'You know that she was plundered as well as others. Her money was sunk in Ophir.'

'I know that she can take her husband's money now. I suppose she has wit enough to keep the keys of his cash-box. Women are not such fools as to omit that.'

'I cannot ask her for money; indeed I cannot, Sampy.'

'Look here, Orange. How the devil am I to get away from this place without blunt? And how am I to live when I get away without ditto? You don't suppose I can dig and plough, do you?'

'I tell you I have nothing.'

'Then you must get me something. I've been overhauling this office and I can find nothing in it. There is a drawer locked in the desk that I have not opened and examined, but I shall know its contents before long, even if I have to break the lock. I don't, however, expect to get much out of it. A man does not leave money in such an uninhabited place as this.'

'If I get you a little you must be content with that.'

'If you get me a little I will be content with it only as long as it lasts, and when spent, then I shall want more.'

'What folly this is! You carried off every penny you could lay hands on, and now you ask for money from those you have plundered!'

'I do not ask you for your own money, I know you have none to give. I want some of Mirelle's money, or her husband's —it is all the same. Get me her diamonds if you can. Do you not understand? I dare not remain here above a day longer; I must be off before the beaks are on my track. How is a man to get away without a penny in his pocket? He must halt and beg on his road, and where he begs, there he is observed. I must double on the hounds on their way hither.

If I make for Bath I shall do. They are sure to run to Port Isaac, whither the " Susanna " was bound.'

'I wish you were safe away. I do not relish your being here. It would be exceedingly unpleasant for me were you taken whilst I am at Welltown. I do not want ugly stories to get about this neighbourhood, for here my mother and I will have to live.'

'I don't suppose you do,' answered Sampson; 'more the reason why I should be given facilities for clearing off.'

'I really do not know what to do. I might represent to Mirelle that you had lost everything, and ask her for a little money, a few pounds; but I cannot, I will not, entreat for a large sum.'

'Why not?'

'Because it is against my own interest. I am not yet settled into the house. I have but arrived to-day, and if my mother and I are to take up our quarters here, I must not begin by making myself disagreeable to the hostess. You know what Mirelle is. She is simple in some things, but when you think you are going to turn her round your fingers, you discover that she is the most impracticable person you ever had to deal with.'

'I say, Orange, what about those diamonds of hers?'

'They are paste.'

'I don't believe it.'

'She gave me part of the set; the pendant and the stones in that were all artificial.'

'You fool,' said Sampson, 'that was why she gave you the brooch. If they had been real, do you suppose that she would have made you such a handsome present?'

'I do not know,' answered Orange, sullenly. She was angry with Sampson, and she wanted to get rid of him. It would suit her very well to live with Mirelle. She hated Launceston, and wished to leave it. She trusted that something was going to be done for her by Mirelle in fulfilment of the promise made by John Herring on the wedding day, but she was not certain. At all events it was most convenient for her to live with Mirelle, and, if she were given money, to lay it by. She had indignantly rejected the suggestion of taking Captain Trecarrel, but she loved him still, and she entertained a lingering hope of future reconciliation. If he wanted her, he would come after her. She had sufficient sound sense to know that he could not marry her if she was without private means, because he was poor himself. She was jealous of Mirelle. The Captain had hovered about her; Mirelle had drawn him off from her. She was not at all sure that the Captain would desist from his attentions now that Mirelle was married. She wished therefore to be with her rival so as to watch her.

'Orange!'

'Well, Sampson.'

'I say. We were always allies.'

'To what does this introduction lead?'

'Where does Mirelle keep her diamonds?'

'I do not know. I have come here to-day for the first time.'

'I wish you would find out.'

'I can find out fast enough.'

'I say, Orange. If I could finger them, you wouldn't see much of me for many a day, and that is what your sisterly heart desires.'

'I wish I could be sure of that.'

'You are not over fond of the Countess Candlesticks, I reckon.'

'I hate her,' answered Orange, vehemently.

'You would not mind getting those diamonds for me, would you? She don't want them. What use can she make of them in a desert like this? She would not miss them.'

'I tell you, Sampy, I do not know where they are, and what is more, if I did know, I would not give them to you. I am not going to risk my place in the house for you.'

'Who is to see you take them? Lay the blame on me. Find out where they are and tell me, and if accessible I will work my way into the house and get them.'

'It won't do; it won't do, indeed. If I knew where the stones were, I would not mind telling you; and if you could get them without risk of detection, and without in any way involving me, I would not care. But I will not help you to them.'

'If I had them, I'd be off to America at once.'

'There—I must go now,' said Orange, rising. 'I will try to get you something, but you must not expect much.' She turned to go out. She was flushed and annoyed. The presence of Sampson was vexatious to her, and might prove inconvenient.

'Stay a moment, Orange. Have you any keys about you?'

'I must go—yes, I have. I brought away the bunch from Dolbeare, in my haste. What will mother do without them?'

'She can send for the blacksmith, I cannot. Leave them with me. I want to look inside that drawer. There is a file in the cupboard, and I can make a key fit the lock I intend to open. Thank you, Orange. You are a good sister—worthy of me. You do credit to your father also. Now you may go.'

In the night a tap sounded at the door of Willapark office. Sampson had been working hard and was tired. He was snoozing in the chair over the fire. He started instantly to full consciousness and in alarm. His fears subsided when the door opened, and he saw Orange enter, very white and trembling.

'Well,' he said, 'what have you brought me?'

'A little money,' she answered, 'not much. I could not get much for you. I have had a quarrel with Mirelle—about you.'

'Have you brought me the diamonds?'

'No, and did not intend to do so; but I know where they are, and they are where you cannot get them.'

'Where is that?'

'In a very strong oak bureau in the room over the porch, and in a secret drawer in the well of that. That room cannot be entered except through the hall, main stairs, and Mirelle's bedroom. So put the thought of the diamonds out of your head. The bureau is always locked, and Mirelle keeps the key. Even if you got into the room, which is not possible, unobserved, you would not be able to open the cabinet. There—that is the end of that foolish dream, and I am glad of it. Had you taken them, I might have been suspected. I have had a quarrel with Mirelle—about you. But I must sit down a moment, Sampson, and then run back.' She was out of breath; she spoke in short sentences, breathing hard between each. 'When we were together, she began to speak about the pendant she had given me, and to ask for it back. She said she would have the paste diamonds removed, and real stones put in their places. She told me that her necklace had been examined, and that it had been found that some only of the stones in it were false. A lady's maid of her mother had tampered with the jewels. Then she desired to compare my brooch, with its paste diamonds, with the real stones in her necklace; she got up and went to the bureau; she took the key out of her purse. There was a secret drawer opening out of a sort of well in the middle, and she brought the set of stones out of that. After that we had compared the false with the real diamonds she returned the necklace to its place, re-locked the cabinet, and replaced the key in her purse. Then we began to speak about you. I told her that you were without any money, that you had lost everything in the ship, and had been further robbed by the men who saved your life. She asked what of?—of the stolen money? I then begged her to let you have something to help you to get away. She set her lips and put on that stubborn look I know so well. She would give nothing. You had robbed Mr. Flamank and many others, and it was your duty to surrender yourself and suffer for your misdeeds. If you had any conscience and honour, that was what you would do, and she would not help you to evade the consequences of your own acts. My blood rose, and I spoke sharply. She was cold, hard, and obstinate. At last I got her to give me something, not for you, but for myself. She and her husband had made me a promise on their wedding day to give me some trifle, and I asked her if she purposed fulfilling that engagement, or whether it was only an empty promise. Then she replied that Herring had made the promise and would fulfil it, and that, if I was in immediate want of money, she would give me a small sum, all she could spare, for she had not more coin in the house. I was forced to be content. Here are twelve guineas; take them and be off. I can get you no more. There is no more to be got.'

'Well, Orange, I must take what I can get. The diamonds can wait. I have found something better than them in the locked drawer.'

'What is it, Sampson? Money?'

'No, not money. Do you like John Herring, Orange?'

'No.'

'I hate him,' said Sampson. 'You do not love Mirelle, I believe?'

'I hate her!' answered Orange, passionately.

'What I have found may serve to wipe off mutual grudges.'

'I am glad of it; use your knowledge.'

'I intend to do so on the proper occasion.'

'Well, good-bye, Sampson; I must return. Mirelle must not know that I have been here. I hope I have seen the last of you for some time.'

'I do not know. I must have a word with John Herring before I disappear entirely.'

O foolish Mirelle! Herring, before leaving, had laid on

her two injunctions—to entrust no one with the secret of where she kept her jewels, and to allow no one to enter his office unattended by herself. She had disregarded and disobeyed both injunctions.

CHAPTER LI.

TWO EXITS.

JOHN HERRING said nothing to Cicely in allusion to what had passed; he could not do so. He was naturally reserved about himself, and he could not tell her of his marriage without telling her also of his separation from his wife. The questions would spring to her lips: 'When were you married? Why have you left her? Why are you now staying at West Wyke instead of at Welltown?' These were questions she would naturally ask, and which it would be impossible for him to explain to her. His trouble was his own; the heart knoweth its own bitterness, and a stranger intermeddleth not therewith. A woman delights in pouring forth her griefs into a sympathetic ear; a man hides his sufferings, and resents sympathy as an insult. Herring had said enough to let Cicely understand the position in which he stood towards her—that of a brother, a position he would never abandon; she had recognised this, and had accepted it.

Herring thought night and day of Mirelle; he could not shake the burden off his heart, and, whatever his distractions, it remained oppressing him, an ever-gnawing pain. He wondered what Mirelle was doing; whether she liked Welltown— that place he loved so well. When the sun shone out of a clear sky, he thought, it is fine to-day at Welltown, and Mirelle will go upon the cliffs and hear the gulls scream and look at the twinkling sea; she will inhale that wondrous air, which to him who breathes it is the inspiration of life in long draughts. Would she dare to go in a boat to Blackapit, when the sea was still, and look up those walls of inky rock striped with ledges, on which the sea birds nested, up into the blue sky above, in which even by day stars can be discerned? Had she wandered to Minster Church, down in a valley embowered in trees, with the ruins of the old monastery crumbling about it? O how happy he would have been to be able to accompany her to the loved spots, wild and picturesque, that had been his delight in boyhood! Would she venture on an excursion to S. Kneighton's Kieve, and pick there the maiden-hair fern, dancing in the draught of the falling water? Would she visit Pentargon, that glorious cove, with precipitous walls of rock black as night, over which a stream bounds in a long fall to meet the sea?

He thought of her sitting by the fire, in her white bridal dress, so lovely, so sad, so like a phantom from another world. Mirelle haunted him; she filled his whole heart. Later he would return to Welltown, when he and she had had time to realise the relation in which they stood to each other, and the first poignancy of the disenchantment was past.

Mirelle was to him the ideal of purity and perfection. He knew his own unworthiness; he was not the man who ought to own her as wife; he was rude and simple. She should be placed on a pedestal in a temple, to be approached by worshippers on bended knees. The snowdrops were out in the West Wyke garden; Herring plucked one every morning and wore it all day. Mirelle had worn snowdrops in her bosom when she married him. The snowdrop was her appropriate flower, white and fragile.

Herring was at Upaver all day. The mine was turning out better than even he had anticipated. There was no question now about the extinction of the debt on West Wyke. Mr. Battishill's profits would blot that out and redeem the mortgages. Mirelle's money sunk in the machinery would yield a dividend before the year was half out. Herring saw to everything himself; he inspired the men with energy. The contractor's bad work at the buildings was made good. His mind was occupied from morning to night; but he never forgot his trouble for one moment. It was ever there rankling in his heart; it took the gloss off success.

Mr. Battishill had sunk into a condition of mental feebleness and bodily exhaustion that engaged his daughter's constant attention. The old man could not be left alone; he no longer rose from his bed to take his old seat in the hall.

When Herring came back from Upaver, he went upstairs to the Squire's room, where he found Cicely knitting, and he sat there for an hour talking to the sick man, trying to interest him in what was going on at the mine. After dinner with Cicely in the hall, he went up again and read Shakespeare to Mr. Battishill. The squire was always ready for that. He had his favourite passages, and these he repeated after Herring, but his power to follow the movement of a scene and to distinguish characters was gone. Old familiar sentences caught his ear, and he murmured them after Herring, as he might follow a prayer, but his mind did not take in the sense. Yet he never wearied of this Shakespeare reading; it was like well-remembered melodies striking his ear, and lulling him to sleep.

When the Squire had had enough, he always laid his thin hand across the book, and said in the words of Coriolanus, 'I am weary; yea, my memory is tired.' Then Cicely, John Herring, and Joyce knelt together by the old man's bed, and he folded his hands and said the one familiar prayer; and then Cicely and the rest bade him good night and left him.

Sometimes the old man would become uneasy, and ask John whether he would protect Cicely. 'You will always stand by her, will you not, John?'

Herring was obliged to give him the assurance he required.

'You are my children.'

'Yes, sir; brother and sister.'

'Brother and sister,' repeated Cicely.

Then the old man murmured, 'And she is fair, and, fairer than that word, of wondrous virtues.'

The Vicar of Tawton, the Reverend Harmless-Simpleton, was frequent in his calls. He was an amiable and well-intentioned man. The Simpletons are a large family, that have never thriven at the bar, in medicine, in the army and the navy, but the Harmless-Simpletons (the two surnames united by a hyphen) have for several generations made the Church their happy hunting ground. They have gone up in the Church like corks in water. The fattest livings, prebendal stalls, and even bishoprics have been showered upon them. As Napoleon won all his battles by one rule, so the Harmless-Simpletons acquired promotion by one simple principle. In the field of doctrine they never taught a truth without first treating it as a taxidermist treats a frog, killing, disembowelling, then blowing out the fleshless, boneless skin with wind, and varnishing the empty nothing. In the field of morals they never attacked a real enemy, but discharged their parks of ordnance, brought down charges of heavy dragoons, and displayed the most skilful strategy against imaginary foes.

When the Reverend Harmless-Simpleton called, he divided his visit into two parts, one of which was devoted to Mr. Battishill and the other to Miss Cicely, in the ratio of three to seven. Mr. Battishill was pleased to see and hear him, and Miss Cicely became deeply impressed with the reverend gentleman's amiability and good intentions.

So, little by little, the old Squire faded away.

There was another old man, who, much about the same time, made his exit from the stage, but in an altogether different manner.

Grizzly Cobbledick had been denied the linney in which to lie at night, 'like a heckamal in a haystack.' He was obliged, much as he objected to it, to return to the Giant's Table. As he feared that his old woman would be disposed to trouble his repose there, he provided himself with the means of sleeping soundly, in the shape of a stone jar full of spirits. Moreover, he paid a libation to her manes every night. He threw some drops of gin into the fire, saying, 'There, old cat! take that, and lie quiet.'

Grizzly was so far civilised by association with men that he knew the value of money. He had lost his shyness in the presence of men and his reluctance to appear in the neighbourhood of houses, and he would go into Zeal and hang about the taverns for drink and tobacco.

Now he had money of his own, and he launched into extravagance. He purchased a jar of hollands, and carried it off with him to the Table, to comfort him at night—that he might lie in the straw and suck and nod, then suck and doze, open an eye and suck once more, and then drop off into a drunken stupor.

That which amused and puzzled him greatly was to see the spirit flame when he cast some drops on the fire. Water quenched fire; how came a liquor to leap into flame? This was more than his dull mind could take in. But it seemed to him that the essence of fire must be in the spirit, that was why it warmed him within, and danced and glowed in his veins. John Herring had been as good as his word. He had sent him straw, and the straw was heaped up at the back of the chamber.

'Take care, Grizzly,' said the man who brought him the bundles. 'Take care that your fire don't get to it; keep it well off.'

Grizzly had sense enough to do this. When he was sleepy the old man went backwards into the straw, disappearing entirely with the exception of his head and the hand that held the stone jar. The only firing was peat, and that did not flame.

When Herring cast him his purse, it was with the words: 'Some men cannot be helped. One must let them go to the devil their own way. You are one, and the sooner you go the better.'

Then Grizzly replied, 'I be going—I be a going as fast as I can.'

He kept his word. He went even faster than he intended, and the way he went was this.

He was sitting over the fire one evening. He had his stone jar under his arm, and he was patting it.

'Her be running dry, her be,' said he. 'Poor thing! let me hold'y up and try again.' He spoke to inanimate objects as though they were endowed with souls as reasonable as his own. 'There!' said he, as he cast a few drops on the fire, and laughed at the flames that leaped up; 'that be the blue blazes I've a swore by all my live and never knowed 'n, to see to, I reckon. Now there bain't another drop left. What ever shall I do? I have got more money, but no more spirits, and what be I to do all night long? Ah! I be a poor lorn creetur, I be. My old woman, her deserted me first, and a mighty shabby trick that were. Do'y hear me a speaking of 'y, old cat? Then my daughter Joyce, her left me—that is, I sold her when her'd a gone of herself. 'Twere good for me I got some money out of the deal: if I hadn't, her'd have cut and run all the same.' He sat and poked the red turves together. 'I wonder,' he said, 'what there be in thicky barrel I took from Ophir? Like enough there be first-rate drink in her. Old Tramplara weren't one to do things by halves. Her be hid away under the fern. I reckon I'll have her out and try.'

He groped beneath the straw to a nether layer of bracken, and from under that rolled a small keg.

'There ain't much comfort to be got out of she,' he said, 'her be so gashly small. I wonder what there be in her? Her be hard to open.'

He put the little barrel down by the fire.

'I reckon I could manage a hole wi' my old stone knife.' Then he got the flint tool, and worked it between his palms on the end of the keg. The fire was getting low; he threw on some more turves. Then he ventured on a wisp of straw to make a blaze and assist his eyes.

'Oh, rallaluley!' he exclaimed, 'I've got the hole drilled through at last.'

He had stolen this little barrel from Ophir during the disorder occasioned by the discovery of the imposition. It was the only thing that he thought might possibly be of service to him. He took it away, and hid it under the fern at the back of the dolmen, intending to examine its contents at his leisure.

'Why, there be no drink here at all,' said he in disgust, when he had put his lips to the hole he had made. 'What be this? I've a got my mouth full of grit; it be black as coal. Blast me blue, but I will let my old woman taste it too.'

He let the contents run out in a little stream; then he gathered a handful of the grains and cast it into the fire to his 'old woman.' The contents of the keg then found their way out in a more expeditious manner than through the hole he had bored. The keg contained blasting powder.

Thus it came about that he fulfilled his promise faster than he had intended. Thus also it is that one of the most interesting monuments of a prehistoric age will not appear on the Ordnance Map of Devonshire now in process of execution.

CHAPTER LII.

THE RETURN OF THE WANDERER.

JOHN HERRING had fulfilled his promise. He had made over five thousand pounds to Orange Tramplara. No sooner was this effected than it was whispered in the ear and the same day proclaimed on the housetops of Launceston. The proclamation reached Trecarrel. When Captain Trecarrel heard it, and had satisfied himself that this was not an empty report, he began to reconsider the state of his feelings towards Miss Orange. Five thousand pounds was a sum for which he might dispose of himself. It was not much, but more was not to be had in that neighbourhood. The Captain was without sisters and cousins scattered over the country, beating the covers for heiresses for him and blowing the horn when they had started one. He was forced to hunt for himself.

Five thousand pounds at five per cent. is two hundred and fifty pounds a year. Two hundred and fifty pounds per annum would enable him to keep his head above water—only his head, not his shoulders, but that would be better than to be overwashed by every wavelet. Now that old Mr. Tramplara was dead, there was no one to look closely after settlements—that was something. Captain Trecarrel was then in very particular want of money, and there was no money to be got through any other channel than the hymeneal ring. The property was already mortgaged, and the Captain could not encumber it further without cutting off his only means of subsistence.

He heard that Orange, followed after a fortnight by her mother, had moved to Welltown, near Boscastle, and was staying with Mr. and Mrs. Herring. The report was not quite accurate, for Mr. Herring, as we know, was not there. Report has the knack of interjecting into the best substantiated information an element of inaccuracy. He knew Herring, and thought that through him he might get the quarrel with Orange patched up—at least, through him he would obtain admission to the house where she lived. Herring would know nothing of the flirtation with Mirelle, and therefore would not scruple to admit him; and, once in, he would manage Orange. What girl could resist his handsome profile, his moustache and blue eyes!

Trecarrel knew that Orange loved him, and he knew also that when a woman loves, her pride and resentment give way whenever it pleases the lover to resume the assault. He would not be precipitate; he would be friendly at first, with a tinge of restraint and a savour of coldness in his manner towards her. This would yield by degrees, and they would soon recover their old intimacy and stand towards each other on the same footing as of old.

'I know perfectly well,' said the Captain, 'that there are hundreds, I may say thousands, of girls with fortunes who would give their ears for me, but the provoking thing is that they have never heard of me, nor can I obtain access to them. There are Birmingham and Manchester manufacturers' daughters, there are the girls of Bristol and Liverpool merchants, without family position, and with vulgar names, who would jump with all their moneybags into my arms, if I could only offer myself to them. But how am I to do so? I know nobody in Birmingham, Manchester, or Liverpool moneyed society, and I am unacquainted with any bridges. Between me and them there is a great gulf fixed, and though I would fain go to them, and they as gladly come to me, yet my tongue must parch in penury, and they must yawn in the bosom of Crœsus. The means of intercommunication fail. I am getting on in life, I am thirty-four, and I ought to be doing something towards paying off my mortgages. I had rather have a girl with ten thousand than one with five, for then I should be twice as comfortable and connubial affection twice as strong; but if the girl with ten be not obtainable, I must be content with her who has only five. I wonder whence that five thousand came? I suspect old Tramplara put away money in his wife's name, and she has it;

and that this five thousand has been placed to her daughter's account as a bait to draw me. If the old woman has money, it will come to Orange in the end; she is bad every winter with her throat, and this is a trying climate for throats, the temperature changes with such rapidity. The old woman would surely not be such a fool as to act the King Lear, and make over all she has to her daughter. She must have a reserve fund of at least five thousand more. By George, I'll risk it!'

So Captain Trecarrel took the Camelford coach as far as 'Drunkards all,' and walked from that point to Boscastle, making a man carry his valise. This was the cheapest way of travelling, and the Captain did everything as cheaply as he could, not because he liked it, but because he could not help himself. He put up at the Ship, where was a cosy little parlour and a clean bedroom. He would be comfortable there. He had brought his drawing materials with him, for the purpose of making water-colour sketches. When making his drawings he painted his subject in Indian ink, and then gave a Prussian blue wash to the sea, and a wash of Prussian blue and gamboge together over the grass and trees, and a wash of sepia to the rocks. Then he imagined a woman in a red cloak to be standing in a suitable position, and the picture would be complete. Gulls could be added ' to taste ' by two little wet dabs with the brush and flicks with his handkerchief. When an evening light was wanted, by way of variety, the picture was submitted to a wash of pink-lake and gamboge in equal proportions. That was how water-colours were managed seventy years ago.

Captain Trecarrel sketched in the harbour, then he sketched in Willapark, and crept on to Welltown, where he found the old house so picturesque that he sketched it also. But the hedge was damp to sit on, so he ventured to the front door to borrow a chair, and having got one from Genefer he seated himself opposite the house, and began his drawing. He was a long time over it, as he was scrupulous about the details, and before it was completed Orange Tramplara came towards him. She was returning from Boscastle, where she had been making a few purchases. It was not possible for her to reach the front poor without passing Trecarrel, and she had no hesitation in doing so, as she had no idea who was there sketching. He had an umbrella open to screen him from the wind; but there was a little hole in the umbrella, and through that he had perceived her. She was abreast of the Captain before she recognised him. He uttered an exclamation of surprise, started, and upset his sketchbook, box of colours, and glass of water into the road.

'I am very sorry, Captain Trecarrel,' said Orange, much agitated. 'I fear I knocked your things over with my cloak.'

'Not at all, Orange. Bless my soul! Who would have expected to see you here? In the name of all the seven wonders, what has brought you to this place, which I supposed was inhabited by wreckers only?'

Orange had recovered herself, and made as though she would pass on with a bow.

'No, Orange, I will not permit you to slip away thus. I want you to be in the foreground of my picture, as you have ever been in my thoughts. A marvellous piece of good fortune has brought us face to face. On a desert island those who have been cast up by the sea forget old grudges and shake hands. I will not be thrust aside in this wild and lonely spot because once upon a time we had a lovers' quarrel.'

'I am surprised to see you here, Captain.'

'The surprise is mutual. I heard that you and Mrs. Tramplara had retired to Falmouth. Are you lodging at this old farmhouse for your mother's health?'

'This is Welltown, the house of Mr. Herring.'

'This! bless my soul! I thought he lived in a stately mansion in a deer park, not in an old ramshackle box like this. The world is smaller than I imagined. I have been making a sketching tour of the North Coast from Hartland to Boscastle, and I intend continuing it to the Land's End. I have some thought of publishing my sketches in mezzotint, coloured by hand. You know my impecuniosity. I thought to turn an honest penny this way without degradation.'

'Have you been long here?'

'Only a few days.'

'Where are you staying?'

'At the Ship.'

'What sort of entertainment do you meet with there?'

'Ham and eggs to-day; to-morrow, by way of variety, eggs and ham. Those are the changes. Nothing else is procurable all down the coast from Hartland to the Land's End. I am told, wherever I go, that next week a sheep or a cow will be killed, and then mutton-chop or beef-steak will be had. But the cow or sheep moves before me as I proceed on my journey, and I never overtake it.'

'We dine early. Will you join us?'

So peace was concluded. The difficulty in concluding it was not great, as Orange was as inclined to meet the Captain as he had been to meet her. Indeed, her readiness to strike hands and forget the past alarmed him. He was of a suspicious character, and her manifest desire to renew the old acquaintanceship made him dread a trap.

He did not know that Orange was getting deadly tired of Boscastle. Of society in the neighbourhood there was little. The only gentlefolks of county position were the Phyllacks of the manor. Old Sir Jonathan was a stately gentleman of the past generation, somewhat pompous, who moved surrounded by his seven daughters, as the judge encircled by the javelin men. The daughters were extraordinarily alike, and though the utmost effort had been made to distinguish them at the first by giving each two or three names, nevertheless Orange felt she might spend a lifetime in their company without being able to know Miss Grace Pomeroy from Miss Anna Maria Amy, or Miss Elizabeth Gilbert from either or from Miss Catherine Penhelligan. They never called separately, but called, all seven together, with Sir Jonathan in the midst. They never walked in batches, but walked in a system rotating round Sir Jonathan like the planets round the sun. When Mirelle and Orange returned their call, they found Sir Jonathan sitting at the fire in a hollow square composed by his daughters, and when one rose to shake hands, her place was occupied by another, whilst Sir Jonathan remained, bowing but inaccessible, behind their petticoats. The extraordinary thing about the Misses Phyllack was that they all seemed of the same age; their manners were alike, the expression of their faces equally sweet, the tones of their voices equally soft, like the cooing of wood-pigeons. They were all equally resolute never to admit a stepmother.

Even if Orange had contemplated it seriously, it was hopeless to break through this bodyguard of daughters, capture and carry off Sir Jonathan. After the call the old gentleman ventured to remark, 'A fine girl that!' whereupon Miss Grace Pomeroy objected that she was coarse, and Miss Anna Maria Amy that she had bad feet, and Miss Elizabeth Gilbert that she had a temper, and Miss Catherine Penhelligan that she was inelegant in her postures, and so on to the seventh, when Miss Grace Pomeroy took up the subject again, and poor Orange would have been picked to the bone, had not Sir Jonathan withdrawn his provocative remark with, 'Very true, my dears, very true; my eyes deceived me.'

Orange would have been glad enough to become Lady Phyllack, but to become Lady Phyllack the knight must be got at, and to get at him the circle must be broken. There was no Arnold of Winkelried at Boscastle to open a road through which Orange might dash in. Not a single Miss Phyllack had been lured from her post, all still were Misses Phyllack and coheiresses. It cannot be said that the ladies looked upon marriage as an evil to be avoided in their own persons, but, unfortunately for them, there were no marriageable young gentlemen in the neighbourhood. To find them they must go afield to Exeter or Bath, but to go there was to expose Sir Jonathan to fascinating widows and designing old maids; and though the knight occasionally suggested a migration to some fashionable resort, the daughters unanimously refused their consent, in their dread of it leading to a stepmother.

The seven young ladies received Mirelle readily into their society, but were cool towards Orange. The seven bosoms instinctively and together felt suspicious of Orange, and, after the remark their father had made, hostile towards her, as a dangerous person who must be kept out of Sir Jonathan's sight.

Orange had found that storm-beaten coast a very dull world. When Captain Trecarrel appeared in it, she felt relief and saw a chance of escape from it. Poor Mirelle was not prepared to receive the Captain with composure. The remembrance of what had passed between them on Christmas morning was too fresh, and she felt too keenly that it was her confession of love for him that had separated her from her husband, and would remain as a barrier keeping him away. She had been living a peaceful and lonely life at Welltown, and from seeing no more of Trecarrel her feelings towards him had become less intense. In time she hoped that this acuteness would be sufficiently blunted to enable her to think more of John Herring. She knew that it was her duty to love him, and she would try to do so, but to do so she must first forget Trecarrel. She was struggling with her heart, to hold it down, and bend it towards her husband. She allowed no thought to recur to Trecarrel. She shut her eyes against every flash of recollection that illumined him, as if to remember him were a sin. None suspected what was passing within, under that frozen exterior. She seemed wholly emotionless, and yet

Orange knew that she was unhappy, was suffering, though she neither knew the extent nor the occasion of her suffering. Orange, who had never striven against any inclination or current of thought, had no suspicion of the systematic, deliberate and obstinate battle Mirelle was fighting with her own heart.

And now, when the first resistance was broken, when she had gained some little successes, preludes of a complete victory, the Captain reappeared, introduced into the house by Orange to turn the scale of battle against her conscience. Mirelle received him with courtesy, but with coldness. She listened to his conversation without seeming to take interest in it, but out of civility she ventured to say a few words and ask a question, and directly dinner was over she withdrew to her boudoir with an apology, and without a request that he would renew his visit. Captain Trecarrel was a little disappointed at his reception. He had been profuse in his expressions of delight at accidentally renewing acquaintanceship, and had been pathetic on his distaste for ham and eggs alternating with eggs and ham.

When Mirelle left the hall, she hastened to her own room, and threw herself on her knees. The trial was more than she could bear. The sight of Trecarrel had undone in one moment the work of months.

Orange made amends for Mirelle's neglect. She begged the Captain to come there again for early dinner, whenever he was sketching in that direction; and as Captain Trecarrel found that the beauties of the portion of the coast south-west of Boscastle were superior to those on the north-east, he was there a good deal. He was surprised to find that neither Mirelle nor Orange knew anything of the sights of the neighbourhood. He volunteered to escort them. He insisted on taking them to S. Kneighton's Kieve, on driving them to Tintagel, and on their exploring the ruins of King Arthur's Castle together. They must visit Blackapit in a boat. There was a seal-cave that ought to be seen—it was a long way off and must be visited by boat—but the weather was splendid, and the sea was as calm as the Atlantic can be on this coast. The weather was indeed delightful, and the saddest heart could not resist the spring influence which swelled the buds and inspired the birds with song.

Mirelle allowed herself to be drawn on these excursions only with extreme reluctance. Orange was bent on going, and it was not proper to allow Orange to go alone with the Captain.

A third person must accompany them, and Mrs. Trampleasure could not be induced to leave the house, her Blair's Sermons, and Rollin's 'Ancient History.' Mirelle felt that the place was dull for Orange, who, with her fulness of life and spirits, needed amusement. She was unable herself to provide her with distractions, and she therefore yielded to Orange's solicitations that they should accept the Captain's offers, and make these expeditions with him. But Mirelle hoped that each would be the last. The Captain was always on the eve of leaving to prosecute his tour, nevertheless there he remained. This was becoming unendurable to Mirelle; the strain on her was too great. Captain Trecarrel was very civil to Orange, but in her presence never more than very civil. Orange gave him every possible encouragement, but he still hesitated. He would not speak till he had sounded Mirelle as to the source and extent of Orange's property and expectations, and Mirelle never gave him the opportunity of speaking with her alone. Till he knew for certain what Orange was worth, and whether the five thousand pounds were really hers, or merely fluttered in his face to lure him on, he would not commit himself. Nor was this the only cause of his hesitation. Since he had come to Boscastle he had heard of the Misses Phyllack, seven coheiresses, and he had done himself the honour of calling on Sir Jonathan. There was some remote connection between the families which justified him in paying a visit now that he was in the neighbourhood. He was graciously received by the young ladies, whose hearts were set in a flutter by his languishing blue eyes, and cordially by Sir Jonathan, who was delighted to have some one to talk to. So he dropped into the manor-house of an evening to take a hand at whist, and to talk about remote cousins, and to be an apple of discord among the seven sisters. If the seven Misses Phyllack had but one hand between them on which he could put the ring, Captain Trecarrel would not have hesitated to marry them all; but one out of seven coheiresses meant one seventh of Sir Jonathan's property when Sir Jonathan was dead, and the old knight looked remarkably robust; it meant also very little indeed, should the old gentleman marry again, and beget a son. Now, over the walnuts and wine one evening, when the daughters were out of hearing, Sir Jonathan had ventured on a remark about Orange: 'Fine woman that—deuced good-looking; my daughters won't let me look at a handsome face, but I may give them the slip some day.' This made Trecarrel uneasy, and next day he redoubled his attentions to Orange, and made no call at the manor.

Orange watched Mirelle, and saw that she loved Captain Trecarrel. She saw it in the struggle made by Mirelle to escape his society, by her reluctance to join in the excursions he proposed. Orange was suspicious of the Captain. Was he there for her sake, or because he was still attracted by Mirelle? She watched him closely. He was attentive to Mirelle, and his eye rested on her inquiringly now and then, when he thought he was unobserved.

Why, unless he still loved Mirelle, did he not ask Orange to be to him what she had been before? What stood in his way? That he was waiting till he knew all the particulars about her five thousand pounds, and till he had made up his mind about the Misses Phyllack, never occurred to her.

CHAPTER LIII.

A PRIVATE INTERVIEW.

For some time the stress of work at Upaver, and anxiety about both the success of the mine and the decline of Mr. Battishill's health, had kept under the yearning of John Herring's heart to see Mirelle again. Love was ever paramount, pain ever present, but he resolutely suppressed his desire to be with her. Duty kept him at West Wyke, and away from Welltown.

When, however, Mr. Battishill's life had ebbed away, and the first grief of Cicely was overpassed, and when Upaver mine was in full working order, when the spring was well on, and earth and sky were full of love, and joy, and hope, then the hunger of his heart became exacting. He must return to Welltown, see Mirelle, and may-be renew his pain.

The spring flowers were very lovely, and he brought bunches of them to Cicely; but that was not the same as offering them to Mirelle. It was pleasant to hear Cicely's gentle voice, with the faintest touch of Devonshire brogue in it; but that was nothing to the delight of listening to the tones of Mirelle's English tinged with French. He must see and hear her again. He could endure his banishment no longer.

The lodestone mountain drew ships to it, and when they came near extracted from them their bolts and nails, and the vessels went to pieces at its feet. Mirelle was his lodestone, and, even at the risk of a final and fatal wreck to his happiness, he must see her.

He still entertained the hope that in time Mirelle might learn to desire his presence, might come to think that life at Welltown would be pleasanter were he there to enliven it, might cease to shrink from him in that vague terror she had shown when he had told her his love, and when he had married her. She regarded him. Might not this regard deepen into a warmer sentiment?

Herring had told Cicely nothing. She had not made a second attempt to force her way into his confidence. It is difficult to say to what extent she suspected the state of his heart. She certainly had no knowledge of his marriage. Mirelle was never mentioned by either of them. He knew that Cicely instinctively disliked her, and she knew that he admired her, though she hardly suspected that he did more than greatly admire her.

Herring's position at West Wyke was anomalous. The people—that is, the workmen at the mine, and the farmers and cotters on the estate—called him the young Squire, and supposed that he was a near relative, and the heir to the property. They sometimes spoke of him as young Squire Battishill. There were few neighbours of the class of the Battishills, and those that were had long ceased to call on the old gentleman and his daughter. They themselves were mounting in the world, and the Battishills were falling. He gave no entertainments, and kept no carriage, not even a gig. This class therefore did not concern itself with the affairs at West Wyke, after it had done the civil thing of attending his funeral. Nevertheless John Herring felt that the situation was unsatisfactory. He would have liked to take Cicely to Welltown to stay with Mirelle, for change of air and scene, and to have persuaded Mirelle to return with them to West Wyke, when he was recalled by the concerns of the mine. But, as matters stood between him and his wife, this was not possible.

At times he fell into a daydream, which brightened his spirits for a few hours. He thought that perhaps now Mirelle might bid him stay by her. Then his future would be changed, the spring would burst forth in his heart, as in surrounding nature. Till then the frost must lie within. He must go home and learn his fate. He could stay away no longer. No—no! West Wyke was not home. He must see if the ice were thawing at Welltown.

So he bade farewell to Cicely and Joyce, set the men at Upaver their tasks, and departed.

There was another motive in his heart drawing him back to Welltown—another beside his desire of again seeing Mirelle. In the locked drawer of his office desk he had left his confession to Mirelle—his confession of the fact that all the money that had been spent to buy up the West Wyke mortgages, that had been sunk in Upaver, and that which had been given to Orange, and that also which Mirelle was now enjoying, was her own, the proceeds of the sale of the uncut diamonds her father had brought to England from Brazil—the diamonds in which he had invested his fortune as a convenient and portable form in which to transfer it from one country to another. He did not wish Mirelle to see this. He did not wish it, for his own sake and for hers. For good or for ill—it seemed wholly for ill—the thing had been done, and could not be recalled. By no means could the effects of the mistake be avoided. If she knew the circumstances, nothing she could do would alter them, and the knowledge would only give her additional and renewed pain, for she might well suppose that had it come to her earlier she would have been saved from taking the fatal step that could not now be retraced. Putting his own wishes aside entirely, Herring could see that the only chance of happiness open to Mirelle was for her to accept the situation, draw towards him, and learn to love him. Were the truth now to break on her, the breach would become irreparable. He knew that he had acted towards her unselfishly and conscientiously, and the error into which he had fallen had been an error of judgment. But would she believe this? Was it not far more probable that she would suppose he had acted with selfish premeditation from the first, and thus become for ever embittered against him?

His anxiety about the confession grew as he thought this over and fevered him as he walked. He resolved directly on his arrival to destroy the document. Why had he not done so before instead of leaving it? Because he had been flurried at leaving, and had thought that it might be useful on some future occasion. The drawer was locked, and therefore he had no cause for fear, but nevertheless he was uneasy. Other keys besides his own might unlock it, and though he did not believe that Mirelle would wilfully and knowingly pry into what he wished to keep concealed, yet it was possible that his words relative to the locked drawer when he left her had been unheeded, and that, finding a key wherewith to open it, she might look in for some mislaid paper or account needed by the foreman of the slate-quarry, and when the drawer was opened she would see the packet lying in it addressed to herself. Herring went accordingly to Willapark first, and with his private key unlocked the office, and then locked himself in. The office was much as he had left it, and yet not entirely. Some one had been there. The chairs were in unusual places. The position of the desk was changed. Probably Genefer had done this in dusting or cleaning. He opened the drawer immediately, and saw that the packet was gone.

Herring sat down on his bed to think. He was almost certain that the letter had been put in the locked drawer, and yet, when he came to revolve in his mind the events of the night and morning when the letter had been written and put away, he found that he could be certain of nothing about it save that he had written, made up, and addressed the packet. He had purposed putting it in the drawer and locking it up. He believed he had done as he purposed, but it was possible that, in the confusion and distress in which he then was, he might have omitted to do so. If the letter had been put elsewhere, it must have been put in his cupboard. This cupboard consisted of a set of shelves that had been run up in a recess, combined with an extemporised wardrobe, where he kept his suit in which he went out boating and shooting.

The cupboard was not closed with a door, but had a curtain on an iron bar in front of it, which latter turned on a crook. He went at once to this closet and thrust the bar and curtain aside so as to get into the recess and examine the shelves. To this place he had gone for the bullets on that turning night in his life. He mounted a stool to explore the upper shelves. He would not leave one unsearched till he had found the missing packet. Whilst thus engaged he heard a key put into the lock, and the door opened. He was surprised, and remained where he was, screened from view.

Then he heard Mirelle say: 'Captain Trecarrel, I sent for you to meet me here in private, as I have something to say to you which I do not wish Orange to hear, because it concerns Orange.'

'Mirelle,' replied the Captain, 'I also have been desirous of seeing you in private, as I also have something to say to you which is not for Orange's ears.'

The first impression on Herring's mind on hearing these words was surprise at Mirelle's indiscretion in arranging a private interview with the Captain. Not a shadow of suspicion of other motives than what were honourable crossed him. It had never occurred to him that Trecarrel was the man Mirelle loved. Had he known this, nevertheless not a thought of anything unworthy of her would have entered his mind. He saw that she had acted in ignorance of conventional proprieties. His first impulse was to step forward and show himself. On second thoughts he refrained from doing so. He refrained for Mirelle's own sake. If he were suddenly to emerge from behind the curtain it would bring home to her at once the impropriety of her conduct, embarrass and distress her, and place both her and the Captain in a very awkward position. The interview was about Orange, and there could be no reason why he should not overhear it, and indeed take a part in it, unless it were, as he supposed, concerning the Captain's engagement to Orange. If that were so it would be kindest to allow Mirelle to have her few words about it with Trecarrel, and he—John Herring—would tell her immediately after that he had overheard the conversation.'

'Je vous donne le pas, Monsieur le Capitaine.'

'Je le prends de bon gré, madame,' replied Trecarrel. 'But as I think in English and not in French, perhaps you will allow me to say what I want in my native tongue.'

'Certainly.'

'In the first place, then, let me speak about my book on the Cornish Coast scenery. I think it advisable that you should possess early copies—proofs before the plates are worn. I think you offered to take three copies at five guineas.'

'I believe I did. Have you secured a publisher?'

'No, not yet, but that is a matter of secondary importance. A publisher can always be secured for drawings such as mine, of scenery that has such historic interest—King Arthur, Uther Pendragon, Gwenever, and so on.'

'No doubt.'

'If not inconvenient to you, would you mind letting me have your subscription at once? I want, you understand, to secure you unrubbed copies.'

'You shall have the money to-morrow.'

'You quite see that I am pressing this entirely in your own interest. There is a material difference between early copies and late impressions, and first subscribers who have paid up will, as a matter of strict justice, be given the best and sharpest copies.'

'Quite so.'

'There was another matter on which I wished to speak to you. A man was saved from the wreck of the "Susanna" in the winter. That man gave out his name as George Bidgood. You, I understand, gave him shelter. You are aware who he is?'

'I saw him brought ashore.'

'You know then that he is no more George Bidgood than I am. George Bidgood was the seaman on board the "Susanna," and was lost in it. The man who was rescued from the waves was Sampson Tramplara, but, as he desired to disguise the fact that he had been saved and was alive, he took for the occasion the name of the drowned man, and there was no one in Boscastle who knew otherwise except yourself. Sampson disappeared after that, but he has just turned up again, as it happens, at an awkward moment for himself, for the "Chough" has come into harbour, and the mate of the "Chough"—a little smack that trades between this place and Bristol—knew Bidgood intimately, and the same man had learned in Bristol that a swindler had made off in the "Susanna," and was supposed to have been lost in her. Last night Sampson was at the Ship Inn drinking, when the mate of the "Chough" came in and joined the party. In the course of conversation Sampson was spoken of as Bidgood; this led to an explanation, and then the mate charged him with being the man whom justice was pursuing, disguising himself under Bidgood's name. There was a disturbance, Sampson was drunk, and in the scuffle he stabbed the mate, and made his escape.'

'Mon Dieu! le pauvre homme! est-il mort?'

'No. The man is not dead, but he has been mortally wounded. However, the condition of the mate concerns us only in a secondary manner—the fate of Sampson is that with which we have to do.'

'He must suffer for what he has done.'

'Will you speak to Orange, and tell her what has taken place?'

Mirelle hesitated a moment, and then said, 'If necessary I will do so.'

'It is necessary. Sampson must not be taken here. The mate is mortally wounded; Sampson must be helped to escape. If he wants money and means of escape he must be provided with them.'

'I will not assist him with money or means of escape. He has done wrong, and must take the consequences.'

'You are right, no doubt, in principle, but the world cannot go on upon principle; it must have its workings eased to suit convenience. It will never do that he should be taken here, and your relationship to the scoundrel come out.'

'It cannot be helped.'

'But you must consider Orange and her mother. By the way, there is another matter I must mention. I have had a talk with Sampson—of course, before this last unpleasant affair with the mate of the "Chough." He was not shy of me, for he knew I would not betray him. During our conversation he let drop some insinuations against your—against Mr. Herring. He says that Mr. Herring robbed you of the greater portion of your fortune, without either you or Mr. Tramplara, your guardian, knowing or suspecting it.'

'Stop,' said Mirelle haughtily; 'not another word, Captain Trecarrel. Mr. John Herring is incapable of acting otherwise than honourably, and I refuse absolutely to listen to slanders that issue from the mouth of Sampson Trampleasure.'

'You are right, Countess, quite right. I was as indignant as you are now. I positively refused to believe it. But he proceeded to enforce his hints with circumstances.'

'Captain Trecarrel, you must have understood me very imperfectly. I refuse to hear another word on this offensive and insulting topic. If you have done speaking about the escape of Mr. Sampson Trampleasure, let me say what I desire to say. Mr. John Herring is an honourable man, and in his absence I am the guardian of his honour.'

'I also shut my ears when Sampson said what he did,' continued Captain Trecarrel; 'I had no intention of saying anything to you about the reflections he cast on the character of your husband, which might be disagreeable for you to hear. I mention this only as supplying an additional reason for getting Sampson Tramplara out of the way, even by helping him with money. It would be most unpleasant for you were he to make disclosures affecting John Herring's character——'

'He can make no such disclosures. John Herring's character cannot be impeached.'

'Certainly—I used the wrong term; were he to hint——'

'The hints of such as he can do no harm.'

'There you are wrong; they would be eagerly listened to, and believed. John Herring is not here to defend himself, and as you say you are the guardian of his honour, I think it is your duty to save him this annoyance.'

'If that be so, let him escape. It goes against my conscience, but, to save my husband unpleasantness, I will do what you ask. I will give him money. You may take my purse.'

'Excuse me. I shall not see the fellow. He is not likely to show again at the Ship, nor am I likely to come across him anywhere in my walks. But he will not leave without having seen Orange. She must have provided him with money before, and his return to Boscastle now means that he has spent all she let him have, and wants more.'

'I will speak to Orange, and give her money. But now that this hateful subject is settled, you will allow me to speak to you about Orange.'

'I am ready to hear anything you may say.'

Mirelle hesitated. She began to tremble, and cast her eyes on the ground. 'Orange,' she began—'that is to say, I mean—but, Captain Trecarrel, it is hard for me to say what I want, and you ought not to have put the necessity on me of saying it. You are not acting fairly by Orange, or—by me. I am sure that—that Orange regards you very, very much; you were engaged to marry her, and I think—I do think you are bound in honour to do so. She is not happy; I can see that she frets. You are trifling with her heart. Why are you here? Why do you not prosecute your journey? Time presses; you must finish your series of sketches whilst the fine weather lasts. Why, then, do you remain here, and come up to Welltown every day, and make excursions with us, and—why do you not leave us in peace?'

'You, you, Mirelle, urge me to make Orange Trampleasure my wife after——'

She cut him short. 'You are bound to marry her. Do you not see that yourself? You were engaged to her before that miserable affair of Ophir intervened to destroy her happiness.'

'After what I told you, Mirelle, that Christmas Day?'

'Forbear!' said Mirelle; 'never recur to, nor allude to that again. I have forgotten it—that is, I try, I pray to forget it. Yes, I entreat you to take Orange.'

'There are several objections,' said Trecarrel. 'In the first place, I cannot afford it.'

'Orange has five thousand pounds,

'Has she no more?'

'Not that I am aware of.'

'What puzzles me is, how did she come by the money? I thought everything had gone when that scamp Sampson bolted.'

'That is easily explained. John Herring gave her the money.'

'He gave Orange five thousand pounds! This is incredible. What claim had she on him?'

'She had been kind to me. I asked him to do it.'

'An exemplary husband! But how the deuce did he come by so much money? I know what Welltown is worth. He cannot have saved it—men in the army spend, they do not save; he cannot have made it. He did not inherit it. Whence did it come?'

'That concerns neither you nor me to know.'

'Orange then really has, of her own, five thousand pounds.'

'Yes.'

'Has she prospects of more?'

'I believe not.'

'Five thousand pounds! By the way, would it be possible to organise a picnic conjointly with the Misses Phyllack to Crackington Cove? The old knight to stay at home.'

'Captain Trecarrel, you are evading the point. You are trying to turn the subject. I am anxious; I am troubled. Do not play with me. It cost me a severe struggle to make up my mind to speak to you alone, and on this subject.'

'Why should it cost you a struggle?'

'It has—that is enough. Do you not see? I am pleading for a—a sister; for her happiness. Can you not understand that I am shy of doing this, and that I only do it as a duty, and for the sake of a sister?'

'Mirelle!' said the Captain, slowly. He looked hard at her. 'That is not it. I can read your heart more clearly than you think. You are desirous of getting me to marry Orange so as to erect a double wall of duty between yourself and me—it is because you doubt your own fortitude unless double-steeled with a sense of twofold duty——'

'Captain Trecarrel!' exclaimed Mirelle, in deadly terror—for he had divined and given expression to her real motive. 'I pray you, say nothing about me. Put me altogether out of your thoughts. Speak only of Orange.'

'You see there is this confounded business about Sampson in the way. Suppose the fellow be apprehended—and the whole of Boscastle is alive and out after him—and suppose the mate dies, as is most probable, Sampson will swing. Do you not see that I cannot well quarter the chevronels with a gallows?'

'He shall escape—he must escape. Orange shall have the money! Captain Trecarrel, either take Orange or go your way to the Land's End.'

'I want time to consider.'

'Take time, but not too much. Now leave me.'

'Oh, Mirelle, is not this cruel of you—of you who knew the state of my heart, what I have suffered, and am suffering still——'

'Leave me!' said Mirelle. She trembled in every limb. 'Leave me!—leave me!'

He hesitated a moment, and then went out.

She stood looking at the door. Then her pent-up feelings burst forth. She cast herself on her knees, and sobbed and cried, 'My God! my God! forgive me! I love him still! I have striven against it! Thou knowest the secrets of the heart. I love him still!' Then the door burst open, and Orange came in, her face livid with rage, and her large eyes flashing hate.

'What is this?—is this?—you meet Captain Trecarrel in secret and alone here?'

'I beg your pardon, Miss Trampleasure,' said Herring, stepping forward; 'not in secret nor alone. I have a right, I presume, to see any one or two in my own room that I choose.'

Mirelle looked up dazed. Her eyes were blind with tears. She understood nothing of what was going on, neither how Orange had come in, nor whence Herring had risen.

Orange looked first at Herring, then at Mirelle, still kneeling and with tears in her eyes and on her cheeks, and laughed scornfully.

'I apologise, Mr. Herring. I have intruded on the confession of a penitent.'

CHAPTER LIV.

THE PORCH ROOM.

HERRING gave his arm to Mirelle to conduct her back to Welltown. He did not say much to her, as his own heart was full, and she, he knew, needed time to recover herself.

Now he knew all. He had never suspected an attachment for the Captain, but had supposed that she had lost her heart to some one in France. What he now learned increased his trouble. Separation from a lover on the other side of the Channel might, in time, have effaced or obscured his image, but Trecarrel was too near to be forgotten. Herring saw that Trecarrel had perceived that Mirelle's efforts to bring about a reconciliation and re-engagement with Orange were dictated by alarm for herself, by her desire to erect a double barrier between herself and the man she loved, so as to afford her conscience a double reason for mastering her affection for him.

Herring did not wish to speak with Mirelle on this subject till later—till he had had time to think over the situation in which he and she were now placed. He therefore said a few words on ordinary topics during the walk to Welltown. He observed that she seemed even frailer and more bloodless than before. The strong air of the coast had not braced her into vigorous life, but seemed to overpower the feeble life that pulsated in her veins.

'You do not grow stronger, Mirelle?'

'I am well in body,' she said.

'I do not think so. You ought to see a doctor—you look so thin and white.'

'The only doctor I need is the sun,' she answered, 'and his visits are so few that they must be costly.'

'But this wonderful stimulating air——'

'There is too much air. It is never at rest—always blowing. I dislike the wind. And the sea is always tossing and thundering. The leaves on the plants, the blades of grass, are never still, but always fluttering and swaying. The waves are ever battering and gnawing at the rocks. Oh for a Mediterranean—a tideless sea! I want peace, stillness, a calm; with the sun shining, and no sea near, and no noise save the hum of bees. Here there are no bees; the wind carries them out to sea, and they drown in the brine. You do not understand me. Here there are no butterflies; the wind breaks their wings. You do not comprehend my state of mind.'

'Yes, I think so. You like a hot climate.'

'I love warmth, but I love stillness better. That is what my soul craves for and cannot obtain. Here the flowers do not bloom—they blow away. Here the birds do not sing—they scream. Here we have weeks of gloomy skies. I want no shadow at all, save that of a cross flung over a hot, white road.

But one sees no crosses here, only signposts. We bear our own crosses hammered red-hot into our lives.'

The evening was beautiful. The sun was setting over the sea, making a road of quivering gold upon the waves. The air was warm. Herring looked round. The scene was grandly beautiful. He wondered that Mirelle could not love it.

He went into the house, and had tea in the hall with her and Mrs. Trampleasure. Orange feigned a headache and did not appear.

Then he ascended the stairs with Mirelle to the little boudoir or porch room; he must have a conversation with her in private before again leaving.

The room was small; it was pleasant, prettily furnished with rose-coloured satin curtains, the walls white and gold. But the damp had come through the paper and formed black fungoid stains, disfiguring all one side. There was no fireplace in the room, so that it could only be used in summer. In the corner stood the bureau in which Mirelle kept the jewels, a bureau of inlaid wood, with ornamental brasswork about the locks and handles. The chairs were white and gold. Herring had spent a good deal of money on this room, hoping that it would please Mirelle, and that she would be happy in it.

He took a chair. She seated herself in the window on the low seat. She opened the casement, and the summer air was wafted in, bearing on its wings the murmur of the sea.

'Mirelle,' he said, 'I overheard all that passed in the office on Willapark. I was there when you came in, but I did not show myself, lest by so doing I should cause you embarrassment. Excuse my saying it, but I do not think you acted wisely in inviting Captain Trecarrel to meet you there.'

'No, I do not think I did, but I could not in any other way get a word in private with him.'

'And you wished to urge him to marry Orange. I think with you that in honour he is bound to take her.'

'Yes, I wish that very much.'

'At the same time I think your interference ill-calculated to advance the cause you have at heart. It was indiscreet of you, Mirelle.'

'Perhaps so. You are always right, and know what ought to be done, and do it.' After a pause, she said: 'Yes, it was not wise of me. I will never do it again. But then, consider, I was alone, and had no one to advise me, for in this matter I could not consult Orange. When I was at the Sacré Cœur, I knew my way about the dear home in the dark, but here I am in a world without orientation. All the familiar landmarks fail me, all the ways lead in unknown directions. I am translated, morally, into a country that I am expected to travel through without a map or a guide.'

'Mirelle, if you like, you have only to say the word, and I will stay here as your adviser. You are too weak.'

'No, my good friend, I am not weak.'

'Weak in body, Mirelle—not weak in character.'

'No; I will always do my duty, as I see it.'

'You are too inexperienced to be left alone.'

'I have Orange with me.'

'But what is Orange as an adviser? You confessed as much just now when you admitted you were without a guide. Mirelle! I am sure Orange does not like you. She is'—he was about to add 'jealous,' but he checked himself—'she is not a desirable person to have about you perpetually. I do not trust her sincerity.'

'I do. I have never done anything to make her dislike me.'

He remained silent. It was difficult for him to speak the truth, and yet it must be spoken for her sake.

'Orange is strongly attached to Captain Trecarrel; that you know,' said Herring. 'Now a loving woman is a suspicious woman. He will not renew his engagement with her, he shirks doing so; and she seeks an explanation of his conduct, and finds it where she has no right to look for it.'

Mirelle turned her face to Herring.

'I told you all, that evening after we had been married. You know that something passed between him and me, not much, just enough to——'

'Yes, Mirelle, you told me that your heart was a treasure I might not possess, but you did not inform me to whom you had surrendered it.'

'I did not! I failed in my duty. I intended to do so, my friend.'

'You did not, but now I have found it out.'

'Oh, John Herring, do not say that I surrendered my heart. That I never did. It was drawn from me, and I fought against it, I prayed against it. God help me! I have been very miserable: I am miserable still. You are not angry with me? I could not help myself.'

'I—I angry with you? No, Mirelle, never; you have

done me no wrong. If wrong has been done, it has been done by me to you.'

'I have suffered, because since I married you I knew it was wrong to think of another man, and I do believe I should have conquered in the end had not Captain Trecarrel come here. I thought he came after Orange, and I have done my best to promote her interests. I want him to go away, and then I will begin my battle over again. He will leave now, and in time I shall have conquered the thoughts I ought not to harbour.'

'Mirelle—one word. Shall I stay here? I shall not trouble you with my presence more than is absolutely necessary. My old office shall be my home, but I shall be at hand to advise and to help you.'

She shook her head.

'I have no right to say Go, or Stay. You must act as you see fit. You are master here; you are my husband; this is your house. But if you will listen to my prayer, I will ask you to go away again—not for long, for a little while. I want rest; I want to be quite alone with God and my own heart. I have got a wrestle to go through, and I had rather undertake it without a spectator. Do not be afraid for me. I shall come out victorious in the end, I do not doubt that. Only, these wrestles take a great deal of strength out of me. When I feel better, and know that the worst is over, I will write to you, and then come, and I shall be able to see you. You are still my friend—nothing I have said or done has altered that?'

'No, no—Mirelle.'

'I always respect and honour you. I know that you are upright and good, and I would love you if I could. I may do so some day, but the weed must be rooted out before the grain is sown.'

'Very well, Mirelle. You said as we walked back from Willapark that here we have the cross hammered into our lives. You have yours, I have mine. It must be so. Perhaps a better time may be in store for both of us.'

'Perhaps.' She looked sadly out of the window. The sun had set, and the golden path on the sea was turned to quicksilver. She rose and moved towards the door into her own room.

'I am very tired. Shall we say Good night?'

'And good-bye. I leave before morning.'

'It is best so.'

She hung about the door, looking timidly at him. Her

hand was on the latch, and it shook; she removed it, but presently put it on again.

'When am I to return? In a month, or two months?' he asked.

She shook her head. 'I cannot say; I will write to you. Give me your address before you leave.'

'There are one or two little matters connected with our affairs here that ought to be discussed.'

'Here is the key of my bureau. Will you write your instructions? They shall be carried out faithfully. I am very tired. You said I was weak; I am weak in body. Write at my desk, and leave the note in it, and the key in the lock.'

'Very well, Mirelle; good-bye!'

'Then she raised her great dark eyes to him, and came tremblingly towards him.

'Kiss me,' she said; 'you have a right to that.'

He took her pale face between his hands, and reverently kissed her cheek, and a salt tear off it was received by his lips. He knew that she did not love him, he knew that her cheek was offered him only because of the strong sense of duty at her heart, and because she felt that some reparation was due for the bitter pain she had caused him.

When he had let her go she bowed her head, and with lowered eyes and a hectic spot of colour on the cheek that he had touched, without another word or look, she disappeared through the door.

Herring sat for a few moments with his hands over his face, and then went to the bureau, opened it, and, taking some paper, wrote on it his address, and various memoranda relative to the house and quarry. When he had done he closed the desk, turned the key, descended the stairs, and left the house. As he went through the gate he thought he saw a man behind the wall near the entrance to the yard, and, supposing this was Hender, Herring cast him a good night. There was no reply, but this caused him no surprise; Hender was a surly man, not addicted to the courtesies of life. Herring did not give him another thought; he had enough to trouble his mind without care for Hender's manners.

His conversation with Mirelle had been, in a measure, satisfactory—as satisfactory as he could expect. There was some faint hope before him; she was doing her best to overcome that unfortunate passion which stood as a dividing wall between them. Time would assist her efforts, which Herring knew were sincere, and then perhaps she might come to care for him. She valued him now; she had not shrunk from him as before, but had freely volunteered a kiss. She had assured him that but a short while would elapse before she would recall him. When the weed was eradicated, then the corn would grow. The hope set before him was not a great one; still it was something to have a hope at all. He went back to Willapark, resolved to examine the quarry accounts, write instructions to the captain, and depart that night on his return to West Wyke. He would walk back, and therefore not go by Launceston, but strike across country into the Holsworthy and Okehampton road.

Not many minutes after Herring had left Welltown, that man whom he had observed behind the yard wall crept forth with a ladder that he had taken from an outhouse. He looked cautiously about him, and then planted the ladder noiselessly against the porch. He threw off his shoes, and swiftly ascended. The window of the boudoir was open, as Mirelle had left it, and the man lifted himself in through it. He stole across the room over the soft carpet to the bureau. The sky was full of twilight, and everything in the room could be distinguished. The window faced north, and the northern sky was illumined with silvery light. A streak of yellow light beneath the door showed that Mirelle's candle was burning in her bedroom. The man listened. He heard steps coming along the passage. Then a door was opened. It was that into the adjoining bedroom, and a voice was heard speaking. The man smiled; he knew the voice well—it was that of Orange Trampleasure, and she was speaking to Mirelle.

Then he turned the key in the bureau, opened it, and searched the well. He soon found the secret drawer, and removed from it the diamonds. He was about to close the desk, when he noticed the papers Herring had written, his address, and memoranda. The man caught these up hastily, and then with a low, bitter laugh, and a look full of malignity in the direction of Mirelle's door, he put in their place the packet containing Herring's confession to his wife, written the night of his marriage, and stolen from his drawer by Sampson Tramplara. That man who now placed the letter where Mirelle must find it was the same who had stolen it—Sampson Tramplara.

All this was the work of a few minutes. As rapidly as he had ascended the ladder and entered the room, so did he descend, replace the ladder where he had found it, and disappear.

CHAPTER LV.

NEMESIS.

John Herring was engaged on the accounts in the office for some hours. Whilst thus engaged he heard the door open behind him, and, when he turned to look who had come in, saw Sampson Tramplara.

'What brings you hither?' he asked, springing to his feet, and flushing with anger.

'What brings me hither?' repeated Sampson, and laughed. 'You, Mr. John Herring. I want a quiet talk with you.'

'Go away at once; I have nothing to say to you.'

'But I have something to say to you, Mister John. In the first place, I want a change of clothes.'

'You must go elsewhere for them.'

'No, I am going nowhere else. I have set my heart on a boating suit hanging in yonder cupboard, or wardrobe, or whatever you call it. I have come for that. There are reasons that prevent my appearing in public, and in the costume that I now wear, becoming though you may think it. Those reasons are that, if I am seen, I shall be arrested—first, for that confounded Ophir, and, secondly, because last night I stuck a knife into a man with whom I had a brawl in a tavern. So now I call you to find me the suit of clothes in which I may escape. The reason, because it is not to your advantage that I should be taken here. Remember, I am the cousin of your wife; you have married into my family. Mirelle gave me shelter when shipwrecked, and though she knew who I was, like a sensible girl, she held her tongue. My mother and sister are your guests. If you refuse me clothes, I shall go to your house, and be taken there, in the society, in the presence, of Mrs. John Herring and her cousins. That will be nice and creditable to the family, will it not? That will be highly entertaining to the ladies, will it not? I reckon that fellow whom I stuck will hardly recover, and if he dies I must swing for it. Creditable to the family, to be able to boast of Cousin Sampy who was gallowsed. I suppose I shall be hung in chains here. Pleasant to have a cousin of Mrs. John so exalted within a sniff whenever she walks abroad.'

'Take the clothes you want,' said Herring; 'be quick, and be off.'

Tramplara went to the recess, and took the garments he required, and proceeded to divest himself of his own clothes, and invest himself in Herring's boating and shooting suit.

'They fit me as if made for me,' said Sampson. 'A good substantial suit this. And here is J. H. on the buttons; that is in style. Look at me. We are the same height, and about the same build; we have about the same coloured hair. It is a d—d pity that I have not your luck. I want something more now.'

Sampson proceeded to roll up his old suit.

'It will not do to leave these garments about; they would betray my change of skin. I must throw them over the cliffs. It is a fortunate thing that there are no sands here, on which a bundle confided to the waves can be washed ashore. Here the waves and rocks worry what is given them past all recall, within a surprising short time. Look at me. This suit becomes me. We might be brothers. Now, brother John, I want something wherewith to line the pockets, which I find are empty.'

Whilst talking, Sampson transferred the contents of the pockets of his old coat to the breast pocket of the waistcoat of his new suit—an inner pocket. As he did so he laughed, and looked comtemptuously at Herring, who was not observing him. That which he transferred was the case containing Mirelle's diamonds. He put that in the inner pocket of his waistcoat, which he buttoned tightly over it.

'Look here!' said he; 'this is all the cash I have, a crown and a halfpenny. Is a crown and a halfpenny enough to carry me across Cornwall and out of England? I want some blunt, and I will trouble you to find me some.'

'Go along, you scoundrel! It is enough for me to have allowed you my old clothes—I will give you no further assistance.'

'That is a pretty name to give me—scoundrel! Pray what reason have you for thus entitling me?'

'Every reason. You and yours robbed Mirelle of what her father had left.'

Sampson laughed.

'Oh, this is beautiful! Virtuous innocence condemns impenitent vice. Brother John, we are both in the same box. It don't become you to ride the virtuous horse; it trots beautifully along a smooth road, but I think I can lay something in its way will trip and tumble it over. You have had your pickings, and a d—d richer find yours was than mine.'

Herring looked at him speechless. Was this a random shot, or did he know anything?

'You are a proper person to act the moral character. James Strange left my father sole trustee of everything, did he not? How much of all he left did you allow him to finger, eh? How much did you keep back for yourself?' Sampson paused for a reply. He stood opposite Herring, with his hands on his hips. 'Don't you think it possible that cousin Strange, in leaving Brazil, sent over as much ready money as he thought he might want, and put the bulk of his property into diamonds, which he could dispose of in London at any time? By his will he constituted my father sole trustee of everything—that is, of money and diamonds. My father never caught sight of the diamonds, never laid a finger on one of them, for a very good reason: they were stolen by virtuous John Herring.'

'This is false.'

'No, it is true. You did not rummage the trunk of cousin Strange, or take them out, that I'll allow; but you received the stolen jewels, and the receiver is as bad as the thief, is he not?'

Herring could not speak.

'My father was constituted trustee. If you had been honest, when you received these diamonds you would at once have taken them to him. You were not honest. You kept them.'

'Sampson Trampleasure, I kept them only for Mirelle, in her interest. I knew the character of your father, I knew what he was doing with the rest of the money intrusted to him, and I would not risk the rest of her property.'

'Who authorised you to keep it?'

'I acted as my conscience directed.'

'Conscience!' exclaimed Sampson derisively, 'I like to hear that word pleaded; it always means, when interpreted, self-interest. Some men follow their consciences as a gardener follows a wheelbarrow, by pushing it along before him. Answer me,—would the law have authorised you to keep back the diamonds?'

'No, the law would not.'

'Then who authorised you? Did Mirelle? Did you consult her about them? I am at a loss to know what other authorisation you could find.'

'No, I did not speak of them to her—and that for reasons of my own.'

'No, I know you did not. You acted on what you call conscience, and I, self-interest. I will tell you what you did with Mirelle's money. You were soft and sweet on Cicely Battishill——'

'Hold,' said Herring angrily; 'I dare you——'

'I will not be stayed. You pitied the girl; you were constantly with her; you were tender and foolish. I do not dispute your good taste. White and roses, and auburn hair—a young fellow might do worse than pick up with Cicely. Well, for her sake you sold some of the stones, and bought up the mortgages on West Wyke, held by my father. Was that fair? My father had refused to invest Mirelle's money in that, and you took her money unknown to him and thus employed it—only for the sake of pretty Cicely.'

'I will not suffer such words to be spoken,' said Herring. 'I have never regarded Miss Battishill in any other light than that of a sister.'

'A very affectionate brother you have been! So very fond of this dear pink-and-white sister, that you desert your wife and spend all your time with her. You ran away the day after your marriage, and have not shown your face to your wife since till this day; and now you are off again, allured back to West Wyke by the superior attractions of Cicely Battishill.'

Herring's blood boiled up, and he struck Sampson in the face between the eyes, and sent him staggering back against the wall.

'Dare to say another such word again!'

'I will dare,' answered Sampson, when he had gathered himself together. He quivered with rage. 'I will dare, because it is true. Are you not going back now to Cicely? You know you are.' How did he know this? Herring wondered. He had no idea that Sampson had possessed himself of the address left in the bureau.

'Who bought his wife with her own money, eh?' pursued the enraged Sampson. 'Cobbledick told me once of a man who bought a wife in Okehampton market for a crown. You have bought Mirelle. That man paid a crown for her out of his own pocket; but you, you picked Mirelle's pocket for the purchase money. Is not this true? Was ever a more dastardly act done than that? You called me a scoundrel. I may not have always acted on the square, but, by God, I never did such a crooked job as this. Did you know that Mirelle was over head and ears in love with Captain Trecarrel? Of course you did. You knew that well enough, and, lest he should marry her, you kept from her the secret of her wealth. You let her and the Captain suppose they were too poor to marry, and so he was ready to sell himself to Orange for five thousand pounds, when in heart he was tied to Mirelle. Was that honourable—was that gentlemanly—was that honest? Eh! Answer me that. No, no, my friend, virtuous John. You were too clever. You wanted to steal the fortune and wipe the guilt off your conscience, and so you marry Mirelle whilst spooning that other one. But how do you manage this? Mirelle don't care a snap of the fingers for you. When the failure of Ophir brought ruin on my family, you allowed my lady to feel the misery of beggary, and then you came to the rescue and overwhelmed her with your generosity—mind you, generous you were with *her* money. You relieved her necessities out of her own purse, and never let her suspect it, in the hopes of rousing in her the feeling of gratitude to her great-hearted protector. What could the poor girl do but accept you as a husband? She could not live on your alms; that would not be decent, would it? A lady cannot receive four hundred a year and a house from a young officer and preserve her character. She *must* marry him, or relinquish what he has given her, and that latter alternative she cannot take without involving Orange and my mother in poverty. Thus it was that you drove Mirelle to accept you. A very ingeniously contrived plan, certainly. Look how all the parts hang together, very perfect, and faulty only in this, that I was not consulted. A very ingenious plan, but cursedly wicked. By God! even I would have shrunk from so dirty and scoundrelly a trick, and I am not squeamish. Give me some money.'

Herring held out his purse—a steel purse of interwoven links, with steel clasp, a present from Mirelle. His head had fallen on his breast; he was broken with shame and humiliation. This that Sampson had said was true, but Herring had never seen his conduct in the light that Sampson turned on it. It had never occurred to him that Mirelle could not accept his bounty without accepting him—that he had, as Sampson had said, driven her to take him, using her necessities as the whip, and that he had, in fact, bought her with her own money. He saw this now vividly, and the sight overcame him. He had been led by his conscience into conduct unworthy of a man of honour; he was degraded in his own eyes. Sampson took the purse, counted the money in his hand, returned it to the purse, snapped it, and slipped it into his pocket.

'That will do for a time. Well! you called me a scoundrel. Which is the biggest scoundrel of the two, Blackguard Sampson or Virtuous John? You regard my father as a robber of orphans; which robbed the orphan most? My father lost her six thousand pounds; you plundered her of more than twice that amount, and with it you carried off her happiness. Faugh! Virtuous John! even I turn away in disgust from you. I stand white and shining as an angel beside you. Nor is this all. No sooner is Mirelle yours and you can *conscientiously* keep her money, than you break her heart by deserting her for another girl with more pink in her cheeks than my Lady White Lily.'

Herring looked up; he was deadly pale, and his lips trembled. 'This is false.'

'What! is it false that you left Mirelle directly you had brought her hither?' Sampson waited for an answer. There could be none. It was true.

'Is it false that you returned at once to West Wyke?' He waited again. It was true, Herring had returned.

'Did you inform your wife whither you were going?' Silence again. Herring had not told her; he had declined to do so.

'No, you evaded telling her. You went back to West Wyke—to Cicely the rosebud, and you have been with her— your pretty pink-and-white sister—ever since. How kind to Mirelle to rescue her rival from ruin with her money! You think Mirelle will appreciate this when told. And told the whole story of your dealings she shall be this very night.'

'Have done,' said Herring, in a low tone. 'Leave me alone.'

'No, not yet,' answered Sampson triumphantly. 'You have insulted and injured me, and I shall not leave you till I have made you sting and writhe. You robbed Mirelle of that which ought to have been put into the hands of my father and me, her diamonds; that is offence number one. You insulted me at West Wyke, and threatened me with a ruler; that was offence number two. I took a fancy to Mirelle, and might have contrived to win her and her money, but you stood in the way by retaining her diamonds, and with them you kept a hold over her destiny; that was offence number three. You exposed Ophir—you brought that pretty and flourishing affair to an end before it was ripe; that was a bad offence, number four. To you I owe the vagabond life I have been living ever since, number five; and to you a blow just now received, to make up the number to six. Shall not I repay these when I may? Do you not know that, now my father is dead, I step into his position as trustee of Mirelle's fortune, till she is three-and-twenty? There is no provision in the will relative to marriage. If you, curse you, had not brought the dogs of justice out of kennel and set them after me, I would claim the diamonds of you, and exact every penny you have spent. I cannot do it now, situated as I am. You have hunted me down for that very reason—you dreaded me, lest I should find out your fraud as you found out mine; you forestalled me, and now you drive me out of England to prevent me from reclaiming from you what you have no right to retain. You are very clever; I never gave you credit for half your talent. But for all your cleverness, you shall not escape. You think that your wife need know nothing of what has taken place. She shall know everything. Do you remember a confession you wrote to her? Well, I took it from the drawer where you had hidden it, and I have given it into her hands. That was the first mouthful; she shall receive next my commentary on it.'

'What!' exclaimed Herring, white, trembling, the sweat standing in beads on his brow.

'Ah! you may well be scared at the thought. That trustful Mirelle, who believed in you as the most honourable of men, has learned this night what you are—a despicable thief. She has discovered what you really are, and how you circumvented her, and robbed her of her liberty, and forged out of her own gold the chain that binds her to you. She knows now the man she has married—and from this night forward she loathes him.'

Herring could not speak; his heart stood still.

'She is now, I doubt not, pacing her bedroom, cursing that man whom she once respected, but whom she now knows to be dishonest, untruthful, and treacherous, the man who has blighted her entire life.'

Then Sampson laughed at the poor, paralysed, broken wretch before him, eyed him from head to foot, turned his back, and with his one hand in a pocket, and the other swinging his bundle of old clothes, he left the office.

Without was night, black and starless.

'I have given him a worse blow than he gave me, I guess,' said Sampson; 'now all I have to do is to dispose of this bundle and then make off to Falmouth as fast as I can. By heavens, I wish the night had not fallen so dark; I cannot make out whither I am going. I can hear the sea, and when I reach the edge I shall see the foam, and then over goes the bundle. It makes me laugh to think how John Herring looked. I might have been stabbing him all the time with a little knife; but faith, I reckon my words went deeper than knives. I wish it were not so confoundedly dark. Curse it!—where am I?'

Where?

Below was Blackapit, with the waves leaping in that cauldron of darkness.

One minute more and the leaping waters were flinging Sampson Tramplara from side to side, and the gulls were flapping their wings and screaming applause over a bruised and lifeless body.

CHAPTER LVI.

A DEAD MAN.

HERRING was back at West Wyke. Everything went on there as usual. The mine was worked systematically. The absence of John Herring for a few days mattered little. West Wyke never altered. Since it had been built, no squire had added a room or an out-house. But from year to year it ripened and mellowed, the lichens spread over the stones in wider patches of orange and white, and the stones became more wrinkled, and the ribs of the roof more prominent through the slopes of small slate.

Cicely was the same—sweet, sunny, simple. Herring thought that nowhere in the wide world could a more restful spot be found than this, or more soothing society. Cicely saw that he looked more broken after this last visit to Welltown than after the former. What was the mystery that hung over his life—what the grief that consumed his heart? His former visit had transformed him from a youth to a man, but this had aged him almost to decrepitude. Cicely observed this, but she said nothing. She troubled him with no inquiries, she did not even allow him to perceive that she noticed a change. The change was not so much in his exterior as within. A cleavage had gone down into his moral nature. On the former occasion his hopes had been shattered, now his faith was shaken. Before he had been broken-hearted, now he was broken-spirited. His interview with Sampson had shaken his confidence in himself, he could no longer rely on conscience as a safe guide, and he knew of no other prompter to action. He reviewed his course of conduct again and again, and always came to the same conclusion, that he was justified in what he had done. What was the alternative course—the course from which conscience had turned him? That was to have given up the box to Trampleasure and washed his hands of all responsibility. But that would have been selfish conduct; it would have been cruel as it was heartless. No doubt he had been influenced by his love for Mirelle when he concealed his discovery from the legal trustee, but he would have done the same for any other helpless person similarly situated, knowing as he did that to betray the secret was to ruin the ward. And to what had he been led? To the wrecking of two lives, of his own and that of Mirelle. If he had acted according to legal instead of moral right, this would not, perhaps, have taken place. How is a man to govern his life— what is to be the mainspring of his actions? The statute law, or the law of God written in the heart? Herring had lost faith in the guidance of conscience, in the directing hand of Providence. He remembered the words of Mirelle on the walk to Welltown, 'All the familiar landmarks fail me, all the ways lead in unknown directions, I am translated into a country that I am expected to travel through without a map or guide.' Those words, which were void of meaning to him when spoken, precisely described his present condition. The framework of his moral consciousness was shaken and out of joint. In time, perhaps, he would recover, but at present the shock had thrown him out of his perpendicular. In Japan, the land of earthquakes, every tower is held upright and together by a huge pendulum of beamwork hanging free. The moral conscience is the pendulum in man. When that is strapped and braced to the girders and buttresses without, a little shock throws the whole system into ruin. It must hang free if it is to serve as a source of stability; otherwise, it precipitates ruin. The human heart can endure any amount of disappointment so long as it maintains its faith in the eternal Providence, but when that fails, its powers of endurance are at an end. Then the wave of bitterness rises and washes over the soul and leaves it like the Desert of Nitre, strewn with bones. The dew of heaven may drop, the showers may fall on it, but the white, bitter surface thenceforth can never laugh into verdure.

John Herring did his work mechanically. He took neither pleasure nor interest in it. The mine might prosper, it probably would, and the result would be evil. He would clear the estate of Cicely from its encumbrances. What for ?—good ? nothing led to good—to find that he had done mischief in his effort to help her. Everywhere men and women are striving to amend wrongs, and only succeed in shifting the suffering from the shoulders of one class on to another. Everywhere dirty pools are being scraped out, only to discolour and defile the water that is disturbed. Everywhere tortured humanity is being inoculated with matter that will expel one disease by preparing the soil for another,

'Please, miss,' said Joyce, one Sunday, to Cicely, who had just returned from church, 'there be that fool of a Jim White from Coombow have a come all the way, and what he be come for I don't know.'

'What Jim White ?'

'A buffleheaded sort of a chap,' said Joyce, in a tone between shyness and disgust; 'he it were as brought me and the master here that day as he were nigh upon killed by Sampson Tramplara.'

Herring looked up, he was at the table. He had not been to church; why should he go to church to be bidden follow conscience when conscience leads astray ? Why should he seek for light when the only light afforded is that of Jack o'lanthorns that lead into mires ? He said bitterly, 'Joyce, why did you bring me hither ?'

'I couldn't do nort other—I did it to make you well again.'

She had followed her conscience, and her poor light had led her to save his life. What for ?—to make Mirelle miserable and himself miserable. Better a thousand times had he died then.

'But, Joyce, what about Jim White ? What does he want ?'

'Well, miss, I dunnow exactly what he wants, but he've a walked all these miles, and he've a got to go back again, so what I want to know is, may he have his meat here, as he ain't a going to get nort else?'

'Certainly.'

'And he may have a drop o' cyder to his meat ? Jim

White be one as can't get on without that. And he smells o' cyder now like as old vaither's cask did when it were fresh.'

'By all means, Joyce,' said Cicely, 'and you may invite him to come here once a month.'

Joyce flushed up. 'I—I don't want the bufflehead to be coming here. I've a told 'n so scores and scores o' times, and I'll tell him if he comes again he'll get neither meat nor cyder. He were here about a month ago, I reckon, and he sed he'd that partikler to say as could only be sed between four eyes. So he sat in the kitchen on one chair, and I on another, a full two hours by the clock, and he never opened his mouth all that time but once, to ax why the great beam went across the ceiling. There! he shall have his meat this Sunday, and, by the blue blazes, he shan't have it of me no more.' Then she stepped up to Herring. 'Please, maister,' she said, 'Jim White have a brought you a paper from Okehampton, a "Saturday News"; he sez he thought you'd a like to see 'n. I didn't think the chap had it in 'n.'

'Thank you, Joyce, and thank Jim White, and here is a present to him for his mistaken kindness to me on a former occasion.'

'But,' said Joyce, 'I may tell 'n that you don't want the paper again. He be that stupid he might make the bringing of a paper an excuse to come here every Sunday. I know,' she exclaimed brightly—'I know what I'll do. I'll tell 'n if he comes again you'll up with your gun and bang off wi' it as you did at me to Welltown that night.'

'Very well; as you like.'

When Joyce had retired, Herring took up the paper indifferently. It could not interest him, for nothing interested him now.

'I wish you had been at church to-day, John,' said Cicely; 'Mr. Harmless-Simpleton preached us a very good sermon.'

'Indeed—on what text?' asked John Herring, carelessly.

'After death, the judgment.'

Herring laughed bitterly. 'Cicely,' he said, 'the order is inverted. The judgment comes first, and after that—after a long and weary interval—death. At least that is my experience.'

She looked at him with a distressed and puzzled expression. 'Dear Cousin John, what has come over you? you are so different from what you were.'

'What has come over me?' he echoed; 'the judgment and

condemnation. There! ask no more questions. Take the paper and look at it; there is nothing in it to interest me.' He pushed it across the table to her.'

'Do you take no interest in politics, John?'

'No; they are only Ophir over again.'

'John, I cannot understand you. Why are you so changed in your view of life? At one time you were hopeful and believed in good, and now you despair and believe only in evil. You make me unhappy.'

'Then I am fulfilling my destiny. The curse is laid on me to blight all I come across.'

'That is utterly untrue.'

'We see life in different lights, Cicely. In after years you will recognise that my view is the true view. Fortunately, the young who start in life are nursed in delusions, or they would refuse the race.'

'John,' said Cicely, 'what is the meaning of this?' She had been turning listlessly over the paper, listening to Herring's words, and troubled in her mind about him. 'Here stands your name—and Welltown, your place in Cornwall.'

'What!' he asked; 'let me look.' And he took the paper hastily out of her hands.

He read of the discovery of Mr. John Herring, late of Welltown, who had disappeared from home on a certain night, but without any suspicions having been raised till his body was found in Blackapit at low water a few days later, terribly mangled and defaced. It would not have been possible to identify the body but for the clothes worn by the deceased, and which had been taken from the place in his office where they usually hung. Moreover, the pocket contained a steel purse known to have belonged to the deceased gentleman, and in the breast-pocket was discovered a magnificent set of diamonds, the property of his wife, which she always kept in a concealed drawer, the secret of which was known only to herself and Mr. Herring. According to what had transpired, the last time the deceased was seen alive was by his wife, seated at the bureau in which these diamonds were. Apparently he had removed the jewels before leaving; for what purpose it was impossible to conjecture, especially as it was suspected that the deceased gentleman had committed suicide. It was reported that he had written a farewell letter to his wife at the bureau where she saw him, intimating his intention; but this letter she absolutely refused to produce at the inquest. This melancholy event had cast a deep gloom over the entire neighbourhood, &c., &c.

Herring read this paragraph over twice before he could understand it, and even then he understood it only imperfectly. But the main points flashed out. Sampson Tramplara had fallen over the rocks, and his body had been mistaken for that of himself because of the clothes he wore and the purse in his pocket. How Sampson had obtained the diamonds he was unable to divine, but he suspected that the letter alluded to was that containing his confession, which Sampson had told him he had given to Mirelle. He sat looking mutely at the paper, his mind working.

'What is it, John?' asked Cicely; but he did not hear. Then she came to him and looked over his shoulder.

'John,' said she, putting her hand on him and shaking him; 'John, what is the meaning of this?'

'Cicely, it is as I said—after judgment, death. Do you see? I am a dead man.'

There was silence in the room. She was collecting her thoughts. What did this all mean?

'John,' she exclaimed, 'what is this?—you have a wife!'

'No—a widow.'

Then he stood up, and walked twice up and down the room, his face white as ashes, his hands behind his back, and his head bowed. Cicely followed him with her eyes; she was bewildered.

'It is best as it is,' said he to himself. 'Mirelle is set free. John Herring is dead.'

Then the truth rushed in on Cicely's mind.

'Oh, John, John! Was she—Mirelle, your wife?'

He looked at her. He did not answer; she saw the mute agony in his face.

'Oh, John, poor John! now I understand all! Now I know why you have been so unhappy. I am sure she never loved you.'

'No, Cicely, she never loved me.'

'She could love no one.'

'You are wrong; she loved another.'

Again there was silence. Cicely's eyes filled.

Herring paced the room again. Cicely could not see him now, her eyes were too full.

'Oh, John! dear, poor John!'

'Cicely,' he said, standing still in the midst of his tramp, 'what has happened is best for every one. Let it be. From henceforth John Herring is dead. If you will, I am John Battishill, your brother.'

CHAPTER LVII.

AN ARREST.

A BLUSTERING day; the rain splashing against the windows of an inn at Plymouth. Mirelle sat in the window; there was a balcony with balustrade before it, and the water dripped incessantly from the rail upon the swimming balcony.

Mirelle was in mourning; her face looked preternaturally white in her black dress. Her eyes were sunken, her lips thin and tremulous; but there were spots of almost colour in her cheeks, speaking of feverish excitement, not of health. Genefer Benoke was with her.

'Mistress,' said the old woman, 'be it still too late to bid you turn back? I tell'y I don't believe as the master be dead. I don't believe it, though I saw him dead with my own eyes. For the eyes of the understanding be keener and clearer than they of the flesh. When Saul the persecutor were cast to the ground on his way to Damascus, he opened his eyes and saw no man. That be the state of most. They've their eyes open, but they sees naught that they ought to see. They goes through the world and they don't see the snares that be set on every side, and the angels that compass them about, and the Providence as is leading of them. The eyes of the flesh be open, but the eyes of the understanding see nothing. With the eyes of the soul I see the master still alive. Afore you came to Welltown I saw you; and I saw what was to be, in a vision, and whether I were in the body or out of the body at the time I cannot tell—God knoweth; but this I do say, that what I then saw with the spiritual eye don't accord no ways with what the natural eye declares. But what do I speak of this to you for as if you knowed naught about the spiritual eye? Sure alive, you lead a life of prayer as do I. Well, I will tell'y what were revealed to me. I fell into a trance, having my eyes open, and I saw the master with his arms round you—the Bride of Snow—and he looked up to you, seeking in you that he never saw.'

Mirelle bowed her face in her hands.

'And with the warmth of his heart you melted away,

drop by drop. I've a seen how you've a been thawing right away ever since the day he brought you to Welltown, tear by tear—as see! you be melting now. And in my vision I saw that you dissolved clean away and your place knew you no more; but, nevertheless, the master remained, with his arms extended and his eyes uplifted, as though still seeking you, till he grew cold, and his hair white, and his tears ice, and his heart were frozen dead. You was gone first, and, after a space, he; it be against the truth of my vision that he should die first and you after.'

'Geneviève, there can be no doubt whatever about what has happened. I would cheerfully give my life to restore his, but that cannot be. I know for certain that he is dead. I have many and weighty reasons for so believing.'

'What reasons? It be true enough that your diamonds and the purse were found on him, as well as his own old clothes that I've a sewed the brass buttons on—I know them well. But what about that? The devil be crafty, and given power to deceive.'

'I have other reasons.'

'I ask you what? You may tell me, for we shall never meet in the flesh again.'

'He wrote to me the night he died. He had been talking to me in my boudoir, and was very unhappy. Then he told me he would write me something, and I gave him the key of my cabinet, where were my diamonds and my writing materials. When I opened the desk next morning the jewels were gone, and I found his letter. In that letter he told me that he bade me farewell for ever.'

' He meant to go abroad.'

'No, Geneviève, the letter said more than that. It intimated that, when I received it, I should be————'

' What? '

' What I now am—a widow.'

' It be a temptation of the devil,' said Genefer, 'who is mighty to deceive, who be come down with great wrath for that he hath a short time. You never let no one see the letter?'

'No. Unfortunately I spoke of it to Orange, and that is how anything came out about it. I thought she would have been more discreet.'

'Well, well!' sighed Genefer; 'the world be full of delusions. Now you be going back to France and to wicked idolatry. There be no call of God in that, to leave the land of light for that of darkness.'

'Geneviève, do not speak on this subject. You and I cannot see alike. I am seeking rest, I am weary, utterly weary of the life I have led in England. It is useless your attempting to argue with me, and to dissuade me from it. I am weary of the wind and the clouds and the rain and the roar of waves without, and of the troubles that toss and overcast the soul within. I must go back. I must find peace. I count the hours till I am within those blessed happy doors of the Sacré Cœur again; and, when once within, I will never, never, never leave that home. Come, Geneviève, help me on with my cloak and hood. I must go out; the rain has ceased, and I will see if there be a chance of the storm abating.'

'Mistress, the packet won't sail with a gale on shore such as this. It would be tempting of Providence.'

'You will come with me. I am impatient of the delay. I must see what the sky and sea look like, and you must attend me, as I cannot stand unassisted against the force of the wind. Oh, Geneviève! where I am going I shall feel no storms—I shall be in perfect shelter, and at rest.'

Mirelle was, as she said, on her way to France. From the time that she knew she was free, one absorbing desire had taken hold of her—the desire to fly from England and return to the convent of the Sacred Heart, there to bury herself from the world. The world, against which the sisters had warned her, she had seen. It was full of unrest, brutality, self-seeking, and imposture. She thought all day of her escape, she dreamt of her return all night. So completely had this idea taken hold of her that it excluded all other thoughts; it possessed her like a fever. She could not think of John Herring. Even Captain Trecarrel was far from her mind. She wanted nothing for the future but perfect quiet within the sacred walls of the Sacré Cœur.

Those of old who were accused of witchcraft were kept without sleep till they confessed. They were denied a moment's doze, till, in the craving for rest, they admitted whatever they were charged with, ready to face the flames if only they might first fold their hands and close their eyes and sigh away their spirits into oblivion.

Some such a craving had come over Mirelle. She had been denied the rest she desired, she had been distracted by responsibilities she did not understand, buffeted by rude associates, placed in situations full of bewilderment, deprived of the ministrations of religion, and, now that the possibility of escape opened to her, she became almost mad to seize it.

Mirelle had told her intention to Orange, who warmly approved of it, and Orange and Genefer had accompanied her to Plymouth, where she was to take passage to France. They had spent a night on the way at Dolbeare, and Genefer was to return with Orange the day after Mirelle had departed.

An arrangement had been proposed by Orange, and readily acquiesced in by Mirelle, that Mrs. Trampleasure and Orange were to remain at Welltown, at least for a while, and take charge of the estate; they were to retain a certain portion of the receipts, and forward the rest to Mirelle.

Mirelle was to have sailed on the day when we have reintroduced her to the reader, seated in the inn window at Plymouth, but the storm had prevented the packet from sailing. Her passage was paid, her berth taken, and her luggage was on board. If the weather abated, she would leave England for ever on the morrow.

Attended by Genefer Benoke, Mirelle went out upon the Hoe and looked forth on the noble bay. There was then no breakwater across its entrance, arresting the violence of the swell. The waves, driven by a southwesterly gale, rolled in from the sea and foamed about the headlands that jutted into the harbour. They tossed and danced about Drake Island and Mount Batten, and ran hissing upon the white marble shore beneath the Hoe. The rain had abated, but fresh showers were coming on, stalking over the angry sea and staining it to ink beneath them. There was no sign of a cessation in the gale. It came on in furious gusts, before which Mirelle cowered and clung to Genefer. As she turned on one occasion, a gentleman standing near, also observing the sea, saw her face, and uttered an exclamation of surprise. She raised her eyes and met those of Captain Trecarrel.

'Mirelle!' he exclaimed, and hastened to interpose his umbrella between her and the wind. 'How unexpected! What brings you to Plymouth? It is my fate to light on you where least anticipated. I have completed my excursion and filled my portfolio. I returned by the south coast to see whether it furnished material for a second issue of pictures, and here I am at Plymouth meditating a return to Launceston as soon as the weather clears. I was so shocked to hear of your loss. I always respected John Herring as a worthy, well-meaning man.

There was no pretence about him, no affectation of being other than he was. I have no doubt that his death was an awful blow to you—so sudden, and the manner so dreadful. You have my warmest sympathy. Poor fellow! poor fellow! Well, well, the world is short of a good sterling man it could ill afford to lose. I hope his circumstances were all right, no money trouble?'

Mirelle shook her head.

'You do not think that distress about over-expenditure can have affected his brain? Inability to meet calls?'

'He was well off—rich—much richer than I thought,' said Mirelle, sadly. 'But pray, Captain, spare me now.'

'Allow me your arm,' said Trecarrel; the wind is so high that I am in momentary fear of your being blown off the cliff and being carried out to sea.'

'The wind is on shore,' said Mirelle, drily.

'True, true; I had not observed it. Bah! here comes the rain, driving as you say on shore and irresistible. Under these circumstances there is no cowardice in beating a retreat and evacuating the Hoe to the enemy. Shall we descend? Where are you staying? At the Royal? Let me accompany you home. What! Genefer Benoke here? How do you do, Genefer? Sad time you have had at Welltown. My heart has bled for you all. I would have flown to the spot to offer my services, but some sorrows are too sacred to be intruded on. I never was more shocked in my life than when I heard of the accident, if accident it may be called, but I suppose it really was that, if he was unembarrassed in circumstances.' So talking, asking questions and getting no answers, Captain Trecarrel accompanied Mirelle back to the inn. He did not wait to be invited to enter, but accompanied Mirelle upstairs.

'Now, tell me all about it,' he said. 'I would not return to Welltown after the sad event through delicacy of sentiment; I thought it might augment your trouble. So I continued my sketching tour, and really made some capital drawings. The weather, however, proved detestable, and after a while I gave up the north coast and took a flying survey of the south. And now, tell me why you are here. What can have brought you to Plymouth?'

'Captain Trecarrel, I am on my way to France, to the convent of the Sacré Cœur, where I was educated.'

'Nothing of the sort. You are going to stay in England.'

Mirelle shook her head. 'No; my mind is made up. Indeed from the moment that I knew my husband was dead, and that I was a free agent, I had no doubt as to what I must do.'

'You are not dreaming of shutting yourself up in a convent?'

'I am going home.'

'Home! What do you mean by home?'

'I mean whatever you associate with rest and fragrance and holiness, with love and innocence and happiness. Some find this ideal in a family. I have never had any experience of home in this sense; the only family I have been with was that of the Trampleasures, and that in no way comes up to my ideal. I will not say more about that. No; what I mean by home is that which I know—the convent of the Sacré Cœur.'

Trecarrel rubbed his chin musingly, and then pulled his moustache. 'If you become a nun, what is to become of Welltown? You are, I presume, well off. Herring had no brothers and sisters, and that falls to you I suppose. Are you thinking of selling John Herring's property, of calling in all your available funds. and bestowing everything on the convent and the beggars of Paris?'

'I have not this thought. Orange and her mother will reside at Welltown and manage the estate, and let me have the money I need.'

'And who will check their accounts—who look after your interests?'

'Orange will send me what I want. I do not require much.'

'What did my poor friend John Herring die worth—that is, how much has come to you, Mirelle?'

'I do not know the value of the Welltown estate.'

'But I do,' said Trecarrel, sharply. 'Six hundred nett, on the outside. Is that all?'

'No,' answered Mirelle; 'there is a great deal more money than that. Many thousand pounds. There are the mortgages on West Wyke, and there is a mine somewhere about there, and money beside.'

'All yours?' asked Trecarrel, turning his melting blue eye on Mirelle, and stroking his moustache.

'I suppose so.'

'And this is all to be left to the unchecked management of Orange.

'Yes; Orange is so kind and sensible, she will know better than I what ought to be done, and how to do it.'

'Mirelle,' exclaimed the Captain, standing up, and placing himself before the fire, occupying the entire rug, 'you are not going to leave England; you are not going to shirk your duty!'

'My duty? I have done that to the best of my powers, which are small. No, Captain Trecarrel, I must go back whence I came. You cannot conceive how abhorrent to me has been the life I have led since I came to England; it has nearly killed me. Look at my hands; they were plump when I left France, compared to what they are now. My strength is gone; a very short walk now tires me out. I was strong before. I have had no illness whatever except that fever at Dolbeare before I was married, but my soul has been sick ever since I left France, and now I feel a sort of instinct in me that if I am to live I must spread my wings and escape over the water to dear France and nestle into the old convent home again.'

'No, Mirelle, you would not find rest there, you may take my word for it. You would carry thither something in your heart which would forbid your finding rest there. Look me in the face and say that this is not so.' She could not do this; there was truth in his words. 'No, dear Mirelle, that old convent life is no more to be returned to than childhood. You may, as an adult, go back into the nursery, and buy a rattle and feed yourself with pap out of a spoon; but you cannot revive the old childish buoyancy of heart and brightness of hope—you go back into infantine surroundings with the care-furrowed heart of age. You would not be happy in the convent, because you return to it a woman, and you went out a child. There is something more to be considered; you have contracted obligations which you have no right to cast off. You own an estate and a fortune, and this gives you influence and power for good. This you have no right to ignore. You have been transplanted by Providence to a place where religion is as dead or diseased as when Saint Morwenna came to the same coast twelve hundred years ago. Do you suppose she came to it by choice? Do you think that she never yearned to be back in the stillness and indolence of her dear convent at Burton? She came to our Cornish coast from a sunny home in the midlands, among lime-trees and buttercup pastures, and from a church where there was sweet music and rich sculpture and all the splendours of Catholic worship, and inhabited a rude hovel overhanging the sea, into which the storm drove between the ill-jointed stones; away from trees and flowers, and music and worship, simply and solely because she was called to live there, and duty tied her to the spot. Now we venerate Saint Morwenna as a Virgin Apostle of the Cornish Coast, as one who brought light to those in darkness, the truth to those in error. You are a Catholic. Was it any choice of yours which took you to Welltown? You were taken there by Providence, and Providence has set you a task which you have no right to leave undone, has given you a post which you dare not desert. Those poor wretched Cornish are like shipwrecked men lost in night and storm, not knowing whither to steer, and led astray by wreckers' lanthorns. You are sent among them as a second Morwenna, to lead them to the true port, to show them the only true light.'

'I—I—I!' Mirelle trembled, and her heart sank within her; she had not strength and courage to execute such a task.

'Yes, you. With your means and position you can do a great deal. Who is there at Boscastle to oppose you—Sir Jonathan? He will do nothing. How do you know but that you may win his daughters and so save their souls? Who is there of influence for miles round except yourself and the Phyllacks? Build a Catholic chapel at Boscastle, down in the midst of the people. Establish there a priest and a mission, and every soul brought into the true fold will bless you.'

Mirelle was silent.

'I am pointing out to you a duty. You have seen no priest since you were married; you must suffer me to be your director. Has not what I urge struck you before?'

'No,' answered Mirelle, faintly. 'But see! I can do much that you say, and yet live in France. I will endow a mission at Boscastle and build there a church.'

'You cannot set a missioner there without a soul to support him; he must have one or two Catholics near, or he can do nothing. Now you understand what I said. If you fly abroad you take trouble along with you, and you will not rest in your convent. It is the story of Jonah over again, and see—see this storm sent to arrest you, to send you back to Nineveh, from which you were flying.'

'How cruel you are—how cruel! I have been so hoping, longing, sighing to escape.'

Cruel indeed he was, and mean beneath conception. He used the words and arguments which he knew would tell with her, not that he cared for the souls of the Boscastle people, or for the advance of the Catholic Church, but because he coveted her money and the estate of Welltown.

'That is not all,' continued Captain Trecarrel, and his tone changed from that of exhortation to that of pleading; his voice melted, and sounded as though tears were welling up in it—it became soft and tremulous. 'You have no right to run away, dear Mirelle, for another reason. You know—you know'—his voice became broken; then, with a gulp, swallowing his agitation—'you know what I mean.'

Mirelle trembled. She did not know what he meant.

'You have no right to sacrifice another as well as yourself. You know, Mirelle, how I have loved you——'

'Stay, stay!' exclaimed Mirelle, piteously. 'Do not speak to me again like this. I must—I must go. If only to pray for my poor husband's soul, I must go.'

'Mirelle, tell me—do you believe that he wilfully destroyed himself?'

'I do.'

'For what reason? There were no money troubles?'

'None whatever.'

'Why, then, did he commit suicide?'

She was silent. She could not explain. He considered for a while, and then said, 'How is it that there had been such an estrangement between you from the beginning? I understand he left you the day after the marriage, and did not return till that day which ended in his death. This is very mysterious, and points to some great cause of trouble between you. Did he love you?'

'Indeed he did. Too well.'

'Did you love him?'

She did not answer, but her head sank on her bosom.

'Tell me, Mirelle—is it true that he wrote to you the night of his death? I heard a report to that effect.'

'Yes, it is true.'

'What did he say in that letter?'

She hesitated. 'He said that he bade me farewell for ever. He said that when I read the letter I should be free.'

'Why did he write thus?'

She made no answer, but covered her face.

'Tell me, Mirelle—did he know of my—of our——'

'Spare me—spare me! Oh, Captain Trecarrel, if you must know all, he knew that I did not love him in the way in which he loved me, and the knowledge of this made him so miserable that—— You know the rest. And now, do you not see that I have his death on my conscience, and I must do what I can to expiate this sin, and do what I can for the poor despairing soul that I drove to despair?'

'Set your mind at ease. I do not in the least believe in his self-destruction. A man about to commit suicide does not first fill his pocket with diamonds worth several thousand pounds. The finding of the jewels upon him is conclusive evidence that he did *not* meditate self-destruction, but, on the contrary, meant to live comfortably on the proceeds of their sale elsewhere. John Herring—you may take my word for it—made up his mind, as he could not be happy with you, that he would go elsewhere, probably to America. Now, a man cannot start afresh in life penniless without great inconvenience and discomfort: so he laid his hand on that which was convertible into money, to start him in the New World. You do not suppose John Herring intended to strangle himself with a diamond necklace, do you? If he did not, the supposition of his having meditated self-destruction is untenable beside the fact of his having taken the jewels. No; he possessed himself of them because he had not sufficient cash in hand, and as he made his way over the cliffs—it was a dark night—he missed his path and fell down Blackapit. There you have the solution of the entire mystery. Set your mind at ease; the guilt of his death does not weigh on you, and there is no need for you to expiate it in a convent.'

Mirelle breathed more freely. This explanation did really seem the correct one, and the relief it gave her was great.

'Now, then,' said the Captain, 'I have knocked this nonsense of cloistering yourself on the head.' He rang the bell, and, when the servant appeared, he said, 'Send to the packet, and have the Countess Garcia's boxes brought back. She is not going to sail in her.'

Mirelle raised her hand in protest, but in vain. The strong will and determination of the Captain was more than she could resist in her present weak condition.

'Listen now to me, dear Mirelle,' he said, and, leaving the fire, came towards her. 'The barrier that has stood between us has fallen. What is there now to hinder you from becoming my wife? I have loved you from the first moment that I saw you, and—do not deny it—you have loved me. You married a man for whom you did not care—a worthy man, but not one a heart like yours could cling to, even if disengaged; and disengaged it was not. Duty obliged you—obliged both of us—to smother and conceal our mutual love. But the fire was not

E E

extinguished, and now that the obligation to keep it under exists no longer, it bursts forth in flame once more. You shall not go to France. If you do, in spite of me, I will follow you, and claim you from the Sisters of the Sacred Heart. You have no right to run away; you owe me reparation for the suffering I have undergone. Shall I own to you something? I knew that you were going to sail in the packet; I knew what you purposed doing; and I came to Plymouth to prevent it.'

Mirelle looked up at him with surprise.

'Yes, dearest, when I knew that you were free I had no rest. I saw my hopes of happiness revive. Hender Benoke was in my pay. He kept me informed of what was taking place and what was meditated at Welltown. In love as in war, all things are lawful.'

Mirelle was now standing near the window, leaning against the angle of the window splay, with the curtain behind her. Her face was turned away. She could not look at the Captain, but she saw nothing through the window panes.

Captain Trecarrel came towards her. She felt his approach, she did not see it, and she trembled violently. She was powerless. The events of her short life in the world had broken down her force of character and power of resistance to a superior and resolute will.

'Mirelle, dearest Mirelle,' he said, in a voice vibrating with pathos, 'you said, a little while ago that the only knowledge you had of home was a cloister; there is another and a fonder home—in the arms, on the heart, of a good and honourable man.' He put his arms round her and clasped her to him.

At the same moment the door opened, and Orange came in, very wet, with cheeks glowing with exercise; but when she saw the Captain holding Mirelle in his arms, and stooping to imprint a kiss on her lips, she turned the colour of parchment.

'Orange!' exclaimed the Captain, recovering himself at once. 'Delighted to see you. Mirelle is not going to France; she is not going to immure herself in a cloister; she returns to Launceston, and thence to Welltown to-morrow, and she has very kindly offered me a place in her carriage as far as Launceston. I do not in the least object to a seat with my back to the horses.'

CHAPTER LVIII.

R.I.P.

The chaise was ready to take Mirelle back again. She was depressed. A strange sinking, a sickening fear had come over her heart, the reaction after the excitement she had gone through, the eager expectation of a return to the convent, and then the arrest on the threshold of escape. She had painfully schooled herself not to think of the Captain, and even now she shrank from thinking of him lest she should be committing a mortal sin. Even now, with the knowledge before her that he whom she had loved would claim her and be to her more than friend and support, she failed to feel anything but disappointment that she was not on her way back to the Sacré Cœur. She loved Trecarrel, but her love for him was not now the predominating feeling of her heart; her craving for rest and shelter prevailed over the other passion. Even now, if she could, she would have prosecuted her journey, and it was with a lingering, longing look that she gazed on the sea. Only duty, that supreme sense of submission to duty, drove her back. Captain Trecarrel knew her character perfectly when he appealed to this. The prospect of enjoying his love, of leaning on him, blunted the edge of her disappointment: it did no more than that.

Mirelle had not slept that night. Indeed she had not slept for several nights. Hitherto she had been kept awake by her fever of excitement at the prospect of return to the home of her childhood; last night she had been wakeful from other causes, disappointment, and bewilderment at the new landscape spread before her eyes. She looked like a girl convalescent from a long and dangerous sickness.

'Do you think, miss, her be fit to travel?' asked the hostess, compassionately, of Orange. 'Her looks a'most like death herself.'

'She suffers from the heart,' answered Orange coldly.

Orange Trampleasure was not herself. A hard look had come over her face. The ripe, sensual lips were set and contracted, and a threatening light glimmered in her eyes.

'That other young lady do have a temper. I wouldn't bo

the one to cross her,' said the hostess to the chambermaid when the chaise departed.

Nor was Genefer herself the confident person she had been. Genefer was wont to speak as the oracle of the truth, to speak and act as though whatever she said and did was inspired. She had no doubt about her own infallibility, and every contrary opinion to hers she regarded as instigated by the devil. But this morning her confidence was gone; almost for the first time in her life she did not see her way clear before her. She had urged Mirelle to return to Welltown, and Mirelle was returning; but now Genefer doubted whether the advice she had given was wise and good. She did not like the Captain, and the Captain had succeeded in convincing her mistress when she had failed.

'The Lord have hid the thing from me!' she muttered as she mounted the box. She sat looking before her, waiting for the light, that she might see her way; but it did not come. At intervals she sighed, and muttered, 'I misdoubt me sore. But the Lord have closed my eyes that I cannot see.'

Strange as it may seem, the old woman had taken a strong liking for Mirelle, and it was not only because she thought Mirelle's object in returning to an idolatrous land was wrong that she opposed it, but also because in her rugged but warm heart she was attached to her and did not like to lose her. There was a singleness of mind and a spirituality of vision in the Snow Bride which impressed as well as puzzled Genefer. How one who was not a Dissenter could live an inner life, and pray much, perplexed her, but she recognised in Mirelle a good deal that was akin to herself, and she found that Mirelle entered into her spiritual experiences with interest and sympathy.

Orange sat by Mirelle, and Captain Trecarrel was opposite the latter. He made himself very agreeable, had a fund of conversation on a variety of topics, but found his companions in no responsive mood. He tried to interest Mirelle in the scenery, which was lovely, but Mirelle was absorbed in her thoughts and disinclined for conversation. The day was fine, the views looking back over Plymouth Bay and the woods of Mount Edgcumbe, the Hamoaze crowded with ships, and the winding estuary of the Tamar, were charming—hardly less beautiful were those in front, of Dartmoor. Mirelle leaned back in the chaise, the hood of which was thrown back, and the air fanned her face and soothed her.

Captain Trecarrel could hardly withdraw his eyes from her;

she seemed to him the most lovely woman he had ever seen. He had an artist's appreciation of beauty of feature. The delicate and perfect chiselling of the nose and nostril; the finely formed, sensitive mouth; the pure brow, and, when she looked up, the solemn depth of her large eyes; filled him with admiration. A little lock of her dark hair had strayed over her forehead, and the soft warm air trifled with it in a tender, playful manner. Mirelle put up her fingers to put it in place, but unsuccessfully; it stole forth again, again to flutter in the light air.

Orange watched Trecarrel jealously; she saw how his eyes turned to Mirelle whenever he dare look at her without rudeness, and how his admiration of her beauty grew. The Captain spoke to her occasionally, but only by the way, his remarks were mainly directed to Mirelle, and when he turned to Orange she felt that he was doing so out of civility alone. His thoughts were not with her, but with her companion. Orange was not herself on this day; her usual colour had deserted her, and the sensuous fulness of life which throbbed in her seemed to have ebbed, and left her flaccid and pulseless.

Captain Trecarrel was aware that he had behaved badly to Orange, and had incurred her resentment; this made him nervous in her presence, and to hide his discomfort he redoubled his efforts to be agreeable. Finding that no conversation was to be got out of Mirelle, he finally turned his efforts to Orange, and endeavoured to amuse her with his adventures at the little inns on his sketching tour.

But still, as he talked, his eyes reverted to the face of Mirelle, and Orange's life returned in a throb of spleen. She rose in her seat and said sharply, 'We will change places, if you please, Captain Trecarrel.'

'Hush!' said he; 'do not disturb her. She sleeps.'

The fresh air puffing in her face, and the warm sun, after the sleepless nights, had operated on the weary brain, and Mirelle had dropped off into unconsciousness. Orange was aware of this without looking round, by the confidence with which the Captain allowed his eyes to rest on her face. Mirelle was breathing gently, and her face had become wonderfully peaceful and deathlike under the influence of sleep. The stray lock wantoned in the air on the pure white brow, but could not wake her.

'Do you really wish to sit with your back to the horses?' asked Trecarrel in an undertone. 'You will then have the sun in your eyes.'

'Yes, let us change places.' Her voice was metallic.

'Then, for the love of Heaven, do not wake her with moving. Stay! here we are at a long hill. I will get out and walk up it to relieve the horses, and then you can change without disturbing Mirelle.'

'If you are going to walk, I will walk also.'

They both alighted at the bridge over the Walkham, and fell behind the carriage. Trecarrel was uneasy; he feared that Orange was going to speak to him unpleasantly, on an unpleasant subject.

'She is so deficient in breeding,' said he to himself, 'that she persists in forcing herself and what she regards as her wrongs upon one.'

'How lovely she is!' exclaimed the Captain, with want of tact; 'but terribly fragile. She looks as if she were as likely never to wake out of the sleep into which she has fallen, as she is again to unclose her beautiful eyes.'

Orange made no answer. Her heart was beating; the rush of life had returned to her veins. She walked at his side in silence for some little way, then suddenly burst forth with, 'What is the meaning of this, Captain Trecarrel?'

'The meaning of what, my good Orange? You must be more explicit.'

'Why is Mirelle returning? How have you succeeded in changing her from her purpose? What inducement have you held out to her to lure her back to hated Welltown?'

'The highest, the purest of all,' answered the Captain, with dignity. 'For what is higher and purer than duty?'

Orange looked round at him.

'What do you mean by that?' she asked harshly. 'Duty—duty to whom?'

'To self—to conscience. I have pointed out to her obligations she must not cast off.'

'Duty—obligations!' echoed Orange, roughly. 'What farce is this? Have you turned preacher?'

'I have advised Mirelle as a friend. She has no one else capable of giving her counsel.'

'Indeed? I am nothing?'

'I beg your pardon, Orange. I do not ignore your high qualifications for advising her as to her social duties; but when we step out on moral ground, there I must beg leave to observe that only one of her own faith is calculated to direct her.'

Orange stood still and stamped her foot. Her hands clenched convulsively.

'Captain Trecarrel! do you suppose me such a fool as to believe you when you take up this tone? I know you too well. I have suffered too severely from your selfishness and cruelty not to know that you are working in your own interest, disregarding everything and every one save some mean and selfish aim. Captain Trecarrel, you were bound to me by the most sacred vows, short of those made at the altar; you took a base advantage of my misfortunes to shake me off, when a man of honour and chivalry would have blushed to desert me. I humbled myself before you into the dust. I am covered with shame at the thought of such self-abasement before one so unworthy. You were without feeling for me, without love, without compassion, without generosity. After that you sought me again, when I had fled from Launceston to conquer my own heart in seclusion. You sought me out, you followed me to my place of retreat, to trifle with me again, to waken up in me what was going to sleep, to torture me, and to sting me to madness. Take care! take care! What have I done to you, that you should do this great wrong to me? I was a good-hearted and gay girl, without gall and bitterness, and you have turned my heart into a cauldron boiling with furious and hateful passions. Take care, I say; take care lest you drive me to desperation.'

' My dear, dear Orange——'

'Have done with "my dear, dear Orange!"' she almost shouted. The anger was boiling in her heart and puffing out the veins in her throat and temples. 'I am "dear" to you no more. Captain Trecarrel, you have had no mercy on me, and I appeal no more to you to consider my wrongs; but I do appeal to you on behalf of Mirelle, whom you so greatly admire, whom you profess to consider so lovely, whom you are guiding in the way of moral obligation. Have you no pity? Do you know to what you are driving her back? Can you not let her alone and allow her to escape whilst she may? Her heart is set on return to France and to her convent. Why should she not follow her heart and go? Why should you stand in the way, and lay your hand on her and arrest her? Let her go. It is not now too late. Let her follow her own wishes and leave England. Do you not see that, tossed as she has been into a turmoil of troubles, they are killing her? It is a whirlpool sucking her in and suffocating her. Do not you incur the guilt of her destruction as well as mine, you moral instructor! You have ruined my happiness, and with it my moral sense. You are thrusting her back out of happiness into death. She has been like a captive escaping from a dungeon, catching a glimpse of sun and laughing for joy, and now you, as a savage gaoler, come and drive her back into the rayless vault again, and cast a stone over the door. Cruel, cruel man!' She panted for breath. 'See,' she continued, 'see how fine the day is! The packet is now at sea with her prow turned towards France. But for your interference Mirelle would be on board, she would be standing on deck looking eagerly forward to catch the first sight of the loved land, her heart beating high with hope, her eye bright with returning happiness, her cheek flushed with renovated life. Let her go back to Plymouth and take the next packet.'

Captain Trecarrel said nothing, but, drawing a silk handkerchief from his pocket, he dusted his boots and faintly hummed a tune.

Orange's passion increased at his insulting indifference.

'Captain Trecarrel,' she said, 'have you no regard for anyone but yourself? You think, do you, that some day Mirelle will be yours, and with her all she has?'

'Orange,' said the Captain, coldly, 'as you pretend to know me, I may return the compliment, and admit that I know you. Now what is the meaning of this sudden sympathy with Mirelle? I know you do not love her; I have eyes in my head which have long ago convinced me that you do not even like her. This outbreak of zeal for her welfare and happiness, I am led to believe, covers—as you were pleased coarsely to remark to me—some selfish aim. And that aim I can discern without difficulty. I understand,' he added with a sneer, 'that Mirelle had constituted you treasurer and agent and plenipotentiary over all her property, landed and funded and invested, with perfect liberty to deal with it as you listed, and without anyone to control your proceedings and check your accounts. And *that* after her experience of how the Trampleasure family deals in trust matters! *O sancta simplicitas!*'

Orange looked at him sullenly.

'Think so if you will, but I tell you you are mistaken.' She stepped before him, barring his road, and held out her hands. 'Captain Trecarrel, I give you one chance more. Let her go. Send her to her convent. Have pity upon both her and me.' Then her rage swelled into a paroxysm; she grasped his shoulders with her strong hands, and shook him. 'Captain Trecarrel, will you be advised, will you be ruled? Do not think in your heart that ever she will be yours, and Welltown joined to Trecarrel! That will never, never be. Let her go. You alone can save her. The carriage has halted for us at the top of the hill. Now call to the postillion to turn his horses and drive back to Plymouth.'

Captain Trecarrel released himself, with a feeling of disgust at her violence and ill-breeding.

'Let us catch up the carriage, Orange,' he said coldly; 'we have dropped far behind. You are excited, and hot, and unreasonable. If you wish to hear what directions I shall give to the driver, you must wait.'

They walked on hastily, side by side, without speaking. Orange's breath was like a flame between her lips.

The post-boy had drawn up the horses at the head of the hill. As they prepared to step into the chaise, Captain Trecarrel remarked—

'She is asleep still. Bless me, she looks as if she might sleep away into death without those looking on being conscious of the change.'

Orange took her place opposite Mirelle, and Captain Trecarrel sat by the sleeper's side.

'You really wish this?' he asked of Orange.

'Yes; give the word to the post-boy,' she answered, looking him hard in the face.

'Drive straight on,' shouted the Captain; 'we are ready.'

Orange sank back in her seat and said no more. Trecarrel looked about him, and admired the richness of the scenery, as the road descended to the beautiful valley of the Tavy, rich in woods, with glimpses of granite moor ridges rising picturesquely above it, and below the little town of Tavistock, with its grey church and abbey nestling by the foaming moorland river. The scene was charming, and the Captain wished he had time to sketch it.

Presently Mirelle woke—woke with a start and shiver.

'Orange!' she said, 'you frighten me. Why do you look at me in that strange manner?'

'I did not know that I was looking at you at all,' answered Orange, and she turned away her face.

'I am cold,' said Mirelle; 'we have our backs to the sun.'

'You have been asleep, and have become chilled,' said the Captain, sympathetically. 'Let me wrap my warm cloak about your shoulders; you must not catch cold. We are now half-way to Launceston.'

Then Genefer murmured, 'The Lord put a lying spirit into the mouth of the prophets, and they said unto Ahab, Go up unto Ramoth Gilead and take it; and he went up and fell there. I cannot see; my eyes are holden. The Lord hath not spoken unto me by word or sign or revelation, and I know not if I counselled right when I said, Return.'

Nothing of interest and worthy of record occurred during the rest of the journey. Mirelle was brighter, refreshed by her sleep, and she tried to enter into conversation with the Captain, but Orange remained obdurately mute. At the gate of Launceston Trecarrel descended and offered profuse thanks to Mirelle for the drive which had saved him the expense of coaching home. The evening had fallen and it was dusk; the chaise was driven rapidly into the gate of Dolbeare, and drew up on the terrace.

The house was locked; no one now lived in it. Orange had taken the key with her to Plymouth; she handed it to Genefer, whilst the post-boy let down the steps, and she descended. Genefer went, with the key in her hand, towards the door, when suddenly she stopped, uttered a cry of terror, and fell back.

'What is the matter?' asked Orange, impatiently.

'Do'y see un? Do'y see un? There he stands.'

'Who? what? No one is there,' answered Orange in a tone of irritation. 'You foolish woman, go on.'

'I see an old man in red; he be there standing with his walking-stick waving it, and signing to us not to come in. He has his hand out, as though to thrust us back. He stands in the doorway.'

'This is sheer crazy folly,' exclaimed Orange. 'Here, give me the key!' She snatched it from Genefer's hand, and thrusting her aside went forward.

Genefer turned her head and uttered another cry. Mirelle had fainted.

'She saw him too, I reckon—that man in a red coat, with the white hair and the gold-headed cane,' said the old woman. 'O Lord, enlighten me! What be the meaning of all this, I cannot tell.'

Orange threw the house door open, and the unconscious Mirelle was borne into the hall by Genefer and the post-boy, and placed in an arm-chair, where she gradually recovered.

'I'll be quick, darling,' said Genefer, 'and get a fire lighted and something warm, and I'll bring you your supper up to your own room.'

'You are over-tired,' said Orange. 'Genefer is right; go to bed.'

When the Trampleasures had removed to Welltown nothing definite was settled as to where they would permanently take up their abode; the furniture and all the contents of Dolbeare had therefore been left there undisturbed, to be removed should they elect to live elsewhere. It was convenient to them to have the house in condition to receive them at any time for a short or lengthy stay as suited them. On their way to Plymouth Mirelle and Orange had spent the night there, and Genefer had attended to their requirements. Now that they had returned, the old servant's hands were full of work. She lighted the fire in the kitchen and in the dining-room, filled the kettle and set it on to boil, and began to prepare for supper. This occupied some time, during which she was unable to attend to Mirelle. When the supper was ready she brought it into the dining-room, and found Orange there seated musing by the hearth.

'How be the mistress now?' asked Genefer.

'I do not know. I have not been upstairs.'

Genefer looked up at the pastille portrait above her head, and said, 'Him it was that I saw in the doorway with a warning wave of the hand, and he sought to bar the door entrance with the stick, that we might not come in. I durst not have passed, but when you went forward, Miss Orange, then he seemed to vanish away like smoke. I reckon the mistress saw un too, for her fainted with fright at the same moment. Did'y ever hear, now, who he might be?'

'No, I know nothing of him,' answered Orange, shortly.

'I reckon he don't come for naught,' said Genefer. 'But a veil is on my face in the reading of events, as there be on the hearts of the Jews in the study of Scripture, and till that veil be taken away I see naught plain.'

'Go about your work,' said Orange, impatiently, 'and do not trouble me with your foolish fancies.'

Genefer looked at Orange, and shook her head, and muttered, 'There be some folks like the fleece of Gideon on which the dew never falls though the grass around be wet.'

Then she prepared a tray, and carried some supper upstairs

to Mirelle. 'Ah!' she continued, 'and there be others on whom the dew drops in plenty whilst all around is dry.'

She found her mistress seated in a high-backed, old-fashioned chair covered with red baize. She had her shawl wrapped about her. 'There, my pretty,' said the old woman; 'see, I've a brought you something at last.'

'Oh, Geneviève, I am very cold,' said Mirelle.

'Shall I light the fire, darling?'

'I should like it. I do not think I am well. I am exhausted, and sick at heart. Feel my hand how it shakes.'

Genefer took the little white hand between her own, stroked it, raised it to her lips and kissed it.

'You love me, Geneviève?' Mirelle lifted her large eyes and looked earnestly into the old woman's face.

'Ah, I do, I do, sure-ly.'

'I am so glad, Geneviève, because I do not think there are many who love me.'

'Do'y think it was the red man in the doorway that frightened you?' asked Genefer. 'You seed un, did you not?'

'I do not know,' answered Mirelle. 'I hardly remember what occurred. I had a sense of a great wave of terror coming over me, but what caused it I no more remember, for my consciousness went from me.'

'He've a got a kindly enough face, there be no vice in it,' said Genefer, as she knelt at the hearth and was engaged on the fire. 'I reckon he don't walk for naught; it ain't only the bad as wanders. Samuel appeared to Saul before the battle of Gilboa. Many of the saints that slept arose, and appeared in the holy city. We have Scripture to show that it be not the bad only as walks. I've a seen my mother scores of times, and her were a God-fearing woman. But father were a darning blaspheming drunkard, and I've never seen him once. I reckon the red man were a peaceable sort of a chap, and if he walks, 'tain't along of his sins, but because he be sent to fulfil the wise purposes of Heaven.'

Genefer put the poker against the bars of the grate.

'There, mistress, I hope you'll be warmer soon, but the kindling be damp and the chimney has cold air in it, and the fire won't draw kindly. Now I must go.'

'Oh, Geneviève, must you really go? I do not like to be alone, I am frightened.'

'Is it the red man you fear? Do'y think he'll walk through the room while you are lying bed? Lord bless'y, I think naught of such spirits. It be the black devils is the chaps to scare one; I've a seed them and hunted 'em many a time.'

'No,' said Mirelle, 'I'm not afraid of him. I do not know exactly what I fear, but something that I cannot describe has come over me. Oh, Geneviève, I wish that you could sleep in this room with me.'

'I don't see how to manage that, my dear. I couldn't move my bed myself up here. But you've no occasion for it, neither. There be Miss Orange close at hand, and only a door between. You ask her, and her'll leave the door open between you.'

'No, no,' said Mirelle, nervously. 'Could you fasten that door, Geneviève?'

'Which? There be but two doors, one is on to the landing, and the other into Miss Orange's bedroom.'

'I mean the latter door.'

Genefer went to it.

'I cannot fasten it. It be locked already, and the key on the other side.'

'Is there no bolt?'

'No, mistress.'

'Never mind, it cannot be helped,' with a sigh.

Then the lock was turned, the door opened, and Orange came through carrying a bolster.

'You like to lie with your head well raised. I have brought you this; you will sleep the sounder for it.'

Then she went up to Mirelle's bed and placed it with the pillows.

'Thank you, Orange. How very kind and thoughtful you are!' said Mirelle.

Orange went up to her. Orange had lost her colour, and a hard, restrained look had come over her face.

'How are you now?'

'A little better; not much. I feel very cold.'

'It is heart,' said Orange, 'that ails you. That will stop some day—or night. Stop in a moment when least expected.' And without another word she went back through her door and re-locked it.

'Shall I unpack your box, mistress?' asked the old woman. 'It won't do for you to stoop. It might bring the swimming in your head again. It is only for me to stay up a bit later to finish the housework.'

'Thank you, dear, kind Geneviève. I am much obliged, I shall be very glad of it.'

Genefer uncorded and unlocked the trunk and removed from it what she thought would be necessary for the night.

'Shall I bring out this Christ on the cross?' she asked, holding up the crucifix Herring had bought for his bride.

'Oh, please do so. I shall be glad to have it.'

'Ah!' said the old woman, 'if the fear and sickness of heart come over you again, you can look to that and take comfort. I be not that set against images such as this, that I would forbid and destroy them. Since you've been to Welltown I've a looked on this here many scores of times, and it have done me a deal of good, it have.'

Then she planted the crucifix in the middle of a small table at the head of the bed, between a couple of wax lights that were burning there.

Mirelle shivered. 'Oh, Geneviève! what have you done? Do you know that with us we put a crucifix and candles in that way at the head of a bed where some one is lying dead?'

'Let be,' said Genefer. 'Sleep is a figure of death, and if you cannot sleep under the cross you are not fit to die under it. Remember what Miss Orange said. You suffer from the heart, and it may stop at any hour; so be always ready.' She went again to the hearth. 'Drat the fire, it won't burn, leastwise not readily; there be too much cold air in the flue. There, mistress, now I must go; I've my work to do downstairs.'

'May I have a rushlight for the night, Geneviève?'

'My dear, there be none in the house; I'd go gladly and fetch you one, but the shops be all shut in the town. There, good night, and God be with you.'

'Where do you sleep, Geneviève?'

'At the far end of the house, up the other flight of stairs.'

'If I should want you? If I should call in the night?' Mirelle looked anxiously, pleadingly at her.

'My darling, it would be no good. I should never hear. But what do that matter? Miss Orange be close at hand, and you've but to call if you feel ill, and her'll run and wake me up, and I'll go for the doctor fast as lightning, so there, don't'y fear any more.'

Mirelle sighed. 'Give me a kiss, Geneviève, before you go.'

'With all my heart, precious!' and the old woman kissed

her fondly on the cheek, and then raised and kissed both her hands in succession.

Then Genefer left. It was not possible for her to tarry longer with Mirelle. There was much that had to be done; the supper things to be removed and washed up, some kindling to be got ready for the fire next morning; the kitchen fire to be put out, and a little tidying to be done in the parlour and the hall. Genefer would have enough to do next morning, getting breakfast ready, and she would leave nothing till then that she could possibly get done that night.

Whilst she was in the dining-room clearing away the supper things, she looked hard at the pastille portrait.

'Whatever did the old man mean by walking and standing in the doorway with that warning gesture?'

She stood in front of the picture for some time, trying to decipher something in it which escaped her. At last, hopeless of discovering what she sought, she resumed her work.

'There, there!' she said, 'I've been wasting the one bit of candle I have, and her'll hardly last me out all I have to do. Whatever be hidden now from me, the day will bring forth.'

After the old woman had finished the washing-up in the kitchen and had extinguished that fire and raked out the fire in the parlour, she went into the hall, which was littered with packages, boxes, trunks, cloaks, and calashes. Genefer disliked disorder, and she set to work putting the sundry articles into some sort of order, though the next day all would again be removed to the carriage for the continuation of the return journey to Welltown.

'I wonder what time of night it be!' she said, as she looked up at the clock. 'Twelve! But no, sure it cannot be. Her's not ticking. Her's standing still. To be sure, her's not been wounded up for ever so long. Loramussy! the candle will never last me out. I shall have to go to bed in the dark, and that ain't pleasant where there be spirits of dead men walking. But'—she shook herself—'is that seemly of thee, Genefer Benoke, to be afeared of spirits? The Lord is my light and my salvation, whom shall I fear? The Lord is the strength of my life, of whom shall I be afraid?'

Genefer's confidence was somewhat shaken by hearing a door opened, and by seeing a white figure on the stairs, slowly descending.

'Lord, mistress!' she said, after she had recovered from

the first shock of alarm, when she recognised Mirelle; 'sure enough you did give me a turn.'

Mirelle was in her long white nightdress, her dark hair was unbound, and fell over her shoulders. The white, delicate feet were bare.

'What be the matter, darling?'

Mirelle took each step on the stair hesitatingly, with foot poised before her, as though feeling in the air, before she lowered it. She descended in this way very leisurely, as one walking in a dream, or one blind, groping the way in an unknown place. Her hand was on the banister, and the bar trembled.

She reached the landing, and stood under the clock. She made no attempt to descend farther.

'Oh, Geneviève, the fire is gone out.'

'I reckon the wood were damp,' said the old woman. 'It be too late, and not possible to light it again now.'

'And the candles are flickering in their sockets.'

'There is not another in the house. Look at mine.'

'It will be so dark.'

'Do not be afraid. The Lord will give you light.'

'It will be so cold.'

'You will be warm in bed.'

'O no! it is colder there than outside.'

She remained without speaking, waiting for Genefer to say something, but the old woman offered no remark, not knowing what to say.

Still she stood there, hesitating, and the banister rattled under her hand laid on it.

'There, there,' said Genefer, 'lie down and shut your eyes, and you will soon be asleep.'

'I cannot sleep.'

She still stood there, irresolute.

'Is the fire burning in the parlour? I should like to go in there, and sit there.'

'I've just put him out.'

'Then—that in the kitchen.'

'He's out likewise. There, there, go to bed like a good dear. There is no help—it must be.'

'Geneviève, I asked Mr. John Herring to send you away. You frightened me. I am very sorry. Will you forgive me for doing so?'

'To be sure I will. I am not one to bear malice.'

'Do you really think, Geneviève, that he is alive?'

'I do. I cannot doubt it.'

'Oh, promise me, if ever you see him, and I not, tell him '—she paused—'tell him that now I wish, with all my heart, I had loved him as he deserved.'

Then she went upstairs again, in the same slow, reluctant manner, step by step, ascending backward, feeling each step behind her with her bare foot before planting it, and raising herself to the higher level, and she kept her eyes fixed on Genefer as though dreading to lose sight of her. At last Mirelle's hand, feeling behind her, touched the latch of her door, and the chill of the metal sent a shiver through her.

Slowly, very slowly, she pressed the door open behind her, walking backwards still, with a sad despairing look in her large dark eyes fixed on Genefer.

And Genefer, standing below, said, 'Sweetheart, go to your bed, and, MAY YOU REST IN PEACE!'

CHAPTER LIX.

DIVIDING THE SPOILS.

'NEVER was more shocked in my life!' said Captain Trecarrel, 'I really have not recovered it yet. So young, so beautiful, so good! and you, my sweet Orange, I observe, are greatly overcome. It does you credit; it does, upon my life.'

Captain Trecarrel was seated in the parlour at Dolbeare with Orange; the latter was looking haggard and wretched. 'And it was heart that did it,' said the Captain; 'I always said that heart was her weak point, and that it must be economised to the utmost, spared all excitement, everything distressing. There has always been that transparent look about her flesh that is a sure sign of the heart being wrong. Poor angel! I have no doubt in the world that she was greatly tried. She has not been happy ever since she came to England; one thing or another has risen up to distress her, circumstances have conspired to keep her in incessant nervous tension. She felt the death of poor John Herring severely; that alone was enough to kill her. Do not take on so much, Orange; there is moderation in all things, even in sorrow for the dead.'

'Leave me alone,' said Orange, hoarsely. 'Do not notice me.'

'I see this painful occurrence has shaken you,' continued

Captain Trecarrel. 'I knew you regarded her; I had no idea that you loved her. Indeed——'

'Leave me alone,' said Orange, emphatically.

'Well, well? When will be the funeral?'

'To-morrow.'

'I shall certainly attend, to show the last tribute of respect to one whom I greatly esteemed. Indeed I may say that next to you, Orange, I never admired any woman so much. She has taught us one lesson, poor thing, and that is not to trifle with the heart, which is a most susceptible organ, and must be guarded against strong feeling and excitement. Do not be so troubled about this matter, Orange; it is bad for the health, over much sorrow debilitates the constitution. You are really not looking yourself. Think that every cloud has its silver lining, and this fleeting affliction, I make no scruple to affirm, is trimmed throughout with gold. Have you reversed it? Have you studied the other side? Have you looked into matters at all?'

'What matters?'

'Well, to put it broadly, pecuniary matters. One is reluctant to advert to such things at such a solemn time, but it is necessary. The sweet luxury of grief cannot be indulged in till these concerns are settled, and they considerably accentuate or moderate it. You and I, Orange, are practical persons: we feel for what we have lost, but we do not let slip the present or overlook the future. You are her nearest of kin, and therefore, of course, everything she had will fall to you. By the greatest good luck her husband predeceased, and Welltown came to her, and from her will doubtless pass to you. Besides Welltown, what was she worth?'

'I do not know—I do not care,' answered Orange, in a tone of mingled impatience and indifference.

'This will not do, Orange,' said Captain Trecarrel; 'you really must not succumb. Good taste imposes its limits on sorrow as on joy. If you come in for ten thousand pounds you do not dance and shout, and if you lose a friend you do not sink into the abyss of sulky misery—that is, if you make any pretence to good breeding. I know what a sensible, practical girl you are. Come, pluck up heart and help me to look into her concerns. I have done my best, my very best, for you so far, and I will not desert you now. The moment I heard of the event I flew to your assistance, I offered my aid, and I have been invaluable to you. You cannot dispute it. But for me there might have been an inquest, which would have been offensive to your delicacy of sentiment. I explained to the doctor her constitution, and the troubles she has gone through; how she felt her husband's sudden death, the languor that has since oppressed her, her fainting fits, the swoon into which she fell after her exhausting journey; and he saw at once that heart was at the bottom of it all. I settled with the undertaker, saw to everything, made every arrangement, and you have not been troubled in the least. I even went after the milliner about your mourning. You cannot deny that I have been of service to you, and I am ready to do more. All that is nothing: now comes the most trying and difficult task of all—the settlement of her affairs; but I am ready to undertake that also, to save my dear Orange trouble; only I ask, as a preliminary, that all the requisite information shall be placed at my disposal.'

'Later,' said Orange, uneasily; 'after the funeral.'

'No,' answered Captain Trecarrel, 'not after the funeral, but now. My time is valuable. I shall have to go to Exeter in three days, and I should like to have everything ready to take with me. If there be a will—which I do not suppose there is—I will prove it for you; if there be not, I will obtain letters of administration for you. You must really let me know what her estate was worth. Have you the means of ascertaining?'

'I do not know.'

'But you must know, or rather you must put me in the way of ascertaining. Have you looked whether there is a will?'

'No, I have not.'

'Have you got her desk?'

'It is upstairs.'

'Bring it down, and we will overhaul it together.'

Orange rose and left the room. She returned a few minutes later, with the large desk that had belonged to Mr. Strange, and after his death had been appropriated by Mirelle. Mirelle had removed from it all his Portuguese letters, tied them in bundles and put them away, and had transferred to it her own treasures from a school writing-desk full to overflowing. It was a strange thing that this desk was thus explored in search of a will at so small an interval of time since we saw John Herring seated at it, at the opening of this story.

'This is the sort of thing I detest,' said the Captain. 'It jars with one's feelings, and vulgarises bereavement. However, it does not become us to give way to our emotions; we must do our duty. Give me the key.'

He unlocked the desk, and turned over the contents; he removed many articles and placed them on the table. What trifles were there!—trifles that had been collected at school and were preserved as treasures, each made precious by some innocent association and sunny memory. A little book in which her school companions had inscribed verses and signed their names. Wrapped up in silver paper and tied with white silk, a lock of hair from the head of Marie de la Meillerie, cut on the day of her first Communion. In a pill-box a raisin out of Mirelle's birthday cake, many years old. Some lace-edged pictures of saints, spangled red and blue and gold with foil stars. A medal of Notre-Dame de Bon Secours. Some feathers off a pet bullfinch that had died and cost many tears. A twig of blessed palm. John Herring's notes and some little presents he had made her; but not one relic of Captain Trecarrel—all such had been burned on her marriage; she had kept them till then. Also a little deal box, in which, softly nested in cotton-wool, was a glass peacock, with spun glass tail—a memorial of one happy day spent at the house of the Countess La Gaye, who had taken Mirelle and her daughters to see a glass-blower, and the man had made the peacock under their eyes, and had presented it to Mirelle. All this rubbish Captain Trecarrel tossed aside carelessly. If it ever had any value, it had it only to her who could appreciate those trifles no more. Then he pounced, with trembling hand, on a paper in John Herring's handwriting —a statement of the property of the Countess Mirelle Garcia de Cantalejo, and with it a much larger paper in many folds. He opened this latter, glanced at it, and tossed it aside with an expression of disgust. It was a pedigree of the family of Garcia de Cantalejo, with heraldic blazonings. The smaller paper soon engrossed his whole attention; Captain Trecarrel's eyes opened very wide. John Herring's confession was not there; Mirelle had destroyed it, lest it should ever be seen by anyone but herself. She had, however, preserved the statement.

'My dear Orange!—my dear, dear Orange!' his voice shook with emotion and excitement. 'I had no idea that the lining was so warm and so rich. There are the West Wyke mortgages, there is a silver lead mine, about which I knew nothing —well, I was aware some time ago that he was paddling in something of the sort near Ophir, but I did not know that it was being worked; when I heard of it, it was not begun. Then there are uncut diamonds. Bless my soul! uncut diamonds! How did they escape the fingers of your excellent father, I wonder? Where can they be? Oh, I see, at the bank. We must take out letters of administration to authorise you to withdraw and realise. Why Orange! my dear, dear, dear Orange,' he put his hand under the table, took that of Miss Trampleasure, and pressed it with fervent affection; 'the barrier that has stood between us has fallen. Happiness is in view before us. You will forgive and forget any little past lovers' quarrels. *Amantium iræ amoris integratio est*, as the syntax says. Let me tott all up as well as I can. Welltown is worth six hundred nett, as far as I can judge, and it is unencumbered. Then there are your five thousand, which will bring in, say two hundred and fifty. It is impossible for me to estimate the value of Mirelle's own property, as the silver lead mine is only now beginning to give dividends, I suppose—I see by the paper that money has been sunk, and there is no entry of return, but then Upaver is quite a new affair. What it is worth I cannot conjecture. Then there are the West Wyke mortgages, and the uncut diamonds, and I suppose money in the bank. The estate must be worth at least a thousand per annum, without including Welltown. My dear, dear, dear Orange, my heart overflows with affection. I will tell you, Orange, what will be the best plan of all for both of us. Let us get a special licence and be married at the earliest time possible, privately, of course, because of the affliction under which you are suffering, and then I can manage all the matter of Mirelle's estate with the utmost simplicity, as my own. It will save a world of trouble, and possibly some expense. By Jove! this is not all. We had left out of our calculations the set of diamonds. Where is it? Oh, here it is in its *étui* on the other side of the desk. Orange, do look at the stones! they are magnificent. They must be worth a great deal of money. I am no judge of stones, but these strike my uninitiated eye as being of the purest water—not a tinge of yellow, not a flaw in them. I can see this, Orange, that our income is likely to be some two thousand a year. I could cry tears of joy at the thought. Did you ever hear anything so ridiculous as the supposition that John Herring had committed suicide with this set of diamonds in his pocket. The thing is psychologically impossible. With such a source of wealth in one's pocket one would begin to live; all previous existence would be tadpolism, now only would one stretch out legs and arms and begin to jump. My dear, dear Orange, I do believe that you and I are only now about to sip the nectar of life. Here—try on these jewels.'

'I had rather not,' said Orange, shrinking back.

'I insist. I want to see you in them. Lord bless you! they never could become that pale little thing; colour, warmth, flesh and life are wanted to carry this. Here, Orange, let me try it on.'

He rose to put the diamond chain about her neck, when a hand interposed and grasped it.

Trecarrel and Orange looked round, startled, and saw John Herring standing before them, with hard, bitter face, very pale, with contracted brows. He had entered the room without their hearing him. The Captain had been too much engrossed in his discoveries to have ear for his footfall on the carpet, and Orange too abstracted in her own gloomy thoughts.

At the sight of Herring, Trecarrel drew back, and his jaw fell. He looked at Herring, then at Orange, then at the diamonds, and, lastly, at the schedule of Mirelle's property.

'By heavens!' he gasped. 'Confound it! you alive! Then Orange is only worth five thousand.'

Orange had recoiled into a corner, blank, trembling, speechless.

Herring was perfectly collected.

'Put everything down,' he said in hard tones. 'Do not lay finger on anything again. Leave the house at once.' He looked at the Captain with contempt and anger.

'And you, Orange Trampleasure, already engaged in dividing the spoils of the dead before she is laid in her grave! You will find a carriage at the gate. Rejoin your mother at Welltown, and leave me in the house alone with Genefer and—my wife. I cannot suffer another presence here.'

He gathered the little scattered trifles together, the lock of hair, the raisin, the glass peacock, the tinsel pictures, with soft and reverent touch, and placed all together in the desk. The jewels he re-laid in their *étui*, and relegated it to its proper compartment. Then he locked up the desk. His face was cold, collected, with hard lines about the mouth, and a hard look in the eyes, in which no sign of a tear was manifest. He removed the desk to a shelf in the cabinet, then he went out and ascended the stairs.

At the sound of his step, a door at the head of the staircase opened, and Genefer came out, with her eyes red, and tears glittering on her cheek.

'It be you, to last, Master John. I knew it. I knew you wasn't dead. God be praised! Even out of the belly of the whale; when the waters compass me about, even to the soul; when the depth hath closed me round about, and the weeds are wrapped about my head, I will say, Salvation is of the Lord.'

Herring was about to pass her, but she stayed him, barring the door, looking hard into his face.

'Oh, Master John! you must not go in looking like that, as the fleece of Gideon without dew. Stay and let me tell you, afore you see the sweet flower of God, His white lily, what was her message to you, the last words her uttered in this world. Her was standing where I be now, and her said to me: " Promise me, if ever you see him, to tell him that I wish with all my heart I had loved him as he deserves." That were the olive leaf in the mouth of the dove as her flew back to the ark.'

The old woman opened the door and went forward, leading the way, with her arms uplifted, saying, 'The dove found no rest for the sole of her foot, and she returned into the ark, for the waters were on the face of the whole earth: then He put forth His hand, and took her, and pulled her in unto Him into the ark.' As the old woman said these last words, she touched the crucifix and the right, transfixed hand of the figure on it.

Genefer drew back.

The white blinds were down in the room, the atmosphere was sweet with the scent of violets. At the head of the little bed was a table covered with a linen cloth, and the crucifix between bunches of white flowers and lighted wax candles was on it. Upon the bed lay Mirelle, her face as the purest wax, and a wreath of white and purple violets round her head, woven by the loving hands of old Genefer. The hands, contrary to the usual custom, were crossed over the breast. Genefer had seen this on a monument 'of the old Romans,' and she had thus arranged the hands of Mirelle, thinking it would be right so for her.

Herring stood by the bed looking at the pure face. Then he signed with one hand to Genefer to leave. The old woman went out softly. Herring still looked, and drawing forth a little case, opened it, and took out a sprig of white heath and laid it in the bosom of his dead wife.

'Mirelle! once you refused it when I offered it you, once you refused it when offered you by Trecarrel, now you will keep and carry with you into eternity my good luck which I now give you.'

CHAPTER LX.

INTRODUCTORY.

SEVERAL weeks had passed. John Herring was back at West Wyke, grave, calm, with a gentle expression in his face and a far-off look in his eyes. The hardness and bitterness had gone, never to return. The Snow Bride would not freeze him to ice. He, in time, would thaw away like her. On his first return to West Wyke he had come back with blasted hopes, on his second with dislocated faith. Now he returned with recovered moral balance, not indeed hopeful, for hope is a delusion of youth, but able to look life in the face without a sneer.

Cicely received him with her usual brightness and sympathy. It was always pleasant to see her kind, sweet face, and to know what a good and honest heart beat in her bosom.

Herring had never been to her other than uncommunicative, partly out of natural modesty, partly because they were out of harmony over Mirelle. But Cicely had a woman's curiosity, and would not be left in the dark as to what had taken place; and she felt real sympathy for John Herring, only she did not know how to exhibit it, because she did not know what course it should take. So she put to him questions, and with tact drew from him the entire story.

'Where does she lie, John?' she asked in her soft tones, full of tender feeling for his sorrow. They were sitting together in the porch, looking out on the old walled garden, with its honesty, and white rocket, and love-lies-bleeding all ablow. 'Have you laid her in Launceston churchyard, or removed her to Welltown?'

He shook his head. 'No, Cicely; neither under the shadow of Launceston church, nor exposed to the winds and roar of Boscastle. She lies in the sunny cemetery of the Sacré Cœur.'

Cicely said nothing. Indeed, neither spoke for some time. Presently, however, Cicely, who had laid her needlework in her lap, and had rested her folded hands on it, and was looking dreamily across the garden, said, 'Mirelle was your ideal, John.'

'She *is* my ideal, Cicely.'

Miss Battishill looked round at him. She was very pretty,

with her copper-gold hair, and the reflection of the sunlight in the garden illumining her sweet face of the most delicate white and purest pink. 'I remember your speaking to me—almost when first I knew you—about Mirelle as your ideal, and I thought what you said was extravagant and unreal. But I was in fault. There was no exaggeration, and all was real to you.'

'It was, and is so still.'

'Now, tell me the truth, honestly, cousin; does the possession of such an ideal in the heart conduce to happiness?'

'On the contrary, it saddens.'

'Then why do you not shut your eyes to such alluring but unsatisfying fancies? Why are you not satisfied with what *is*, instead of sighing after what *may be*?'

'Cicely, it seems to me that the world is divided between those with ideals and those without. When I say without, I mean that the great bulk of mankind are, as you say, content with things as they are. They are without ambition after the perfect; they are satisfied with the defective. Such men put forth their hands, and without effort gather happiness. They ask for nothing very high, and certainly nothing above them. They are vulgarly happy, enjoying what is on their level and attained without effort. But there are others who are not thus easily satisfied. They form in their minds an ideal from which every imperfection is cast off, and the formation of this ideal in their hearts deals it its death-wound. The ideal is the ever-unattainable, and if happiness consists in obtaining the desired, happiness can never be theirs, because the ideal can never be reached. Hope also is killed along with happiness, for how can you hope for the unobtainable? The ideal may be of various sorts. It may be sought in moral, social, political, religious perfection; in Woman, in the State, in the Church, in Art; but is always pursued with disappointment—I had almost said with despair. When I was a child, I was told by my nurse that under the root of the rainbow lay a golden bowl, and many is the rainbow I have run after in hopes of finding the golden chalice from which could be quaffed immortality. As I grew older and always failed, I found that the rainbow moved before me as I advanced, and that the cup of supreme felicity could never be pressed by my lips. That is the picture of all idealists. We have given up every hope of attaining the Iris we look on, but we still follow it.'

'I think yours is a sad story, John.'

'Perhaps so, but I do not know. Mirelle has been my ideal, and therefore unattainable.'

'But, John, suppose she had really loved you, and been everything you could wish as a wife—you would have been happy.'

'I should have been happy—yes; but my ideal would have died. I remember a story that Genefer—by the way, you do not know her—my old nurse, told me many years ago of a man of Trevalga, who saw a pixy, a beautiful fairy who haunted the glen and waterfall of S. Kneighton. He saw her when she was bathing, and took away her white garment, and refused to restore it till she allowed him to kiss her lips. She wept and pleaded, but in vain. Then she suffered him to draw her to him and to touch her lips, but the touch of mortal flesh withered her. She shrivelled like a faded rose and lost all beauty, and became as a wizened hag; and he went from his mind and drowned himself in the Kieve. I cannot conceive of Mirelle other than one far, far above and distant from me. It is possible, had things been as you say, that I might have discovered imperfections.'

'Of course she had her imperfections,' interrupted Cicely, with a slight touch of impatience in her tone. 'I do not wish to say a word that may wound you, but, my dear John, nothing human is perfect, and certainly Mirelle had her short-comings apparent enough to me.'

'Then, better a thousand times that things should be as they are, that these imperfections should not have been seen by me; and now, I know they are swallowed up in a faultless splendour. If Heaven gave me my choice, I would choose this.'

'Do you mean seriously to tell me that you would not have Mirelle restored, and restored to be yours entirely?'

'I would not. I had rather have my unapproachable ideal shining down upon me from afar, than have my ideal dissolve in my arms into the commonplace. The ship sails by the star but never attains to it. I can look up, and I am content. I ask for nothing more.'

'This frame of mind is to me inexplicable. It is unworthy of a man of reason to strive for the unreachable. When a person of sense sees that what he or she has wished is not to be had, that person makes an effort and accommodates herself to circumstances.' She coloured a little.

'That is to say—some weary of pursuing an ideal, and settle themselves down to enjoy what they can obtain. I can quite understand that; and perhaps it is the most practical course, but it is, to some, impossible.'

'But that is the most—it is the only, sensible course. The other offers a mere treadmill round of duties, without hope to spur you on, and happiness to reward you.'

'No doubt you are right; and yet it is impossible to some. I have set up pure and perfect womanhood as my ideal; but others have ideals of different nature. The young politician starts with an ideal of a perfect commonwealth before him, and he is sanguine of redressing grievances, of elevating politics to a noble patriotic passion instead of mean party rivalry. But after a while he finds that every reform brings in fresh evils, and, if it does away with some wrongs, it inflicts others; he finds that it is impossible to be patriotic without partisanship, and that those whom he strives to raise are unworthy of being raised. I believe the leaders of the Revolution in France were earnest men with their ideal before them, and, striving after a perfect state of liberty and fraternity, they called up a Reign of Terror. I saw once an enthusiast who had taken to educate a pig; he taught it letters, he washed the beast clean, and dressed it in a coat, but, when left to itself, it wallowed in the next mire and forgot its alphabet. I have no doubt that a young curate starts on his sacred duties with the sincere hope and belief that he will do good: he preaches with earnestness, thinking to waken the religious sense of his people, he establishes schools to instruct the young, and presently finds that all he has done is absolutely useless—the people will not be regenerated, his sermons are profitless, and his educated children read only vicious literature. It is the same——But I see I weary you.'

'I do not understand you.'

They were silent awhile.

Presently Cicely said: 'John, do you not think your own weakness may be at the bottom of all the trouble you have met with? I do not speak with any intention to be unkind. You will allow that.'

Herring thought a moment. 'I do not know, Cicely, that I could have acted other than I have, and been true to my conscience. I might have taken the selfish line, and cast aside those responsibilities which seemed to me to be forced upon me, and, no doubt, then I should have been light-hearted and boyish to the present moment, laughing, shooting, riding, spending money, a careless young officer without much thought of the morrow. But I had rather have my sorrows and walk uprightly.

I am better for having an ideal and following it, though I shall never catch it up.'

Cicely did not pursue the subject: she stooped over her work, took it up, and averting her pretty face said, as the colour mantled her white throat and deepened in her rosy cheek, 'John, you have been candid with me: I will be equally frank with you. I will make a confession to you.' She hesitated a moment, and then said, 'Mr. Harmless-Simpleton has asked me to be his wife.'

'I wish you joy with all my heart, dear Cicely,' said Herring, warmly. 'He is a good, well-intentioned, amiable man, with whom you are sure to be happy.'

'Vulgarly happy,' said Cicely, drily.

Herring coloured. 'I beg your pardon. I meant no disparagement when I used that term. I meant only ordinarily happy, happy as the buttercups, and the birds and bees, as all nature that is content with the place God has given it, and the sunshine and sweet air that surround it. Why should you not be so? It is no privilege to have an ever-aching void in the heart, to be ever stretching after the moon. You will be happy in a sphere where you will do good and be beloved. When do you intend to be married?'

'I do not know. There is no occasion for delay, and there is nothing to precipitate matters. But now—when I am married and settled into the Vicarage at Tawton, what is to become of that queer Joyce? Is she to come with me?'

'I—I!' Joyce was there in the door to answer for herself. 'Wherever the maister be, there be I too. He sed as how he'd never wear no stockings more but what I'd knit; and you wouldn't have he go barefoot?'

John Herring turned his head, and looked at Joyce.

'You had better remain with Miss Cicely. I do not want you.'

'I will not,' answered Joyce, resolutely. 'I go with you.'

'Then, I dare say, Genefer will find work for you on the farm, or in the house at Welltown. But you will not be so comfortable or happy as here.'

'I care not,' said the girl. 'I *must* follow you. I belongs to you. You bought me of vaither for shining gold. No, Miss Cicely, I follow the maister.'

'Go your ways,' said Cicely: 'you are each of you, in your several ways, idealists, and each following the unattainable.'

'And now, beginning life,' said Herring, 'all that has gone before is introductory to the real life; a rough and painful initiation into the axioms on which the problem will have to be worked out. We know now where we stand, and which is the direction in which we must set our faces, to plod on our way forward, hopeless indeed, but still, conscientiously forward.'

www.ingramcontent.com/pod-product-compliance
Lightning Source LLC
Chambersburg PA
CBHW022137300426
44115CB00006B/233